This text is dedicated to Kathleen J. Moyer, PhD, my mother, who worked on her dying process in conjunction with the writing of this edition. During her life, she taught me how to be a committed professional woman; during her illness, she taught me patience, silent communication, and new priorities.

—Judie McCoyd

Emily and Hannah, my beautiful daughters; Nina Seigelstein, my "love" who continues to support me in everything I do; and Amy Koller, my beloved mom who has been an inspiration to me throughout my life.

—Jeanne Koller

My family: Bruce Bryen (my husband) has provided immeasurable support for all of Carolyn's writing; Kim Remley, Brian Walter, and my grandchildren, Matthew, Connor, Hazel, and Matilda, who have brought me incredible joy during midlife and now older adulthood.

—Carolyn Ambler Walter

Register Now for Online Access to Your Book!

SPRINGER PUBLISHING
CONNECT™

Your print purchase of *Grief and Loss Across the Lifespan, Third Edition*, **includes online access to the contents of your book**—increasing accessibility, portability, and searchability!

Access today at:
http://connect.springerpub.com/content/book/978-0-8261-4964-0
or scan the QR code at the right with your smartphone
and enter the access code below.

X6BJ34NA

Scan here for
quick access.

SPRINGER PUBLISHING
View all our products at springerpub.com

Judith L. M. McCoyd, PhD, LCSW, QCSW, is an associate professor at Rutgers University—School of Social Work, teaching in the MSW advanced clinical curriculum and working with both the PhD in social work and the DSW doctoral programs. Before academia, she worked in perinatal, emergency department, and oncology settings, and she continues to maintain a small private practice with perinatal and end-of-life care as specialties. She is coauthor of *Grief and Loss Across the Lifespan: A Biopsychosocial Perspective* (all three editions) and coeditor (with Toba S. Kerson) of *Social Work in Health Settings: Practice in Context* (third and fourth editions—2010, 2016). She presents at national and international conferences, such as the Council on Social Work Education, the National Association of Perinatal Social Work, and the Society for Social Work and Research, and she has journal publications about perinatal complications and loss, genetic testing and decision-making, technology and health care, societal aspects of bereavement, and social work education. Her current research explores how perinatal technologies affect the experience of childbearing and bereavement.

Jeanne M. Koller, PhD, MSW, LCSW, is an assistant professor at Monmouth University School of Social Work, primarily teaching in the graduate clinical curriculum. She previously was on faculty at the Rutgers School of Social Work. At Rutgers, she served as coordinator for the MSW Aging & Health Certificate. Over the years, Dr. Koller has taught courses related to aging and health, MSW foundation level courses, and undergraduate level courses. In addition to her work in academia, Dr. Koller has over 26 years of clinical social work practice experience specializing in grief and loss, depression, relational issues, aging, and issues related to the LGBT+ community. Dr. Koller is a member of the Board of Trustees for the Visiting Nurse Association of Central Jersey (VNACJ) Community Health Centers; the coordinator for the New Jersey Radical Age Chapter; the cochair for the Monmouth/Ocean National Association of Social Workers (NASW) Unit; and on the Executive Committee of Garden State Equality's "Elders for Equality." Dr. Koller also serves on the American Society on Aging's Editorial Board for the LGBT Aging Issues Network (LAIN) and regularly serves as an abstract reviewer for The Gerontological Society of America. She is an active presenter on issues pertaining to work with LGBT+ families, aging and the LGBT+ community, and ageism.

Carolyn Ambler Walter, PhD, LCSW, is a professor emerita at the Center for Social Work Education at Widener University, Chester, Pennsylvania, where she taught MSW and PhD students. Dr. Walter is the coauthor of *Grief and Loss Across the Lifespan: A Biopsychosocial Perspective* (2009, 2016) and the author of *The Loss of a Life Partner: Narratives of the Bereaved* (2003). She is the coauthor of *Breast Cancer in the Life Course: Women's Experiences* and the author of *The Timing of Motherhood*. Dr. Walter has published many articles in professional journals on such topics as women's issues, grief and loss, and social work education. She has given presentations at state and regional hospice conferences throughout the United States and at the Association of Death Education & Counseling (ADEC), National Association of Social Workers (NASW), and Council on Social Work Education (CSWE) national conferences. She is currently serving as a consultant on grief, loss, and transformation and life transitions. Her current interests involve teaching courses in Restoring Your Life After Loss to retirees, older adult communities, and volunteer organizations.

GRIEF AND LOSS ACROSS THE LIFESPAN

A Biopsychosocial Perspective

Third Edition

Judith L. M. McCoyd, PhD, LCSW, QCSW

Jeanne M. Koller, PhD, MSW, LCSW

Carolyn Ambler Walter, PhD, LCSW

 SPRINGER PUBLISHING

First Springer Publishing edition 2009; subsequent edition 2015.

Springer Publishing Company, LLC
11 West 42nd Street, New York, NY 10036
www.springerpub.com
connect.springerpub.com/

Acquisitions Editor: Kate Dimock
Compositor: Amnet Systems

ISBN: 978-0-8261-4963-3
ebook ISBN: 978-0-8261-4964-0
DOI: 10.1891/9780826149640

Qualified instructors may request supplements by emailing textbook@springerpub.com
A Casebook supplement is available from **connect.springerpub.com/content/book/978-0-8261-4964-0**

Instructor's Manual ISBN: 978-0-8261-4966-4
Instructor's PowerPoints ISBN: 978-0-8261-4965-7
Instructor's Syllabus ISBN: 978-0-8261-4967-1
Casebook ISBN: 978-0-8261-4968-8

20 21 22 23 24 / 5 4 3 2 1

Library of Congress Cataloging-in-Publication Data

Names: Walter, Carolyn Ambler, author. | McCoyd, Judith L. M., author. | Koller, Jeanne M., author.
Title: Grief and loss across the lifespan : a biopsychosocial perspective / Judith L.M. McCoyd, Jeanne M. Koller, Carolyn Ambler Walter.
Description: Third edition. | New York, NY : Springer Publishing Company, LLC, [2022] | Carolyn Ambler Walter's name appears first on first edition. | Includes bibliographical references and index.
Identifiers: LCCN 2020029068 (print) | LCCN 2020029069 (ebook) | ISBN 9780826149633 (paperback) | ISBN 9780826149640 (ebook) | ISBN 9780826149664 (instructor's manual) | ISBN 9780826149657 (instructor's PowerPoints) | ISBN 9780826149671 (instructor's syllabus) | ISBN 9780826149688 (casebook)
Subjects: MESH: Grief | Attitude to Death | Adaptation, Psychological | Human Development | Social Support | Counseling
Classification: LCC BF575.G7 (print) | LCC BF575.G7 (ebook) | NLM BF 575.G7 | DDC 155.9/37—dc23
LC record available at https://lccn.loc.gov/2020029068
LC ebook record available at https://lccn.loc.gov/2020029069

Printed in the United States of America by Gasch Printing.

Contents

Preface

This third edition of our book brings a new coauthor (JK), a well-deserved retirement (CW), and a continuing labor of love. Our first edition came as a result of Carolyn and Judie's work together as consultants and our shared frustration about the dearth of texts that could meet the needs of the grief and loss classes we each taught. Our work was animated by our beliefs that loss is at the heart of growth and that death loss is only one type of loss. We were happy to share new information about continuing bonds, meaning-making, disenfranchised grief, and the dual-process model in our first edition and enjoyed updating it all in the second edition. This third edition brings in Jeanne Koller with new perspectives and approaches, while maintaining allegiance to the original approach to the text that students, instructors, and clinicians have assured us they find helpful.

Death and dying courses in social work, nursing, counseling psychology, and medicine traditionally focused on topics such as the experience of dying, the delivery of healthcare during the end of life, and the experience of mourning after a death. Classic texts such as Rando's (1993) *Treatment of Complicated Grief*; Worden's (2002) *Grief Counseling and Grief Therapy*; and Parkes, Laungani, and Young's (2000) *Death and Bereavement Across Cultures* have been joined by newer ones, yet we believe our text still offers a unique perspective. We include neurobiological aspects of development and grieving as we truly believe our students need to understand these aspects of biology if they are to claim a bio–psycho–social–spiritual perspective in the 21st century. In addition to the sections on psychological and social development, we have added a section on spiritual development in each life phase and have also added a section called Special Considerations in Risk and Resilience to describe aspects of marginalization that may affect development. We include factors that promote resilience, maintaining our strengths-based approach to all of this material. We continue our identification of maturational losses, incorporating these nondeath losses into a section renamed Living Losses found in each life phase chapter. Having been told by readers that they most enjoyed the more memoir-ish readings that end each life stage chapter, this edition has more readings of this sort to add additional dimensions to the text. We have developed ancillary materials available to qualified instructors (email: textbook@springerpub.com) that include outlines, PowerPoint slides, and activities for each chapter as well as the readings from our earlier editions. We hope this third edition helps each reader feel prepared to help grievers of all ages and types.

Judith L. M. McCoyd, Jeanne M. Koller, and
Carolyn Ambler Walter

**Qualified instructors may obtain access to supplements by
emailing textbook@springerpub.com**

**A Casebook supplement may be accessed at http://connect.springerpub.com/
content/book/978-0-8261-4964-0 (see the opening page for details)**

Acknowledgments

We have many to thank for their help with this text. First, we would like to thank the instructors, students, and clinicians who have given us feedback on earlier editions. All have helped us to improve and update this edition. Second, we thank our Readings Writers, who contributed the readings at the end of each chapter and are experts, sometimes academically and often experientially. We appreciate your willingness to share your stories to enliven this text. Third, we want to thank the clients and research participants who have shared their loss experiences and meaning-making, teaching us ever more about the subtleties of multiple types of loss. Fourth, we owe gratitude and respect to the people who taught us about grief and loss experientially: for Judie McCoyd, they include Judy Achuff (high school "best friend"), Eunice and Ben Maurer and Jonathan and Erma Forry (grandparents), Mary and Walter McCoyd (in-laws), Doug Moyer (sibling), and Kathleen and Ivan Moyer (parents). For Jeanne Koller, they include all her grandparents, especially maternal grandmother Dorothy Robertson; Bernard T. Koller (father); and Thomas J. Koller (sibling). For Carolyn Walter, they include Joseph Penrose Ambler (father) and John Walter (first husband). Fifth and very resoundingly, we thank Jim Baumohl for his close editing of every one of these chapters, multiple times, to help us clarify our points and protect us from garrulousness, vagueness, or inaccuracies. As goes the saying, we recognize that any remaining mistakes are our own.

We give deep thanks to our family and friends who have supported us in this endeavor. Judie McCoyd thanks Corey Shdaimah and Anne Dalke, who remain trusted allies; Susan Turkel, a great walking buddy; the Mothers of Boys (MoB) group; and the Wild Flowers, who all provide distraction and a safe holding environment. She also thanks Mariah Duphiney for research assistance, reference checking, and chapter mapping. Great thanks to Jim Baumohl for attentive and rigorous editing, and indispensable help with parent care and the household during stressful times. Jeanne thanks her spouse, Nina, who put up with the time Jeanne spent holed up in her computer nook and yet was always supportive, and dear family, acknowledged here previously, who have died but inspire her every day. Finally, we note Carolyn's full retirement, described in her reading in Chapter 9, "Grief and Loss in Retirement and Reinvention." We hope she has enjoyed the chance to watch the process rather than feel the stress of participating. Finally, we wish to thank Kate Dimock at Springer Publishing Company for believing in us and this book enough to ask for a third edition. We are grateful to be working with her.

Grief and Loss: Theories and Context

INTRODUCTION

This chapter starts with a bio–psycho–social–spiritual overview of loss and grief, segueing into aspects of risk and resilience as they affect loss and grief. It covers classical grief theories such as Kübler-Ross's stages of dying and Worden's tasks of grief through postmodern, current theories. The concepts of continuing bonds, dual-process model (DPM), disenfranchised grief, ambiguous loss, and meaning-making are discussed for their utility in working with grievers in a culturally attuned manner. The concept of maturational loss, a type of nondeath, living loss, is also introduced. Maturational losses are experienced when an individual matures, often in positive ways, yet has a lingering sense of loss as a response. Consideration of how theory drives intervention and description of effective interventions in loss and grief complete the chapter.

OBJECTIVES

After studying this chapter, the reader will be able to:
- Summarize biological impacts, psychological experiences, social contexts, and spiritual aspects of grief.
- Identify the way adverse childhood experiences have changed our understanding of loss and stressors in childhood and how genomic changes and neurobiological impacts play a role in the outcomes of ACEs.
- Consider how the aging of the population in Western nations (along with other population trends) changes some of the ways in which we approach loss and human development.
- Trace the evolution of classical grief theory, including task- and stage-based grief theories of the modern era.
- Describe postmodern grief theories and concepts, including the dual-process model (DPM), meaning-making, continuing bonds, disenfranchised loss, and ambiguous and nonfinite loss.
- Discuss third-wave therapies with application to loss, including mindfulness practices and acceptance and commitment therapy (ACT).
- Utilize the perspective that loss is a normal and inevitable part of life that may promote growth.

CONTEXT

Loss is at the heart of life and growth. We believe this as much now as when we wrote that opening line in the first edition of this text.

We define loss broadly to include death losses as well as nondeath losses of jobs, relationships, capacities, and even the status quo. By definition, any new state of being involves a break with—a loss of—the past. All change, for better or worse, involves loss. Normal maturational changes represent growth that is often celebrated in ritual, but we should not ignore the loss with which it is joined.

Growth and loss proceed together. Practitioners must therefore understand not only that a variety of losses can stimulate grief but also that not all loss provokes grief. Attachment, whether to a person, an object, a skill set, or a way of being, is critical to the experience of loss. Losing any person or thing to which one is attached will elicit a sense of loss. Yet each loss has the potential to stimulate new growth and maturity in the bereaved. Still, we are cautious and observe Klass's (2013) admonition to avoid approaching grief as if it will *always* create growth, and we recognize that sorrow, especially after a death loss, may linger.

This text is for reflective practitioners of all levels of experience and for educators desiring a text on loss that explains developmental differences in how individuals create and lose attachments of various sorts. In this third edition, we incorporate recent research about how adverse childhood experiences (ACEs), risk and resilience, genomic understandings, and the changing demographics of aging affect loss and grief. We amplify material introduced in the second edition, including more information about how technology, social media, neurobiology, genomics, and trauma intersect with grief and loss. We continue our focus on loss as a normal (though uncomfortable) destabilizing experience with the potential to stimulate growth and resilience capacities through the opportunity to learn about one's strength and ability to cope. This is consistent with recent research indicating that resilience is promoted by exposure to an optimal range (in the number and types) of stressors (Crane et al., 2019), a finding to which we will return in discussions of risk and resilience.

Throughout this book, we convey the most recent developments in theoretical understandings of loss and grief, trauma and attachment, and developmental aspects of grief from a bio–psycho–social–spiritual perspective (including neurobiological and genomic information). We discuss how ACEs effect responses to loss, risk, and resilience. We review research on specific responses to loss situations and discuss intervention strategies supported by practice wisdom and empirical research.

Human development proceeds from both biological blueprint and individual response to the influences of social and material environments. In this book, we define chapters by developmental tasks that are tackled at the more or less predictable ages to which our chapters are loosely bound. However, because development is contingent and variable, the age markers to which we refer are *typical*, nothing more. For example, most infants walk at around age 1, but biological development requires that they crawl before they walk. Infants confined to cribs with little stimulation or opportunities for "floor time" in which to crawl (problematic social influence) will not likely walk by the age of 1.

In our first edition, there was no chapter for emerging adulthood; young adulthood was viewed as beginning after adolescence. By the second edition, emerging adulthood had become a newly defined life phase ranging from 18 to 25 (Arnett, 2007), largely as a response to societal factors such as changing sexual and educational norms that expanded the time during which people were still accomplishing the murky tasks of building intimate relationships, careers, and more independent lives. The Great Recession of 2008 to 2009 cast a long shadow over the economic prospects of those entering the labor market at that time. Thus, we now view emerging adulthood as persisting until 30 (and for some, well beyond that), though there are many who achieve stable, independent lives at earlier ages. This illustrates the fluidity and overlap that can be obscured by defining our chapters by developmental tasks and typical chronological ages of their achievement.

The dilemma becomes even more apparent in older adulthood. As biological and social forces interact to promote longer lives for many, the phases of older adulthood often map onto people's socioeconomic status more than chronological age or the tasks theorized to occur during that phase of life. People whose bodies were tested by poverty or the physical work they did for many years may not have the good health to enjoy a "reinvention" in retirement or an "encore" older age.

In short, no age or phase will apply to everyone. Similarly, the many psychodynamic generalizations we address include assumptions and assertions to which there are significant exceptions. Additionally, historic events such as the Great Recession or the recent COVID-19 pandemic affect people differently. One of our aims is to get beyond old rules about grieving and provide the developmental foundation that encourages attention to the contexts of loss experiences and the important dimensions of potential individual variation in reaction to them. To this end, we give a set of typical experiences in each age group and describe how development and circumstances contextualize loss, providing the basis for typical and atypical reactions. Often, the atypical response will tell you much about who your client is.

In this text, we identify losses common to different developmental stages, understanding that loss and subsequent grief are normal. We use the term *normal* in the sociological sense to reflect statistical norms and common experience, not to indicate any judgment attached to the loss. For each life phase, we identify customary death and nondeath losses (which we now call living losses) that include maturational losses, those losses that come as a result of growth/maturation. Although we address instances when grief is out of the norm, we do not focus on pathologizing diagnosis. We believe that loss and grief, though often distressing, can be (and usually is) managed without professional help. Even so, we believe that most people process losses more easily when they have people to talk with who care about them and listen intently and well. Although complicated and prolonged grief reactions occur, most grief is not pathological. We have learned through our clinical practices that most people can cope with even tragic loss when they have someone empathic to accompany them on their grief journey. To enable better practice, we aim to promote a better understanding of how individual development intersects with experiences of loss. We will incorporate intervention models along the way; however, for deep discussion of counseling skills, we recommend Darcey Harris and Harold Winokuer's text *Principles and Practice of Grief Counseling* (2016).

We intend this text to help practitioners understand how the experience of grief is influenced by biological responses to stress, psychological responses to loss in view of previous attachments, and social norms and the greater environment in which the griever is located. A bio–psycho–social–spiritual perspective guides practitioners to conceptualize their work in ways that enable grievers to make meaning of the loss and process it in their own way. We envision a practitioner who may *seem* passive in not pushing one grief model but who actively helps the mourner explore a new identity in the aftermath of loss. Good grief work allows mourners to learn more about themselves and how they fit in the world—and to grow as a result.

TEXT STRUCTURE

This text has a standard organized structure for each level of development from infancy through older adulthood. Each chapter opens with a brief introduction followed by the objectives for the chapter. These are followed by a vignette about an individual who is experiencing losses characteristic of that age group. These are followed by a review of normal developmental issues (bio–psycho–social–spiritual) for that age, particularly the abilities and challenges that are specific to it. As developmental task accomplishment lags for some people and is accomplished early by others, some developmental tasks overlap chapters, and there is fluidity in the ages assigned to each chapter. A section on special considerations in risk and resilience follows that review. The next section describes how an individual of that age tends to cope with a death loss. Consideration of the living losses follows and includes how an individual of that age may experience atypical,

typical, and maturational losses, including their own life-threatening illness. This is followed by a section about how significant others tend to react to and mourn the death of someone in that age range. We close each chapter with a discussion of interventions found to be useful for that age group. Each chapter ends with short readings by people with experiential or clinical knowledge, providing a firsthand account of a particular type of loss.

Throughout the book, we will use some jargon that needs to be understood at the outset. *Typical losses* are those relatively common to a specific age group but often met with little support precisely because they are "normal." Pet loss, for example, is likely to occur during the school years, just as the loss of a romantic relationship is common in emerging adulthood. These are typical losses. *Off-time losses* occur during a stage of life where they are not expected. Although parents often die when children have reached middle age, it is considered an off-time loss when a parent dies during a child's adolescence or emerging adulthood. Off-time losses are more challenging because few peers are available to provide role models for grieving, peers may distance themselves because of unfamiliarity and discomfort, and formal support resources may not be appropriately responsive because the loss is off-time.

Other typical losses result from development (growing up), and we refer to these as *maturational losses*: examples include when a toddler loses unconditional positive regard and is no longer viewed as "cute" for misbehavior but is held accountable or when a young adult marries and must give up the freedom of single living. We believe maturational losses can lead to "illegitimate" expressions of grief, known as "disenfranchised grief" (Doka, 2002). This text names such losses, recognizing that until named, they cannot be acknowledged and their emotional resonance considered. We also sound a note of caution that while recognition of the loss is necessary, overt mourning is not always required.

BIO–PSYCHO–SOCIAL–SPIRITUAL ASPECTS OF GRIEF

We adopt a bio–psycho–social–spiritual perspective on grief and loss across the life course. As spirituality is a core part of development for many people, we incorporate discussion of spiritual aspects of loss throughout this edition of the text and encourage practitioners to assess the degree to which spiritual perspectives and practices are important to each individual with whom they work. We explicate the biological aspects of human development, including neurobiological, genomic, and other physical changes, along with the more typical psychological and social aspects of development. Much of the biological material will be new to many clinicians, but to understand how grief is embodied, clinicians must appreciate the immunological, hormonal, and other biochemical responses that humans have to stressful events; genetic, genomic, and epigenetic effects and influences; and neurobiological impacts of grief and trauma. We provide ample citation so that readers may explore this material in more depth.

Biological Effects of Grief

There is a strong association of higher mortality with bereavement (Parkes et al., 1969; Stroebe et al., 1981). Although some older studies found no statistically significant risk of death after loss (Clayton, 1974), recent and better-designed studies confirm that individuals can and do "die of a broken heart" at double the rate of nonbereaved people matched for age and other demographics (Carey et al., 2014; Dande & Pandit, 2013). Bereavement effects are not transient as first thought but can lead to lingering cardiac problems (Schwarz et al., 2017). Additionally, widowers die at higher rates than widows (Stroebe & Stroebe, 1993). How and why does that happen? What are the biological mechanisms that function to put grievers at risk? How might practitioners intervene to promote health after the death of a loved one?

Explaining the complex mechanisms of morbidity and mortality due to a "broken heart" is beyond the scope of this book. However, a basic understanding of how immune systems, genetic/epigenetic factors, neurological systems, and cardiovascular (and other organ) systems can be affected by stress and grief (and by depression and anxiety) helps practitioners recognize the impact of psychosocial factors on physical health and think about how to promote health despite bereavement. For those interested in more detail, Koch (2013) provides a useful summary of diseases caused by mind–body interactions including "broken heart," otherwise known as Takotsubo cardiomyopathy.

In Western countries, the Cartesian separation of body and mind still rules common understandings; physical health is deemed "about the body," and psychological well-being is "about the mind." Yet the interaction of mind and body has been assumed in many other cultures for eons, and the recent embrace of mindfulness and other practices originating in contemplative religious and cultural practices has shed light on those interactions (Siegel, 2010a, 2010b). Often, people have associated positive emotions with good health (Seligman, 2012), yet recent findings strongly indicate that a mix of positive and negative emotions (tempering bad with good and good with caution) actually seems to promote health even better (Hershfield et al., 2013). The interactions of emotions, stress, trauma, and physical health are mediated through immune, genomic, hormonal/biochemical, and neurological functions, all of which affect organ functions.

The immune system is one of the most potent mediators of mental and physical health, and levels of expressed emotion are associated with changes in immune functioning (Brod et al., 2014; Salovey et al., 2000). A significant body of work (well summarized in Salovey et al., 2000) shows that negative emotions decrease secretory immunoglobulin A (S-IgA) levels, which then causes individuals to be more susceptible to infection by viruses such as the common cold. Likewise, the negative emotions of grief reduce the immune system's efficiency and provoke inflammation and decreased activity of T lymphocytes and natural killer cells (Buckley et al., 2012), reducing the ability to fight everything from short-term viral diseases to cancer. These changes are also associated with higher levels of inflammation, which itself is associated with cardiovascular disease and cancer over time (Buckley et al., 2012).

Although genetic endowment is frequently viewed as static, new knowledge about how genes are "turned on and off" has led to new understandings of how genetic expression changes as a result of environmental stresses (Rothstein, 2013). Furthermore, the genome is actually changed over time in ways that can be passed down to offspring (epigenetics; Bienertová-Vašků et al., 2014; Zucchi et al., 2013). These genomic effects have clear implications for people stressed by grief over long periods of time. Some suggest genomics play a part in the differences between people who experience complicated (prolonged) grief and those whose grief follows a more customary trajectory (O'Connor et al., 2014; Schultze-Florey et al., 2012). Mindfulness practices used for managing grief have been shown to help calm the inflammatory response believed to negatively affect both immune system function and genetic expression (the inflammatory response is regulated by genes; Creswell et al., 2012). In short, we should not neglect the reciprocal relationship between genomics and grief.

Neurotransmitters and other neurochemical interactions also play a role in the interaction of mental and physical health. The major mediator of brain chemistry under stress is the hypothalamic–pituitary–adrenal (HPA) axis, which, when activated, causes a release of cortisol, the stress hormone. Norepinephrine and adrenocorticotropin hormone (ACTH) are also released when the HPA axis is activated, with rises in ACTH typically creating a feedback loop with cortisol (which then rises, ideally leading to lowered ACTH production). This feedback loop seems to break down in depressed and stressed individuals, with cortisol staying elevated (Buckley et al., 2012). Children and youth are reported to have disturbed cortisol functioning after the death of a parent. The cortisol-awakening response becomes blunted, and heightened levels of cortisol remain in their systems (Dietz et al., 2013; Kaplow et al., 2013). Cortisol is associated with sleep–wake cycles, and sleep disturbance is highly associated with grief reactions in most age groups. This lack of good sleep may also contribute to poor health during bereavement (Buckley et al., 2012).

Neuroanatomy also seems to be affected by grief. Using functional magnetic resonance imaging (fMRI) to scan acutely bereaved individuals' brains after interviewing them about their loss, researchers found indications that the posterior cingulate cortex, the cerebellum, and the inferior temporal gyrus are all affected (Gundel et al., 2003; O'Connor et al., 2007). Each brain structure has a role in autobiographical memory and creation of the "storyline" of individuals' lives, a capacity increasingly implicated in good mental health (Boddez, 2018; Siegel, 2010a). Freed et al. (2009) showed that differing levels of attention to one's grief are associated with changes in the way the amygdala (the "emotion center" of the brain) interacts with the dorsolateral prefrontal cortex (where "thinking" and executive functions process emotions and meaning). These changes suggest that rumination (attention focused unremittingly on grief) may create neuroanatomical changes over time. O'Connor et al. (2008) have shown that the reward center, where attachment "shows up," is stimulated when individuals with prolonged grief are examined with fMRI: Both pain and reward centers are stimulated as reminders of the attachment figure who died, whereas those with customary grieving show only the pain. Grieving affects both the neurochemistry and structure of the brain.

With such issues in mind, it is important for the grief counselor to promote physical health. Regular exercise, balanced diet with an increase of B vitamins and antioxidants, increased omega-3, and exposure to light (Zisook & Shuchter, 2001) should all be encouraged. Urging an examination by a physician is recommended, along with encouraging self-care particularly aimed at resuming good sleep habits, avoiding alcohol and other drugs, and decreasing risks during the bereavement period. A useful short video about the biological impacts of grief can be found at www.youtube.com/watch?v=eEcaUhxAH2g (How Grief Affects Your Brain and What to Do About It: NBC News).

Psychological Effects of Grief

Cognitive and emotional development play important roles in processing loss and understanding death. Every loss is framed within the griever's stage of development. When a loss happens in childhood, that loss will need to be reworked as development proceeds; the loss of a sibling at the age of 7 will need to be reassessed in adolescence and young adulthood as the secondary losses inherent in the death evolve. The 7-year-old will miss a brother as a playmate, but the 35-year-old may miss the help of a sibling with aging parents' needs.

The attachment style of the person generally and the specific nature of the attachment between the griever and the deceased (when a death loss occurs) constitute a further psychological dimension of grief. Bowlby's stages of loss are described later, but Bowlby's theory is premised on loss being a function of a broken attachment. He suggested that the intensity of loss is directly related to the level of attachment (both as a sense of connection and as an activation of the evolutionary attachment system; Bowlby, 1980/1998). Many researchers have explored how attachment styles inform the grief process (Field & Wogrin, 2011; Smigelsky et al., 2020; Zech & Arnold, 2011). Ainsworth et al. built on Bowlby's work to identify attachment styles developed as a result of the infant–caregiver relationship. Secure attachment is characterized by the individual feeling lovable and able to give love without high levels of anxiety or distance. Insecure attachment of the anxious-preoccupied style is characterized by individuals feeling less lovable and highly anxious about maintaining others' love; insecure attachment of the dismissive-avoidant style is characterized by the individual rejecting attachment relationships and working to maintain emotional distance. Insecure attachment styles are correlated empirically with difficulties in grieving, but research at the intersection of attachment and bereavement has been challenged by inconsistencies in measurement of attachment styles (Shaver & Tancready, 2001). Recent research (Smigelsky et al., 2020) examines attachment styles (using a fourth, fearful attachment style, characterized by high anxiety and avoidance of attachment) and assesses the nature of the grievers' specific relationship with the deceased, including levels of conflict in that relationship. They find that higher levels of attachment anxiety (fearful or preoccupied styles) in the context of a closer relationship with the deceased predict a higher level of risk for more debilitating grief reactions. Ironically, people with more avoidant and dismissive attachments have less risk for problematic grief reactions, and individuals with secure attachment styles have higher risk for problematic grief when the specific relationship was fraught with conflict. For both groups, conflict in a close relationship with the deceased was associated with more problematic grief reactions (Smigelsky et al., 2020). Smigelsky's group suggests, along with others (Kosminsky & Jordan, 2016), that an attachment-informed approach to bereavement is important to creating effective tailored intervention with grievers.

It is widely understood that grief nearly always entails psychic pain; it challenges coping and typically includes feelings of irritation, sadness, and rumination. Less commonly appreciated is the heightened sense of vulnerability and fear that accompany grief (Sim et al., 2014). Bereaved individuals commonly fear another loved one dying and are often afraid to go out into the world or sleep alone at night. Loss stimulates an acute sense of vulnerability and subsequent hypervigilance, just as trauma does (Lopez Levers, 2012). Rando (1993) captured this in her extensive list of symptoms of grief, yet vulnerability is seldom recognized as an expected aspect of grief. Helping grievers recognize this customary part of grieving helps them to feel less frightened and "crazy" when they feel anxious.

Uncertainty about the future is a facet of grief closely related to vulnerability. Loss and separation change many plans abruptly. Such rapidly changed expectations lead to uncertainty about one's future. Uncertainty provokes anxious behavior, heightened vulnerability, and stress (Hirsh et al., 2012). This is part of the discomfort experienced by grievers, and it may inspire attempts to defend against attachment, potentially leaving people isolated just when they most need support.

Rando (1993) echoed Simos's (1979) observation that major losses are made up of many smaller, secondary losses. For example, the death of a parent during childhood not only is a tragic loss of an attachment figure but also incorporates losses of guidance, economic support, a sense of a secure base, a protector, and so forth, not to mention losses of friends and a familiar school if adjustment requires a new living situation. For a griever to fully mourn the primary loss, these secondary losses must be recognized and validated.

Rando (1993) also described how time and grief interact. Although many try to put a time limit on grief, she recognized that it continues long after the acute phase has resolved. The "anniversary reaction" is an example: The griever has a sudden temporary upsurge of grief (STUG) reaction (1993, pp. 64–77). The griever may not even be conscious of the occasion yet feels dysphoric every April, the month a loved one died. STUG reactions can be set off by a song, a familiar scent, or encountering an unexpected reminder of the loved one.

Practice wisdom has long held that multiple losses accumulate, giving more intensity to grief. However, while the nursing literature is rife with discussion of cumulative grief because nurses experience loss when patients die (Marino, 1998; Shorter & Stayt, 2010), few empirical studies have explored it. Some of the better-designed research does not find the expected negative outcomes of cumulative grief (Cherney & Verhey, 1996). Nursing literature notes the possibilities for burnout and compassion fatigue, but Cherney and Verhey (1996) suggested that there could be adaptive habituation to grief. This is an area where much more research is necessary.

Still others note the accumulation of grief from losses in addition to those caused by death (Brave Heart, 1998) and persuasively argue that a history of cultural and other prior losses impedes coping with new ones. Individuals likely manage cumulative losses differently, but the clinician should take a thorough and accurate history, including identification of all kinds of prior losses and the griever's responses to them. We believe that maturational losses will be part of this cumulative load.

Boddez (2018), synthesizing understandings of attachment theory, behavioral theory, and grief, suggests that "appetitive conditioning" (p. 19) involves a pairing of positive feelings and safety when one is in the presence of a loved person (attachment), and this regular pairing yields strong appetites for the pairing to remain constant—a situation that changes with a death. Boddez illustrates how conditioning and extinction responses fit the experience of grief, including the initial yearning/craving responses immediately following a loss. He suggests interventions such as association splitting and extinction, common behavioral interventions, can help extinguish the yearning grievers feel in connection with cues that bring the deceased to mind.

In sum, psychological theories about grief attribute it to attachment styles; to conditioned responses; and to experiences of change, uncertainty, and vulnerability. All have value for helping clinicians understand grief. Each theoretical approach stipulates different approaches to intervention. The following sections on theories of grief illustrate more fully the connections of theory to intervention methods.

Social Aspects of Grief

We tend to think first, and sometimes only, about the psychological impacts of loss, ignoring how the collective processes of culture and the patterns of relationships we call social structures tell us about what loss is, what it means, and how to mourn. Grief is fundamentally social in that it involves mourning a loss of connection or a place in the social order of life (Thompson & Cox, 2017). The deep social aspect of grief extends to the support mourners need to process their grief.

Social rituals are fundamental to most important transitions, including those provoked by loss and death. Traditionally, funerals were grounded in religious practice and a community of believers that provided a deeply social way of mourning losses (Parkes et al., 2000). Yet, as Parkes et al. observed, by the 1990s, fewer U.S. citizens participated in organized religion and its mourning rituals. Recent studies suggest that fewer U.S. or European citizens engage in religious funerals than in previous generations (Norton & Gino, 2014). Even so, Norton and Gino (2014) show that specified performed behavior defined as ritual is useful in allowing a griever both to have a sense of control and to lower the levels of grief and mourning. Thompson and Doka (2017) suggest that rituals have the power to validate disenfranchised losses and that interventions that help grievers develop rituals of transition, reconciliation, and affirmation can all help grievers reflect upon and process the pain. In lieu of religious rituals, creative activities that memorialize the deceased, assist the grieving, and support the caregivers are increasingly being used to aid mourning (Bertman, 2015).

Undoubtedly, technology is changing the way people are socialized generally (boyd, 2014), including in the realm of death and dying. Granek (2017) argues that grief has become medicalized, psychologized, and isolated from others. She asserts that grievers have resisted the privatization of mourning by finding community online. Instead of shared religious rituals, many turn to Facebook, Instagram, Snapchat, and internet cemeteries to share their grief (Lingel, 2013). Sites that maintain the deceased's previous social media presence and internet cemetery sites arranged in advance of a death can conflate death and presence. They create new rituals where the bereaved can not only elicit and receive support but also maintain an ongoing degree of involvement with the deceased (Dilmaç, 2018). Indeed, group intervention modalities for support after loss are rising on the internet despite some resistance from traditional group work practitioners (Lubas & De Leo, 2014). These secular technological rituals are becoming common forms of memorialization, ritual, and grieving in developed countries.

The concepts of disenfranchised grief and ambiguous grief (both discussed in the following sections within postmodern theories) reveal other fundamentally social features of loss and grief. Both ideas derive from inconsistencies between the feelings of the griever and what is culturally recognized as a "real" loss and an "allowable" state of grief. Such "feeling rules" (Hochschild, 1979) vary by religious, national, ethnic, and generational contexts. The "sympathy biography" (Clark, 1997) encompasses the idea that people keep a mental running ledger of who owes them sympathy and whom they owe. Clark (1997) discusses what losses and events generate sympathy and how sympathy is exchanged over time among friends and family with an awareness of what constitutes adequate reciprocity. Norms and rules about losses to be mourned, sympathy to be extended, and the people entitled to mourn (and for how long) are social creations, not artifacts of biology or individual psychology.

Each of us holds assumptions about how the world works. These assumptions (e.g., my husband will be there to kiss me good night; children outlive their parents; my house will be there when I get home) make the world familiar and predictable, thus seemingly safe. This is known as the "assumptive world," and we seldom think about it until the assumptions are violated. Traumatic events violate it and trigger distress (Janoff-Bulman, 1992). For many, the recent COVID-19 outbreak revealed our assumption that modern medicine in a developed country would be able to stem any pandemic and people would get the care that they need—our assumptions were violated. Grief usually forces the griever to actively revise the assumptive world by recognizing the assumptions that have been violated by the loss and reflecting on what assumptions still hold. Similarly, Attig (2011) asserts that bereavement requires that mourners "relearn the world." He challenges the notion that "time heals" passively and argues that one must relearn the world actively, reflecting and grappling "intellectually and spiritually, emotionally and psychologically, behaviorally, socially, and biologically" to adapt to a world without the loved one in it (p. 49). Attig views this as a much more holistic process than revising assumptions; it requires pragmatic relearning of how to function in the world without the lost entity or person.

The assumptive world includes "taken-for-granteds" that can be approached in much the way social workers use an ecological perspective. Working with a griever, we might explore the different layers of assumptions. For instance, on the micro level, assumptions exist along the lines of "I'll predecease my child"; on the mezzo level, one may hold assumptions such as "my child will be safe at school"; on the macro level, one may believe that public health resources will remedy any epidemic—and then be disoriented by an epidemic of gun violence or a viral outbreak that shatters all of these assumptions. Grievers may need help to identify the varied assumptions they have at differing societal levels. When assumptions require revision at multiple levels, we would expect greater challenges to adapting and revising or relearning the assumptive world.

Spiritual Aspects of Grief

Earlier, we noted the movement away from religious rituals, but spirituality and religion are not the same. Distinctions vary, but the most useful is that religions have institutionalized structures (leaders/clergy) and dogmas (beliefs to which adherents of a religion subscribe), whereas spirituality encompasses more idiosyncratic ways in which individuals make sense of metaphysical questions about the existence of God(s), life after death, or the meaning of life. Religious identifications are generally falling in the United States, Western Europe, Australia, and in many developed nations (see globalreligiousfutures.org), and more people identify as atheist or agnostic than ever before. This means that assessment of spiritual as well as religious beliefs (or lack thereof) must be part of a full assessment of any griever in order to understand meaning-making structures and processes of importance to that person. Such an assessment should be bounded by Knitter's (2010) "prerequisites for dialogue" (pp. 260–262): humility, commitment (exploration of the client's spiritual commitments, not the counselor's), trust in our common humanity, empathy, and openness to change. These prerequisites should be part of any respectful counseling relationship.

Religious and spiritual beliefs give meaning to human existence and suffering (Thompson, 2017). Thompson notes that religion and its rituals bring "a sense of order to a time [of bereavement] characterized by chaos and disorder" (2017, p. 338). He traces the ancient connection between grieving and religion to their common struggle with meaning-making; for in the presence of terrible grief, life's meaning is questioned. Religion typically provides an established and narrow range of answers to these existential questions of why we live, suffer, and die, whereas spiritual and secular approaches require that people grapple with meaning-making in the absence of ready-made answers.

Like theists (people who believe in God[s]), atheists have beliefs and commitments. Schnell and Keenan (2011) found that atheists fell into three groups: those strongly committed to self-actualization as a form of meaning-making and who exhibited no crises of meaning in their large-scale study among Germans; those who have broad commitments to varied meaning-making strategies (particularly commitments to well-being and/or relatedness) who have few crises of meaning; and those with low levels of commitment to any forms of meaning-making and who tend to have more crises of meaning. They found that the atheists experienced about the same levels of crisis of meaning as the religious members of their sample. Similarly, Sawyer and Brewster (2019) compared bereaved theists with atheists and found demographic and loss-related variables to be much more important predictors of distress after a death; more surprisingly, they found belief in God to be more predictive of distress than atheism. They also found that both theists and atheists who reported an active search for meaning after a death were more likely to exhibit posttraumatic growth.

Christian et al. (2019) recently examined how religious and spiritual beliefs explain prolonged grief. They found that a report of "somewhat important" spiritual beliefs was associated with a small but statistically significant rise in prolonged grief disorder; religious beliefs and spiritual beliefs deemed "not at all important" or "very important" did not show any impact on prolonged grief. They speculated that people with somewhat important spiritual beliefs may have more unanswered questions of meaning—greater uncertainty—than those who find answers in religious beliefs, or whose spiritual practices either are not very important or, to the contrary, are highly developed and capable of answering such meaning-related questions.

Attig (2011) asserts that death of a loved one has the potential to be spiritually transformative: "As we recognize the gift-like character of the life of the deceased, we may wonder at the mysteries of the universe itself within which such gifts are provided through no dessert or effort on our part" (p. 184). In sum, the human impulse to make meaning is heightened during grief. Spiritual and religious understandings and practices (or rejections of them) must be assessed to help grievers of all types consider how those aspects of their worldview affect their experience of loss.

RISK AND RESILIENCE AND GRAPPLING WITH ADVERSE CHILDHOOD EXPERIENCES

In the late 1990s, Kaiser Permanente conducted a large study of patients' problematic childhood experiences and their associations with health in adulthood. These experiences came to be known as ACEs, an acronym, as noted earlier, for adverse childhood experiences. In the original study, Felitti et al. (1998) collected data about respondents' childhood abuse (physical, sexual, and psychological) and their difficult household situations (violence against their mother; or living in a household with members who were substance abusers, mentally ill or suicidal, or ever incarcerated). They found that more than half of respondents experienced at least one of these ACEs and about one quarter had two or more ACEs. Individuals with four or more reported ACEs had much higher incidence of many health problems, substance use disorder, and mental health problems (Felitti et al., 1998), a finding that has remained robust as multiple research groups continue to explore these outcomes (Centers for Disease Prevention and Control, 2019). ACEs certainly inflict losses (of safety, secure parenting, and well-being) and are one mechanism for how risk is conveyed across generations and across time. See Figure 1.1 to identify ACEs and structural challenges that affect development.

Risks are real, yet so is resilience. From Tedeschi and Calhoun's classic work on posttraumatic growth (2004) to the observation that resilience may be strengthened by systematic self-reflection upon coping with stressors (Crane et al., 2019), it has been illustrated that not all individuals at risk of poor outcomes experience them. Indeed, Seery et al. (2010) found that those who experience two to four ACEs seem to fare better than those who experience more than four, or none. A growing group of researchers now argues that learning to cope with and reappraise stressors as

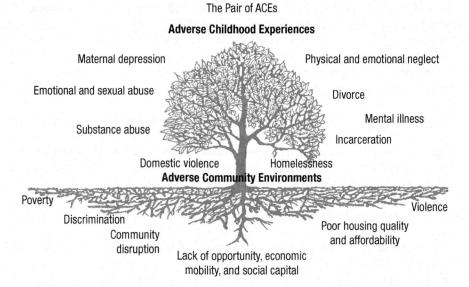

FIGURE 1.1 ACEs in Childhood and Community. This image illustrates the many sources of ACEs to which people are potentially exposed in childhood. Although the ones around the tree crown are typically known, the ones around the tree roots are just as devastating and often not as recognized. ACEs, adverse childhood experiences.

Source: Reproduced with permission from Ellis, W., & Dietz, W. (2017). A new framework for addressing adverse childhood and community experiences: The building community resilience (BCR) model. *Academic Pediatrics, 17,* S86–S93. doi.org/10.1016/j.acap.2016.12.011

challenges to be overcome (Lazarus, 2006) may be a crucial key to avoiding negative outcomes. Some adversity seems to foster developing skills necessary to coping with varied stressors and promotes belief in one's capability to survive an adverse event and subsequently thrive. One commonly identified "lesson learned" from grief is that one can survive what seemed to be unendurable. Crane et al. (2019) assert that promoting systematic self-reflection on abilities to cope, regulate emotional responses, and reappraise stressful events is an effective strategy to promote resilience. We have seen that those likely to move through grief authentically and to eventually engage in life again are those who reflect upon the loss, their coping, and their emotional regulation.

It is important to note that population-level characteristics are closely associated with higher exposure to risks of impaired well-being and poorer long-term health and economic status. In the United States, people of color are at higher risk for low socioeconomic status in every age group and more likely to have poorer health. Asians, undifferentiated by origin in the statistic, are the exception. They have the highest rates of medical insurance coverage and better health outcomes than Whites (HealthyPeople.gov, 2020a). The Healthy People 2020 goals for the United States (HealthyPeople.gov, 2020b) specify the reduction of racial health disparities, but in 2015 a Black adult still had double a White adult's chance of dying of heart disease; Black adults also have the highest death rate from every type of cancer and from homicide (Centers for Disease Prevention and Control, 2015). These disparities both expose people at risk to more potential losses and may impact the way individuals process loss disparities made even worse as losses accumulate.

A WORD ABOUT THE CHANGING DEMOGRAPHIC OF THE UNITED STATES AND THE WORLD

The United States is rapidly becoming an "aging" society. The number of adults 65 and older has steadily increased since the 1960s and is growing at a faster rate than ever as the "baby boomers" (those born 1946–1964) are getting older (Mather et al., 2015). In 2030, all living baby boomers will be over 65; 20% of the U.S. population will be of what is now customary retirement age (U.S. Census Bureau, 2019). In 2030, older adults will outnumber children for the first time in U.S. history (U.S. Census Bureau, 2019).

The U.S. older adult population is also becoming more diverse than ever before. According to the Administration for Community Living (2018), racial and ethnic minority populations will increase from 19% of the older adult population in 2006 to 28% in 2030. Although there have been some significant improvements for all older adults since the 1960s in economic security, health status, and postponements of disability, these positive trends are not evenly distributed. For example, in 2014, just 8% of non-Hispanic Whites 65 and older lived in poverty, compared with 18% of Latinxs and 19% of African Americans (Mather et al., 2015). Like health disparities, structural inequalities do not spare older adults.

There is also a growing "diversity gap" between older and younger people in the United States. While each successive birth cohort is becoming more diverse, diversity is concentrated in the youngest age groups due to historical trends in immigration (Mather et al., 2015). This gap is sharpening intergenerational political conflict in powerful ways that are hard to predict. If history is a reliable guide, the older, White members of U.S. society are likely to practice a politics rooted in fear of losing control of a country they believe should be defined by their material and cultural interests (Boyer, 1978). This conflict among generations and cultural groups threatens cooperation and limits tax support for social welfare and public health measures. Cooperation among countries on important matters such as climate change and pandemic disease is also threatened as diversity concentrates in younger generations, and ethnonationalism becomes widespread among older established groups who want to maintain their power. On a grand scale, this could lead to tragic losses.

The fact that we are living longer than ever contributes mightily to these changes and conflicts. In 1900, U.S. life expectancy at birth was 47.3 years, and by 2014 it was 81.3. A surge in deaths by suicide and drug overdose decreased life expectancy slightly from 2015 to 2017 but rose slightly again in 2018 (Centers for Disease Prevention and Control, 2018). This short-term phenomenon should not obscure the larger trend toward greater longevity, which applies throughout the world.

Longer lives require more income and care for a burgeoning population of older people in the United States who will be disproportionately White and will require high levels of medical care as they age. The resources to support care for aging people will come from taxes paid by a disproportionately smaller population of younger, more diverse workers whose life prospects are narrowed by technological changes (Ford, 2015) and climate change (Kolbert, 2014).

To some degree or another, each of these demographic trends applies across Europe, large parts of Asia, many parts of South America, and some parts of Africa. Each can influence what we perceive as loss, what losses we deem meaningful relative to others, and how we react to what is lost or slipping away. All change involves loss, and there is a lot of change on the horizon.

INTRODUCTION TO GRIEF THEORY

Classical Grief Theory

Task-Based Theories

> *Mourning is regularly the reaction to the loss of a loved person, or to the loss of some abstraction which has taken the place of one, such as one's country, liberty, an ideal, and so on—Freud, 1917/1957, p. 243.*

Grief, ancient as consciousness, is a modern subject of scholarly attention. Freud was one of the first to address grief, melancholia, and mourning in a scholarly manner. He observed that we can mourn for things, values, and statuses, not only as a response to a death. He also assures that grief and mourning are "not pathological," even when psychotic thoughts, feelings, and behaviors occur in reaction to loss.

Freud proposed a "task-based theory" predicated on the idea that the mourner must decathect from the lost entity. Freud's theory of behavior held that the psyche cathects people and loved entities with libidinal energy and that that same libido must be withdrawn in order for mourners to heal after loss. He believed people experiencing melancholia (what we might now call dysthymia or depression) had not successfully withdrawn the libidinal energy (decathexis) and needed help to do this. In Freud's understanding, the next task was to transfer libido to a new love object via cathexis. He asserted (Freud, 1917/1957) that mourning is only completed when the ego becomes free by virtue of decathecting libido from the lost love object. He suggested a year as the customary time necessary for this to be achieved. (Despite his religious skepticism, as a person of Jewish heritage, Freud may have adopted the year of mourning ritualized in Jewish faith.)

Freud's was the primary theoretical paradigm for early grief work. Usually couched in the language of "letting go," counselors have long believed that mourners must separate from their attachment to the lost entity, even if they did not necessarily follow Freud's theory of decathexis. Though simplistic, this task-based model for grief work has periodically reemerged in other forms. Indeed, this task of decathexis, separation, or "letting go" continues to inform practice wisdom despite new understandings of loss and grief. Freud himself set the context for some reinterpretations of grief work. He wrote to a friend who like Freud had experienced the death of a child:

Although we know that after such a loss the acute state of mourning will subside, we also know we shall remain inconsolable and will never find a substitute. No matter what may fill the gap, even if it be filled completely, it nevertheless remains something else. It is the only way of perpetuating that love which we do not want to relinquish. (Translated letters, Freud, 1961)

He implies that decathexis may occur but that recathexis is not likely to fill the gap, that the original attachment "remains something else" that mourners do not relinquish. We will return to this idea in connection with theories of meaning-making (Neimeyer, 2001) and the concept of continuing bonds (Klass et al., 1996).

Some of the first empirical work to explore the grieving process was done by Erich Lindemann (1944), who studied the responses of grievers following the Cocoanut Grove nightclub fire in Boston in November 1942. He designed the study in advance to be fielded immediately after a tragedy so that there would be no anticipatory grief but a sudden loss. He believed this would allow him to assess mourners' responses more accurately. He theorized that grief normally includes somatic distress, preoccupation with the deceased, guilt, and sometimes, hostility. He asserted that 8 to 10 sessions with a psychiatrist over the course of a month and a half were sufficient to manage grief work. This was based on his findings, yet few would agree with him today. Evidence can enlighten or mislead, and research does not always produce conclusions that stand up over time. The evidence in support of any "best practice" is always the best evidence at the time and always subject to revision.

Lindemann believed that the following traumatic death tasks of grieving, which he postulated, must be accomplished, but he moved beyond Freud's tasks of decathexis and recathexis:

1. Emancipation from bondage to the deceased
2. Readjustment to the environment in which the deceased is missing
3. Formulation of new relationships

In some ways, Step 1 mirrored decathexis and Step 3 mirrored recathexis, but Lindemann contributed the idea that this was not a totally interior, psychological process. He acknowledged in the second task that bereft individuals must adjust to a social world in which their loved one is no longer living. He proposed 4 to 6 weeks as necessary to accomplish these tasks. The unfortunate consequence of his time frame was that mourners, wanting to seem healthy, avoided expressing grief after 4 to 6 weeks and grief work practitioners began to regard grief that lasted longer as pathological.

The time frame of grief has long been contested (Kendler et al., 2008), and the "normal" duration of grief remains controversial (Penman et al., 2014). Penman et al. (2014) note that while more variability in grief trajectories is acknowledged today, uncertainty remains about how to define grief that seems out of the norm. The most recent *Diagnostic and Statistical Manual of Mental Disorders,* Fifth Edition, of the American Psychiatric Association (*DSM-5*; American Psychiatric Association, 2014) no longer included what was called the "bereavement exception." Previously, depressive symptoms that might rise to the level of a major depressive disorder (MDD) were excluded if there had been a death loss up to 2 months before. Many declared the 2-month cutoff unrealistic as mourning often extends well beyond that (Wakefield et al., 2011). Now, *DSM-5* recommends diagnosing MDD when criteria are met (recognizing that grief seldom includes the level of self-loathing and feelings of worthlessness that generally accompany MDD.

J. William Worden (2009) has become known for a task-based grief theory and intervention framework that encompasses the following steps (Worden & Winokuer, 2011):

1. Acknowledge the reality of the loss.
2. Process the pain of the grief.
3. Adjust to a world without the deceased.
4. Find an enduring connection with the deceased while embarking on a new life.

Worden adds the experience of processing pain, and his tasks provide a way to work with grievers without the assumption of "cure" but with the expectation that grievers can be assisted in working through their grief. Worden's task-based strategy is widely embraced because it provides an action plan and a way of guiding a process that often feels out of control.

These task-based theories of grief and intervention were a major step forward from assumptions that the bereaved were pathologically affected if they could not move on with their lives as if little of import had occurred. Freud depathologized grief, and the other task-based theorists explicated what the bereaved needed to accomplish in order to heal. In the undisciplined, untidy world of grief (Foote & Frank, 1999), a structured response lends a sense that there is a map to guide the way.

Stage-Based Theories

Like Lindemann, Kübler-Ross (1969) was interested in empirical data. As part of a seminar on death and dying at the Chicago Theological Seminary, she and her students talked with dying patients about their thoughts, feelings, and expectations about their conditions at a time when medical practice wisdom held that patients were not to be told their illnesses were fatal. Her book *On Death and Dying: What the Dying Have to Teach Their Doctors, Nurses, Clergy and Their Own Families* (1969) was the source of the now widely accepted and reified stages of "denial and isolation," "anger," "bargaining," "depression," and "acceptance." Following these stage-based chapters in her book, there is a chapter entitled "Hope," a characteristic that she identifies as crucial. Eliott and Olver (2007) interrogate how hope is used both as a noun and as a verb, illustrating how hope for a cure ("having hope"—a noun) creates hope as something one has or does not have, but as a verb hope is something one does. This hope is an active state with desired goals like living until a special event or dying without pain (Eliott & Olver, 2007).

Kübler-Ross's (1969) stages of adjustment to a terminal diagnosis are now widely applied to all types of losses, but her stages were developed for people who are losing their lives, not those who have lost loved ones. These are different experiences. While she has become known as the mother of grief theory, empirically speaking, her stages have little to do with grief (Stroebe et al., 2017).

The stage of denial is particularly misunderstood. Kübler-Ross originally conceptualized it as a stage during which the diagnosed would "shop around" to ensure an accurate diagnosis and/or express hope that medical test results and a terminal diagnosis were incorrect. She viewed this as a healthy adaptation to allow the person to slowly adjust to the idea of a life-threatening illness. This stage has been widely misinterpreted and misapplied in grief counseling. It has often been viewed as a stage to be "broken through" or confronted, with counselors often applying Draconian methods to ensure that denial is not maintained in connection with a death loss. Indeed, Volkan (1985) developed "regrief therapy" as an intervention for the pathologically bereaved. His useful concept of a linking object, an object that reminds the mourner of the lost one, is used within a therapy designed to cut through any "denial" that may remain:

> Throughout treatment, patients experience a variety of emotions as they gain insight into their inability to let the dead person die. . . . The use of the linking object brings about special emotional storms that are not curative without interpretation that engages the close scrutiny of the patient's observing ego. (Volkan, 1985, pp. 289–290)

This assertive confrontation of denial has become one of the suspect interventions associated with early grief work counseling. That denial is viewed as a stage to break through, rather than as the protective adjustment time that Kübler-Ross described, reveals one of the difficulties of stage theories more generally. Both the bereaved and less reflective practitioners can view these models as a recipe, an intervention plan to be broadly applied. This assumes a one-size-fits-all quality to mourning. It also implies that knowledge of the stages can allow one to move more quickly through them—a fallacy with major implications.

Kübler-Ross's model of moving from protective denial to a state of anger and irritation (in her study, often directed at caregivers) is usually viewed as a one-way journey. It is portrayed as if an individual, once in touch with the reality of their loss, will then become angry (either at the lost loved one or at others) and move into a bargaining stage. Clinical work with bereaved individuals shows that anger and irritation flare throughout bereavement. Furthermore, the bargaining that was so intuitive with the terminally ill patients Kübler-Ross interviewed (e.g., if I make amends to everyone I have wronged, I will get well) seems inapplicable to the bereaved who have nothing to bargain *for* as they are aware that the loved one is, according to the resolution of the denial stage, already dead. Yet grief work counselors sometimes believe that expressions of bargaining are necessary before a client can move into the depressive states so characteristic of grief. Once bereaved individuals exhibit sadness, tearfulness, and depressed activity, their family and friends (as well as professionals) then recognize this as classic grief and mourning.

Bereaved individuals may fluctuate among the various stages, and "acceptance" comes gradually (if ever), not in one bright flash. The stages imply a progressive, linear movement through the stages (characteristic of theories of the "modern" era) rather than the oscillation seen most commonly among the bereaved. Recognize, too, that "acceptance" for Kübler-Ross's dying population has a very different quality than acceptance of loss by a bereaved person. For Kübler-Ross (1969, p. 113), acceptance is the point at which a patient accepts that they are dying and they start to withdraw a bit from the world at large.

This differs from acceptance in the bereaved, from whom we expect *more* breadth of emotional expression (including occasional happiness), *more* involvement with prior interests, and *more* engagement with the wider world. These differences are seldom acknowledged in the simplified formats often provided as stage theories for loss. Kübler-Ross was quite clear that these were stages characteristic of dying people and might not apply to others, although she later said they could apply to the bereaved as well (Haupt, 2002), a claim about which we are skeptical. She also cautioned against belief that stages occur in exact sequences, but this caution is seldom incorporated when people learn the stages she postulated, with the result that a fluid and complex process is given a mechanistic cast. Kübler-Ross's stage theory, though once a widely accepted discourse of grief, is now rejected by well-informed grief theorists, researchers, and practitioners (Stroebe et al., 2017).

A second classic stage theory grew from the empirical data of John Bowlby (1980/1998), who followed the children of World War II as they were separated from their parents in war zones and cared for in safer areas. He later studied widows (and a few widowers) and believed that this population confirmed his findings in the study of children. He postulated stages of the following:

- Numbness—defined as being shocked and stunned, not as denial; Bowlby identified the protective nature of this stage.
- Separation anxiety (yearning/searching)—defined as an alternating state of despair and denial, with anger folded in, much like that found in children separated from parents. He claimed that pathological grief is characterized by being stuck in one of these modes— either yearning, or angry and detached.

    Thus, anger is seen as an intelligible constituent of the urgent though fruitless effort a bereaved person is making to restore the bond that has been severed. So long as anger continues, it seems loss is not being accepted as permanent and hope is still lingering on (Bowlby, 1980/1998, p. 91).
- Despair and disorganization—as the loss sinks in, bereaved people attempt to recognize the loss and develop a "new normal." It is a time of lost objects (keys, etc.) as well as lost thoughts and lost time.
- Acquisition of new roles/reorganization—when the bereaved gives up attempts to prepare for the deceased's return (gets rid of clothes, etc.) and moves into new aspects of life and relationships, the bereaved has achieved reorganization.

Bowlby's (1980/1998) stages recall what he recognized in children: They yearn and pine for their parent when separated. He theorized that the attachment style the child exhibited—secure, anxious, avoidant (Ainsworth et al., 1978)—would influence the impact of loss and that children less secure in their attachments would be more likely to exhibit anxious or detached feelings when experiencing a loss. He and others have speculated that these influences extend into adulthood, with adults' grief reactions influenced by their attachment styles. Additionally, he recognized that anger is a barrier to processing grief and that the bereaved begin to move through their grief only once anger subsides.

Since Bowlby's observations about the direct relationship between the level of attachment to the loved object and the degree of loss, many researchers have explored how attachment styles inform the grieving process (Maccallum & Bryant, 2013; Smigelsky et al., 2020). As noted earlier concerning psychological aspects of grief, anxiety is said to be higher, giving subsequent intensity to grieving and yearning, when the bereaved has an insecure attachment style (Smigelsky et al., 2020; Zech & Arnold, 2011). Regardless of attachment style, clinical experience indicates that the level of fondness and connection correlates with the level of grief and mourning.

Maciejewski et al. (2007) explored the stage theories of Kübler-Ross (1969) and Bowlby (1980/1998) and found more support for Bowlby's stages, though aspects of Kübler-Ross's stages were present. They studied 233 bereaved individuals over the course of 2 years and concluded that stages of disbelief, yearning, anger, and depression all had discrete peaks over time. They found that "acceptance" ran as a linear, positive trend across the entire timeline, with acceptance happening anywhere in the grief trajectory and increasing as time elapses. Stroebe et al. (2017) bemoan how Kübler-Ross's stages continue to be used and misapplied in multiple arenas, despite ample evidence that they do not apply to grief. Concerns about stage theories remain: The biggest problem is the idea that they are applicable to all and that they seem like recipes for grieving. We acknowledge the irony that we critique stage theory but then organize our book using age and developmental stage and task theories, which may have arbitrary boundaries. We recognize that these are fluid categories for the purpose of ordering the material in this text rather than reifying ages, stages, or tasks.

A recent classic comes from the work of Therese Rando (1993). Rando argues that individuals move through similar phases that are fairly universal. These are framed as processes rather than stages. She identifies them as constituted of the six "R" processes that she asserts lead to the healthy completion of grieving. Her model (Rando, 1993, p. 45) consists of tasks for mourners to accomplish in each phase. It is prescriptive in that it describes a process the bereaved must experience to proceed toward healing. Here, note that the titles of the phases and subphases are Rando's (1993), followed by our summaries of their meaning.

Avoidance Phase
1. Recognize the loss—The bereaved must acknowledge and understand the reality of the death.

Confrontation Phase
2. React to the separation—The bereaved must experience the pain of the loss, give it expression, and mourn secondary losses.
3. Recollect and reexperience the deceased and the relationship—The bereaved is to review and remember the relationship realistically and also review and reexperience the emotions that arise as they remember the relationship.
4. Relinquish the old attachments to the deceased and the old assumptive world—The bereaved must let go of previous bonds and beliefs and develop a "new normal" with new relationships and attachments.

Accommodation Phase
5. Readjust to move adaptively into the new world without forgetting the old—The bereaved must revise the assumptive world; develop a new relationship with the deceased; adopt new ways of being in the world; and form an identity not predicated on the presence of the deceased.
6. Reinvest—This is a time to actively invest in new relationships and roles and indicates a resolution to active grieving.

Rando's (1993) model has room to tailor the treatment process, and she suggests that the model is useful when grief is deemed to be complicated in some way. Despite Rando's obvious compassion and concern for bereaved people, her model is subject to some of the same criticisms noted earlier. These models are of the "modern" era: All progress is forward, and the map is the same for all. The model is "normal," and deviation is considered abnormal. Pathologizing variation in a highly variable process like grief seems rather obtuse from the "postmodern" perspective that eschews essences and "natural uniformities" in the social world.

The Transition to Postmodern Grief Theory

Some theorists in the tradition of Michel Foucault critique grief theorists and counselors for "disciplining grief" (Foote & Frank, 1999). They say

> grief, like death itself, is undisciplined, risky, wild. That society seeks to discipline grief, as part of its policing of the border between life and death, is predictable, and it is equally predictable that modern society would medicalize grief as the means of policing. (p. 170)

Grief counseling is viewed here as a way to pathologize grief in the service of therapeutic intervention (or use of psy disciplines, according to Granek, 2017) to produce conformity to societal norms. The medicalization of grief, a form of Foucault's "technologies of the self," tends to lead grievers to believe that good self-care requires grief work within a therapeutic context. Granek (2017) suggests that viewing grief as a disease leads to individuals hiding their grief in private (or psy discipline's offices) in ways that separate them from the social support that enables them to heal.

Walter (2000) also recognized how policing grief can be destructive. He traces the evolution of policing grief from the Victorian era's enforcement of contained, formalized, and time-limited grieving to a current expectation of expressive grief with a tendency toward medicalization of the grief process. He asserts that mutual aid groups have evolved to resist policing and medicalization while they themselves have evolved norms that contain an expectation of grieving like other group members.

Postmodern theories of grief grow from a social constructionist understanding of the world (Berger & Luckmann, 1967), which asserts that humans construct an understanding of the world that they then see as self-evident and true. This "trueness" is deeply felt yet differs from how others will construct their truths. For example, in some traditions (Jewish and Amish), the dead are buried solemnly and usually within a day, whereas in others (Irish), the dead are "waked" with viewings and parties before burial occurs. Members of each group believe their traditions to be "natural" and others' to be odd. Postmodern understandings hold that there are many truths, each created within historically specific social milieu. This approach is embraced by grief theorists and therapists (Neimeyer et al., 2014) who assert that "grieving [i]s a situated interpretive and communicative activity" (p. 496) during which grievers work to make meaning of their loved one's life, find their place in a changed social context, and perform (or resist performing) grief in ways consistent with the relevant cultural context.

The narrative tradition of therapy (White & Epston, 1990) grew from social constructionist and postmodern understandings and is predicated on individuals developing their own stories with the help of the therapist. A narrative project to make meaning of the deceased's life, death, and relationships is critical to processing grief (Neimeyer, 2001). Along with the evolution of this meaning-making approach to grief work, theorists and practitioners questioned the classic models of grief and templates for grieving. Social constructionism and postmodernism more generally imply that no individual's grief must follow a preset path; further, decathexis, resolution, closure, and/or acceptance should not be envisioned as desired outcomes for all grievers. This perspective allowed Klass et al. (1996) to theorize what many mourners had been saying all along: The end of active grieving does not have to entail detachment from the deceased. Most often, it entails continuing bonds, which change in quality. Foote and Frank (1999) assert that postmodern meaning-making approaches provide a basis for resistance to disciplining grief—at least until those strategies are institutionalized too and become an updated form of policing grief.

From this vantage point, the notion of "closure" must also be challenged. Analogous to Kübler-Ross's "acceptance," closure is often thought necessary for grievers to heal. Even if one sets aside the idea that acceptance is the desired outcome of grief, the construct of closure is knotty when explored through a sociological lens (Berns, 2011). "Closure" arose in the popular narrative during the 1990s and developed multiple meanings, all of which reflected the hope of grievers to be relieved of pain and suffering. Perhaps most insidious (if predictable), closure came to justify myriad commercial endeavors from "burials" in space to "diamonds" made of cremains (Berns, 2011). Berns notes that the word *closure* is used to mean closing a chapter, remembering, forgetting, getting even, knowing, confessing, and forgiving; such broad usage allows many services and products to be sold—and laws to be made—in pursuit of closure. Yet, as a concept, closure is as slippery and suspect as most other "natural" outcomes of grief. Just as Klass (2013) cautioned not to assume that all grief leads to growth, we emphasize that not all loss experiences (nor even most) will or should lead to closure.

The following postmodern, conceptual approaches to grief allow grievers and supporters to tailor their interventions, avoid thrusting uniform models on grievers, and support therapeutic or informal healing strategies without insisting on closure or acceptance.

Dual-Process Model

A deceptively simple grief theory that is not prescriptive and can be tailored to individual grievers came from the work of Stroebe and Schut (2010). Their theory drew from Bowlby's ideas (1980/1998) about disorganization and reorganization. Although Bowlby conceptualized these as discrete stages, Stroebe and Schut (1999, 2010) envisioned continuous oscillation between loss orientation (LO) and restoration orientation (RO). This differs from Bowlby's stages of disorganization and reorganization in that the bereaved person sometimes experiences grief actively and focuses on the loss and at other times moves toward building a new life. Both these usually alloyed orientations have value. One allows for distraction and restoration time that frees mourners to move into new roles and activities while the other allows processing time for the loss. Both are necessary.

Notably, rumination (a typical aspect of early LO) is often portrayed as the *sine qua non* of grief work (Bonanno, 2009), yet Stroebe et al. (2007) developed the DPM to show how excessive rumination is actually a mode of avoidance (Figure 1.2). They identify excessive rumination, particularly focused on one's emotions and a refusal to believe one can recover, as antithetical to healing, not part of the fruitful work that occurs in LO or RO.

Stroebe and Schut (2010) built on their original model to show how it can be used as both an assessment tool (How much of the bereaved's time is spent in each orientation? How does the proportion gradually change toward more RO?) and an intervention. (Therapeutic guidance can help grievers move into whichever orientation they might be avoiding.) We think different developmental stages may also affect this process as children seem to spend more time in RO (particularly utilizing distraction) and seem to oscillate naturally between orientations more quickly. Research is necessary to explore whether our impressions are generalizable and useful.

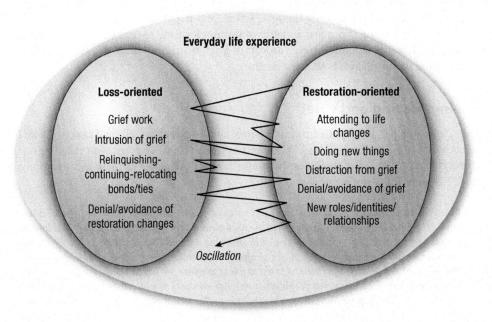

FIGURE 1.2 Classic Dual-Process Model. This graph (Stroebe & Schut, 1999) illustrates the activities of each orientation and the irregular oscillation as the griever moves between activities in loss orientation (LO) and restoration orientation (RO).

Source: Reproduced with permission from Stroebe, M., & Schut, H. (1999). The dual process model of coping with bereavement: Rationale and description. *Death Studies, 23*, 197–224. doi.org/10.1080/074811899201046

In a volume of *Omega* devoted to empirical examination of the DPM, Carr (2010) observed that some did not find the expected response to DPM interventions (e.g., those involved in DPM groups fared no better than those in typical loss-oriented support groups). She speculates that grief groups may meet the more universal needs of LO but that RO requires new individualized skills. She also raises Shear's (2010) hypothesis that some avoidance of active grief is adaptive. However, no one can specify optimal lengths and times for periods of avoidance, and thus the optimal balance between RO and LO remains unresolved (Carr, 2010).

Stroebe and Schut (2015) more recently revised the DPM to incorporate the recognition that individuals' grief is influenced in many ways by the family constellations in which they live. Although the familial cultural context has long been understood to influence grieving (Walsh & McGoldrick, 1991), the Dual Process Model- Revised (DPM-R; Stroebe & Schut, 2015) now integrates family LO and RO along with tasks individuals and families undertake in each orientation (based on Worden's tasks, 2009). Problems of incongruent mourning and varied forms of interpersonal interactions within families can be better identified and assessed using the DPM-R.

Revision of the Assumptive World or Relearning the World

The assumptive world is the set of fundamental beliefs people hold, often unconsciously. A major loss violates this complacency and challenges the griever to revise and relearn their assumptions (Parkes, 1988). This relearning occurs during DPM-R's RO when grievers work to understand previous assumptions and restore a sense of predictability, safety, and continuity by adopting new assumptions and defenses against fears evoked by the loss itself and the associated unraveling of the assumptive world. Attig clarified how "relearning the world" differs from revision of the assumptive world (Janoff-Bulman, 1992). Revising the assumptive world entails revising cognitive assumptions about the way life works—a primarily intellectual task. Attig asserts that relearning the world requires actively relearning a sense of safety and belonging along with a new way of negotiating life, a process requiring thought, action, and negotiation (Attig, 2015). Attig (2011) emphasized that grieving is not just a matter of waiting for time to pass but an active process of continuously choosing to work through aspects of grief, managing varied senses of vulnerability, and relearning the world as it is after the death.

Meaning-Making and Grief

Robert Neimeyer has ably applied to grief theory and intervention Viktor Frankl's (1946/1984) insights about meaning-making and White and Epston's (1990) concern with meaning-making and storytelling in narrative therapies. Neimeyer traces the lineage of these ideas to Immanuel Kant (1724–1804),

> who emphasized that the mind actively structures experience according to its own principles and procedures. One contemporary extension of the argument is that narrative—the distinctly human penchant for storytelling—represents one such ordering scheme (Bruner, 1986). . . . Significant loss—whether of cherished persons, places, projects, or possessions—presents a challenge to one's sense of narrative coherence as well as to the sense of identity for which they were an important source of validation. . . . Bereaved people often seek safe contexts in which they can tell (and retell) their stories of loss, hoping that therapists can bear to hear what others cannot, validating their pain as real without resorting to simple reassurance. Ultimately, they search for ways of assimilating the multiple meanings of loss into the overarching story of their lives, an effort that professionals can support through careful listening, guided reflection, and a variety of narrative means for fostering fresh perspectives on their losses for themselves and others. (Neimeyer, 2001, pp. 263–264)

Neimeyer's (2001) lucid explanation nicely fits our view that understanding grief in the context of grief therapy is a mutual project. Grief therapy is a respectful process of hearing and witnessing the stories people tell of their lives and their losses, questioning in ways that encourage appreciation of other perspectives, and leaving room for them to reject those perspectives. At its best, grief work encourages mourners to construct and reconstruct stories of meaning that enable them to move into new lives and develop new assumptive worlds in the aftermath of loss.

Clinicians working with grieving people must recognize that their stories will take multiple forms and that the therapist should *not* force adherence to a "true" or "real" version. Instead, we are to help clients create their own coherent stories while illuminating blind spots. New understandings can enable a story that fits the client's evolving worldview and creation of meaning in evermore useful and function-promoting ways. This is a relational project involving a practitioner's willingness to engage the client in an authentic and caring manner and exhibit genuine curiosity about how the client tells the story. Successful grief therapists convey realistic hope that this process will help clients return to full engagement with life and loves.

Early in the development of grief theories of meaning-making, Davis et al. (2000) questioned whether it could be assumed that most bereaved individuals find meaning in loss. In their sample, only about half reported finding meaning in their loss. They suggested that clinicians might intervene more effectively by helping the bereaved to understand (a) the risks of staying stuck in their grief, (b) how to use the therapist as a "container" during the early phases of intense grief, (c) the benefits of using rituals and traditions that have meaning and comfort for them, (d) how to move ruminations/obsessions into a flowing narrative, and (e) how to set attainable goals that allow choices and a sense of accomplishment. Neimeyer et al. (2006) built on these and other suggestions to assist meaning-making while incorporating continuing bonds and other postmodern concepts. Even more promising, these ideas are being applied in related fields such as genetic counseling (Douglas, 2014), thus allowing more people struggling with loss to receive needed support.

Continuing Bonds and Grief

A pivotal insight in contemporary grief theory came when Klass, Silverman, and Nickman each examined data from their disparate research populations and realized that bereaved people maintained a sense of relationship with deceased loved ones instead of "letting go" (1996, p. xviii). They challenged the notion that disengaging from the deceased or lost entity is the goal and asserted instead that a major aspect of grieving is the transformation of the relationship with the deceased to allow a continued bond between the bereaved and the deceased (p. 16). In the introduction to their important book, they explained that their data illustrated that bereaved people did not need to sever ties or bonds with the deceased, but instead find new meaning in how those relationships helped to shape their own lives and those of the people and communities around them. Memories, prayers, connections, and other ways of internalizing an ongoing bond with the deceased were viewed as helpful rather than hurtful. Although it may not sound so now, this was a revolutionary shift in how grief theorists and therapists would subsequently approach the nature and goals of grief work. The continuing bonds concept allows each individual to have a highly personal outcome to their grief, founded in the relationship they had with the person who died and how they internalized that relationship. This is also influenced by the beliefs they have about life after death. Nevertheless, this understanding also carries a caution. Just as bereaved people were "policed" into nonexpression of their grief (or more recently into full expression even when this did not fit their needs), we must remain cognizant that while some grievers may find comfort in continuing bonds, others will find them unnecessary. Although not all continuing bonds relate to grievers' beliefs about an afterlife, for grievers who do not believe in any sort of ongoing existence, being encouraged to maintain a relationship with the deceased may feel disturbing. Instead, a continuing bond based on memories and incorporating qualities and skills of the deceased into their own lives can be a more acceptable way of maintaining the bond.

Research on grief after traumatic loss differentiated types of continuing bonds. Field and Filanosky (2010) indicated that externalized continuing bonds (hallucinating the deceased loved one; hearing voices of the deceased) are associated with poorer adjustment over time. Internalized continuing bonds (having an internal sense of the deceased still comforting and caring) seemed protective (from complications of grief) and comforting.

Cultural differences are important here. Mexican "Day of the Dead" celebrations and Buddhist worship at shrines of deceased loved ones are only two of many rituals that foster continued bonds. Japanese ancestor worship (Shinto and Buddhist) also maintains continuing bonds with the deceased (Valentine, 2010). Individualized assessment of the client, discussion of cultural aspects of the grief process and customs, the intuitive and respectful stance of the clinician, and the awareness of the wide range of ways people process grief are imperative for competent grief work.

Disenfranchised Grief

Doka (1989, 2002) coined the term *disenfranchised grief* to conceptualize grief that is not recognized, validated, or supported in the mourner's social world. It is grief that does not conform to social norms of grief in the griever's culture. Hochschild (1979, 1983) referred to norms that guide "appropriate" emotions in a given situation as "feeling rules." Disenfranchised grief violates feeling rules or occurs when feeling rules are not established or are discrepant (McCoyd, 2009). Unclear norms leave grievers uncertain about how their peers will react to their sadness and whether their loss will be recognized. Furthermore, ambiguous norms may leave grievers wondering if they may call their experience a loss.

Doka (2002) defined five categories of disenfranchised grief: (a) grief where the relationship is not recognized, such as gay and lesbian relationships, extramarital relationships, and other relationships that lack social sanction; (b) grief where the loss is not acknowledged as legitimate by societal norms, for example, grief following abortion, relinquishing a child for adoption, pet loss, and other losses that are not viewed as worthy of sympathy; (c) the grief of individuals like children, the very old, or people who are developmentally disabled who are (inaccurately) not believed to experience grief; (d) grief where the circumstances of death cause stigma or embarrassment, such as when a person dies of AIDS, alcoholism, suicide, or while committing a crime—deaths viewed as the result of moral failures; and (e) grief expressed in nonsocially sanctioned ways, as when a griever is deemed to be either too expressive or not expressive enough. Each reflects a way in which the policing of grief still functions.

The nature of disenfranchised grief means that grieving individuals do not receive the social support and degree of sympathy from others that they need to process grief. The very core of grief (for most) is to actively process the pain of loss. Yet the circumstances of disenfranchised grief exacerbate the pain by rejecting the griever or offering little or no support. Many of the losses discussed in the following chapters fall into one or more of these categories of disenfranchised grief. In such cases, validating the event as a loss and normalizing the grief response can allow the griever to move through the loss response without complications. Because societal norms bring the grief into question, drawing on the social acceptability and experience of others having similar losses is more powerful than merely asserting a right to grieve. It seems likely that the most effective forms of intervention for disenfranchised grief use support groups of similarly situated people to create a social space where norms support recognition of the loss.

Thompson and Doka (2017) recently added categories of "workplace losses" (the workplace fails to offer support suitable to the griever's needs), "suffocated grief" (the expression of grief is penalized, as in legal settings), "forbidden grief" (grief is actively disallowed and punished if expressed), and the experience of cumulative trauma (ongoing oppressive isms or poverty, for instance). These categories join Doka's original typology of disenfranchised grief as experiences for which support is insufficient to meet the griever's needs.

Robson and Walter (2012) criticized the notion of disenfranchised loss for failing to reflect the hierarchy of grieving rights found in most situations (determining who is considered entitled to support and sympathy). They noted that the language of disenfranchisement implies a binary distinction: One has freedom and legitimacy as a voting citizen, or one does not. As an alternative, they developed a tool to measure the levels of grief that allowed those in different relationships to the deceased (for example, the parent of the deceased is viewed as a legitimate mourner more than the deceased's friend). They found substantial agreement across groups that there is a relatively well-accepted, even if not explicitly defined, hierarchy of mourning. They observed: "Our contention therefore is that disenfranchisement is not a norm, but a feeling experienced by mourners whose personal grief exceeds their position in the hierarchy either as generally perceived or as perceived by one or more significant condolers" (Robson & Walter, 2012, p. 109). They noted that clinicians tend to work with grievers whose grief outstrips the sympathy allotted to them. The clinicians may assume that their work is to enfranchise all grief, an assumption Robson and Walter question. Even so, mourners are often in the situation where their need for support following a loss is not viewed as legitimate. It is the work of the clinician to help the griever secure that support.

Ambiguous and Nonfinite (or Chronic) Grief

Ambiguous loss (Boss, 1999), also called "frozen grief," is difficult to process because of the uncertain definition of who or what is lost. In ambiguous loss, the lost entity is

- physically present but psychologically absent—for instance, a loved one with Alzheimer's or head trauma/brain injury; or
- physically absent but psychologically present—such as when someone is kidnapped or missing in action during a war.

It is unclear how to adjust to such losses. Without a death (the first case), it seems premature and even cruel to grieve as if there has been one; in the second case, grieving would remove the hope of return. Boss points to the following difficulties with ambiguous loss:

- Adjustment to the loss cannot occur as it is uncertain what one is supposed to adjust to.
- Rituals are not available, and there are few social supports.
- The irrationality of life is on display. It is hard to feel the world is rational when nothing seems clear or rational.

Critically, ambiguous loss seems potentially unending. The uncertainty drags out, and there is little ability for resolution and no end in sight. These losses also confuse support people, who are perplexed about whether to express sympathy or to maintain a stolid sense of normalcy and hope. Because the loss has not fully happened (yet), people lack social support, yet they struggle with the fact that their loved one is slipping away. Boss reports a case where the mother of a veteran of the Iraq war with significant head trauma struggles with the fact that her son is alive, yet certainly not the same son she raised and loved (Boss et al., 2011). Central to managing ambiguous grief is learning to live a life that has become utterly different from the one planned, unpredictable and incomprehensible (Boss et al., 2011).

This may be why peer support groups seem so efficacious with these grievers. Group members share a similar experience of confusing loss over a protracted period. Although similar loss does not guarantee similar response, the group can discuss obstacles to social recognition, validate the struggles, and talk about strategies for coping with the lack of support.

A similar type of grief, chronic sorrow (sometimes referred to as nonfinite grief), reflects the living nature of the loss (as in ambiguous grief). This type of grief is characteristic of parents whose children are born with (or contract) disorders that affect their development and ability to participate in typical society. This grief tends to be "permanent, periodic, and progressive in nature" (Boss et al., 2011, p. 165) and reflects the losses parents experience when they see other children accomplishing goals their children have not or cannot.

ISSUES OF INTERVENTION

Grief theorists tend to identify phases and associated tasks through which mourners must move in order to heal. Newer theories avoid the prescriptive nature of many earlier ones, yet the onus remains on the bereaved to move through some process. Interestingly, students and others who want to assist those who are grieving often ask "What can I do?" not "What should the bereaved do?" Asking what we, the clinicians, can do to help is actually the much more important question.

Mourners seldom have family and friends available and sufficiently skilled to provide the nondirective approach necessary to accompany them as they review these opposing urges and reflect upon prior experiences. Today, we are increasingly geographically separate from our families, and people often need help coping with grief. Grief counselors have numerous professional titles used here interchangeably (practitioners, clinicians, therapists, etc.) to emphasize that they are united by the requirement to patiently be with and witness grievers' pain and encourage the possible growth that comes from loss. This style is not rigid and allows for the integration of many evidence-based interventions.

Therapist Activity When Intervening With Grief

Lloyd (2002) provides a general intervention strategy for customary grief after death loss. The practitioner is to (a) explore attitudes toward death and dying from psychological, sociological, and philosophical/religious perspectives; (b) explore and analyze the bereaved's constructions of life; and (c) explore the bereaved's processes of adjustment to the world without the deceased. Within each area for exploration, attention should be paid to how the bereaved is redefining roles, rebuilding identities, negotiating transitions, surviving trauma, and maintaining morale. Nearly all losses entail a need to revise one's identity. The death of a spouse turns one into a widow; the loss of a job leads to identification as unemployed; and the birth of a child means a new identity as parent. Clinicians can provide a safe space for reflecting upon the varied facets of loss and identity, encouraging grievers to process the cognitive, psychosocial, spiritual, and emotional aspects of their losses.

Boss et al. (2011) suggest how to assist those with ambiguous and nonfinite loss. The clinician should work respectfully with the griever to (a) name and validate the loss; (b) help the client find meaning in their new role; (c) address trauma when it is present; (d) temper mastery—by which they mean tempering the mourner's expectations of controlling the situation; (e) help the griever reconstruct identity; (f) normalize ambivalence—that is, help the griever recognize that it is normal to both love and hate the person who is the object of the ambiguous loss, changed from their previous persona; (g) revise attachment; (h) discover new hope; and (i) identify resources for support.

A newer "third-wave" therapy is directed toward living with unpleasant circumstances not amenable to change. Acceptance and commitment therapy (ACT) evolved to grapple with the concrete, unchangeable, and functional contexts in which people find themselves (Hayes, 2016). Whether experiencing chronic pain, mental health crises, or grief, individuals are often in situations they cannot change and must find ways to cope with them. ACT draws on the recognition that the more people try to suppress awareness of an unpleasant circumstance, the more likely they are to maintain focus on it and increase their suffering. ACT challenges people to recognize that attempts to avoid fear, or resistance against the uncontrollable, actually enhances discomfort, whereas openly accepting phenomena such as pain, anxiety, or other uncontrollable experiences can enhance coping ability. Acceptance involves recognizing that life is challenging and that adaptation must rely on whatever works, rather than be stuck on "shoulds" or what others find reasonable. ACT aims to help clients let go of trying to control the uncontrollable (Hayes, 2016). Using cognitive diffusion techniques (much like exposure) or mindfulness strategies, clients are helped to quit resisting and avoiding the painful stimuli (for our purposes, a death or loss) and instead nonjudgmentally embrace the here and now; clients are encouraged to commit to moving forward despite discomforts.

Although both Holly Prigerson and M. Katherine Shear developed criteria for prolonged grief and complicated grief, respectively, *DSM-5* did not adopt diagnoses for grief. Empirical work has strongly confirmed a grief form that includes extended times of yearning and grieving in ways that disrupt grievers' ability to move through their grief (Boelen, 2016). Strong empirical support for an intervention developed by Shear (2015) has indicated specific elements that assist the 2% to 3% of grievers who exhibit extended and intense grieving. This 16-week intervention includes the following elements (Shear, 2015):

- Establish the lay of the land (provide psychoeducation about grief).
- Promote self-regulation (help grievers learn how to oscillate between LO and RO and "dose" themselves, thus helping to approach whichever aspect they are avoiding).
- Build connections (promote social relationships).
- Set aspirational goals (look toward the future and goals that can be realistically attained).
- Revisit the world (specifically confront aspects of the loss that have been avoided).
- Include storytelling (enhance review of the story of who/what was lost and promote re-membrance).
- Use memory (focusing on positive memories too).

These practices can be used with all grievers and, in the more structured version developed by Shear, show promise for helping those who are struggling with their grief response.

Mindfulness as an Intervention for Grief

Mindfulness has become widely known and accepted as a practice for becoming more attuned to one's internal sensations, emotions, and responses to them, as well as becoming better attuned to others. Starting as mindfulness meditation, popularized in Jon Kabat-Zinn's (1990) work, mindfulness has many new iterations that apply to the work we do with grievers and to our self-care practices. Cacciatore and Flint (2012) synthesized much of this work in their ATTEND model of bereavement care, making the point that it is for use by the practitioner/therapist; it is for use within the therapeutic relationship; and it is for the client's use. The pillars of the ATTEND model are attunement, trust, therapeutic touch, egalitarianism, nuance, and death education. Attunement comes first and is likely the integrating principle of mindfulness. Attunement requires attending to oneself and others' well-being. It entails empathy, responsiveness, intentional attentiveness, and allowing each person to observe and accept pain and suffering as well as positive emotions. Dan Siegel puts this at the heart of being a mindful therapist (2010b) and notes that "presence" is a sense of being open to the other (the client) while attunement requires presence and also includes "focused attention and clear perception" (Siegel, 2010b, p. 35).

Cacciatore and Flint (2012) define trust as compassionate communication that allows the client to know there is safety and care within the relationship. The second T in ATTEND is therapeutic touch, which they acknowledge is controversial. Nevertheless, therapeutic touch conveys caring with a gentle touch on the hand or shoulder or a willingness to sit side by side as a griever cries. Egalitarianism focuses on the idea that the mindful relationship is humble and takes place between equals in a collaborative and safe relationship. "Nuance" reflects all the unique aspects of the client and the practitioner as they come together to work on the client's challenges. They note that nuance rejects assumptions and one-size-fits-all answers. All work together is tailor-made within the mindful relationship. Death education encompasses knowledgeable provision of psychoeducation to assist the dying and the grieving to know what to expect during the process.

Similarly, the acronym SIFT (Epstein et al., 2008) helps practitioners to be mindful within the therapeutic relationship. SIFT refers to how the practitioner must review sensations, images, feelings, and thoughts. By doing so, the practitioner gets in tune with concerns about how the client is feeling and what responses the practitioner is having that may create barriers to staying attuned. This awareness allows the practitioner to stay fully engaged with the client. In psychodynamic education, we refer to this as attending to our countertransference so as to avoid "bringing our own stuff" into the relationship in harmful ways. Siegel also uses the acronym COAL to reflect the importance of curiosity, openness, acceptance, and love, which infuse the mindful therapeutic relationship. Regardless of which acronym frames the work one does with grievers, mindfulness requires intense connection and attunement with one's client and with oneself. Such intense work can only be done well when the practitioner attends to their own self-care. Whether practicing mindfulness exercises on one's own, engaging in contemplative practices, or finding routines that help one stay healthy, it is imperative that practitioners be aware of their own well-being and responses. Throughout this text, we describe various mindfulness and other practices for use with clients. Practitioners would do well to become familiar with mindfulness practices and to utilize them day to day. Kabat-Zinn's *Full Catastrophe Living* (1990) is a great place to start, and many of Siegel's works involve mindfulness practices as well (2010a, 2010b).

A FINAL WORD ABOUT GRIEF WORK

In 1991, Stroebe and Stroebe asked the question, "Does 'grief work' work?" Their answer was "maybe." Findings that widowers who avoided emotional expression had worse outcomes than those who did not gave tepid support for grief work; however, widows did not exhibit this same association. This led the authors to conclude that "the view 'everyone needs to do grief work' is an oversimplification" (p. 481). Indeed, Bonanno et al. (2004) found that the majority of widows and widowers did well after spousal death. In short, most people feel pain but are able to cope, even after major losses. See Figure 1.3 for approximate percentages of grievers who require treatment for their grief.

The grief work hypothesis assumes that emotional ventilation (crying, mourning, anger) needs to be expressed before one can begin to heal from a significant loss. It assumes that if emotional ventilation did not occur and the person was seemingly healthy, either they were grieving pathologically or the attachment to the lost one was not strong. Multiple studies have found this to be inaccurate (Bonanno, 2009; Carr et al., 2006; Currier et al., 2007; Konigsberg, 2011). A significant group of bereaved people actually become worse if emotional ventilation is pushed upon them; many do quite well without professional intervention. This reminds us once again that even with evidence-based interventions, directives that include "must," "should," and "require" may not fit every griever. The appropriate prescription is to attend to the particular experience of each griever and recognize that most will heal without professional help.

Earlier, we raised the concern that classic theories may create a tendency to police grief. We also raised questions about the efficacy of grief work. Nevertheless, reflective practitioners must avoid the paralysis that can result from giving so much weight to these concerns that we neglect to provide support for those who ask for our assistance. Remaining open, mindful, and reflective about new understandings in grief theory, while also using empirical data derived from interaction with clients, will guide us toward meaningful work with grievers. Whether a griever perceives the work to be useful (or not) permits modification to fit that person's developmental and mourning needs. These are requirements of ethical and sensitive practice in the world of grief support.

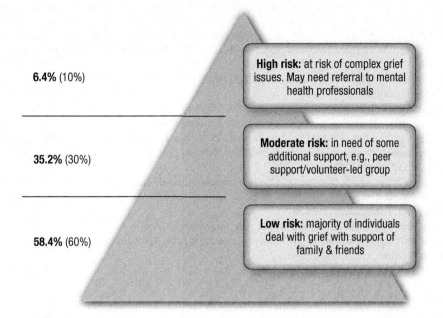

6.4% (10%)

High risk: at risk of complex grief issues. May need referral to mental health professionals

35.2% (30%)

Moderate risk: in need of some additional support, e.g., peer support/volunteer-led group

58.4% (60%)

Low risk: majority of individuals deal with grief with support of family & friends

FIGURE 1.3 Percentages of People Needing Grief Intervention. This image illustrates the percentages of grievers estimated to be at risk for problematic grief reactions. Predicting who fits which category is more challenging.
Source: Aoun, S., Breen, L., Howting, D., Rumbold, B., McNamara, B., & Hegney, D. (2015). Who needs bereavement support? A population based survey of bereavement risk and support need. *PLoS One, 10*, e0121101. doi.org/10.1371/journal.pone.0121101

DISCUSSION QUESTIONS

1. What rituals do you typically engage in after a death in your family and how do you believe this helps or hurts the mourners?
2. Consider the disenfranchised losses you have experienced in your lifetime. If each one were actively mourned, how might that change the way you feel about those losses?
3. How would you approach a client who comes into a first session and says, "My spouse just died and I know I'm in anger right now but I want to get to acceptance"?
4. In light of the tepid support for grief work for all losses, how do you think most death losses of close people should optimally be managed?

KEY REFERENCES

Only key references appear in the print edition. The full reference list appears in the digital product found on http://connect.springerpub.com/content/book/978-0-8261-4964-0/chapter/ch01

Administration for Community Living. (2018). *Projected future growth of older population.* https://acl.gov/aging-and-disability-in-america/data-and-research/projected-future-growth-older-population
Attig, T. (2011). *How we grieve: Relearning the world.* Oxford University Press.
Boelen, P. A. (2016). Improving the understanding and treatment of complex grief: An important issue for psychotraumatology. *European Journal of Psychotraumatology, 7*(1), 32609. https://doi.org/10.3402/ejpt.v7.32609

Bonanno, G. A. (2009). *The other side of sadness: What the new science of bereavement tells us about life after loss.* Basic Books.

Boss, P. (1999). *Ambiguous loss: Learning to live with unresolved grief.* Harvard University Press.

Doka, K. J. (Ed.). (2002). *Disenfranchised grief: New directions, challenges and strategies for practice.* Research Press.

Klass, D., Silverman, P. R., & Nickman, S. L. (Eds.). (1996). *Continuing bonds: New understandings of grief.* Taylor & Francis.

Neimeyer, R. A. (2001). *Meaning reconstruction and the meaning of loss.* American Psychological Association.

Rando, T. A. (1993). *Treatment of complicated mourning.* Research Press.

Stroebe, M. S., & Schut, H. (2015). Family matters in bereavement: Toward an integrative intra-interpersonal coping model. *Perspectives on Psychological Science, 10*(6), 873–879. https://doi.org/10.1177/1745691615598517

Stroebe, M. S., Schut, H., & Boerner, K. (2017). Cautioning health-care professionals: Bereaved persons are misguided through the stages of grief. *Omega (United States), 74*(4), 455–473. https://doi.org/10.1177/0030222817691870

U.S. Census Bureau. (2019). *2020 census will help policymakers prepare for the incoming wave of aging Boomers.* https://www.census.gov/library/stories/2019/12/by-2030-all-baby-boomers-will-be-age-65-or-older.html

2

Grief and Loss in the Context of Perinatal Attachment and Loss

INTRODUCTION

This chapter reviews normal biopsychosocial developments during pregnancy and the neonatal period. The development of perinatal attachment is emphasized. Loss as a result of the death of a fetus or neonate is examined as a form of disenfranchised grief, and perinatal losses, such as infertility, assisted reproduction, abortion, adoption, and learning of a fetal anomaly, are explicated. Typical maturational losses associated with customary pregnancy such as loss of the idealized child, loss of sleep, and changes in the partner relationship are reviewed. Interventions including the Five Vs and the Meaning of Miscarriage Model are explained.

OBJECTIVES

After studying this chapter, the reader will be able to:

- Understand the prenatal and postpartum attachment process as a frame for how loss is experienced during and soon after pregnancy.
- Describe how biological changes in pregnancy impact attachment and the subsequent experience of loss.
- Understand how technology mediates perinatal attachment, diagnosis, and loss.
- Analyze how social norms define perinatal loss and constrain options and sympathy after such losses.

VIGNETTE

LaVonne, a 26-year-old teacher, and her husband Lamar, a 30-year-old business executive, were referred for grief counseling after a late stillbirth at 32 weeks' estimated gestational age (EGA). They eagerly anticipated the birth of their first child and were stunned when the baby died. LaVonne was astonished by the intensity of grief she felt and surprised by how little support she received from friends, who seemed to believe that her grief was out of proportion to her loss. A close friend reminded her that they each had abortions during college and the friend did not see how this was different. LaVonne tried to explain how much she enjoyed the pregnancy and bonding with the "baby in my belly," but the friend could not understand her grief. Lamar also seemed impatient with her frequent tearfulness. She struggled to resume her regular activities and get-togethers with friends. Adding to their concerns, they learned that their baby had a genetic condition, sickle cell anemia, not uncommon among African Americans. This did not directly cause the stillbirth, but it could be inherited by a future child. Their insurance would not cover in vitro fertilization (IVF) and pre-implantation genetic diagnosis (PGD), the only sure way to avoid a baby affected by sickle cell. Their friends and family members, accustomed to people living with sickle cell disease, seemed reluctant to support their wish to avoid having a baby with the condition. LaVonne and Lamar felt sad and unsupported.

After some psychoeducation about grief and its common presentation after stillbirth, the couple worked hard to express their concerns and feelings to one another. Although Lamar feared it would "make LaVonne worse," LaVonne's feelings were actually soothed by talking about the loss. They used the support of their counselor very well and used the time to work through some of the "disconnects" between what their physicians suggested they do and what their family and friends thought they should do. They had to make challenging decisions about whether to pursue the assisted reproductive options their perinatologists told them about, especially because they were expensive. Additionally, some members of their church and wider community asserted that such options were offensive because "they were playing God." In the end, they decided to try one round of ovulation stimulation, IVF, and PGD. They had a little girl who was a carrier but not affected by sickle cell disease. They felt they made the right decisions and worked with their counselor to reconcile themselves to the disapproval of some family and friends.

DEVELOPMENTAL ASPECTS OF PREGNANCY

Pregnancy begins with anticipation, uncertainty, and hope. LaVonne's experience highlights how emotionally charged the experience of pregnancy and childbirth can be. Success in achieving pregnancy is often complicated. Once pregnant, a woman's attachment to the dreamed-of baby usually grows rapidly, while technologies (ultrasound, genetic screening, and testing) may generate knowledge requiring difficult decisions in the face of that attachment. Here, we will consider the development of prenatal attachment in typical pregnancy, focusing primarily on the mother as the pregnancy occurs in her body. This process differs for women who were not planning to get pregnant or who create their family in less typical ways, but each of these experiences entails potential loss.

The development of an emotional bond between the mother and growing fetus is a primary task of pregnancy. Nearly all credible behavioral theory focuses on the relationship between the infant and the mother or primary caregiver as the formative force behind most relational behavior (Spierling et al., 2018). Research and theory exploring how that bond develops prior to the birth (which Bowlby identified as the beginning of attachment) has exploded (Brandon et al., 2011; Spierling et al., 2018).

Obviously, parental attachment to the fetus frames the experience of perinatal loss. Here, we will explicate what is known about the biological, psychological, and social aspects of the formation of the bond with a fetus during pregnancy and what is lost when a pregnancy ends prior to birth. The mother's perspective on that bond is critical to how the mutual attachment process begins once the baby is born, a process shaped by the mother's biopsychosocial context during pregnancy.

Biological Developmental Context of Pregnancy

The beginning of pregnancy causes radical changes in a woman's body. Instead of moving through a roughly 28-day hormonal cycle to which she has been accustomed since adolescence, she is suspended in a phase of her cycle during which high levels of estrogen and especially progesterone are secreted. Other hormones, including human chorionic gonadotropin (HCG), are secreted in ever-increasing amounts. Aside from the physical effects of breast tenderness, bloating, and nausea that accompany these hormones, emotional effects such as increased irritability, labile moods, and an increased sense of vulnerability are believed to be related to them as well. Research suggests that pregnancy-related nausea may actually be associated with both HCG and progesterone, priming women to be averse to the smells, flavors, and textures of foods and other substances that are unhealthy during pregnancy (Hahn-Holbrook et al., 2012).

The physical changes of pregnancy clearly influence a woman's emotional life and can have implications for attachment to the fetus. On the one hand, these changes provide palpable evidence of the fetus's presence in her body; on the other hand, they can lead to feelings of less control over her body. These body changes can inspire resentment and blame of the fetus if the changes are overwhelming or unwelcome. In short, the physical changes of pregnancy can be a reassuring reminder of the fetus's presence or a burden to bear. How a mother feels about these changes will likely influence her emotional state generally and her attachment to the fetus specifically. Likewise, she (and likely her partner) may be creating "representations" of the fetus (ideas about its characteristics, motivations, and growth—e.g., "He's such an active little guy!") that seem to underlie the development of secure or insecure attachments after birth (Ammaniti et al., 2013).

As the fetus grows, it makes its presence increasingly known, first by gentle brushings (quickening) often experienced as "butterfly wings inside," progressing in later stages to stronger effects as the fetus moves and tries to stretch in confined spaces. This coincides with the woman's body getting larger, a development often connected to her sense of attractiveness (or lack thereof). A new center of gravity and increased weight alter body dynamics so as to increase the sense and actuality of vulnerability. Feeling like a stranger in her own body may lead to high levels of psychological discomfort, particularly for women whose self-image is strongly tied to physical appearance or for women who have great need for control. These physical effects may impact the way a woman perceives her growing fetus.

Progesterone (a primary hormone of pregnancy) is believed to help prime "nesting" behavior—the tendency to create a safe place to house the newborn—and obsessive nesting is a normal aspect of late pregnancy (Feygin et al., 2006). As prolactin is secreted along with oxytocin at the time of birth, the reward system of the brain is stimulated, fear is buffered, and women have increased affiliative motivations (Hahn-Holbrook et al., 2012), meaning they generally want to remain close to the newborn as well as friends and family. Interestingly, rats raised to be addicted to cocaine, when primed with their newborn pups to promote oxytocin release, actually prefer closeness to their pups over cocaine (Mattson et al., 2003), indicating the strong level of reward new mothers get from physical closeness with their newborns. (In the reading by Zimmerman-Levitt at the end of this chapter, we see how adverse birth events interfere with this early physical closeness in ways that inspire loss.)

Sleep problems bridge the physical and psychological aspects of pregnancy. The aches and pains associated with a growing uterus combine with frequent urination and hormonal influences to deprive pregnant women of easy sleep, and loss of sleep is consequential. Sleep patterns are affected in early pregnancy by hormonal changes and in late pregnancy by changing fluid volumes and physical discomforts such as gastroesophageal reflux, all of which combine to mean that nearly half of pregnant women experience sleep disturbances (Pengo et al., 2018). These sleep disturbances are associated with poor pregnancy outcomes such as preterm birth and gestational diabetes (Pengo et al., 2018), making good sleep a crucial aspect of pregnancy.

Many women are fascinated by the development of the fetus as it goes from a recently fertilized egg to a newly born baby (neonate). Many websites help parents track growth, from the hipster pregnancy site The Bump, which tracks embryo and fetus growth by food size (starting out as a poppy seed; pregnant.thebump.com/pregnancy/pregnancy-tools/articles/how-big-is-baby. aspx), through Baby Centre, which gives details of development at each week of gestation (www. babycentre.co.uk). Envisioning the growing fetus allows women and their partners to promote prenatal bonding and strengthen attachment, but it may also make the woman more susceptible to intensified grief if she experiences a loss.

It is notable that assisted reproductive techniques such as IVF have given more couples the chance to pursue biological parenthood. A less known implication is that these pregnancies are more likely to experience adverse pregnancy outcomes and complications (Nagata et al., 2019). Although these technologies open doors to parenthood for many, their use brings some degree of increased risk.

An unfortunate biological aspect of pregnancy is that virtually anything to which a pregnant person is exposed affects the fetus. In a world where substance use disorder is common, particularly opioid dependence and its attendant neonatal abstinence syndrome, fetal effects are a highly publicized and moralized concern. The public health dimension of the concern is legitimate: In utero exposures such as nicotine and alcohol have well-established, long-term effects on infants' well-being (Zuckerman et al., 2002). However, moral panics over more exotic substances often divert attention and resources from substances such as nicotine and alcohol and result in Draconian policies such as charging new mothers with felonies. It is important to remember that in the drug-panicked 1980s, cocaine-exposed infants were initially viewed as hopelessly impaired and held up as the ultimate victims of maternal abuse, yet most follow-up research failed to show the detrimental long-term impacts that were forecast (Zuckerman et al., 2002). Nonjudgmental interventions directed toward general health during pregnancy allow us to help both the pregnant person and the fetus.

Psychological Aspects of Pregnancy

The complex psychology of pregnancy is grounded in the development (or not) of a relationship with the developing baby, both the physical fetus growing in the uterus and the image of the baby developing in the mother's (and others') mind(s). Attributions about the growing fetus play a large role in parents' growing attachment to the fetus and the baby they conceive in their dreams. When a pregnancy is desired, attachment tends to grow; when a pregnancy is not desired, varying levels of attachment evolve and affect how loss will be perceived.

Raphael-Leff (2005) combines psychoanalytic understandings about pregnancy with ideas about the permeability of maternal body boundaries in pregnancy to develop phases women go through as pregnancy progresses. She also incorporates maternal longings for infantile security with the seeming invasion and violence of birth and theorizes a typology of women's experiences with pregnancy. She defines three phases of pregnancy. In the first, the mother's thoughts and emotions are defined by a "psychological slippage" (2005, p. 62), where the mother at times feels consumed by the changes of pregnancy and at other times forgets that she is pregnant. She often focuses on emotional nurturance and nurturance by food during this time. Psychoanalytic understandings of this phase focus on the reactivation of the mother's emotional past, particularly the ways she was mothered (or not) and the fantasies she may have about her growing pregnancy. Indeed, research shows that women's recollections of care by their own mothers are key to how they provide care to their children (Spierling et al., 2018). Raphael-Leff's second phase of pregnancy happens after quickening (feeling fetal movements). The pregnant person's sense of fusion and oneness with the fetus changes as they realize that the fetus moves independently in their body. Raphael-Leff views this as a time when pregnant women start to imagine the personality of the fetus and to have a sense of "twoness." By the third phase, when the fetus has achieved viability and the birth experience looms large, negotiating with her care provider becomes a woman's focus to ensure the health and safety of the baby-to-be.

Raphael-Leff (2005) asserts that a woman's relationships with her fetus and her care providers fall into three categories that frame the psychology of pregnant women. "Facilitators" are delighted to be pregnant and gestating. They experience fusion in Phase 1, communion in Phase 2, and relinquishment in Phase 3. "Regulators" see pregnancy as a means to an end and try to keep its mundane realities out of mind. Phase 1 is a time of heightened self-control, to avoid being overcome by physical effects or sentimentality. Phase 2 is also defined by self-control, in addition to a perception of the fetus as a kind of parasite. Phase 3 is characterized by detachment and the desire to get through the birth. "Reciprocaters" balance between the former two types, experiencing some ambivalence in Phase 1, while being able to tolerate the uncertainty of pregnancy in Phase 2; ultimately, they prepare while taking a "wait and see" approach during Phase 3.

John Bowlby, a founder of attachment theory, considers patterns of infant attachment as shaping how an individual will form relationships in adulthood. The clear implication of his theory is that mothers, driven by both species-survival forces and their own attachment patterns, will attach to newborns quickly. This implies that some process went on before the birth to prime the woman for the attachment. Walsh (2010) suggests this process be called development of the caregiving system rather than prenatal attachment or bonding because it is one-sided (parents toward fetus), yet *prenatal attachment* remains the prevailing term.

Depression and anxiety symptoms are common during typical pregnancy (Kirby et al., 2019) and even more likely during high-risk or medically complicated pregnancies (White et al., 2008). Research shows preterm birth and low birth weight to be highly correlated with anxiety in pregnancy (Doktorchik et al., 2018) and that depressive symptoms and other stressors result in poor pregnancy outcomes and poorer maternal–infant attachment (Ding et al., 2014), although others find the connection a bit more tenuous (Lima et al., 2018). Levels of stress are particularly high when a mother has had a prior pregnancy loss (Gaudet, 2010), and to protect themselves emotionally, women who have experienced pregnancy loss often try to avoid early attachment (Cote-Arsenault & Donato, 2011). Mindfulness, yoga, and other meditation techniques assist pregnant women to reduce stress (Beddoe et al., 2009; see also the websites www.noetic.org/education/self-study/mindful-motherhood-course and www.mindful.org/mindful-magazine/mindful-pregnancy). See Figure 2.1 for an illustration of the ways comfort and complaint should flow for new mothers, their baby, and their supporters.

Social Aspects of Pregnancy

Societal messages about pregnancy and the reinforcement of gender roles during youth (playing house, babysitting) can influence a woman's feelings and behavior regarding pregnancy. The culturally derived lessons generally fit a woman's ethnic, racial, religious, and generational contexts. In countries where women are lacerated or flogged during labor to scare away bad spirits or told to confess if they are having difficult labors, they learn to avoid medical care because it is believed merely to cause problems (Evans, 2013). Yet even in Westernized nations, cultural heritage and religion influence expectations, attitudes and practices regarding pregnancy, beliefs about the fetus, and childbirth (Schott & Henley, 1996). Societal messages in the United States in postcolonial times through the 1950s dictated that pregnant women (who could afford it and generally who were of European White heritage) avoid physical labor, be coddled, and turn their focus inward. When these societal messages changed, pregnant women expected to work until the onset of labor, give birth, and continue with work as soon as physical recovery was complete. Women

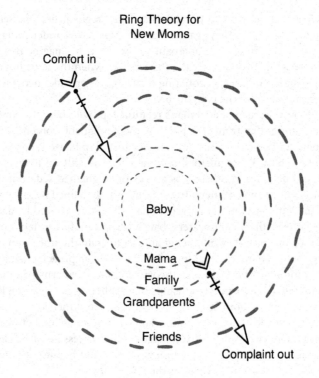

FIGURE 2.1 Ring Theory for New Moms. This image illustrates how support should flow in toward the middle, while the chance to complain and be comforted should flow from the middle outward.
Source: Reproduced with permission from *The Post Party New Mom Blog.* https://thepostparty.com/freebies/

who step outside the norms of their culture or are caught up in rapid cultural shifts are likely to be ostracized (Schott & Henley, 1996), enduring a shaming that reinforces the norms for others by dramatizing the transgression. The relatively rapid changes in U.S. culture that normalized alcohol consumption by pregnant women in the 1970s turned quickly toward defining alcohol consumption in pregnancy as a public health problem that might warrant criminal prosecution for child abuse by the 1980s (Golden, 2011).

Similarly, in the United States, early-stage pregnancy was socially ignored until the 1970s, when it became ever more imbued with notions of "life" and value (Freidenfelds, 2013). Cultural components play an active role here. Some social environments (consider poor, developing countries) give very clear messages that pregnancy loss levels are high and that it is best to avoid giving much thought to a pregnancy until very close to delivery. Other social environments (especially current U.S. culture) encourage early pregnancy testing, visualizing the fetus on ultrasound and often naming the fetus from the moment pregnancy is confirmed. Again, failure to adhere to the given norms brings sanctions from family members, friends, and pregnancy-care providers. When messages about norms are in conflict or discrepant, women's coping capacities are challenged, and decision-making is more complex (McCoyd, 2009a).

Emotion work (Hochschild, 1979) is socially guided and consciously used by pregnant women motivated to maintain their health, cope with negative events, manage pain, and achieve the desired birth (Carter & Guittar, 2014). Emotion work involves women bringing (or pretending to bring) their emotions and emotional behaviors into congruence with socially derived rules about how to feel (Hochschild, 1979). Feeling rules related to gender roles and "good patient" behavior influence how pregnant/birthing women (and their midwives) behave (Carter & Guittar, 2014). Women hospitalized with medically high-risk pregnancies (MHRPs) draw on socially constructed discourses about how to be a mother. Through sacrifice, nurture, and worrying, they show that they are tending to their pregnancies and practicing maternal virtues (Curran et al., 2017).

Research and theoretical logics suggest that everywhere a woman has lived since her birth, the exposures she has had, and her endurance of poverty or other stressors mark her body in ways that affect perinatal outcomes (Kane & Margerison-Zilko, 2017). Social relationships during her lifetime may have been supportive and ameliorated stress, or their difficulties may have contributed to social isolation, known to negatively affect pregnancy and birth outcomes (Kane & Margerison-Zilko, 2017). Geronimus (1996) suggested that some of the racial differences in pregnancy and birth outcomes relate to the "weathering hypothesis": Non-Hispanic Black women experience cumulative stress that wears them down, leaving them more vulnerable to poor health outcomes.

In sum, women's social contexts powerfully shape their pregnancies and births. As social feeling rules change, so too does women's behavior during pregnancy. Whether due to impacts of the social context on one's body or the way one interprets appropriate behavior during pregnancy, the social world strongly influences perinatal outcomes.

Newer technologies such as genetic microarray testing, noninvasive prenatal screening, high-resolution ultrasound, nuchal fold testing, and chorionic villi sampling are used frequently in developed countries and often viewed by pregnant women as bonding tools (as opposed to fetal health testing, their true intent; McCoyd, 2013). The technological imperative that may be characteristic of highly developed countries (McCoyd, 2010a) interacts with variable community norms about pregnancy and childbirth. Hearing fetal heart tones, visualizing the fetus on ultrasound, and identifying the fetus's sex are now all typical experiences for pregnant women that connect them more strongly to the fetus. This may enhance bonding in normal circumstances but may also intensify the grief that comes with perinatal loss.

SPECIAL CONSIDERATIONS IN RISK AND RESILIENCE

The biggest recent story in perinatal circles is the dramatic increase in the United States of maternal mortality (death during and 1 year after pregnancy) and severe maternal morbidity (SMM—significant illness in or after pregnancy), both of which have more than doubled since the late 1980s. Ironically, during the same time period, maternal mortality rates in developing countries fell dramatically (though they remain higher than U.S. rates; UNICEF, 2015—data.unicef.org/topic/maternal-health/maternal-mortality). In the United States, the rate of maternal death was 7.2 per 100,000 pregnant women in 1987 and rose to 18 in 2014 (Centers for Disease Control and Prevention [CDC], 2019). According to the CDC, the death rate of non-Hispanic Black women (42.8/100,000 in 2011–2015) is over three times that of non-Hispanic White women (13/100,000 in 2011–2015). The poorer maternal outcomes of illness and death are a recent development in the United States, often attributed to later-life pregnancies and women having more chronic health conditions prior to pregnancy (CDC, 2019).

Infant mortality (death of the infant at birth or within the neonatal period) follows similar trends, with non-Hispanic Black infants dying at a rate of 11.4 per 1,000 live births in 2016 in contrast to 4.9 deaths per 1,000 live births in non-Hispanic Whites and 3.6 per 1,000 live births in Asians (CDC, 2019). Although the infant mortality rates have been falling in the United States and around the world, the U.S. infant mortality rate is nearly double that of comparable countries (Health System Tracker, 2015).

Maternal and infant health is also affected by adverse childhood experiences (ACEs) such as abuse, neglect, and/or family dysfunction (Racine et al., 2018), which we know affect racial and socioeconomic groups in patterns similar to those previously discussed. Just as people of color and those with lower socioeconomic status (SES) are more likely to experience multiple and higher intensity ACEs, they are also more likely to experience poorer health outcomes, in this case, more premature births, low birth weight, and pregnancy complications as a result of exposure to ACEs when the mother was a child (Racine et al., 2018). Notably, Racine et al. found a connection between ACEs and poor obstetrical and neonatal outcomes with a relatively resourced population (mostly White and higher SES). The impact is not just on neonatal outcomes; Sancho-Rossignol et al. (2018) found that women who had seen domestic violence in their households when they were children had poorer prenatal attachment and higher levels of heart rate reactivity when the baby cried once born; additionally, the infants of those mothers also had poorer behavioral regulation. Hudziak calls these findings "a sobering call to duty for health care professionals" (2018, p. e20180232). We support that call. Although we cannot change people's history of exposure to ACEs, we can provide good obstetrical care that is easily accessible and affordable, supportive, and trauma informed so that every mother and baby are able to get a healthy start.

SUMMARY OF DEVELOPMENT IN THE PRENATAL PERIOD

Pregnancy involves the development of both the fetus (from multicelled blastocyst through embryonic stages and into a fetus that is eventually capable of living independently) and the woman (from individual through pregnant woman through mother with responsibilities toward another person). The development of a woman from a nonpregnant individual to a first-time mother holding a baby is an exemplar of maturational loss as we are defining it. Maturational loss is a form of both growth and maturation, but these developments also entail loss because a known and (usually) comfortable stage of life is left behind for a new, unknown stage. Even in ideal circumstances—a planned pregnancy lovingly accepted by prepared parents (and extended families) who traverse pregnancy and delivery with no real complications—people experience losses. The woman loses true independence in that she must consider how her self-care and nutrition affects her pregnancy. She loses sleep, her nonpregnant body, and possibly her sense of autonomy. Her partner may feel a similar loss of independence as the partner is now tied more tightly to the pregnant woman and may be relied upon more extensively for economic, emotional, and other support. Although these losses are generally welcomed as a sign of maturation and movement toward a chosen goal, they are losses nonetheless. The greatest loss is experienced by the fetus at delivery as the baby is thrust from the womb: prior to birth, the fetus' every need had been met. The moment of delivery requires the baby to breathe, do the work of swallowing to get nutrition, respond to stimuli, and lose the protected, dark calm of the uterine environment. We tend to focus only on the growth of maturation, but nearly all maturation involves these types of poorly recognized losses.

LOSS AS EXPERIENCED BY A FETUS

Little is known about the experience of a fetus. The time of conception (when egg and sperm join to become one cell) through the development of multicelled spheres that exist after cell reproduction for approximately 2 weeks is a time called the germinal period. From 2 to 6 weeks postconception (8 weeks from the time of the last menstrual period), the embryo grows and primitive nervous and circulatory systems develop. At the beginning of the third lunar month, the rudiments of all systems are present, and the entity is called a fetus. The fetus is approximately one and a half inches at this point (12 weeks of gestational age) and grows to approximately 20 inches by the end of the 40th week of gestation. The genitalia and facial features develop during the third to fourth lunar months, and bones begin to harden. The fifth and sixth months are a time of rapid growth. Sensory development occurs, and eye movements begin between 16 and 24 weeks, with patterned eye movements that indicate sleep–wake cycles occurring by around 36 weeks of gestation (www.webmd.com/baby/interactive-pregnancy-tool-fetal-development). Despite these developments, most sense-making and meaning-making processes rely on experience with the environment; the stimulus of light changes or auditory input likely makes no sense when the fetus has no context (or cortex for that matter) with which to interpret the sensations.

Some speculate that the mother's emotional state has a bearing on fetal experience because the chemical and metabolic substances that cross the placenta via the mother's blood supply can have physical effects on the fetus, such as increased heart rate (Ding et al., 2014). Some research shows strong associations between mother's anxiety and depression and the neonate's birthweight and temperament, as well as other complications of pregnancy (Glover, 2014). It is possible that the fetus experiences physical aspects of maternal emotions (oxytocin leading to warm and comfortable feelings; adrenaline leading to anxious feelings), yet, again, with no prior experience through which to interpret these sensations, it is unlikely that the sensations affect the fetus in cognitive or emotional ways. Development of the cortex (thinking part) of the brain occurs in the last weeks before delivery and rapidly during the first 3 months of after birth.

REACTIONS OF OTHERS TO THE LOSS OF A FETUS

Biological Changes Associated With Intrauterine Fetal Death

Pregnancy loss is remarkably common. Macklon et al. (2002) reported that only about 30% of conceived pregnancies lead to a live birth and about 60% are lost around the time of implantation, before "clinical" pregnancy is recognized (see Figure 2.2). Because another 10% are lost to miscarriage and stillbirth, truly a small minority of fertilized eggs go on to create a baby.

The experience of miscarriage, intrauterine fetal death (IUFD), or other pregnancy loss leads to an abrupt change in the biological status of the pregnant woman. If labor must be induced, the experience of laboring to produce a dead fetus/baby is physically and emotionally grueling. Hormone levels drop dramatically, just as with delivery of a live child. Prolactin release will signal oxytocin release, and the woman will have to cope with breast enlargement and milk production until bound and unused breasts quit secreting milk. Endorphin levels are high during late pregnancy and delivery to blunt the pain of labor, but these also drop off dramatically after delivery (https://www.nct.org.uk/labour-birth/your-guide-labour/hormones-labour-oxytocin-and-others-how-they-work). These hormonal and other metabolic changes happen regardless of whether the fetus is born alive or not. Most obstetricians and perinatal observers assume that hormonal changes promote feelings of depression ranging from "baby blues" to postpartum depression. The drop in hormone levels creates a propensity toward depressive moods that a pregnancy loss will exacerbate.

Biological characteristics affect both the experience of loss and the tendency toward it. Kenny et al. (2013) used a cohort of over 270,000 English women to examine the effects of advancing maternal age on pregnancy outcomes and were able to control for SES (social deprivation in their study), BMI (obesity), and other risk factors. They found that poor outcomes increased as maternal age increased, an important consideration as women often delay childbearing due to education and other factors. Additionally, although many assume that the length of the pregnancy (gestational age) affects grief intensity, most research finds that loss even in early pregnancy leads to significant grief for many women (Bellhouse et al., 2018). Nevertheless, scores on the Perinatal Grief Scale (PGS; Toedter et al., 1988) indicate that people with later pregnancy losses have higher scores (more active grieving, difficulty coping, and despair), just as women tend to have higher scores than men generally (Toedter et al., 2001). Perinatal loss is also strongly tied to depression and anxiety even up to 10 years after the loss (Kokou-Kpolou et al., 2018) in ways that are associated with whether the loss happened before a live birth or immediately after. Additionally, depression and anxiety seem to negatively affect future pregnancies when no intervention is available (Hunter et al., 2017).

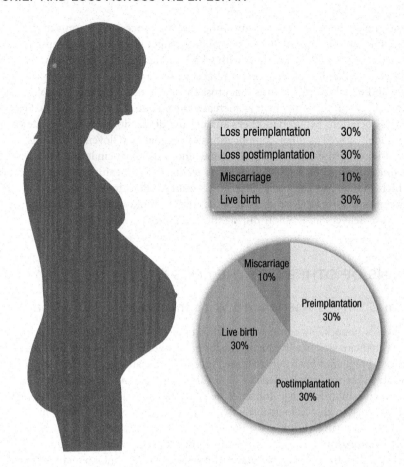

FIGURE 2.2 Pregnancy Outcomes of Conceptions. This image illustrates the approximate percentages for conception outcomes. Approximately 60% of conceptions are never recognized as pregnancies, happening before a woman knows of the pregnancy.
Source: Data from Macklon, N. S., Geraedts, J. P., & Fauser, B. C. (2002). Conception to ongoing pregnancy: The 'black box' of early pregnancy loss. *Human Reproduction Update, 8*(4), 333–343. doi.org/10.1093/humupd/8.4.333 (p. 335).

Women who lose a pregnancy often experience a sense of failure, and their body image is likely to be affected (Bennett et al., 2005; Cacciatore, 2010). Women seem to interpret their inability to provide a "safe nest" as a personal failure. Clinical experience shows that women frequently mistrust their body's ability to sustain future pregnancy. They often generalize this into a broad mistrust of their bodies. Certainly, the medical language of perinatal loss—"failed" IVF cycles, "mis"carriage, "incompetent" cervix, and "elderly" primigravida (older first-time mothers)—carries implications of fault.

The lay support literature (Davis, 1996; Layne, 2003) frequently mentions physical sensations such as aching arms, a feeling of an abdominal void, and occasionally hearing baby cries when no babies are around. These sensations have provoked little interest from the medical community; however, many peer counselors (parents who have had previous perinatal loss) believe that these are biological phenomena. They explain that the mother's body was primed to respond by holding the baby, with the weight of the baby supported by the mother's arms and abdomen, and that her body is mourning the loss of these sensations. Some even speculate that hearing baby cries is due to a heightened awareness (with the implication that this is also biologically primed) that either allows one to hear at great distance or interprets other sounds as the sounds one was expecting to hear.

Psychological Aspects of Intrauterine Fetal Death

Before the early 20th century, women seldom responded very emotionally to an early miscarriage as these were common, and childbirth threatened women's health (Freidenfelds, 2013). More recent norms in Westernized countries include early diagnosis of pregnancy and valorization of even the fertilized egg, which has changed the psycho-emotional experience of miscarriage for many women (Freidenfelds, 2013). Miscarriage (loss of the pregnancy before the 20th week of gestation) and stillbirth (pregnancy loss after the 20th week EGA) have become more recognized as sources of emotional pain (e.g., www.nytimes.com/2019/10/02/parenting/after-a-miscarriage-grief-anger-envy-relief-and-guilt.html). Robust lay literature and an extensive network of support groups for perinatal losses of many sorts have evolved since the early 1980s.

A Cochrane Collaboration systematic review observed that historically women were separated from their dead and dying infants due to the belief that if they did not see the neonate, there would be no attachment and hence no grief (Koopmans et al., 2013). Contemporary understandings about prenatal attachment are very different, of course; perinatal practice has changed, and women are now encouraged to acknowledge their attachments, keep mementos (ultrasounds and bills when a fetal body is not available), and see and hold their baby's body if the state of development and delivery method allow this. Yet none of these measures have been rigorously tested and found to be effective at preventing complications of grief, which occur in about one of every five bereaved mothers (Koopmans et al., 2013). These supportive approaches, often carried out by social workers and chaplains, have been widely commended, even if not considered "evidence-based practice," due to a lack of randomized trials that compare varied forms of care (Bennett et al., 2005; Koopmans et al., 2013). Indeed, it is difficult to imagine the ethical justification for refraining from certain empathic interventions in order to assure randomization of treatments when women have just experienced perinatal loss.

Attachment theorists identify psychological impacts of loss. Bowlby (1979/2000) theorized that people are strongly motivated to maintain affectional bonds and that "all the most powerful forms of attachment behavior become activated" in the face of loss (p. 42). These behaviors and attempts to recapture pregnancy erupt when women are told that their fetus has died in utero. Bowlby wrote:

> In the case of the anxiously attached, mourning is likely to be characterized by unusually intense anger and/or self-reproach, with depression, and to persist for much longer than normal. In the case of the compulsively self-reliant [the avoidant], mourning may be delayed for months or years. (1979/2000, pp. 139–140)

This provides an interpretation for why some women experience chronic, complicated, or delayed grief reactions that have nothing to do with gestational age. One might assume that the securely attached would grieve in a healthy manner. Furthermore, women who have anxious attachment patterns may grieve in an extended and self-reproaching manner, whereas women who have avoidant attachment styles may delay or refrain from mourning. It is clear from clinical practice that women differ in the intensity of their grief and their level of anger directed at self or medical providers (as well as at women currently pregnant). Generally, the due date after a loss is a challenging time, yet it is also often a point when emotions and longing begin to give way to restoration orientation.

Klaus and Kennell (1976) seem to have been the first to study perinatal loss empirically. They were pediatricians influenced by Bowlby's conceptualization of maternal–infant bonding. They likened perinatal loss to the loss of a spouse. To posit such a serious equivalence was quite unusual because, at the time, pregnancy loss was something to be hidden and forgotten. Klaus and Kennell supported the development of hospital protocols to allow contact with the stillborn or deceased infant and to avoid tranquilizing medications (noting that they interfere with grief work).

They introduced the idea of "group discussions," observing that bereaved mothers benefit from reading other bereaved mothers' diaries (pp. 235–239).

Bowlby acknowledged that perinatal bereavement includes "[n]umbing, followed by somatic distress, yearning, anger, and subsequent irritability and depression . . . [and] preoccupations with the image of the dead baby and dreams about him" (1980/1998, p. 122). He supported changed hospital protocols allowing women to hold their dead babies and encouraging women to name them and conduct simple funerals. He recognized a parent's need to acknowledge the baby's existence as a separate entity in order to effectively mourn it. He notes that "this loss becomes a non-event with no one to mourn" (p. 123). Bowlby acknowledged the need to attach to the deceased baby in order to mourn. This chance to see and hold the baby had been implemented in most hospitals by the early 1980s but came into question again following a study by Hughes et al. (2002), which concluded that women who held their stillborn infants experienced higher levels of anxiety and depression in subsequent pregnancies. Critics of this research observed that all bereaved women in the sample were compelled to see their baby rather than merely being told that they might do so. Also, while anxiety in subsequent pregnancies is likely for those with previous pregnancy loss, the comparison group in the Hughes et al. study consisted of women who had not had a previous pregnancy loss. Erlandsson et al. (2013) conclude that when contact between mothers and their dead babies is managed as a matter of course, yet given a choice in the face of strong resistance, women fear the encounter with their dead baby less and tend to feel better supported.

Klaus and Kennell (1976) asserted that "replacement pregnancy" may occur after fetal loss when the mother is unable to work through separating from the expected child. They wrote:

> We strongly encourage the parents to refrain from having a replacement infant until they have completed their mourning reaction. We explain that it is difficult to take on a new baby at the same time one is giving up the baby who has died. (p. 237)

They suggest a waiting period of at least 6 months. There is no well-developed theoretical or empirical basis for such a prescription, and Grout and Romanoff (2000) have called "the replacement child" concept a myth. As Koopmans et al. (2013) note, our knowledge about effective supports for families affected by perinatal grief is still incomplete; becoming prescriptive about whether and when to have another pregnancy is surely premature.

Social Aspects of Intrauterine Fetal Death

Pregnancy loss is common. When preimplantation loss and loss before a first missed menses are included, the level of loss may be as high as 60% to 70% (Larsen et al., 2013). Although more often acknowledged in recent years, social recognition of perinatal grief remains limited. Although not all women grieve early miscarriages, women who have actively attached prenatally are likely to do so. With social norms and prenatal technology that promote such attachments and a political culture that increasingly views embryos and fetuses as "persons," not only do many women benefit from some level of support and validation for mourning after miscarriage or stillbirth, but others may need legal support if they are blamed for the losses they endured (Browne, 2018).

Race, class, religion, and ethnicity all have a bearing on how prenatal attachment is viewed and how perinatal grief is enacted. For instance, research indicates that African American bereaved parents have higher rates of pregnancy loss overall, have more cumulative stress in the form of marginalization and oppression over their lifetimes, and typically adhere to cultural norms that encourage continued bonds with the deceased, and greater emotional expression, but less overt familial dialogue about grief and loss (Boyden et al., 2014). These circumstances would seem to make grieving more challenging, and traditional therapy is not widely viewed as a legitimate form of health seeking in the African American community, leaving grievers alone in trying to cope with difficult emotions. It is possible, even likely, that religious and other communities provide support when parents are connected, but the academic literature is silent on this point.

In a study that explored miscarriage in several cultures (Wojnar et al., 2011), lesbian couples were found to experience complex grief reactions more frequently because they had navigated many barriers to pregnancy, dealt with disapproving social contacts, and negotiated who would carry the pregnancy (Wojnar, 2007).

Family members are affected by perinatal losses as well, and some of the "forgotten grievers" are living siblings (Avelin et al., 2011). The death of a newborn in the neonatal intensive care unit (NICU) has been shown to have lifelong effects on some siblings (Fanos et al., 2009). It is likely that siblings who are aware of a miscarriage or stillbirth will react similarly to those who experience the death of a sibling in the NICU: They will likely have raised anxiety and worry about their parents' health and coping and feel like they are "not enough" for their parents (Fanos et al., 2009). Working to avoid family secret-keeping and promoting rituals such as scrapbooking and other memorialization seemingly assist siblings in coping with perinatal death (Youngblut & Brooten, 2013).

Grandparents are often "forgotten grievers" too (Gilrane-McGarry & O'Grady, 2011). They have "double grief," mourning the grandchild that will not join the family and also grieving for their son or daughter. Gilrane-McGarry and O'Grady observe that as most grandparents have experienced many other losses due to their age, they experience cumulative grief as well as double grief.

Family and peers sometimes offer little comment, assuming that everyone can move on as if nothing of real importance has happened. The absence of rituals for enlisting support and saying "good bye" in perinatal loss make the latter drastically different from other types of death loss, where funerals, memorial services, and social support are common. This lack of ritual has consequences. The mother and her supporters try (mostly in vain) to either move on without acknowledgment (difficult because the mother is feeling loss) or find new ways of observing the loss.

Social recognition of loss is complicated further when the mother has a fetal anomaly diagnosed and subsequently ends the pregnancy. These are desired pregnancies, "electively" terminated (McCoyd, 2007, 2008, 2009a, 2009b; Rapp, 1999), and if miscarriage and stillbirth are silently disenfranchised losses, the termination of a pregnancy affected by fetal anomaly is actively hidden because of privacy norms and the stigma associated with abortion in U.S. culture (McCoyd, 2010b). Although women may disclose the loss to their intimates, they often do not provide the full story. They then feel that what support they receive is the result of deception and they have difficulty utilizing it effectively (McCoyd, 2007).

Even more concerning, women are sometimes legally prosecuted for miscarriages and stillbirths (Paltrow & Flavin, 2013). Some may have wished for their pregnancies to end, but regardless, women have been prosecuted for everything from practicing medicine without a license to delivery of controlled substances to a minor and homicide. Punitive and shaming responses to miscarriage and stillbirth are being deployed more and more frequently, especially against women of color (National Advocates for Pregnant Women [NAPW], 2019). This has become especially alarming in view of narrowing reproductive rights and the organized campaign to limit accessibility of contraception and abortion in the United States and beyond.

Perinatal bereavement is experienced and expressed in a variety of ways, influenced strongly by social norms. The level of prenatal attachment has much to do with the way the loss is experienced and mourned, just as the responses and support of friends, family, and medical care providers' are crucial to how bereaved parents grieve. Only a full bio–psycho–social–spiritual assessment prepares the clinician to practice intelligently and sensitively in such cases.

OTHER TYPES OF PERINATAL LOSS

Perinatal loss is experienced most often in miscarriage, stillbirth, and neonatal death. Infertility and abortion are types of disenfranchised perinatal loss. Here, we briefly address these losses, as well as the alternative (and ever-expanding) pathways to parenthood that entail loss of the typical and highly valued pregnancy and childbirth experience.

Infertility

Infertility is defined as a year of unprotected heterosexual intercourse that does not lead to pregnancy, and it is believed to affect 1 in 7 couples in the developed world and 1 in 4 in the developing world (Borght & Wyns, 2018). It often leads to psychosocial distress. The rate of infertility varies based on race, social class, age, nulliparity (whether one has ever been pregnant before), and other demographics but is estimated to affect 7% to 15.5% of "eligible women" (women who are trying to get pregnant) in developed countries (Thoma et al., 2013). With more women postponing pregnancy due to changing economic and social norms for emerging adults, the rate of infertility has been rising as more women who want children age beyond their optimal fertility (Borght & Wyns, 2018).

Couples feel the loss deeply when they are unable to become pregnant. Many people begin to visualize their hopes for pregnancy long before they pursue it. Infertility invalidates these expectations and creates an increased sense of vulnerability, a loss of self-esteem, and a belief that one's body is defective and/or apt to betray (Lind et al., 1989). This is a private, disenfranchised loss, often hidden from family and friends, who are not expected to know about or understand it. This silence self-disenfranchises the loss.

Although a painful loss, research that tracked couples who remained infertile after 10 years and those who achieved pregnancy using assisted reproductive technologies (ARTs) found that quality of life in both groups was fairly similar (Wischmann et al., 2012). Most infertile couples found advantages in being childless over time. Women from those couples tended to have greater work satisfaction and had lower rates of divorce than typical parent populations (Wischmann et al., 2012). Like most losses, infertility brings emotional pain, yet its sufferers survive and move on after sufficient time to process their new assumptive world and recreate meaning in their lives.

Losses Related to Unintended Pregnancy

Rates of unintended pregnancy vary tremendously by age, race, and educational status. Until about 2008, almost half of all pregnancies were unintended, decreasing to about 45% in 2011 (most recent available data; Guttmacher Institute, 2019). When parents elect to give birth as a result of unintended pregnancy, life changes for better or worse, depending largely on their ability to mobilize resources to support their own health and the family's economic circumstances (Kavanaugh et al., 2017). Even when pregnancy was not intended, some parents derive happiness from the birth despite stressors because they feel that God provided them this fate or that children are a blessing and they could rise to the occasion (Aiken et al., 2015). For many with an unintended pregnancy, resources do not seem forthcoming, and they consider relinquishing their baby for adoption or terminating the pregnancy via abortion. In 2011, more than half of unintended pregnancies yielded a birth (58%) and 42% ended in abortion (Guttmacher Institute, 2019). According to the Adoption Network, only about 4% of those who carry unintended pregnancies relinquish their babies for adoption (Adoption Network, 2019).

Readers may notice our attempt to avoid referring to only women as pregnant. Although it is beyond the scope of this text to cover a deeper discussion of healthcare needs and psychosocial aspects of pregnancy among transmen, it is also important that the experience of erasure (Hoffkling et al., 2017) be recognized as a form of loss. We will use the term *pregnant people* in this section because many pregnancies experienced by transmen are unintended. Furthermore, even when intended and desired, a transman's pregnancy can stimulate losses, from erasure and gender dysphoria to rejection by friends/family.

When an unintended pregnancy yields the decision to abort, accessing reproductive healthcare services can become part of the stress burden of following through with the decision, as abortion services in the United States are highly stigmatized and multiple states have passed laws to make abortion services essentially inaccessible. Not only are state laws crimping access, but "gag laws" mean physicians have limited ability to discuss holistic reproductive options with women in their care (Hatcher et al., 2018; Taylor et al., 2013). When pregnant people can access abortion, they are often viewed as not needing emotional support because they made an active choice for that option. Research shows that even 3 years later, the vast majority of those who had abortions (95%–99%) feel they made the right decision (Rocca et al., 2015), and although many have some degree of sadness after the procedure, it is typically tempered with relief (Major et al., 2009). It is clear that abortion counseling is useful during the process to help clarify values and provide emotional support (Joffe, 2013), but abortion stigma (Major & Gramzow, 1999) and political prohibitions linger and add to individuals' sense of disenfranchised grief after abortion.

Adoption also leaves people with sadness, lowered sense of self-worth, and other painful emotions, even when they are later reunited with the child they relinquished (March, 2014). This disenfranchised grief (Doka, 2002) is also a form of ambiguous grief (Boss, 1999) as the relinquished child is physically absent and whereabouts are essentially unknown even though the child is psychologically present in the birth mother's mind. Although less stigmatized than abortion (and seen as highly virtuous by many who oppose abortion), birth parents who have relinquished babies for adoption frequently comment that the stigma and disapproval they experience, along with a lack of social support and counseling, adds pain to an already painful experience (Fessler, 2006). After carrying and giving birth to a baby, the birth mother is expected to break contact. Older-style adoptions meant the birth mother had no communication whatsoever with the adoptive parents and had very little control over any aspects of the adoption (Henny et al., 2007). Yet, even in open adoptions, which are now more common, birth mothers may have only cursory contact after the adoption goes through (Henny et al., 2007). These losses after an unintended pregnancy, resulting from emotionally difficult choices, generate grief that is disenfranchised and therefore challenging to process.

Assisted Reproductive Technologies

A full discussion of the many available ARTs is outside the scope of this chapter, yet anyone using ART experiences the loss of the "normal/typical/customary" way of creating their family. In the United States in 2010, approximately 1.5% of all births were due to ART, with states such as New Jersey, New York, Massachusetts, and Connecticut accounting for the highest rates (between 3.5% and 4% of live births in each of those states; Sunderam et al., 2013). Using the definition of Sunderam et al. (2013), ARTs encompass any measures that require handling of both eggs and sperm. They do not count ovulation-promoting medications that may enable typical coitus to produce a pregnancy or insemination with donor sperm, even though these are also fertility treatments that entail medical assistance and a sense of loss. Now, it is possible, through IVF of one woman's egg with a man's sperm subsequently gestated in a second woman and raised by a third woman, to create a child with three mothers: one genetic, one gestational, and one social/adoptive—see this link to a *New York Times* story illustrating this: www.nytimes.com/interactive/2010/12/22/magazine/20101222-twiblings-audio.html?ref= assistedreproductivetechnology&_r=0.

At each level of technology, losses include a changed sense of body integrity and function; changes in the relationship with one's partner; losses of embryos; and loss of innocence about the "natural ease" of creating a family. Many issues must be resolved: How much ART to use, how long to keep trying, how to assess the ethics of using donors and gestational carriers, and what and when to tell children about their conceptions (Paul & Berger, 2007). Additionally, losses due to the birth of very premature children are common after ART (in the form of either a death loss when not yet viable or the loss of the healthy baby as when multiples are born and have the sequela of prematurity, such as cerebral palsy, vision and hearing impairments, and cognitive impairments). Multifetal selective reduction is recommended when more than three embryos/fetuses "take," and once again, the pain of terminating some to enable the birth of other fetuses creates complex emotions and grief (Evans et al., 2015). Even when the ART goes well and enables a healthy child to be born, losses of having the child "the natural way" increase medical intervention in one's life, and the "burdens of choice" (Galst & Verp, 2015).

Medically Complicated Pregnancies and Loss

Women often expect pregnancy, once achieved, to proceed with little effect on their lives until they deliver. Advances in pregnancy care have reduced maternal death and pregnancy complications over the past century in most developing countries, though recent rises in maternal mortality in developed countries are attributed to aging mothers, more women with chronic illnesses becoming pregnant, anemia, ART, poor obstetrical care, and even the level of governance (effective regulatory capacity; Ruiz-Cantero et al., 2019). Complications occur in 10% to 20% of pregnancies in developed countries and range from hyperemesis gravidarum, placenta previa, and premature labor to pregnancy-induced diabetes or preeclampsia. These conditions have biological, psychological, and social aspects unique to the condition, but all have outcomes in common. Women experiencing these conditions experience loss of control, both because their bodies are not behaving in the ways they would choose and because required medical care limits autonomy (Munch et al., 2020). They are also pulled between opposing forces such as decisions to share their emotions or suppress them, maintain control or defer to medical providers, and meet others' expectations or not (McCoyd et al., 2018), Anxiety, depression, stress, grief, boredom, fear, ambivalence, and guilt are also commonly associated with pregnancy complications (Meaney et al., 2016). Social workers and other caregivers can validate a woman's frustration and fear and also promote control where it is possible (McCoyd et al., 2020). Notably, mental health status prior to conception is a primary determinant of pregnancy outcome (Ding et al., 2014), often affected by prior losses and/or psychosocial contexts. Social workers and other counselors may be able to improve the odds of healthier mothers and babies.

Prenatal Diagnosis and Termination of Pregnancy for Fetal Anomaly

With the advent of ultrasound and amniocentesis, it has become possible to see inside the uterus to assess fetal health. Most pregnant women do not hesitate to engage in prenatal screening (which determines *risk* of an anomaly), particularly in Westernized nations (McCoyd, 2013; Santalahti et al., 1998). Advancing maternal age is known to increase the risk of trisomy conditions (chromosomal abnormalities), yet obstetricians encourage screening for all pregnant women because other fetal anomalies might be detected (genetic, cardiac, and neural tube defects, for example; American College of Obstetricians and Gynecologists [ACOG], 2016). Because many more young women get pregnant than older women, the number of pregnant women under age 35 whose fetus gets diagnosed with an anomaly is greater than the number of "older" women with an affected pregnancy (Choi et al., 2012). Most women who are told that their fetus is at higher risk for an anomaly have not previously considered this possibility (McCoyd, 2007, 2013) and may not understand that they must have a diagnostic test to determine whether the fetus does indeed have whatever condition is of concern.

Positive diagnoses rarely predict the degree of the condition. There is frequently much uncertainty about the viability of the pregnancy, the possibilities of a term birth, and the outcomes for the baby. Complicating matters further, women and their partners have only a brief time to decide whether to trust the information they have (McCoyd, 2010a, 2015) and whether they believe themselves capable of bringing such a pregnancy to fruition and raising the child (McCoyd, 2008). Following the angst of quick decision-making under conditions of uncertainty, when termination is elected, women often feel a short surge of relief, often followed by grief they do not expect. Although most women understand they are losing a pregnancy/fetus they desired and became attached to, they often feel constrained in their grief because the "treatment" of pregnancy termination is, technically, an abortion—a medical procedure fraught with stigma (McCoyd, 2010b). Couples often mourn in secrecy, making an already difficult loss even more challenging. Effective interventions must help couples recognize the reasons for their decision, lower their sense of guilt, and recognize their right to grieve the healthy child they hoped to have.

Delivery of a Premature or Medically Compromised Neonate

Sometimes, a medically complicated pregnancy yields a premature baby or neonate. Other times, premature labor starts and cannot be stopped, or membranes rupture and the neonate is born. *Time* magazine referred to a "Preemie Revolution" (Kluger, 2014), noting that 478,790 babies were born prematurely in 2010 and 462,408 survived (p. 29). Yet of those born at 24 weeks EGA, just over half will survive, and most of these will experience complications such as cerebral palsy, neurocognitive delays, and hearing and vision impairments. By 28 weeks' EGA, most will survive and over half will survive without noticeable complications (Kluger, citing CDC, 2014, p. 29). Even when survival is likely, parents must endure the high-tech environment of the NICU, with its frightening alarms and machines, and manage fears for their child's current and future welfare. Parents are also concerned about how to pay for both the hospitalization and therapies to ensure that the child will catch up with developmental milestones over time. These fears (and loss of the expected joys of having a healthy child) combine with the sense of vulnerability that accompanies most losses; additionally, parents must allow the medical system to take charge of nearly every aspect of their newborn's care, denying them bonding opportunities and the confidence of competence derived from providing the newborn's care.

The losses identified in Zimmerman-Levitt's reading at the end of this chapter are heightened when a baby is born prematurely or with a medical condition. As Douglas's reading at the end of this chapter notes, parents sometimes are aware that their fetus has a diagnosis but hope that the newborn does not show evidence of it or is less affected than predicted. The losses involved in starting the parenting relationship in a medical setting give way to the ongoing losses associated with learning what delays their child is likely to experience.

INTERVENTION

Intervention for perinatal grief is as hidden as the loss. OB/GYN providers seem unfamiliar with resources for psychosocial intervention, whether they be Shear's work with complicated grief, perinatal loss support groups, or other targeted psychosocial interventions (Lacasse & Cacciatore, 2014). In a study of medications used after perinatal bereavement, individuals given either benzodiazepines/other sleep aids or antidepressants were most often given the prescriptions by their OB/GYNs, most frequently within a week of the loss (Lacasse & Cacciatore, 2014). Yet, psychotropic medication has potential for iatrogenic harm, and most clinicians urge a first approach of allowing natural healing (good nutrition, sleep, support) or formal psychosocial treatment (Lacasse & Cacciatore, 2014) rather than medication. The healthcare providers caring for the mother and her family at the time of the birth are also critical. A systematic review showed that parents wish for "privacy not abandonment" (Ellis et al., 2016, p. 6), especially because the actions of healthcare providers are highly memorable for parents (Ellis et al., 2016). Clear, empathic, tailored explanations for the loss are necessary: additionally parents benefit from the opportunity to build memories of their child's brief life and need adequate information about varied delivery and burial options (Ellis et al., 2016).

McCoyd (1987) developed a framework for intervention for use with perinatal loss that has been applied by MSW students to multiple types of loss over the past decades. Called the Five Vs, it provides interventions the practitioner can use to guide the work without resorting to structured, predetermined tasks. The Five Vs provide a model to structure the work, yet allow the bereaved to follow their own needs and inclinations. The Five Vs are validating, valuing, verifying, ventilating, and being visionary. Validating is critical if the loss is disenfranchised. The primary task of validation is to help the bereaved identify areas where they do not feel "allowed" to grieve and to recognize and validate the right to be a mourner. Particularly when a pregnancy has not been revealed, the bereaved parents may not have others who acknowledge their loss. Helping women and couples recognize their right and necessity to mourn is a critical first step toward healing.

Valuing and verifying are elements of validation. By recognizing that the lost entity had value to the mourner, the clinician validates the griever's right to mourn. Helping the bereaved parent discuss all aspects of the lost entity/person's value acknowledges the importance of the disrupted bond (a domain for exploration). Verifying includes any intervention to assist the bereaved with gathering tangible mementos and/or developing rituals that "make real" the loss. These reminders can be used by the parents to stimulate support from friends and family. Creating memory boxes with footprints, handprints, locks of hair, and pictures if possible is useful to parents' own grieving but can also be used to remind others that the baby had a presence in the world.

Most social workers and other grief clinicians are quite familiar with ventilating. They regularly urge clients to "vent," to "let it all out," or in other ways to be emotionally expressive. Ventilation can be done in a variety of ways and does not always need to incorporate tears. Indeed, if the clinician falls prey to the grief work hypothesis and insists on tears as a form of ventilation, they actually risk harming the mourner. Ventilating entails an expectation that the bereaved is able to talk about the loss with authenticity, consistent affect, and content, and such mourning does not require tears. In pregnancy loss, gender stereotypes of mothers mourning with tears and fathers with rigid control often hold true but not always. Mothers often are overtly emotionally expressive until the due date, and then their partners start to express anger, sadness, and irritation. It seems the partners "stay strong" for the mother, and once her emotion has run its course, the partner's authentic response is allowed expression. Ventilating may lead to meaning-making, and the clinician can help explore the many ways the loss has affected the griever's life. The grief therapist practices best by remaining quietly supportive and exploratory, avoiding platitudes or trite phrases that could interrupt the mourner's ability to ventilate thoughts, feelings, and reflections freely.

Being visionary is often part of the ending process but occurs throughout the work (whether formal grief work in a therapeutic setting or supportive friendships). This generally entails assisting the bereaved person to think through likely future events and recognize their potential for intensifying grief feelings (Rando's [1993] subsequent temporary upsurges of grief [STUG] reactions). In being visionary, the grief therapist can share lessons learned from others about when and where grief is likely to be heightened. With perinatal loss, the due date for a lost pregnancy often revives feelings of grief. Grievers often need to reflect and mourn at this time. Likewise, helping the perinatally bereaved anticipate that future pregnancies are likely to be fraught with reminders of the loss can help them recognize and manage anxiety if that comes to pass.

Models to assist with perinatal grief have also been proposed by Wojnar et al. (2011), who suggest that the Meaning of Miscarriage Model (incorporating aspects of Swanson's earlier model) is a useful and culturally sensitive way to assist bereaved parents. The themes for intervention are explored with the bereaved. These themes include (a) coming to know (about the pregnancy and its potential loss), (b) losing and gaining (naming what was lost), (c) sharing the loss, (d) going public, (e) getting through it, and (f) trying again. These explorations are to be combined with Swanson's theory of caring, which includes (a) maintaining belief, (b) knowing, (c) being with, (d) doing for, and (e) enabling (Wojnar et al., 2011, pp. 554–555).

Intervention in perinatal grief will nearly always require attention to the disenfranchised nature of nearly all of its forms. It also incorporates awareness that parental grief differs from other types of grief due to the grieving parent's sense of responsibility for the offspring's well-being. No intervention in perinatal grief is complete without attending to these issues.

READINGS

Daniella and Her Family's Challenging Beginnings
HEATHER DOUGLAS

Heather Douglas, MSc, MS, CGC, CCGC, is a certified genetic counselor in Toronto, Canada. She sees prenatal, pediatric, cancer, cardiac, and adult genetics patients.

In my role as a genetic counselor, I met with Marianne and Daniel (pseudonyms), a couple in their mid to late 20s. Their 6-year-old daughter, Daniella, had a chromosomal condition, and we were meeting to discuss the risks for the couple's current pregnancy.

I asked the couple to tell me about Daniella. They recalled their story in detail, starting with their visit to another genetic counselor when they were pregnant with Daniella. In that pregnancy, there was an ultrasound marker that implied a higher chance of a chromosome condition in the baby, even though this marker is often a false alarm. Though the couple was distraught by this finding, they decided that they would not do any genetic testing and decided to accept whatever health conditions the baby might have.

In their case, the ultrasound finding was indeed an indication that the baby was not well. Daniella was born and soon suffered respiratory distress. She was admitted into the neonatal intensive care unit for 3 months. She needed surgery for serious nasal blockage and a heart defect. It was determined that she has a complex chromosome imbalance that caused these problems as well as developmental delay. At 6 years old, Daniella said only a few words and was in a special-needs kindergarten class. She was not yet toilet-trained and did not dress herself independently. While usually healthy physically, she had had multiple episodes of respiratory distress during which an ambulance was called and hospitalization was needed.

Marianne and Daniel described Daniella as a caring, sociable girl with a good memory. They regaled me with stories demonstrating how sweet and spunky she is, and they seemed excited by my request to see photos and videos of her. I expressed that while their love for her was undeniable, it must be difficult to have a child with special needs. Both Daniel and Marianne became teary and told me that it had "taken a huge psychological toll on the family." They said they would sometimes look at their friends who had healthy, typical children and feel that the world was unfair. However, when describing Daniella, they said, "She was meant to be ours." I asked how they had gotten through the past few years, and they said they relied on their inner strength. Their grandmother has a saying, "A human being is stronger than a rock," and they reminded themselves of this whenever they struggled.

For the current pregnancy, I determined that there was a low chance of having a baby with the same chromosome abnormality or any other problem. They chose noninvasive tests like blood work and ultrasounds rather than invasive tests that would directly check the baby's chromosomes but could cause a miscarriage. All the tests were going well, until an ultrasound found two bright spots in the baby's heart. While usually a normal variant, it is a marker for a higher risk of a chromosome condition, much like the marker found in their previous pregnancy. At this point, they were concerned but still did not wish to put the pregnancy at risk, so they again declined invasive tests. Marianne was still pregnant at the writing of this case study.

Developmental Milestones

Young adulthood is a time when people move away from their families of origin, becoming individuals. Many will then get married or into a serious relationship and start a family of their own.

Generally, parents expect that their baby will be healthy and develop typically, and so having a baby with a disability is the loss of the expected child (Boss et al., 2011). Here I outline the biological, psychological, and social impacts of this loss for the parents in more detail.

Biological Impact of the Loss

The news of a concerning ultrasound marker caused significant stress for Marianne and Daniel in both pregnancies. Stress for an expectant mother can cause preterm labor, low birth weight babies, high blood pressure, and even developmental delays in the child (Cardwell, 2013). In addition, maternal stress in pregnancy is associated with increased anxiety behavior and even adult-onset disease in the offspring years later (Brunton, 2013; Louey & Thornburg, 2005). It remains to be seen how Marianne's stress about her pregnancies will affect Daniella and her younger sibling.

Parenting a child with a disability is associated with elevated levels of stress (Azad et al., 2013), and the stress is a predictor of poorer physical health for the parents (Cantwell et al., 2014). Considering that Daniella will likely need lifelong care, Marianne and Daniel will be at increased risk of health problems for decades to come.

Due to the emotional and financial demands on them, Marianne and Daniel were not ready to have another pregnancy for 6 years. By waiting, they had actually increased their chances of infertility and of having a baby with an unrelated disability like Down syndrome, since both are associated with age. Luckily, Marianne and Daniel were young when they had Daniella, so the risks of these problems were still fairly low 6 years later. In contrast, a couple in their mid-30s may not have time to wait for a second child.

Psychological Impact of the Loss

Parents describe intense initial reactions to having a baby with a disability: numbness, disappointment, isolation, defensiveness, protest, despair, denial, sadness, anger, self-doubt, humiliation, confusion, guilt, and hopelessness (Kearney & Griffin, 2001). In addition, parents' feelings of control can be challenged, affecting their adjustment to their child's disability (Lloyd & Hastings, 2009). Marianne and Daniel acknowledged feeling out of control after Daniella was born. Attachment between the parents and child can also be inhibited or influenced (Douglas, 2014). Having a child in the NICU can enhance the mother and father's levels of stress at a time that is already so difficult (Busse et al., 2013).

While the parents' initial grief reactions may wane, reactivation of grief may occur periodically throughout their child's life. This is called "chronic sorrow," described poignantly:

> Things can be going along just fine, and suddenly out of the blue you might begin feeling sad again. Sometimes it may be little things that set off these feelings—those moments may be trimming the Christmas tree, hearing a special piece of music, seeing your child outside playing—or it may be the big life changes which bring back strong feelings of sadness—such as having your handicapped child begin public school. (Damrosch & Perry, 1989, p. 27)

Marianne and Daniel were experiencing chronic sorrow. The visit to the genetics clinic reactivated the sorrow for them; however, it also seemed to remind them of the great joy they took in parenting Daniella.

Social Impact of the Loss

Like Daniel and Marianne, parents of a child with a disability may feel distance from parents of "typical" children and may feel more supported by other parents in circumstances similar to their own (Kerr & McIntosh, 2000). Interestingly, having a child with a disability may increase the bond the parents feel with their own parents. Grandparents are a common source of emotional and practical support when a child has a disability (Findler, 2000). This conflicts with the developmental task for young adults, which is to achieve independence from their families of origin. Marianne's parents and Daniel's parents were all involved in the family's daily life. It is difficult to know, however, if this was because of Daniella's disability or because they came from a culture that emphasizes a connection with the extended family.

Interventions

Both general and grief-specific counseling strategies would help this couple cope with their grief over Daniella's disability. Paula Boss et al. (2011) provide a template for helping people with ambiguous or chronic grief. Normalizing ambivalent and negative emotions by saying things like "It's natural to feel that way" and "Many parents in the same situation express the same feelings" brings validity to their feelings and provides a safe, supportive, and nonjudgmental space. Naming the loss can validate it for the clients: "Although Daniella is clearly a lovely girl, you have experienced a loss here. You were picturing a typical child and instead your daughter has health and learning problems." Providing hope for the child is important: "Daniella will grow and will keep learning, even if it takes longer than for other kids. She will continue to develop her interests. How do you think she'll enjoy being an older sister?"

One of the most tangible things we can do is to educate our clients about chronic sorrow and provide anticipatory guidance: "Even though it will be nice to watch Daniella grow, there will be hard times too. A lot of parents of children with developmental delay have told me that they can feel sad at any point, but particularly at big life changes, like the start of high school, when another sibling gets married, or even times like now, during a pregnancy. I just want you to be prepared for this and to know it's normal." Asking about social support and linking them with other parents of children with a similar condition allows parents to get support and anticipatory guidance directly from their peers.

"Meaning-making" is a contemporary grief theory that can supplement these general counseling techniques (Neimeyer & Sands, 2011). Most research on meaning-making has focused on the death of a loved one, but some has focused on the losses that accompany having a child with a disability. For instance, work by King et al. (2000) involving parents of children with Down syndrome suggests that the more parents process their experience and make sense of it as a coherent story (in other words, make meaning of the experience), the better their coping. Many parents raising a child with a disability describe the silver linings of the experience, effectively making meaning out of their loss (Kearney & Griffin, 2001; King et al., 2000).

Several years after the initial shock of having a child with a disability tends to be a good time to explore meaning (Shear et al., 2011). Sometimes, asking our clients to tell the story of their child can be enough for them to start processing the meaning of their loss or to reveal how they have made sense out of their experience so far. I knew that Daniel and Marianne had started meaning-making because of their statements, "Daniella was meant to be ours" and "Human beings are stronger than a rock." Questions that can also encourage meaning-making may include the following: "How do you think you've coped with Daniella's health and development concerns? What has been the hardest thing for you? What has gotten you through it?" Asking directly about religion, spirituality, and existential beliefs can help clients to realize how they have been making sense out of their loss: "You've probably heard the expression, 'Everything happens for a reason.' How do you feel about that? Do you think there is a 'reason' that this happened? How might what happened fit with your religious beliefs? Have your religious beliefs changed since you had Daniella?" Asking about strengths and silver linings such as "What strengths have you seen in yourself? Most things in life have both positives and negatives. . . . What are some of the positives?" can help clients identify the silver linings, another type of meaning. Promoting therapeutic writing can help in meaning-making because it is another opportunity for a client to reflect on their experience. Daniel in particular used therapeutic writing through email to discuss his concerns about the current pregnancy, comparing and contrasting it to the pregnancy with Daniella.

This case highlights the grief that surrounds having a child with a disability and how it can be reactivated by important life events like facing a new pregnancy. Further complicating this case, the ultrasound finding in the current pregnancy echoed the parents' experience with their first pregnancy, heightening their anxiety and fear about the new baby's health. As counselors, we can accompany our clients through their grief and anxiety by encouraging them to express their feelings, validating those feelings, providing anticipatory guidance, and supporting them in their journey to make meaning out of their loss.

Jasper's Birth: Accumulated Losses and Elation
EMILY ZIMMERMAN-LEVITT

Emily Zimmerman-Levitt, MSW, DSW, LCSW, is a licensed clinical social worker and substance abuse counselor in the state of New Jersey. When not on newborn mom duty taking care of her beautiful new son, Jasper, Emily works primarily with adults who are experiencing any number of relational, communication, addiction, or mental health issues. Her doctoral work was focused on trauma-informed infertility treatment—information and training for medical professionals. You can find her at her private practice: Guided Growth, LLC, www.guidedgrowth.net.

Most people think the birth of a new baby brings only joy when the pregnancy is wanted and the parents prepared. Yet even under these optimal circumstances, birth can bring a sense of loss. The losses can accumulate when there is a history of loss preceding the birth.

I was 41 and happily married with a thriving clinical social work practice, and in the last year of my doctoral program, I finally got pregnant after years of trying. After more than a year of trying "diligently" but unsuccessfully, I was connected with a reproductive endocrinologist (RE) physician who specialized in infertility. On some levels, my experience was fairly typical and positive—I followed the treatment protocols and became pregnant after their first IVF cycle. Everyone thought I should be happy, yet few understood the invasive treatments I had to undergo to become pregnant. Tracking and then stopping my ovulation cycle so that I could be hyperstimulated (create more ova than a typical cycle) was only the beginning. The regular injections, nearly daily visits to the RE office, and vaginal ultrasounds became such a normal part of life that I did not even think about how I felt about losing my privacy, my chance to have a customary intimate relationship with my husband, or even the money that all these procedures cost. Even so, my losses were already accumulating, even though they were below my threshold of perceiving them. All I could focus on was getting pregnant and having the baby we so desperately wanted. Periodically, a thought would cross my mind that maybe I should have started trying to get pregnant when I first graduated from college, but I also knew that I wanted to earn my MSW and get established in my career before I started having children. These questions about the way I made decisions in life only added to a sense of loss.

The week and a half after the RE transferred the fertilized ovum into my uterus was almost unendurable. There was no way to know whether the pregnancy would "take" and the waiting was excruciating. My husband and I lived in fear that something could negatively affect the pregnancy. I was afraid that exercising, being stressed, or otherwise doing anything beyond the bare minimum might cause me to lose the pregnancy I felt limited and in a constant state of anxiety. More losses accumulated as I felt the vulnerability of waiting to find out whether I was pregnant. And then—*Joy!* We learned that the pregnancy hormones were detected and that the pregnancy seemed to be establishing well. Now we could finally relax, we thought.

The pregnancy was viewed by most as noneventful. Once established, the RE transferred me back to my regular OB/GYN (a bit of a loss too as I had become so accustomed to regular reassuring checkups and ultrasounds which suddenly come to an end once transferred to OB). I liked my OB/GYN but wondered if she understood how vulnerable I sensed the pregnancy to be. We scrimped and saved to afford prenatal gamete screening to have the best chance that the baby would be healthy. Even so, at the 20-week anatomy ultrasound scan, they saw a bright spot on his heart, an echogenic intracardiac focus (EIF). The high-risk doctor warned us this could be a marker for Down syndrome, yet we decided that with the PGS and bloodwork, we (hopefully) had enough information and decided against the diagnostic amniocentesis as we worried about the risks. I kept reading stories about how assisted reproductive techniques yielded more children born with anomalies of various sorts and my husband had to reassure me a number of times that things were looking good, but still I stayed up nights and even experienced self-blame over things that I anticipated could go wrong and how they would somehow be my fault (due to my advanced maternal age, the way I ate during pregnancy, used the wrong cleaning products in the house, or even forgot to take a vitamin or pill). These thoughts were always running through my mind, but I tried to stay focused on working, caring for my health, and using the strategy a friend shared that I should focus on the good things (looking at the baby's development on Baby Center and having fun picking maternity clothes). That was hard. Every item I bought felt like a jinx. I was afraid to plan the baby shower and I missed out on a lot of excitement as I procrastinated on the planning and decorating until the very last minute.

Finally, the prenatal blood screening, ultrasound, and ongoing obstetrical surveillance seemed to show our son was developing typically. Once again, I felt like we could finally relax and await his birth. We did our visit to the hospital where we would give birth, took childbirth classes, and talked with our doula and doctor about how we wanted to avoid too much medical intervention and bond with our son once he was born (rather than have him go immediately to the nursery). We understood that this "birth plan" was provisional and assumed everything went well. Everyone kept assuring me it would: They would say, "Your body is made to do this." I would smile and nod, but in my mind, I would think of how my body did not know how to get pregnant on its own so what if it did not behave with the birth. We had his car seat, nursery, and my "go-bag" ready, and I was looking forward to being away from work for a bit.

Two days short of my due date, the obstetrician recommended that I be induced (my labor started). We agreed, and I planned to go back to the hospital the next day, but then I started having contractions. I labored at home for a few hours and eventually called our doula, who came to the house to provide support. I was doing well and felt like my body and my baby were working in unison to allow his birth. After 8 hours of labor at home, the pain was increasing, and I knew I needed to get to the hospital. Once we arrived, it seemed like everything intensified, and yet every time they examined me, they told me the baby had not moved down. This dragged out for hours, and I began to lose control. It felt impossible to stay ahead of the contractions. I was really in pain, yet still not dilated enough. Time seemed to stretch out, and although I wanted to avoid an epidural, after 30 hours in labor, and still at 8 cm dilation, I had to "give in." I felt such a loss of control over my body at that point and a sense of failure after everything my husband, I, and my doula had planned. I was exhausted and just wanted to get Jasper here safely. I thought this would be the most difficult it would get. I finally was allowed to begin to push.

After 3.5 hours pushing, Jasper's positioning had not allowed him to descend, and I was asked to decide whether I wanted a C-section or a fourth-degree tear. At that moment, I knew my body was not coming out of this without a major surgery. I knew I would look different, ravaged and destroyed with a long recovery. I opted for C-section because I did not want to end up with both a C-section *and* a perineal laceration. During the C-section, we women go in alone. No more husband, no more doula. During the initial prep, the doctors made my husband and doula wait outside. I was shivering so hard from adrenaline and the medication that I could not lay flat. When my husband finally came in, he helped hold my arms down. Talk about loss of control, just the next in *so* many losses.

When they opened me up, they discovered my poor baby was basically swimming in a pea soup of meconium (the fetal excrement), which he aspirated with his first breath and could not breathe. So many mothers eagerly await the first cry and having their baby placed on their chest for connection and skin-to-skin bonding. I wanted that so badly. Unfortunately for me, I lay there helpless with my body still cut open while they suctioned him and whisked him off to the special care nursery instructing my husband to accompany him. That left me alone on the table listening to the doctors' chitchat as they sewed me up and I wondered what was happening with my baby. I told the doctor I was going to throw up. I felt completely helpless and afraid.

My husband stayed with Jasper while I recovered and they moved me to our room. My son was born at 10:42 p.m., yet I did not get to see him until 1 a.m., when they finally wheeled me to the special care nursery. I was upset that because I did not see him come out of me or even get to see him when he was born, I felt like he was a stranger. When I got back to my room, my husband was there asleep. I knew I had become a mother that day, yet in my drugged-up exhausted and completely traumatized state, I could not even fathom what that meant. It was surreal and then got more so. The nurse told me to start pumping my breastmilk. I had no idea what to do.

The next morning, I woke hoping the day would allow us to bond as a family. Instead, I discovered that I could not walk! Not at all. Legs gave out under me. Complications from the epidural, nerve impingement from working to push, and the edema from 30-plus hours of IV fluids meant I could not walk. The doctors ordered physical therapy (PT).

The next days were filled with wheelchair visits to the nursery, continuing attempts to pump my milk (so little and yet so precious!), awaiting PT, and stress. On day 2, we were told that Jasper's organs took such a hit during the birth that he needed to be transferred to a real NICU at another hospital. They wheeled him in his incubator to say good bye to me. Once again, my husband left to be with him, and I was left pumping alone (and failing miserably to get milk). I was also trying to learn to walk again. I certainly felt anger and bitterness as I learned to walk in the hospital hallway while others held their babies in their arms one room away. I remained in the hospital catheterized for days because I could not move yet. I had lost my mobility, my dignity, my chance to have the birth, and bonding experience I planned for, and now I had lost my husband and son too. I was able to log in to a camera a few times a day to see my baby, but it certainly was not the same as having that time to hold him and be with him. I was alone in a room waiting to see a baby I did not feel like I knew, on a screen every 3 hours so I could try and pump the colostrum for my husband to bring to him, but all I felt was a loss of empowerment or ability to nurture him. It was excruciating.

After a week, I was released from the hospital, and I could finally visit my son. I had to use the walker I was provided at the hospital as I traveled to the NICU. Exhausted and stressed one day coming home from the NICU, my legs collapsed under me, and I fell while walking into the house. I just broke down crying. I think I gave in to all the grief in that moment. I had been trying to just keep going, and it was a moment I felt like I just could not manage anymore. I do not know who was more scared, me, or the people around me.

In the end, it took a week before we were all home together. To outsiders, it seemed like the delay coming home was just a blip along the way, but we were traumatized. My husband had been shuttling back and forth between the two hospitals, and I was barely walking. Nursing was challenging as Jasper could not always latch on and my milk supply was not optimal because of the injuries I had endured and the lack of my baby to promote the milk production. I began to wonder if I was up to doing this whole parenting thing—everything kept going wrong. Yet, once he was home, I could not believe what we had survived.

Jasper was recently 1 month old. The birth injuries I sustained mean I still have numbness in my legs and I am only just beginning to be able to go up and down stairs—I still hesitate to carry the baby in case my legs are not reliable. I have a real loss of independence, but I am working on my strength. My milk is finally starting to amp up. And we are bonding. It is hard to believe how much I love this little boy.

Couples in similar circumstance work with counselors to recognize the many losses that build up over the course of the infertility, pregnancy, and birth. Many experience "baby blues" that are stoked by lots of loss, creating a potential for full postpartum depression. Counselors can help people recognize the ways women need to reclaim their body's functioning and health, assure adequate help caring for the baby, and acknowledge that few things had gone the way they planned. Couples need help talking openly and creating circumstances where they can heal and reconnect after such a challenging set of cumulative losses. Although friends and family often just want to focus on how happy the new family should be—and couples are generally elated—couples also need the space to name and process the losses they experience. Telling the story of a traumatic birth experience from conception to pregnancy to birth can help mothers begin to process the trauma that is left over after the whole experience, allowing them to begin to feel like it is containable, rather than a series of events that just keep replaying themselves in a traumatic loop. Naming the many losses potentially involved in this most joyous of events is useful—and that does not even begin to capture the things that are normal parts of the experience: loss of sleep, no time to shower, a brain that feels fuzzy, worries about the baby, and on and on. Yet, the work to name the losses and to move forward from the event can help people who have traumatic birth experiences. That is part of why I am telling my story here.

I hope readers of this text never look at the birth of a new baby the same again. As an educated woman of "advanced maternal age," I thought I had prepared for everything. I wanted a natural, beautiful, and safe pregnancy and birth experience. What I got was surreal, out of control, chaotic, and with some significant complications and losses. I felt my positive birth experience, bonding, flowers, visitors, and happiness were all stolen from me. We are all doing really well now, and my support people have been amazing in getting me through, but the grief was so real and it lingered well after anyone on the outside could see it. Even as my Cesarean scar heals, it remains. I have worked very consciously and mindfully to stay positive throughout. Even so, it is important for all clinicians to understand that even though all ends well and both mom and baby are healthy, the losses involved in pregnancy, birth, and the neonatal period are often significant and lasting.

Releasing Rosie: A Case of Pediatric Hospice
KARIE McGUIRE

Karie McGuire, LCSW, is a 2020 graduate of the Rutgers University DSW Program. She has spent most of her career working with individuals who have experienced trauma, in the form of interpersonal violence, abuse, or loss. She works in hospital and academic settings.

Rosie (all names are pseudonyms) touched many lives. She was the hospital's first infant hospice case. There were many losses experienced throughout the baby's life span by the family members, friends, and hospital staff who cared for her. In my role as the NICU social worker, my goals include meeting the family for the first time after the delivery, developing rapport, and doing an assessment. The assessment includes social history, family dynamics, pregnancy history, and any other pertinent information. During this initial interaction, it was clear the family was emotionally drained, and I immediately provided emotional support. We discussed ways to cope with the NICU admission. I validated the tough decisions they made earlier in the pregnancy, affirmed support for future decisions, and connected them with varied resources.

History: At around 27 weeks of gestation, the baby was diagnosed with holoprosencephaly. This is a rare "abnormality of brain development in which the brain doesn't properly divide into the right and left hemispheres" (rarediseases.info.nih.gov/diseases/6665/holoprosencephaly/cases/27877). Following diagnosis, the parents struggled to understand what it meant for the baby and for their family. They tried to envision their daughter's future. The prognosis was vague, as the doctors were unsure of how severe the condition would be: They would not know until the birth, assuming the baby survived. At nearly 7 months of pregnancy, terminating it was not an option. The parents decided to accept the child however things turned out and love her regardless of the struggles ahead.

As the social worker assigned to the family for the duration of their neonatal intensive care admission, I spent a lot of time getting to know their life story. Together but not yet married, each parent had two children from a previous marriage, yet they were working together well through very demanding times. They left their home and supports to move closer to the pediatric trauma hospital just in case specialty care was needed. The father of the baby, Emmanuel, was the only financial provider. Sabrina, the mother, supported the household and the children. They had little money and were living in a house they found through a nonprofit agency. Immediately after the birth, along with the medical team, they could see the abnormal facial features associated with holoprosencephaly. Shortly after admission to the NICU, Rosie began to experience severe and continuing seizures that had to be controlled with medications, and she needed tube feedings for nutrition.

During the initial assessment, the parents expressed tremendous guilt because they would have terminated the pregnancy and spared Rosie the suffering of birth and the hospitalization had they known early enough to terminate the pregnancy. With the late diagnosis, through no fault of their own, they had no choices. I supported the parents, especially Sabrina, as she visited the NICU every day. Almost every time I interacted with Sabrina, she was tearful, with a varying range of emotions. She shared her feelings of guilt, grief, loss, and fear. She often wanted to talk about her fear that her other children would not be able to meet her daughter. I scheduled weekly meetings at Rosie's bedside to help Sabrina process her emotions and fears. However, she was not only experiencing the grief of watching her daughter gradually decline; she was also trying to manage a life on the brink of homelessness. Trying to minimize chaos at home and maintain her relationship with Emmanuel and the children added more tension.

Both of her biological children had behavioral needs and were getting additional support at school. They needed her devoted attention while home, a challenge since Rosie's birth. One of the physicians put it well, describing the parenting couple as "wealthy in emotional intelligence—but resource poor."

After the medical team spent about a month testing and assessing the baby, along with consulting other hospitals and specialists, I organized a family team meeting. As the social worker on the unit, I ran the team meetings, but they included the nurses and the physician in charge of care. We discussed the possible next steps for the baby and her prognosis. The options were for Rosie to go home with private duty nursing care around the clock; be transferred to a long-term care facility for pediatric patients, where Rosie would remain for the rest of her life; or remove all life supports allowing her to die at the hospital. After contemplation, tears, and time, the parents decided to bring Rosie home to live as long as she could.

During the next few weeks, I worked diligently to find a home care agency that would supply equipment and nursing in the family's home. I found an agency to provide in-home nursing coverage 12 hours a day and which agreed to pursue insurance authorization for this coverage. After the agency explained the process to the parents, we had a team meeting to discuss next steps with the parents and to make sure they were comfortable with the plan. The next day, Emmanuel and Sabrina asked to revisit the plan. They felt unable to manage to her care alone during the hours when nursing care was not available. They were worried, for example, that if she needed to be taken to the ED in the middle of the night, they would have no one to care for the other children; they had no social or familial supports in their neighborhood. They felt overwhelmed by the prospect of administering all the medications to prevent Rosie's seizures.

After Emmanuel and Sabrina brought these concerns to me, we sat down to talk through the other options. We reviewed options: a long-term care facility, withdraw care and take the baby home, or withdraw care in the hospital. The team met often to get the family to open up about their concerns. We were able to answer all of the parents' questions and explain how each scenario could progress, allowing them to make an informed decision. Throughout the meetings, we saw them struggling to make the decision. They did not want to put their daughter through any more pain. At the same time, they did not want to let their daughter go and did not want to seem as if they were giving up. I met with them to validate their struggle and discuss how they were taking care of themselves throughout this process.

As a medical hospital social worker, I often covered other medical floors and was involved in setting up hospice for adult patients; we start referrals to inpatient, home, and unit-specific hospice care. I presented the idea to the team of offering the option to plan a date to start the baby on hospice, which could occur on the unit. With this plan, many of the parent's issues could be addressed, including their worry that their other children would not get to say good bye to their baby sister, that the baby would die alone, and that they would be giving up on their daughter altogether.

The team agreed to involve a hospice care agency to provide supportive services for the family while the baby was dying and also after the hospital experience was over, something that I could not provide them yet felt they needed. Hospice care includes ongoing nursing support, social work support, and faith-based support. At the time, the NICU census was low, which made this plan feasible. After the team agreed with the plan for hospice, we brought the parents back in to present the idea. We felt the parents were hoping for a suggestion that would give them permission to let Rosie go peacefully. We cleared out a space for the team to set up hospice, extended visiting time, and allowed the other family members to come visit. After we explained how it would work, the hospice provider met with Emmanuel and Sabrina and received their approval.

I explained what options were available for funeral services and connected the parents with resources for financial support. Sabrina decided to work on getting her children extra support at home when the time came, and she spoke with a child life specialist to get ideas about how to support her children through their loss.

After reviewing the process, the plan was to have the entire family visit on a Sunday, have a small baptism for the baby, and have the siblings do crafts with the child life specialist to have as keepsakes. After that Sunday with the family, the baby would be placed on comfort care, and hospice would start care. The baby had around-the-clock nursing by the same NICU team the family knew, and Rosie's parents came to the hospital when possible. Sabrina, although tearful throughout the time she spent with the baby, voiced to many staff members that she knew they were doing the right thing and that they could not see their daughter in pain any longer. She wanted everyone who took part in her daughter's care to take a picture holding the baby so she could remember everyone.

On the second day of hospice, while the baby was getting around-the-clock medications for comfort, the nurse and other staff members took turns holding Rosie when her father was at work and her mother was with the other children. Staff members volunteered to take turns holding her so the nurse on duty could get some relief. I held Rosie on my lunch break, and the nurse manager sat with me to keep me company. It was the middle of the day, and according to the medical team, Rosie showed signs she had begun the dying process. She had minutes without breathing but then would take a breath, and her vitals would come back up to normal. Twice while I was holding her, she stopped breathing and after about 5 minutes caught her breath. The third time, it felt different. About 7 minutes passed, and the nurse came back from break; the three of us surrounded the baby in my arms. About 10 minutes went by with no breath, and the nurse called the doctor to come check for a pulse. After about 15 minutes of no breaths, they asked me to place the baby back on her bed to check her without my pulse interfering. They quickly established that Rosie had died while in my arms, and they officially pronounced her as dead.

I was flooded with many emotions. I felt sad that Rosie had died, but I also felt a calmness that came from rocking the baby during her final breaths. I was grateful that she never had to be alone. I wanted Emmanuel and Sabrina contacted immediately, and the nurse called to have them come as soon as possible. When the family came in, Emmanuel and Sabrina asked their children to wait in the waiting room while they figured out what to do next. They did not want to tell the children that the baby died until they were home. To avoid indicating that something was wrong, they spent about 10 minutes alone to hold their baby girl one last time. They spent time with the care team and hugged everyone one last time. Sabrina said she would give me a call when she was ready to talk about next steps.

About 3 days later, Sabrina called wanting to come in and meet with me. She brought the team donuts and coffee along with a thank you card. We sat alone in the NICU family room, and I let her cry and vent. For about one and a half hours, I just let her talk about her decision, her worry about her relationship with Emmanuel, and about whether they could handle this. She asked how she could get connected with ongoing support. I validated her worries and reiterated to her the need to let people help her, as she is the caregiver of the family. She agreed that she felt overwhelmed. I connected Sabrina to a therapist who specializes in child loss and fetal anomalies, and let her know that I would follow up in about a week. When I checked in, she let me know that she had set up a first session with the therapist. I reinforced these strengths.

As a final memorial, Sabrina invited members of the NICU team to a service for her daughter, where we said our last good byes.

Seldom do hospital social workers become such intimate helpers as an infant dies. Even so, we are honored to be with people during these profound and life-changing moments in their lives. Our ability to think empathically while remaining a creative problem solver and to tolerate our emotions while we support the patients/families most intimately involved with the health issue is the indispensable quality we bring to our work with these families.

SUMMARY

Even in the best of circumstances, maturational gains such as achieving pregnancy and getting ready to have a baby also entail losses of accustomed self-image, independence, and couple time. When experiences of fetal diagnosis, pregnancy complication, and/or pregnancy loss occur, innocence is the subsequent loss. In a society where pregnancy complications and perinatal death are hidden, expectations are that every pregnancy goes well. The reading by Emily Zimmerman-Levitt illustrates that even when things go well, a complicated birth involves loss too. Whenever the common expectations about pregnancy and birth are violated, innocence is lost. Once the protection of innocence is lost, the rest of the pregnancy and future pregnancies will require managing fear, uncertainty, and concern for the health of oneself and one's future child. There are no easy answers in these situations. Weighing one's attachment to one's potential baby against the possibilities of harms that could keep that child from living a healthy full life, and considering the capabilities of the caregivers to provide needed care, means that each situation will have a unique calculus. When there is a fetal demise, the parents lose the potential child and the growing attachment they had; yet they also will mourn the hopes, dreams, and fantasies they envisioned in anticipation of a new family member. Even though these losses are hidden from view and seldom acknowledged, they are some of the most potent losses we can have because they occur before the bereaved can formulate memories to enable grieving rituals and active mourning. Interventions need to acknowledge and validate the loss(es) while supporting the parents in their hopes for their family.

DISCUSSION QUESTIONS

1.   What are your own beliefs about the nature of an embryo or fetus? How do you believe this may inform grief work you might do with women after a pregnancy loss?
2.   What are your beliefs about the challenges and benefits of raising a child with a developmental disability? Does the level of cognitive or physical difference or impairment change your assessment about raising the child?
3.   If a friend revealed that she had experienced a recent miscarriage, how would you respond?

KEY REFERENCES

Only key references appear in the print edition. The full reference list appears in the digital product found on http://connect.springerpub.com/content/book/978-0-8261-4964-0/chapter/ch02

Bellhouse, C., Temple-Smith, M. J., & Bilardi, J. E. (2018). "It's just one of those things people don't seem to talk about. . ." women's experiences of social support following miscarriage: A qualitative study. *BMC Women's Health, 8*(176), 1–9. https://doi.org/10.1186/s12905-018-0672-3

Bowlby, J. (1998). Attachment and loss: Sadness and depression. *Attachment and loss.* Vol. 3. Pimlico. (Original work published 1980).

Cantwell, J., Muldoon, O. T., & Gallagher, S. (2014). Social support and mastery influence the association between stress and poor physical health in parents caring for children with developmental disabilities. *Research in Developmental Disabilities, 35*, 2215–2223. https://doi.org/10.1016/j.ridd.2014.05.012

Ellis, A., Chebsey, C., Storey, C., Bradley, S., Jackson, S., Flenady, V., Heazell, A., & Siassakos, D. (2016). Systematic review to understand and improve care after stillbirth: A review of parents' and healthcare professionals' experiences. *BMC Pregnancy Childbirth 16*, 16. https://bmcpregnancychildbirth.biomedcentral.com/track/pdf/10.1186/s12884-016-0806-2

Koopmans, L., Wilson, T., Cacciatore, J., & Flenady, V. (2013). Support for mothers, fathers and families after perinatal death. *Cochrane Database of Systematic Review, 6*, CD000452. https://doi.org/10.1002/14651858.CD000452.pub3

March, K. (2014). Birth mother grief and the challenge of adoption reunion contact. *American Journal of Orthopsychiatry, 84*(4), 409. http://dx.doi.org/10.1037/ort0000013

McCoyd, J. L. M. (2015). Critical aspects of decision-making and grieving after diagnosis of fetal anomaly. In J. P. Galst & M. S. Verp (Eds.), *Prenatal and preimplantation diagnosis: The burden of choice* (pp. 269–286). Springer Publishing Company.

McCoyd, J. L. M., Munch, S., & Curran, L. (2018). On being mother and patient: Dialectical struggles during medically high-risk pregnancy. *Infant Mental Health Journal, 39*(6), 674–686. https://doi.org/10.1002/imhj.21744

Meaney, S., Lutomski, J. E., O'Connor, L., O'Donoghue, K., & Greene, R. A. (2016). Women's experience of maternal morbidity: A qualitative analysis. *BMC Pregnancy and Childbirth, 16*(184), 1–6. https://doi.org/10.1186/s12884-016-0974-0

Racine, N., Plamondon, A., Madigan, S., McDonald, S., & Tough, S. (2018). Maternal adverse childhood experiences and infant development. *Pediatrics, 141*(4), e20172495. https://doi.org/10.1542/peds.2017-2495

3

Grief and Loss in Infancy, Toddlerhood, and Preschool

INTRODUCTION

The needs of toddlers and preschool children (ages 1–5) are often dismissed during times of loss, with many assuming these children do not understand death. This chapter examines growing awareness of loss and death in this age group and considers their growing cognitive and verbal capacities. Temperament, attachment style, and learning ability are all explained as facets of what influences responses to death and loss. The role of religion and other cultural aspects of loss, generally inculcated by caregivers, are also examined. Maturational losses such as loss of the fully attuned caregiver, expectations of "good behavior," and birth of a sibling are described. The importance of consistent caregiving, structures, and routines for older preschoolers is emphasized. Play therapy best practices are reviewed, and the notion of a "grief checkup" is addressed as a form of intervention.

OBJECTIVES

After studying this chapter, the reader will be able to:
- Describe the psychosocial and biological development of humans from birth to approximately age 5.
- Describe how adverse events can affect young children's development and how communities can create circumstances that enhance it.
- Trace the ways cognitive developments affect children's understanding of death and the subsequent impact of that understanding at different young ages.
- Identify how parents and others grieve when a child dies who is not yet well integrated into the community.
- Analyze the maturational milestones from infancy through preschool ages that entail both growth and loss.

VIGNETTE

Becca was angry. All the other girls in her day-care class were going to a Pizza-&-Play restaurant for a birthday party, but her mother would not let her go. All of her life, her mother kept her from doing practically anything fun with other people, especially if it involved food. Becca and all her friends were just turning 4, and Latoya's was the first big birthday party she had ever been invited to attend. She was begging her mom to let her go, but her mother told her "no."

Her mother explained she had "life-threatening allergies" to eggs, milk, tree-nuts, and wheat. Becca remembered the year before when she had sneaked a teeny tiny piece of a friend's granola bar. She started vomiting and broke out in hives. She remembered being scared as the day-care worker kept asking what she had eaten and then gave her an injection in her thigh. Her mother insisted that the day-care worker keep her EpiPen with her whenever Becca was there. Becca hated feeling like the day-care workers and her family watched everything she did. Becca's doctor told her that many children with allergies like hers were not even allowed to go to day care to play with friends because parents were too afraid to let them be on their own. Becca was sort of glad her mother needed to work so that she could go to day care with her friends. Becca's mom finally agreed to talk with Latoya's mother, and they agreed Becca would come for the playtime part of the party. Her mother promised to make her a special food treat once they got home from the party. Once again, she felt different from all the other kids, and she did not like it.

DEVELOPMENTAL TASKS: TRUST VERSUS MISTRUST AND AUTONOMY VERSUS SHAME

Infancy through the time a child typically enters kindergarten (usually age 5) involves tremendous change physically, cognitively, psychologically, and socially. Infants usually weigh around 7 pounds at birth and have no ability to care for themselves, other than to send dependency signals and hope their caregivers are attuned. Erikson (1959/1980) theorized that infants develop (or not) a sense of trust based on the attuned, trustworthy caregiving they receive. Neurobiological findings support Erickson's theory, indicating that having attuned care in childhood is associated with having trusted and caring relationships in the future (Siegel, 1999/2012). The Centers for Disease Control and Prevention has also emphasized the importance of all children, but especially young children, having "safe, stable, nurturing relationships and environments" (CDC, 2019b, p.1). This promotes children's health and well-being and protects them from abuse, neglect, and other adverse childhood experiences (ACEs).

When children enter preschool or kindergarten, they typically weigh around 40 pounds and can walk, run, talk, and articulate requests for care. Erikson posits that they move through a stage called "autonomy versus shame" (1959/1980), during which they begin to gain control over themselves and their behavior and ideally learn to control bodily wastes, experiencing shame at not meeting parental expectations when they do not. They can make friends, play, and begin to form attachments as well as develop the template for relationship styles over their lifetime (Ainsworth et al., 1978). They have not yet entered the broader world of school and judgmental adults. Instead, in ideal circumstances, they have parents and relatives who love them unconditionally and help promote their development, in part by correcting and guiding behavior through encouragement. Even under ideal circumstances, however, infants, toddlers, and preschoolers experience maturational losses involved with growth. Typical developmental milestones can be identified using the CDC's checklists (CDC, 2019a).

Biological Development

Newborns depend on others for the care they need (nutrition, cleaning and hygiene, and stimulation to promote growth), but they are born with a surprising number of reflexes that help them survive. These elicit care from others while priming actions that promote motor skill development (Slaughter, 2014). The Moro reflex is elicited when a newborn's head moves abruptly and the infant throws out the extremities and grasps in response, seemingly to prevent falls. Another reflex involves turning toward a soft stimulus on the cheek to grab a nipple for sustenance. The tight grasp newborns exhibit when anything is placed in their grip is the endearing reflex that helps infants hold on to something solid and elicit a bonding response from adults.

Newborns spend about 16 hours per day sleeping, but they sleep in shorter stretches than adults and new parents often feel sleep deprived as a result. Sleep scientists traditionally use a 5-hour span of sleep (midnight to 5 a.m.) to define "sleeping through the night" (Henderson et al., 2011). As infants learn to self-sooth, they sustain longer periods of sleep, building the ability to self-regulate and fall back to sleep. The first 3 months are very labile, but sleep usually consolidates between 3 and 4 months and infants can generally sustain sleep for 8 hours or so by 6 months. Toddler sleep quality seems to mediate cognitive ability, and there are positive associations between toddlers' parents' socioeconomic status (SES) and the toddler's sleep quality, affecting toddlers' cognitive capacities (Hoyniak et al., 2019). Hoyniak et al. found many nuances to the finding that toddlers of lower SES parents have lower cognitive capacities. Most important, they observe that the later household bedtimes (and more stimulating environments) often found in their lower SES sample mediate the association between SES and toddler cognitive abilities. By preschool, children need to sustain sleep for about 10 hours to avoid impulsivity, obesity, and learning challenges (Jones et al., 2013).

Humans are born with all their sensory abilities, but some require more development and coordination than others. Vision is limited by newborns' inability to focus beyond 11 inches. This promotes the stares of interest when held by a caregiver whose face is at the best point of focus. Other senses appear to be relatively intact at birth, but to make sense of the stimuli, the infant requires experience with the world. By 3 to 5 months of age, generally, infants can manipulate objects in front of themselves (called midline behavior) because they have learned to better control their own stimulation. This is a time of tremendous brain development. Kiser (2015) observes:

> Babies' brains grow at the gallop, making 700 new neural connections a second. By the age of 3, a child has 1,000 trillion synapses, up to 4 times the number in an adult brain; these are later pruned.

She goes on to advocate for educational experiences out in nature, where toddlers can learn faster by manipulating things in the natural environment. Like many others, she believes that smartphones, tablets, and other screens inhibit the very cognitive growth that parents typically want to enhance.

At 5 years old, healthy children master control of most of their bodily functions. They can run, skip, manipulate objects, and use words to express desires. They can bathe themselves, feed themselves, and generally provide basic self-care. Individual differences of "handedness" and interest in being more sedentary or more active are revealed more fully by this age.

Psychological Development

The physical development that underlies greater independence strongly influences the psychology of a growing child. Nurturance in a secure, attentive, and trustworthy environment in infancy sets the stage for an ability to feel safe in beginning explorations of the world (Mahler et al., 1975; Winnicott, 1953/1965). Winnicott (1953/1965) was one of the first to articulate the concept of the "good-enough mother" who adapts to the infant's needs but allows "optimum frustration." She is not perfect and does not meet every infant or toddler desire. She allows the child to be frustrated and "fail" occasionally, within that child's capacity, to permit development of new skills.

Winnicott's thinking represents a critical transition from the Freudian idea that the mother is responsible for disturbances of the child's psychological growth. Freudian theory implied that a mother must be perfectly attuned and informed about optimal ways to help the growing infant discharge drives. Winnicott (1953/1965) believed that mothers need to "fail" occasionally so that infants and toddlers learn to self-soothe. He asserted that "good enough" parenting would promote good mental health. He articulated the concept of "transitional objects" that toddlers could use to maintain a symbol of the calming presence of the mother without having her actual presence. Transitional objects (such as a special blanket) allow the child to develop a sense of self separate from the mother while still feeling the security of the mother's presence (Winnicott, 1953/1965).

Ainsworth et al. (1978) asserted that patterns of ability to tolerate separation from a primary caregiver set the template for future attachments. These patterns were defined as secure, insecure (with subtypes of anxious avoidant and anxious resistant), and disorganized. These attachment styles are said to develop as a result of the mother's (or caregiver's) attunement and adequate caregiving. Children from infancy to age 4 or 5 seem particularly vulnerable to the detrimental consequences of neglect and abuse because attachment styles develop and are reinforced during this time and become neurobiologically encoded (Siegel, 1999/2012). Siegel (1999/2012) posits that toddlers' and preschoolers' budding implicit and explicit memory skills enable their ability to build relationship templates and empathy and to develop the mind. Loss during this time would obviously tax the youngster's ability to encode a sense of security in relationships.

Temperament also emerges between infancy and early childhood. Based on the degree of nine characteristics (activity level, rhythmicity, distractibility, approach or withdrawal, adaptability, attention span, intensity, responsiveness, and quality of mood), Thomas et al. (1970) discerned three categories of temperament: easy, slow to warm up, and difficult. These temperaments are noticed in the newborn nursery and seem to provide a behavioral template for the infant's behavior stretching through early childhood. It seems they can be moderated in later childhood and adulthood only with significant effort.

These temperaments likely have a biological base but are modified by interaction with caregivers. For instance, a difficult and fussy infant will push away from the caregiver, will reject new foods, and will seldom sustain a full night's sleep. A caregiver who is also of a difficult temperament will have a challenging time adjusting to this infant style and may have great difficulty providing attuned care, amplifying the child's difficult temperament and setting the stage for poor attachment. In contrast, a patient, secure caregiver may help the infant feel safe, help contain distress, and gently but persistently provide incremental new experiences without becoming angry and loud with the child. This allows the child to desensitize, learn to accept help in self-soothing, and develop strategies to cope with transitions.

Some readers will notice that Piaget's theory of sensory–motor intelligence (1954) and the preoperational stage are missing from this discussion. Many studies cast doubt on whether children in toddlerhood to preschool really are as egocentric and concrete as Piaget suggested (Rosengren et al., 2014). The ability to understand the *finality* of death, its *universality* and *irreversibility*, and the idea that the body *ceases to function* at death are all concepts necessary to understanding death (Speece & Brent, 1996). Piaget would conclude that youngsters would not be able to understand these concepts, yet empirical work shows that they do (Rosengren et al., 2014). Children as young as 4 are able to talk about death (of a person, dog, and plant) in ways that indicate they understand its irreversibility and finality as well as social norms about sadness (e.g., that plants do not elicit sadness but dogs and people do; Rosengren et al., 2014).

Social Development

The development of language ability is another major accomplishment of the time from birth to entry into school. Language opens other capacities such as imagination, play, memory, empathy, and the beginnings of symbolic thought. Babbling and vocalization combine with gestures and pointing to lead the way toward development of communicative language (Iverson & Goldin-Meadow, 2005). Neuroscience suggests that infants begin to process language they hear long before they can speak and this lays down the pattern for exploring language (Dehaene-Lambertz et al., 2006). Language (signed or vocal) is clearly a major factor in the ability to interact socially. We know that children raised in homes where they are neglected or where they are in foster care at a young age are more likely to have language delays and these delays can impair functioning over their lifetime. Interventions like early childhood educational settings can help to ameliorate these delays and promote development (Merritt & Klein, 2015).

From infancy through early childhood, the family (however constituted in that child's environment) ideally creates social interaction that both promotes infant development and allows development of the mind that will serve that individual over a lifetime (Siegel, 1999/2012). Even when socialization to customary social norms has been unsuccessful, interventions to repair the parent–child relationship appear to improve the child's ability to interact acceptably, as when aggressive children become less so after improved parenting (Granic et al., 2007). Research shows that even a brief antenatal intervention to teach parents how to adapt to and nurture their new baby can have positive impacts as the child moves through toddlerhood (AlphaGalileo, 2014).

When parents are not emotionally available in early childhood (e.g., due to alcoholism, depression, emotional distancing, child welfare removals, or substance use), children exhibit less ability to regulate their emotion and exhibit more externalizing behaviors upon entrance to school (Eiden et al., 2007). Indeed, Luby (2015) reports that among children initially housed in an orphanage during toddlerhood and preschool, the children who moved to foster homes where they received more nurture were less likely than the ones remaining in the orphanage to show callous and unemotional traits (and lack of empathy) during adolescence. When children receive attuned caregiving, they exhibit more empathy, eagerness to perform well, and prosocial behavior (Siegel, 1999/2012). When parents guide children to identify emotions, regulate them appropriately, and use language, they are better prepared to be successful in school (Denham et al., 2012). These same skills, together with socialization into religious and other community norms, help frame children's understanding of death and the rituals connected with it (Rosengren et al., 2014).

Children inevitably are exposed to death in the natural and social worlds around them. Adults often have more difficulty coping with discussions of the subject than do the children (ages 3–6; Rosengren et al., 2014). Indeed, when it comes to teaching young children about death, many adults hold paradoxical views. They believe they must shield young children from death while at the same recognizing that youngsters need guidance to process the meaning of it (Rosengren et al., 2014). This contradiction seems to persist even though clinicians, teachers, and death educators all agree that children benefit from direct, clear communication about death. When designing research on socialization processes related to death, one team of investigators found that even their Institutional Review Board (the ethical oversight board for research) required major modifications because its members believed that young children need preparation and support to answer hypothetical questions about death (Rosengren et al., 2014).

Spiritual Development

Preschool children are generally exposed to spiritual and religious teaching through their parents' faith communities, often through the stories of the faith tradition. Islamic tradition includes whispering the call to prayer (*adhan*, which includes the words that Allah [God] is great) in the newborn infant's right ear immediately after birth. Christian traditions typically include an assertion that the child is beloved of God during the baptism ceremony. Jewish traditions start with a bris or naming ceremony to bring the child into the faith tradition. Research shows that early connections to faith are quite influential and that young children typically develop conceptions of God as loving and caring, even when only one caregiver (who might even be a teacher or other professional caregiver) displays that love and care (de Roos, 2006). In a large study using the Early Childhood Longitudinal Study data set, Bartkowski et al. (2008) found that children whose parents are on the same page religiously (religious homogamy) show more prosocial behavior in their preschool and later years and have fewer behavioral issues. Ford (2017) suggests that preschool children benefit from "spiritual first aid" when they experience catastrophic loss, intervention that must include helping children know they are not responsible and that God (in whatever form the child understands the deity) is still loving. Philosophers and religious scholars have debated the question of theodicy for centuries, so we cannot expect a preschool child to understand how God can be perceived as all-powerful and loving but allow bad things to happen. Even so, according to Ford (2017), children raised in a belief system/faith tradition will likely benefit with reassurance that God still loves them. Little is known about how secular parents manage these issues, though focus on nature's rhythms is often invoked to help children understand death (Rosengren et al., 2014).

SPECIAL CONSIDERATIONS IN RISK AND RESILIENCE

ACEs have major consequences for people over their lifetimes, including higher potential for chronic health conditions, risky behaviors, mental health problems, and early death (Felitti et al., 1998). The sample of the original ACEs study was primarily White and from relatively privileged backgrounds, yet we know that many children experience the same marginalization as their parents, with poverty, discrimination, poor educational resources, and neighborhood violence affecting them just as those factors affected their parents. Challenging social environments and the associated ACEs affect neurological, endocrine, immune, and epigenetic aspects of children's growth, leaving them at risk for health and mental health problems in their futures (Boullier & Blair, 2018). Thus, pediatricians and other professionals want to focus on preventing and/or identifying ACEs early. They want to promote best parenting practices and early intervention programs that may help to both prevent and mitigate adverse events and environments (Boullier & Blair, 2018; CDC, 2019b). Preventing toxic stress is a critical aspect of mitigating ACEs in young children. Effective intervention assists parents to avoid exposing young children to risk and ACEs and helps them promote resilience (Flouri et al., 2015). This requires helping parents overcome the consequences of their own childhood experiences, which in turn allows them to offer their children appropriate authoritative parenting and acceptance as they provide attuned caregiving that modulates developmentally appropriate levels of demandingness (Ben Shlomo & Ben Haim, 2017). Very good videos available at the CDC (2019c) website help parents of toddlers and preschoolers assess their child's development and promote positive parenting practices.

Aside from associated ACEs, some children are at higher risk because they have been born exposed to substances used during the pregnancy. As indicated in the perinatal chapter, many focus on substance use such as cocaine or opioids, yet fail to recognize the damage of alcohol or nicotine (Zuckerman, Frank, & Mayes, 2002). Yet, intuitively we understand that exposures in utero likely have some effect on the children born of those pregnancies. In a large study, Messinger et al. (2004) examined children at age 3 who had exposures to cocaine, opiates, or a combination of both, along with a matched group who were unexposed, and found no significant differences in mental, motor, or behavioral outcomes at age 3 when controlling for birthweight and nonoptimal caregiving. Nonoptimal caregiving does seem to play a major role in poor outcomes for children born to substance-using parents (Winstanley & Stover, 2019).

Other risks come in the form of environmental pollutants such as lead and other toxins in the air, water, and soil. Preschool children, especially toddlers, are at higher risk from these pollutants for at least five reasons, noted by Fisher (2016):

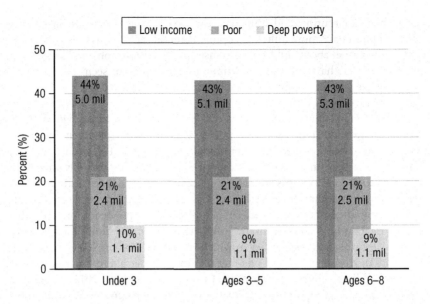

FIGURE 3.1 Percentages of Young Children Living in Poverty, by Age Group, in 2016. This bar graph illustrates the percentages of young children living in low-income families (highest bars), poor families (middle bars), and families in deep poverty (lowest bars), by age group in 2016 (Koball & Jiang, 2018).
Source: Reproduced with permission from Koball, H., & Jiang, Y. (2018). *Basic facts about low-income children: Children under 9 years, 2016.* National Center for Children in Poverty. http://nccp.org/publications/pub_1195.html

1. Pound for pound, infant and toddler bodies need more food, water, and air than older children and adults, so their bodies will accumulate higher concentrations of any pollutants found in those substances.
2. Infant, toddler, and young children's bodies are closer to the ground (and frequently on it), therefore getting heavier exposure where toxins tend to settle and accumulate (e.g., lead paint particulates in house dust on floors).
3. Young children notoriously put things, including dirty hands, in their mouths, increasing exposures to substances in their environments.
4. Young children's metabolic pathways are more immature and not as able to break down toxins and excrete them from the body.
5. Each exposure can break down developmental and maturational processes over time, affecting them in early childhood while also creating circumstances of risk for future health as these breakdowns accumulate over a lifetime (Fisher, 2016).

Environmental pollutants are much more common in geographic areas where poorer people are concentrated. Children already at greater risk because of fewer economic resources and poorer access to good education, medical care, and food are also exposed to higher levels of dangerous pollution. Although environmental justice efforts are under way in many countries (Erickson, 2018; Nesmith & Smyth, 2015), they face powerful opposition in some places. In the United States, the Trump administration has been systematically undoing the regulations critical to minimizing pollutants, creating increased risk for every child, particularly those of lower SES. See Figure 3.1 for the proportions of children living in poverty.

LOSSES EXPERIENCED IN INFANCY AND EARLY CHILDHOOD

Infants' and toddlers' experiences are difficult to know, but the death of a caregiver has an obvious negative impact. Development is a primary factor: Infants under about 6 months cope relatively well as long as their care routines and attuned caregiving continue (Coates & Gaensbauer, 2009), whereas older children have more difficulty coping. Parental separations due to military deployment provide information about children's responses to separation from, and loss of, loved ones. Infants and preschoolers have little sense of time; past and present seem indistinguishable for most toddlers. Yet, separations require a sense of past (when the loved one was here), a sense of present (when the loved one is missing), and a sense of future (when the loved one will return). Time sense evolves in tandem with vocabulary to help the toddler understand it, so until they can use such language and understand time concepts, the separation of deployment (or illness) makes it challenging for a toddler to understand separations from parents (Paley et al., 2013). Similarly, when infants' or preverbal children's beloved caregiver falls ill or dies abruptly, they have no language with which to process this loss and it appears unlikely that they have any concept of death to assist them in understanding their feelings of loss. Developing language skills enables better understanding of complex emotional experiences brought about by separation or death.

Other empirical findings come from the "Mothers, Infants, and Young Children of September 11, 2001" project that studies families in which the father died on September 11, 2001. The surviving parent's degree of initial and ongoing distress and her ability to cope were shown to mediate infants', toddlers', and preschoolers' grief responses (Markese, 2011). When a caregiver dies, children in this age group are more likely to experience parent–child conflict, behavioral problems, and externalizing behaviors as they grow (Markese, 2011). The most important intervention for these young children is to assist the primary caregiver to remain attuned to the child and to provide support, and respite to enable that caregiver's optimal functioning.

Death of a Caregiver or Loved One

Certainly, the most detrimental loss a youngster can experience is the death of the primary caregiver. With high rates of maternal death and an opioid epidemic killing many young adults, more young children are experiencing the loss of a parent during preschool years, often before they have the verbal ability to fully process the loss. After achieving verbal ability, children benefit by revisiting their losses with understanding adults over the years because with each new developmental phase, they bring ongoing language development and new cognitive capacities to processing the loss. In the online resources for this book, an essay by Chris Michael illustrates how the loss of a father at age 3 creates challenges over a lifetime.

There is general consensus that children under age 2 are not able to understand death, particularly its finality, though they do experience separation anxiety and exhibit reactions of protest and despair (Bowlby, 1979/2000, 1980/1998). Research findings are inconsistent about the effect of parental death on bereaved children as they grow. Berg et al. (2016) examined a large cohort of Swedish children and distinguished between parental death due to natural and "external" causes (suicide, homicide, drug overdose) and found that children bereaved due to external causes in very early childhood (preschool age) were at higher risk for future psychopathology. Stikkelbroek et al. (2012) followed a smaller cohort in the Netherlands and found no significantly increased risk among parentally bereaved children. Earlier scholarship indicates that the responsiveness of the child's remaining caregiver and person's ability to provide safe and consistent care are better predictors of resilience or psychopathology than the mere event of a parental death (Christ, 2000; Hope & Hodge, 2006; Silverman & Worden, 1993/2006).

It is unclear whether a child less than 3 years old processes death as anything other than separation anxiety that is not relieved by crying for the caregiver's return. Stevenson asserts that "by age 3, the child understands that there is a thing called death" (2017, p. 4) but still views it as reversible. McKissock (2017), who cofounded the National Centre for Childhood Grief in Australia, states that children ages 2 to 4 experience death as an abandonment, believe that it is reversible, and tend to regress in order to elicit care, whereas those 4 to 7 tend to personify death (Grim Reaper or a monster) and may feel responsible. Responses tend to take the form of bodily symptoms (stomach aches) and regressions to earlier states of functioning. Therefore, the recommendations for care of very young children who experience a significant death loss focus on ensuring that there is a caregiver to provide attuned, nurturing, and consistent care (despite the caregiver's own grief), keep the infant's/toddler's routine predictable and consistent, and allow for regression such as bedwetting and refusal to feed oneself (Hames, 2003; Hope & Hodge, 2006; Willis, 2002). Regardless of whether children under 2 or 3 can accurately conceptualize death, they still grieve, albeit in a manner different from adults. Doka (2017) clearly identifies adults' tendency to disenfranchise children's grief in detrimental ways by ignoring, minimizing, or otherwise not recognizing this different manner of expression as true grief and mourning. This is dangerous for infants and young toddlers; reassurance and nurture are necessary for them to adapt and thrive.

As the toddler grows, concepts of death evolve (Christ, 2000). Children who are 4 to 5 years old understand that death involves the deceased's separation from living people and a cessation of breathing and heartbeat. They may have little sense of death's permanence. One study of children 3 to 5 years old found that their struggle to understand the irreversibility of death led to "befuddlement" (Christ, 2000, p. 75), intensified reactions to other separations, and repetitious questions about the location and condition of the deceased. Furthermore, a sense of interchangeability or a sense that the lost one just needs to be replaced with another sibling/mother/father/grandparent adds to the challenge of the surviving parent's need to support, nurture, and respond while the child asks disturbing questions (Christ, 2000). Yet other research indicates that these questions, when answered directly, honestly, and clearly, including the idea that each individual is special and not replaceable, allow children to make meaning using idiosyncratic blends of biological and religious explanations (Rosengren et al., 2014).

Magical thinking is common at this stage of development, and children may believe their angry thoughts caused the death. Clear explanations grounded in concrete realities provide important ways for children to begin to understand death, particularly the reason for the death and that the child could not have caused it. Attendance at funerals in order to see the body is often a positive strategy as long as the child can be protected from adults' uncontrolled outbursts of emotion that they may find more disturbing than the death itself (Willis, 2002). Preparing the child, answering questions, and providing for the child to be with a trusted adult not severely affected by the death are all useful to assist 3- to 5-year-olds through the mourning process.

A fundamental aspect of childhood loss is the child's need to "rework" the loss at each stage of development. Children can only understand death within the cognitive development (and language capability) they have at that moment in time, yet must live with the loss their entire lives. As they develop emotional language skills, abstract reasoning, ability to anticipate the future, and so forth, they will need to reassess and grieve the loss through their new perceptual abilities, sometimes with professional help. A loss in early childhood requires more developmental iterations of "reworking" than a later loss.

Living Losses: Atypical, Typical, and Maturational Losses

Loss of Caregiving

The literature on infants and toddlers emphasizes the importance of the primary caregiver (generally the mother) to healthy development. During this stage, the infant's or toddler's whole life is tied to the care and stimulation received from caregivers; therefore, the most traumatic loss endured at this stage is the death of a primary caregiver and/or parent. Even without a death, the infant/toddler is likely to experience loss of the caregiver in both normal developmental ways and more dramatic ways. Certainly, optimal frustration, as Winnicott (1953/1965) discussed it, amounts to a temporary loss of the caregiver; the felt need/desire of the child is not met immediately, and the child feels abandoned. This is a normal and healthy experience after about 4 to 6 months of age. Because infants have not yet grasped "object constancy" (that people continue to exist even if unseen), when the caregiver is gone, the baby feels (briefly) as if the caregiver is lost forever. This same phenomenon also allows the baby to adapt to the surroundings of the present moment (after protest, an infant will eventually adapt to the person who is providing care because they have "forgotten" their caregiver). Yet, there is great joy when the caregiver returns. As the infant ages, object constancy is such that the toddler knows their caregiver still exists (somewhere), and protests and yearning may last longer.

Temporarily losing care is a normal, maturational loss that contributes to the child's development. As the child begins to recognize that the caregiver is sometimes absent but returns and generally provides attuned care, object constancy grows and a sense of security develops. These types of maturational loss occur within a secure and trustworthy relationship and promote development. Development is threatened when the separation occurs in ways that are beyond the youngster's ability to cope (for instance, when a parent is drug addicted and unable to be engaged predictably) or where this loss is chronic (as when parental depression limits caregiving).

During the critical first 1 to 6 months of life, children need a caretaker attuned to their physical and emotional state who not only provides care but also can soothe them and verbally reflect their experiences. Infants born to mothers with postpartum depression or other mental health problems may not receive the finely attuned care newborns need. Indeed, children born to depressed and anxious mothers have difficulty with emotional self-regulation in infancy and more likelihood of depression in adolescence (Stein et al., 2014). Ideally, the other parent or surrogate caregiver would meet the needs of the infant at this point. Often, other adults believe that the mother's mere physical presence is enough to keep herself and her baby safe, and she is deemed capable of managing her own and the baby's care. This can lead to tragic outcomes when postpartum depression occasionally evolves into postpartum psychosis without appropriate supports in place (www.webmd.com/depression/postpartum-depression).

Parental depression has ramifications beyond infancy and toddlerhood. Women with early-onset depression are likely to have children with dysregulated emotional patterns at age 4, decreased perceived competence ratings at age 5, and decreased social acceptance when entering school (Maughan et al., 2007). Most women's depressive symptoms include an externalized locus of control and more difficulty managing parenting stress. These symptoms may act as mediators to either lax or overreactive parenting that meets the infant's attachment and attunement needs inconsistently. In turn, this places children at risk for poor attachment, a sense of mistrust, and a defensive detachment (Stein et al., 2014). There is strong and consistent evidence that caregiving attunement and emotional care assist infants to develop the neurobiological substrate that enables them to develop attachments and the ability to learn self-soothing and affect regulation (Applegate & Shapiro, 2005; Siegel, 1999/2012). Put another way, when care is unavailable, the infant's brain has less opportunity to develop, and this negatively affects the infant's ability to engage fully in other attachments and to develop affect regulation (Shapiro et al., 2001). Interventions directed toward helping the primary caregiver stay connected and sensitive to the infant's needs through parent training, infant massage, and home visitor supportive interventions have shown promise in reducing the negative impact of caregiver mental health problems on the infant's development (Stein et al., 2014).

When an infant or preschooler experiences the loss of a caregiver due to parental depression, removal from parental care, or hospitalization, they experience loss that we do not view as normal maturational developmental loss. However, the challenges of such loss are rarely recognized. While the youngster receives care for basic needs such as nutrition, shelter, and hygiene, often little attention is paid to the need for an attuned and consistent caregiver. In highlighting the ramifications of such loss, we aim to validate it so that remediation may become customary.

Loss of a Child's Own Health

As Bluebond-Langner et al. note, "One of the compelling understandings of a child in Western society is as a being with a future" (2017, p. 469). Atypically, young children sometimes lose their health to life-threatening illnesses and, along with their families, are caught up in intense experiences of treatment. Hospitals that provide care for infants soon after birth and in toddlerhood are now much more aware that children of this age need to maintain and continue to develop attachment relationships with their caregivers. They have embraced family-centered care models that encourage parents to be at the baby's bedside (www.ipfcc.org/faq.html). Babies and toddlers in institutional care or in foster care also experience separation from their primary caregiver. Under such circumstances, it is important to promote attachments to consistent and available caregivers.

Families often want to avoid discussion of their toddler's possible death, and the uncomprehending child is focused on the pain, separation from family, and perceptions of their caregivers' stress. Few studies capture the experience of children coping with life-threatening illness at this young age (Bluebond-Langner, 1978; Schwartz & Drotar, 2006; Takeuchi, 2008). A notable exception is Takeuchi's dissertation research, where she asserts that "dying preschoolers . . . have very unique ways of understanding the death concept, ways that are fundamentally different from those who are healthy . . . [that do] not presuppose adulthood for those who may never achieve it" (pp. 13–14). She asserts that even preschoolers come to understand death through discussion with parents and medical care providers, and she observes that "the luxury of being an innocent and immature child is sacrificed and must be mourned" (2008, p. 99), though she also supports open, developmentally attuned communication with the child. With more awareness of the value of open discussion and the fact that more children experience chronic, life-threatening illness, even the resource WebMD (2019) has advice for parents about how to handle children's questions when they have life-threatening illness. Still, parents and healthcare providers often differ in their understanding of young children's prospects, complicating maintenance of an effective working relationship that will benefit the child's care over time (Bluebond-Langner et al., 2017).

Birth and Gradual Loss of Complete Care

Judith Viorst described what is almost certainly a universal experience:

> We begin life with loss. We are cast from the womb without an apartment, a charge plate, a job or a car. We are sucking, sobbing, clinging, and helpless babies. Our mother interposes herself between us and the world, protecting us from overwhelming anxiety. We shall have no greater need than this need for our mother. (Viorst, 1986, p. 9)

After what we might call *original loss*, infancy and toddlerhood are defined by the optimal frustration experienced as the caregiver gently pulls away and allows the child to develop self-soothing and self-entertainment skills. This necessarily involves losing the company and total security the caregiver provided to that point. Even as the toddler moves into early childhood, there are often maturational losses such as when behaviors once deemed cute (putting food in one's hair or suddenly sitting down and refusing to move) are no longer tolerated and can actually anger adults.

Aging from infancy through the beginning of the school years includes many small maturational losses, as we are expected to self-soothe, toilet train, begin to provide for our own hygiene, pick up toys and take on responsibilities in the home, and be held responsible for our behavior. Although few recognize these many small losses as worthy of mourning, it seems likely that the steady accumulation of these losses contributes to the frustrations and temper tantrums of toddlers and preschoolers (perhaps the source of the "terrible twos"?). When parents are sensitized to these losses and learn to help interpret them to their children ("Now that you are a big girl, we are not going to laugh when you act that way"), it helps the child recognize the changes and process the losses more easily.

Birth of a Sibling

Another typical maturational loss deserving mention is the abrupt loss of the caregiver's attention when a sibling is born. The child (hopefully) has been the "apple of the parent's eye" to that point and has received attuned attention and care. When a sibling arrives, the infant or toddler is abruptly moved to the side while family members and friends come to fawn over and bring gifts to the new baby. The older sibling may have been looking forward to having a brother or sister, only to experience a new wish that the baby would disappear. Reactions to this type of loss sometimes include attempts to get parental attention with poor behavior, developmental regressions, or overt aggression toward the new baby and others. Providing reassurance of care and nurture is critical to helping the child process the grief of losing the parents' sole attention and finding ways to accept the new baby (Faber & Mazlish, 1987/1998). These typical losses are often ignored, and toddlers are expected to simply adapt to the changed circumstances. Viewing these changes through the lens of loss allows us to empathize more with the toddler/preschooler whose world has changed. This encourages us to support the youngster along with parents and caregivers as the child reacts to the loss and adjusts to changes.

REACTIONS OF PARENTS AND OTHERS TO THE LOSS OF AN INFANT OR PRESCHOOLER

Loss of the Idealized Child

The bond with a baby starts long before delivery, and parents develop dreams about how they believe their baby will look, act, and progress. The (nondeath) loss of the idealized child is part of nearly all parents' experience as they adapt to the child who has been born rather than the one envisioned. Although seldom recognized as a loss, even factors such as whether the infant has hair or is bald can trigger some mourning for the idealized child.

When a child is born with developmental delays, congenital conditions, or other anomalies, this loss is much greater. Parents who receive such news must mourn the dream child while also mourning the loss of the typical child. Aside from the whirl of medical appointments, diagnoses, and treatments, parents must cope with the social ramifications as family and friends learn about the child's condition/s. The stigma of disability (Goffman, 1963) is not socially just, but it exists nonetheless, and mothers often experience some of the same stigma (Ladd-Taylor & Umansky, 1998). The self-image of the parents is often affected as they wonder why they "failed" to bring a healthy child to birth. When the discrepancies between reality and what was expected become clear, adjusting to the child's condition and bonding with the child who is—rather than the envisioned one—requires a degree of mourning.

Most parents experience the loss of the idealized child even if the actual child is healthy and robust. Parents often picture their children as athletic or attractive or having valued qualities not always evident at birth or as the child grows. When this loss is recognized, it can be acknowledged and lose its power to interrupt the connection between parent and child.

Death of an Infant, Toddler, or Preschooler

The death of a child is always experienced as a life-changing event, usually as a trauma (Klass, 2005; Rando, 1986). Young children are often seen as the most physically vulnerable humans, inspiring a high degree of responsibility for providing life-preserving care, the purported evolutionary reason for attachment behaviors (Bowlby, 1980/1998). Parents typically feel guilt when their care does not keep the youngster alive.

Deaths of preschool children are complicated by the fact that few outside the family knew the child yet, particularly when the child dies in infancy/toddlerhood. The ability of memory to sustain and comfort is limited by the child's short life. Parents must also mourn their lost hopes and dreams for the future the child never had.

Klass (2005) describes the importance of the social world sharing in the parents' grief and acknowledging the parents' loss, yet this is precisely what is often limited, particularly when the infant is quite young. This seems to mirror a myth that the connection a parent feels is dependent on the length of the child's life. This myth may comfort those who remain uninformed and distant from the bereaved parents, but the reality is that parents grieve deeply and intensely regardless of the child's age (Rando, 1993). Klass found that bereaved parents moved through periods he called into their grief, well along in their grief, and resolved as much as it will be. This last term does not imply (as words like closure and acceptance do) that parents will "move on" and forget or accept what has happened, neither of which is possible. Often, grieving is itself a comfort for parents as it aids their continued connection to their deceased child. Parents wonder if continuing with their own lives as usual is disloyal to the memory of their child (Klass, 2005). Parents often maintain the bond by memorializing the deceased child through participation in groups like Compassionate Friends or by promoting legislation related to the child's death (e.g., Megan's Law for Megan Kanka) or starting a charity in the child's name (Alex's Lemonade for Alexandra [Alex] Scott). Parents find many ways to keep the bond active (Klass et al., 1996).

Sometimes, children die in accidents that result from tragic oversights. Infants and toddlers occasionally die as a result of being left in car seats in hot cars; toddlers are run over by the family car or die in an accident in the home. Parents feel intense guilt and have trouble with meaning-making when their child of any age dies from disease, accident, and other uncontrollable events (Lichtenthal et al., 2013). In our experience, when death results from something that can be imagined as preventable, parents will have an even more difficult time finding a way to make meaning and to mourn.

INTERVENTIONS

McKissock and others strongly recommend that bereavement support be available to all children, if only for a "grief checkup" (2017, p. 48). This would entail a meeting during which caregivers receive psychoeducation about normal regressive and somatic responses of preschoolers along with guidance and role-modeling of how to answer the child's questions in a direct, developmentally appropriate and nurturing manner. The key is providing support to the caregiver/s of the child so they can help the child redevelop a sense of security and predictability. McKissock emphasizes that preschool-age children need to be given truthful, developmentally appropriate information in a safe space where they can comfortably ask their questions. They need to hear that they will be valued, safe, and cared for despite changes due to their loss.

READINGS

Latrice's Story
COLLEEN MARTINEZ

Colleen Martinez is a registered play therapist–supervisor and New Jersey licensed clinical social worker. She is a clinical social work associate at Ramapo College of New Jersey and also teaches MSW students at Rutgers University. She has been treating children and families for over 20 years. In her private practice, she provides supervision and consultation to mental health professionals who serve children and families. You can find her as Colleen The Play Therapist on Instagram and Facebook.

Latrice's Referral for Services

Latrice is a 4-year-old African American girl enrolled in a preschool program in an urban public school district in the northeastern United States. Although only 4, she is described at school as a "bully." According to staff and teachers, she frequently pushes and kicks her classmates. She is also described as difficult to teach. She does not respond verbally and frequently does not follow direction. She uses only one- or two-word utterances when she wants something but does not respond verbally to attempts at conversation from her teachers or peers. She was evaluated by the child study team due to her apparent speech delays and behavioral challenges.

At the child study team interview, Latrice's mother, Ginelle, reported that Latrice is an only child who has always lived with Ginelle and Ginelle's mother. Ginelle and Latrice's father were never married, and he has not been involved in Latrice's life for the past couple of years. Ginelle reported that Latrice "was never a noisy child"; she didn't cry much and generally is quieter than other children in the extended family. Ginelle had previously not been concerned about Latrice's lack of speech as she, too, is quiet and did not speak much until she was kindergarten age. While she does not see the aggressive behaviors seen at school, she is concerned that Latrice does not seem happy.

Ginelle reported no problems during pregnancy, delivery, or in feeding Latrice as an infant. Ginelle described Latrice as an easy child. Latrice never really demands much attention at home. She seems to be content watching television or playing by herself. Latrice has always been easy to separate from her mother for babysitting, day care, and school, and Latrice never showed a strong preference for her mother when she was a baby. Ginelle remembers that Latrice was "fine" as a baby being held by her mother, a babysitter, or even a stranger. If she is very upset or hurt, Latrice will cry loudly and seek out her mother or grandmother, but this is an infrequent occurrence.

Ginelle reported no history of substance or mental health issues in her own, or Latrice's father's, family but acknowledged that she is probably depressed herself. Due to her busy work schedule and Latrice's issues at school, treating her depression is not a priority for her at this time. She agrees that after Latrice is more settled in school, it might be good to talk to a professional about her own depression. Ginelle does not see any medical providers regularly, but she does take Latrice for pediatric visits and vaccination appointments at the local hospital pediatric clinic. Ginelle denies any trauma or abuse in her, or Latrice's, history.

Latrice's Child-Centered Play Therapy Experience

Latrice was eligible for special education services. She was placed in an inclusion classroom and referred for speech and play therapy. I observed Latrice in her classroom in my role as her play therapist. She is the tallest child in the room. She engaged in pretend play with her classmates in the play kitchen area and grabbed a toy food item from her classmate's hand. At transition time, she was the last child to leave the play area and only joined the rest of the class for circle time when the teacher took her hand and led her to the circle.

My playroom is a typical one designed for child-centered play therapy (CCPT), with a variety of toys and play materials. CCPT is nondirective, so all sessions are child directed, and child-centered play therapists (CCPTherapists) set limits only when necessary (Van Fleet et al., 2010). In our first session, I told Latrice that I help children with their problems and worries through play and that she could play with whatever she liked in my playroom. Latrice was silent in our first session and for many subsequent sessions. She occasionally glanced tentatively at me but rarely maintained eye contact. In the first session, she engaged with the dollhouse and dolls, and she continued to do so for many sessions that followed.

CCPTherapists follow the child's play, looking for patterns and themes in children's play (Van Fleet et al., 2010). For each weekly session, Latrice separated easily from her classroom, becoming more enthusiastic about going to the playroom. Each week, she focused on the dollhouse, playing with the adult and child female dolls. Over time, she became more enthusiastic to see me and eventually greeted me by name. She was consistently eager to go to the play therapy room, and the only time she ever required therapeutic limit setting was when she did not want to leave when our session was over. This is not an uncommon response (Van Fleet et al., 2010), and eventually Latrice did not test limits about ending sessions.

Week after week, Latrice consistently played with the same materials. She would bring a number of female figures to the dollhouse and move them around, over time increasingly making positive sounds and utterances, such as "Hmm," "Hi," and "Wow." She did not attempt to engage me in her play, so I used empathic listening and tracking (reflecting her actions) to demonstrate my attention and acceptance. CCPTherapists do not rush the process (Van Fleet et al., 2010). After nine sessions of this repetitive play, Latrice introduced a male figure to the gathering in the dollhouse. Up to and including this change, Latrice was calm, with an affect that was neutral to positive. At times in her play, she seemed to be saying pleasant things that I could not understand. She would smile at the figures and seemed to engage them in talking with each other. During this period of her treatment, Latrice interacted more with me, by verbally greeting me, looking and smiling at me, and initiating closer proximity by bringing the toys closer to sit by me while she played.

During the 11th session, there was a significant change in Latrice's play. After the female figures gathered in the dollhouse and the male figure joined them, another male figure was introduced to the house. When this male figure entered, her demeanor changed. She frowned and furrowed her brow, and she moved the male figures around the house abruptly. She grumbled loudly and stamped her feet. Later in the same session, she yelled for the first time in her sessions "No," more loudly than I knew her voice was capable of.

During our 12th session, Latrice engaged with the female figures and the dollhouse with a pleasant demeanor, as she had for many sessions prior. She then brought a male figure to the dollhouse unremarkably. When the second male figure was introduced, she became louder and visibly angry. She yelled "No" and then took the first male figure to the toy kitchen, where she had not played previously. She placed the male figure in the toy oven, closed the door, and began to sob. Latrice stood next to the toy oven with tears streaming down her face for nearly 5 minutes. In line with CCPT, I tracked her behavior and reflected her feelings during this time. I said, "You're standing there and not moving. You're so sad." As had become typical, when I told Latrice that our session time was over, she easily left the room and returned to the classroom.

After this session, I felt compelled to call Ginelle to discuss Latrice's play. She was at work during school days, and while I had never met with her, she always made herself available to take phone calls from me. I told Ginelle that Latrice had been playing a story about females gathering pleasantly, that a male joined them, and that when a second male joined them the tone changed, there was yelling, and then a male was removed and Latrice cried. I told her that Latrice sobbed next to the toy oven, with the male figure inside. Ginelle, always quiet during our conversation, was nearly speechless. She eventually said, "I can't believe she's telling you that." I knew what she meant but clarified that Latrice had played it out rather than verbally telling me anything. Ginelle proceeded to tell me that she never told me or the other school staff about something that happened, because she did not think Latrice remembered. When Latrice was 2 years old, she and Ginelle were at a family party when Latrice's father arrived. It was a happy event, and there were no problems until a man showed up at the party to fight with Latrice's father. The man shot and killed Latrice's father in front of the women and children, including Latrice and her mother. Ginelle explained that while it was a horrible experience, the funeral was even worse. Latrice's father was a young man well loved in his community, and there were many people at his funeral who were despondent and inconsolable. Latrice saw many mourners cry and scream at her father's funeral.

Ginelle and I agreed that even though Latrice was very young at the time of her father's death, she was deeply affected by the trauma of her father's shooting and subsequent funeral. Ginelle was grateful that Latrice was getting an opportunity to "talk" about what happened and thought that she, too, would likely benefit from treatment to process her own trauma and loss.

Play therapy sessions with Latrice continued for the remainder of the school year. She played out the same story a number of times, with decreasing emotional intensity. The last time she placed the male figure into the oven she looked sad but did not cry. Playing out her experience many times may have given her a sense of mastery, and thus she may not have felt as overwhelmed. In subsequent sessions, Latrice began to explore other toys and materials in the room, and at the end of the year, she made pictures with the art materials similar to projects she was making in her classroom.

Within weeks of beginning play therapy, Latrice's aggressive behavior in the classroom became less frequent, and her verbalizations increased. Over time, Latrice became a relatively cooperative, well-liked, and well-integrated member of her preschool classroom. She no longer stood out from her typically developing peers. At her year-end reevaluation, she was found to no longer be in need of special education services due to improvements in her speech and behavior.

CCPT gave Latrice an opportunity to process her experiences of trauma and loss, of which I was completely unaware. Gaining mastery over the violence, grief, and loss that she experienced allowed her to move on to more developmentally appropriate tasks like speech and language development, and social and preacademic skills. Inspired by her daughter's progress, Latrice's mother agreed to seek therapy for herself.

Discussion

Because Latrice was so young when she witnessed her father's killing and funeral, her mother assumed that she did not "remember" what happened and therefore was not affected. This is an example of disenfranchised grief. As Crenshaw (2002) points out, a preschool-age child does not have the ability to conceptualize death and cannot process grief in the same way as adults, but they are surely impacted. Latrice's play clearly indicated that she needed to process her experiences. Future work with this family should include grief work for Ginelle and attention to her ability to comfort and reassure Latrice while she continues to process her own loss.

Attachment is a major factor that I consider when evaluating the complexities of Latrice's life and her presenting symptomology. Reportedly, Latrice rarely seeks comfort from her mother or other caregivers and never indicates a preference for proximity to her mother. These may be indicators that Latrice and her mother never formed a secure attachment. Not only does Ginelle appear to struggle with depression, which can lead to insecure attachment (Cicchetti et al., 1998), but both Latrice and Ginelle have been traumatized. Trauma can affect a dyad's attachment style (Lyons-Ruth & Block, 1996). A child who rarely seeks out interactive regulation (help with calming down) may have weakened her attachment with her mother. An insecure attachment style can lead to less competence in social relationships and more behavioral problems (Fearon et al., 2010). Future work with this family might include attachment-based therapies such as theraplay, or dyadic developmental psychotherapy (DDP). While it is optimal for parent and child to develop a secure attachment very early in life, theraplay and DDP may be effective in improving attachment between parents and older children (Rubin et al., 2009).

If we look at Latrice's life through the lens of Erikson's (1959/1980) stages, we might consider the impact of her experiences on developing a sense of trust versus mistrust. When a parent is unable to provide attuned caregiving, due to trauma, loss, depression, or other factors, the child may develop a sense of mistrust and have difficulties in developing trusting relationships with others (Siegel, 1999/2012). This may have contributed to Latrice's difficulties in relationships at school. Hopefully, our work may contribute to Latrice's successful navigation of Erikson's stage of autonomy versus shame. When referred for services, Latrice was having difficulties with peer and adult relationships as well as preacademic achievement. Had she continued with these challenges, a long-standing sense of incompetence might remain. However, her first year of preschool ended with reports of significant improvement in social, language, and preacademic functioning, laying the foundation for a long-term sense of competence.

Hannah's Story
MAYA DOYLE AND CARRIE OSTREA

Maya Doyle, PhD, MSW, LCSW, is an assistant professor of social work at Quinnipiac University and a rare-disease researcher and advocate.

Carrie Ostrea, MBA, is a "rare mom" who now works as a coach, consultant, facilitator, and program development strategist specializing in rare-disease patient engagement, advocacy strategy, and non-profit growth and sustainability.

Carrie and her husband experienced several years of infertility and fertility treatments before adopting two children internationally and learning they were pregnant (Ostrea, 2003). Two days after their baby girl, Hannah, was born, she was admitted to the neonatal intensive care unit (NICU) with an enlarged spleen and extremely low platelets. By 5 months old, her liver became involved, and she was diagnosed with neuronopathic Gaucher's disease type 2 or type 3 (www.gaucher.org.uk), an extremely rare autosomal recessive lysosomal storage disorder. There are no more than 300 children in the world with Gaucher's at any one time, as most die before they are 2. The devastating (and ultimately incorrect) prognosis was that Hannah would survive only 9 months.

Rare disease creates unique challenges for caregivers (Pelentsov et al., 2015). In Hannah's case, very little was known about Gaucher's, limited research was in progress to improve knowledge, and there were few medical specialists for Gaucher's or similar diagnoses. Caregivers become financially stressed by treatment and have profound feelings of guilt and loss. Hannah's family sent cells to researchers in Canada, the United States, and Israel in hopes of finding life-prolonging treatment.

Even though the neurologic progression had started, charming Hannah persisted. She was able to cruise, crawl, play with toddler toys, eat pureed foods, cuddle, and chase her siblings in her walker when she was 20 months old. She was enrolled in physical therapy, occupational therapy, vision therapy, developmental therapy, and hydrotherapy to preserve her function and comfort.

Siblings of children with rare and life-limiting diseases often take on caregiving tasks and have considerable knowledge of an affected child's condition but may seek to protect parents from awareness of how much they know (Malcolm et al., 2014). At the same time, they must manage normative development tasks and relationships with peers, family members, and other adults. Additionally, siblings often struggle with the family's limited ability to focus attention on them while caring for a sick child. Hannah's parents relocated to be close to her dad's family. They worked to balance parenting Hannah with the needs of her young siblings, trying to give them a "normal" life. Grandparents and friends made sure the kids were able to join activities and events. Hannah received nursing services, gradually needing more hours per week. Her mother stayed up with her for the "night shift," because she required a tracheotomy and g-tube, four to seven syringes of medicine several times a day, and oxygen. The family had a vital window of time together after school each day; they included Hannah in many family activities but would also have her stay with nurses for family activities that were too difficult when she participated.

At age 2, Hannah's condition worsened significantly, and she was hospitalized for 7 weeks. Carrie lived at the hospital, sleeping at the on-site Ronald McDonald house or in the Pediatric ICU lobby. Hannah's primary care pediatrician and her ENT remained involved in her care, providing support to the family even when they could do little medically. The progression of Gaucher's brought new losses. Hannah barely could roll over to move, was unable to sit unassisted, and could not pick things up. She smiled less often, and it was harder for her to sleep or even get comfortable. An MRI of her brain revealed tremendous brain matter loss. Her discomfort and irritability worsened. Comfort and palliative care had been part of Hannah's care from early on; her parents wanted her to be "happy and pain-free." However, the decision to not pursue aggressive treatment options was a challenge for both team and family. Her parents decided that it was time to bring Hannah home to be surrounded by her family and friends when she passed away.

The family met with the only hospice provider in their state, and Hannah and her mother spent a few days at the hospice facility while the agency helped get the house ready and provided support to help her brother and sister understand that their little sister was dying. The children knew Hannah had "special needs," but her parents did not share her prognosis until they decided to bring her home on hospice.

On the first night home, Hannah no longer had wires, leads, nurses, or docs poking and prodding, or x-rays—just peace and comfort. The hospice team worked to find medications to reduce her agitation while allowing her to be awake, aware, and comfortable. Although sedated around the clock, Hannah remained home for 7 weeks. She passed away late one evening, after a weekend of being cuddled, loved, and surrounded by her entire family and close friends. She passed away in Carrie's arms.

After Hannah died, her family decided to create a nonprofit foundation to help other families find information and emotional support to cope with the rare and medically complex conditions of their children. They created an online community for other families impacted by Gaucher's and extended their connections to other advocacy organizations, meeting similarly affected families in the process.

Their goal is for Hannah—and Hannah's impact on the world—to be remembered. Living through a child's rare disease process and subsequent death can provide motivation to share what one learned with others. The child lives on in these efforts, and creating legacy creates meaning for a bereaved family. Even so, ongoing advocacy is daunting even as it maintains memories. Advocate families themselves need support; the demands of foundation and advocacy work can be a productive part of the ongoing process of mourning and remembering, but it can also mask prolonged, complicated, and even anticipatory and ambiguous grief.

Hannah's family also created personal ways to recognize and remember her. They have family traditions that keep Hannah present—going on trips and taking family photos with her favorite Minnie Mouse. Her grave is decorated for the seasons and the holidays. Her brother remembers her in small ways but doesn't talk about her, while her sister is more willing to join in conversations.

At the time of her passing, Hannah's mother ended her eulogy with these words:

We, along with so many of your family, friends, and even strangers, are going to continue this fight in your name. Because of you, other families will be empowered to fight for their children. Because of you, doctors will have more compassion and resources when working with children with rare diseases. Because of you, communities will come together for reasons they never did before.

Source: Hannah's story is adapted from http://littlemisshannah.com.

SUMMARY

The primary caregiver is a critical figure in infants' and toddlers' ability to develop in optimal ways. Although loss of all-encompassing caregiving is a normal maturational loss as the caregiver provides "optimal frustration" to encourage the infant's evolving self-care, nondevelopmentally appropriate loss of a caregiver (through depression, illness, neglect, separation, or death) can have extremely detrimental effects. Parents also experience losses of their private relationship, of the idealized baby and child they thought they would have, and of hoped-for independence when a child is born with conditions that will require close and continuous attention. Assuring gentle, attuned, and empathic caregiving for youngsters and support for their caregivers is a critical aspect of care in the face of losses large and small.

DISCUSSION QUESTIONS

1. A friend calls and says her cousin's 18-month-old son has just lost both of his parents in a car accident. After talking briefly with your friend about her own feelings, she says she thinks you need to accompany her to the home and "start to do therapy" with the child. How should you respond, and why?
2. You work in a day-care setting and one child's mother just gave birth to triplets who are in the hospital intensive care nursery. What concerns would you have for the 4-year-old child and how might you help her?
3. You are a hospital social worker and a young woman approaches you after the death of an older adult on your unit. She explains that the deceased was her mother and that her 3-year-old son was very close to his grandmother and she wants your guidance on how to tell her son about the death. What do you say?

KEY REFERENCES

Only key references appear in the print edition. The full reference list appears in the digital product found on http://connect.springerpub.com/content/book/978-0-8261-4964-0/chapter/ch03

Bowlby, J. (1998). *Attachment and loss: Sadness and depression. Attachment and loss.* Vol. 3. Pimlico. (Original work published 1980).

Christ, G. H. (2000). Impact of development on children's mourning. *Cancer Practice, 8*(2), 72–81. https://doi.org/10.1046/j.1523-5394.2000.82005.x

Flouri, E., Midouhas, E., Joshi, H., & Tzavidis, N. (2015). Emotional and behavioural resilience to multiple risk exposure in early life: The role of parenting. *European Child and Adolescent Psychiatry, 24*(7), 745–755. https://doi.org/10.1007/s00787-014-0619-7

Klass, D. (2005). The inner representation of the dead child in the psychic and social narratives of bereaved parents. In R. Neimeyer (Ed.), *Meaning reconstruction & the experience of loss* (pp. 77–94). American Psychological Association.

Markese, S. (2011). Dyadic trauma in infancy and early childhood: A review of the literature. *Journal of Infant, Child, and Adolescent Psychotherapy, 10*(2–3), 341–378. https://doi.org/10.1080/15289168.2011.600214

Rando, T. A. (1986). The unique issues and impact of the death of a child. In T. Rando (Ed.), *Parental loss of a child* (pp. 5–43). Research Press.

Rosengren, K. S., Miller, P. J., Gutierrez, I. T., Chow, P. I., Schein, S. S., & Anderson, K. N. (2014). Children's understanding of death: Toward a contextualized and integrated account. *Monographs in the Society for Research in Child Development, 79*(1), 62–82. https://doi.org/10.1111/mono.12079

Siegel, D. J. (2012). *The developing mind: How relationships and the brain interact to shape who we are* (2nd ed.). Guilford. (Original work published 1999).

Silverman, P. R., & Worden, J. W. (2006). Children's reactions to the death of a parent. In M. S. Stroebe, W. Stroebe, & R. O. Hansson (Eds.), *Handbook of bereavement: Theory, research, and intervention* (pp. 300–316). Cambridge University Press. (Original work published 1993).

Speece, M. W., & Brent, S. B. (1996). The development of children's understanding of death. In C. A. Corr & D. M. Corr (Eds.), *Handbook of childhood death and bereavement* (pp. 29–50). Springer Publishing Company.

Zuckerman, B., Frank, D. A., & Mayes, L. (2002). Cocaine-exposed infants and developmental outcomes: "Crack kids" revisited. *Journal of the American Medical Association, 287*(15),1990–1991. https://doi .org/10.1001/jama.287.15.1990

4

Grief and Loss in Elementary School-Age Children

INTRODUCTION

The physical, cognitive, character, and spiritual development in elementary schoolchildren (ages 5–10) is rapid and remarkable. Social influences such as poverty, adequacy of schools, and parenting are examined for their ongoing power in molding the child's present and future. This chapter details how grief and loss due to death, as well as due to limited socioeconomic resources, affect elementary school-age children. The effectiveness of organic supports such as teachers, counselors, and coaches are emphasized. The growing number of children considering suicide at this young age is discussed, and the impact of adverse childhood experiences (ACEs) is explicated. Maturational losses such as parentification, loss of magical thinking, and anxiety are all addressed, and interventions such as progressive muscle relaxation, play therapy, and mindfulness-based stress reduction are identified as useful for work with children.

OBJECTIVES

After studying this chapter, the reader will be able to:
- Describe the cognitive, biological, psychological, social, and spiritual development of children from age 5 and entry into school to about age 11.
- Understand factors that affect levels of risk for children and their futures as well as protective factors that help enhance resilience.
- Explain the ways schools' practices affect child development, as well as their vital role in promoting health and well-being among bereaved children.
- Understand the way dual process and continuing bonds may be expressed by elementary school-age children.

VIGNETTE

Douglas was trying to behave, but he was very angry. They were having to move, once again, and this time it was to his grandmother's, far away. His dad was in jail again, and his mom was getting evicted from the fifth apartment they had lived in since he was in kindergarten. Douglas was most upset because now that he was in third grade, he often got to stay with his cousin's family when his mom was working. After the move, he would not get to do that because they would be 4 hours away. His teacher and his mom did not understand why he was so grumpy—he was not sure he understood it all himself. He knew he was angry and scared. He was sick of his mom telling him it would be "a new opportunity" and that he would have lots of pets to play with at his grandmother's. He wondered if it was even worth studying for his spelling test when he would not be at this school anymore. He had always loved his school and classmates; they all stayed the same even when he and his mom moved to different apartments, but now, even that would change. Douglas knew that no amount of being angry was going to change his mother's mind, but being angry seemed all he was able to do.

DEVELOPMENTAL TASKS: INITIATIVE VERSUS GUILT AND INDUSTRY VERSUS INFERIORITY

Children usually enter the school environment at about age 5, when they start kindergarten. Until recently, kindergarten allowed a gentle transition from the home environment to an academic setting, but now kindergartens focus on explicit skill and knowledge acquisition. For some children, this is a first exposure to large-group situations; for others, day care or "pre-K" has socialized them to be part of a large group of children. During early elementary school, children begin to develop confidence in taking the initiative to move out into the broader world, using language skills and imagination to engage with the greater society (Erikson, 1959/1980). Yet some children arrive at school angry about the attention and care they have not received from caregivers and can be extremely disruptive because they have not learned to cooperate with teachers and classmates. In kindergarten and first grade, children begin to leave home for long stretches of time and must perform in different ways from home, where they have (ideally) been nurtured and loved without pressure. For children who have not been in quality day-care settings, these new responsibilities constitute a major transition. Children may experience a loss of positive self-image as they move into the school environment, where peers and teachers judge how well they fit.

Elementary schoolchildren thrive on structure and stability, particularly in their younger years. Neuropsychiatrist and pediatrician Dan Siegel describes this as a time when children learn to navigate between chaos and rigidity and between impulsivity and inflexible adherence to rules (Siegel & Bryson, 2011). Children at this age need help processing their emotions; they must learn to adapt to circumstances, build empathy, and increase their ability to attend to their own well-being (Siegel & Bryson, 2011). Douglas had a chaotic family life, and the moves threatened his stability. Although his mother was trying to assure that he had a place to live, she was moving him away from his school and extended family, where he had found some degree of stability and predictability. Leaving an elementary school where people knew and liked him felt very scary. Frequent moves from schools can place children at risk for poor self-regulation and academic outcomes (Friedman-Krauss & Raver, 2015).

Children who have had unpredictable environments or have not received love and unconditional acceptance from caregivers may find school a haven, where achievements lead to praise and an increased sense of self-efficacy. As children move into the higher elementary school grades, they industriously learn and produce projects and papers and engage in creative, athletic, and other endeavors. The ability to produce in this way promotes a sense of mastery, but the child who is unable to meet this level of industry often experiences a sense of inadequacy and inferiority

(Erikson, 1959/1980). Ultimately, children who meet the social and academic expectations of the school environment will likely thrive in the social world that will encompass their future.

Biological Development

Children nearly double their weight and height between the ages of 5 and 11. Fiftieth percentile 5-year-olds weigh 42 pounds and are about 43 inches tall. By age 11, a child in the 50th percentile weighs 82 pounds and is 57 inches, or nearly 5 feet tall. At the same time, the brain becomes more complex. Children's brains show growth in the prefrontal cortex as well as the temporal and occipital cortices (Sowell et al., 2004). Sowell et al. also found changes in the relationship between gray matter and white matter in the brains of children as they age from 5 to 11. Some of these changes were highly correlated with the development of verbal skills and are believed to indicate more complex connections that permit higher cognitive skill development and further learning.

Lenroot and Giedd (2006) identified the prefrontal cortex as the site of children's growing ability to control impulses, make rational decisions, and integrate the brain's activities. These abilities are often called "executive functions." Research indicates that children who have experienced abuse/neglect have a 17% smaller (by area) corpus callosum (the brain structure that helps integrate both sides of the brain) than nonabused children (Teicher et al., 2004).

Brain development and impulse control are critical to the ability to learn, to interact appropriately in social settings, and to develop peer relationships. When the biological substrate (the brain) not developed, children are at a great disadvantage. The typical school environment requires an ability to remain seated, raise one's hand before speaking, and generally think before acting. These are very difficult tasks for a large percentage of 5-year-old children, but they usually master these skills by the time they move into second or third grade, likely because brain development is sufficient. Theories of brain development posit that children's growing ability to learn from previous errors (Grammer et al., 2018) and to cognitively regulate themselves (Friedman-Krauss & Raver, 2015) are mediating capacities for learning more generally, especially during the first through third grades. Children who have experienced abuse and neglect may have structural and functional brain changes that impair these executive capacities, often in an intergenerational pattern. When children's own parents were neglected or abused, the parents may have difficulty creating an optimal environment for their children (DeGregorio, 2013).

Along with brain structure and function, cortisol (the body's stress hormone) and its management through the hypothalamic–pituitary–adrenal axis (HPA) are known to be affected by chronic stress and trauma (Bevans et al., 2008). Chronic stress during childhood affects the hippocampus, prefrontal cortex, and amygdala, impairing memory, concentration, and executive function in negative ways (Boullier & Blair, 2018). Research with parentally bereaved children found their cortisol response was blunted, leaving them at higher risk for depression and other health and mental health problems in adulthood (Kaplow et al., 2013).

Biological development also involves genomics. Genetics was once understood as unchanging DNA, either inherited or not, like a gene for brown eyes. Epigenetics now illustrates how genes are turned on or off via methylation due to environmental exposures. Essex et al. (2013) found strong associations between ACEs and gene methylation. In a prospective study, Essex et al. (2013) showed how maternal stress during infancy and paternal stress in the preschool years yielded changes in the methylation patterns of children later in life. Although the science of epigenetics is still developing and cannot always predict outcomes, it seems that stressors (e.g., parental substance use disorders, parental death, exposure to violence, poverty) may all affect children's genomes.

Physical play, another aspect of children's lives from ages 5 to 11, is important for developing healthy bones and muscles, as well as imagination. Due to a proliferation of video and computer games, and fears for their safety in many neighborhoods, children may have fewer opportunities to use their large muscles, and pundits have expressed concern about the development of children's bodies and growing levels of obesity in the United States (Wallis, 2006). Children need physical activity to maintain their health. Touch—whether gentle and nurturing or as playful roughhousing—seems related to learning gross motor skills and may have beneficial epigenetic effects analogous to the thriving of rat pups licked and handled by their mothers (DeGregorio, 2013).

Childhood obesity causes physical effects that can limit children's development and is highly correlated with later development of type 2 diabetes and cardiovascular disease. Subica (2018) notes that obesity rates remain highest for children in African American and Hispanic communities and that although rates seem to be plateauing or even falling, great health risks remain for obese children. Subica strongly supports limiting access to sugary drinks via caregiver supervision (behavioral intervention) and taxation of soda (policy-level intervention), for instance. Caregivers should also limit screen time while increasing vegetable and fruit consumption and physical activity. He suggests community-based interventions to encourage physical activity, even the use of state tobacco tax money to install speed bumps that enhance the safety of outdoor activity.

Poverty weighs heavily on children. It is associated with low birth weight and prematurity in infancy (making school success more difficult) and with poorer mental and physical health (Xue et al., 2005). Child poverty rates cannot be compared across countries due to divergent definitions and methods of calculating poverty. Child poverty rates in the United States have decreased since the Great Recession (December 2007 to June 2009), but they remain sobering and starkly reflect the inequalities associated with race in the United States. Data released by the U.S. Census Bureau in September 2018 showed that while the overall poverty rate in 2017 was 17.5% (a statistically insignificant change from 18% in 2016), the 10.9% rate for White children under 18 was dwarfed by those of Native (31.5%), Black (28.5%), and Hispanic (25%) children. The figures for children living in "extreme poverty" (families with incomes less than half the poverty rate, or $1,053 per month for a family of four) were even sadder, with Native (16.4%), Black (15.3%), and Hispanic (10.5%) rates higher than the White rate (5%) by multiples of 2 and 3 (Children's Defense Fund, 2018).

Psychological Development

During their elementary school years, children undergo rapid growth in academic ability as the result of improved processing and integrative cognitive skills. Social skills also develop considerably. The ability to navigate academic and social demands has a great positive impact on children's sense of self-efficacy and self-image.

Erikson (1959/1980) posited that in the elementary school years, children must resolve the crisis of initiative versus guilt followed by industry versus inferiority. Although we typically use the language of developmental tasks rather than crises, we still find that children who have difficulty succeeding in school and peer relationships risk developing a sense of guilt and poor self-image. Piaget (1954) theorized that children between the ages of 5 and 7 move from preoperational thought processes to concrete operations processes, which remain with them to age 11 or 12. The preoperational stage is characterized by egocentric thinking and (according to Piaget, though questioned by others) an inability to put themselves in the position of others. They tend to attribute human characteristics to inanimate objects, and magical thinking (a belief that their thoughts can influence events) is strong. Clearly, if a loss due to death occurs, children are at risk if they believe that their hostile thoughts may have caused the death.

By the concrete operations stage, children have more understanding of causation, quantity, and symbolic action. They can take the role of the other and are able to play games and do role-taking activities. Developing language skills allows children to process their thoughts and emotions with others in ways that were not possible previously. If preschool children are often able to grasp the concept of death (Rosengren et al., 2014), elementary schoolchildren certainly seem able to do so. Massat et al. (2008) suggest that elementary school–aged children are often abruptly returned to school after a major loss, disturbing their dual-process oscillation (between restoration and loss orientations) as they must stay in restoration orientation to function at school. They suggest that psychological sequelae of loss in elementary school may be related to this abrupt reentry with little help to process their loss. Massat et al. (2008) emphasize the important role of school social workers in the amelioration of children's grief.

Children with learning disabilities (LDs) are particularly at risk for poor outcomes such as lowered self-esteem and efficacy because they have difficulty meeting academic demands. If learning differences are not diagnosed early, children may grow to believe they are incapable of success and their expectation of failure can become self-fulfilling (Lackaye & Margalit, 2008). At a time of life when acceptance by peers is critical to the sense of self, children with LD struggle with peer relationships and feel devalued in the eyes of their teachers and possibly their parents.

Bitsko et al. (2018) found that the proportions of children diagnosed with anxiety disorders rose from 1 in 28 in 2007 to 1 in 24 in 2011, with indications that these proportions were continuing to rise. They tie some of this to high levels of parental stress. They suggest that helping children to manage their anxiety (rather than avoid triggers) is the most helpful strategy. An intervention called Supportive Parenting for Anxious Childhood Emotions (SPACE) targets the parents of children with anxiety. It helps parents express a belief that children can face their fears, rather than allowing children to avoid what scares them or focusing on children's fears (Hathaway, 2019). By giving children space and support to handle their fears, children learn that they can survive both what makes them anxious and the anxiety itself.

More disturbing is a rise in childhood suicide, which, although still uncommon, is becoming more frequent among children of ages 5 to 11 in the European Union (Kovess-Masfety et al., 2015) as well as in the United States (Sheftall et al., 2016). Suicide among elementary school-children in the United States is most common among Black male children, who typically took their lives by suffocation or hanging (Sheftall et al., 2016). Helping children manage relationship problems with family members and assuring adequate management of attention deficit disorder symptoms are viewed as likely helpful in reducing the suicide rate among elementary school-age children to the low rates previously seen.

Social Development

Children who have not entered school generally have social relationships that are mediated by their caretakers. Even in school, much of the activity is structured and supervised until the first "recess" at school or the initial unsupervised play date with a peer. This new peer interaction demands enhanced social skills. Learning to take turns, engage in give-and-take conversations, share possessions for the good of the group, and even the ability to name emotions and display attention are associated with success in the first-grade child's future (Rhoades et al., 2011).

Skill with language is an important factor in a child's acceptance or rejection by peers (Menting et al., 2011). Menting et al. found that higher levels of externalizing behavior (aggression, etc.) among Dutch children from kindergarten to 4th grade were associated with poor receptive language skills and peers' rejection. This is important to understanding loss in two ways. When children experience a loss, they have varying ways of expressing their hurt and fear, particularly at younger developmental stages. Younger children may act out aggressively (or alternatively withdraw) in ways that create peer rejection. This then creates a second loss as bereaved children now lose the social support cushion that can promote resiliency (Criss et al., 2002). In later elementary school, this peer network is used more for distraction and engagement with other activities than to verbally process feelings about loss (Christ, 2000). In either case, impaired communicative abilities, or a tendency to act aggressively, will limit bereaved children's ability to mobilize support after a loss, leaving them vulnerable to grief complications. Notably, tightening school budgets and "return to basics" educational policies mean that many children live in school districts where classes are large and educating students is secondary to keeping them off the street and giving only a modicum of needed mathematical and communication skills (Carlson, 2008). These

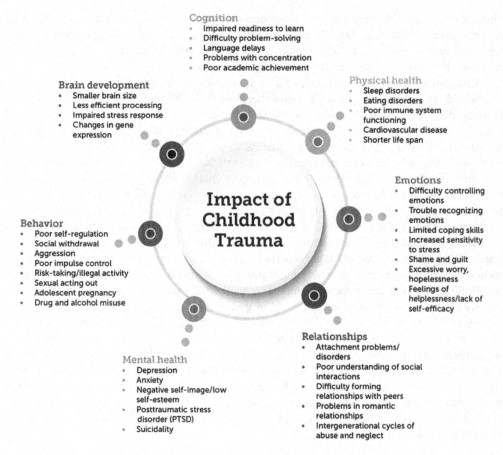

FIGURE 4.1 Impact of Childhood Trauma. This model illustrates the varied impacts of childhood trauma on aspects of a child's development.
Source: Reproduced with permission from Bartlett, J. D., & Steber, K. (2019). How to implement trauma-informed care to build resilience to childhood trauma. *ChildTrends.* https://www.childtrends.org/publications/how-to-implement-trauma -informed-care-to-build-resilience-to-childhood-trauma

conditions do not promote the optimal education of students, much less provide the emotional support that bereaved children need.

Spiritual Development

Children in elementary school become accustomed to learning what adults tell them to learn, and this applies to their spiritual lives as well. In a comprehensive review of research related to children's spiritual development, Mata-McMahon (2016) distinguished between nonreligious spirituality, directed toward transcendence and unity in relationships and/or with nature, and religious spirituality, which entails transcendence beyond the individual into the sacred along with religious stories, dogma, and practices. She observed that studies looking at children's spirituality tend to find that younger children (6–11), even in secular environments, find comfort in a belief in God and tend to pray as a way of finding comfort or expressing desire. Her own research with kindergartners found them being kind, connecting to their environments, and pondering deep questions in ways she defined as spiritual. Further, she notes that Wills (2011) tied spiritual development to music and children feeling as one with something bigger than themselves (chorus), hence not requiring religious content. Indeed, definitions of spirituality often draw from Fisher's (1999) classic assertion that spirituality derives from an individual's relationship with four entities: themselves, others, the environment/nature, and the Transcendent (or something beyond oneself). Others note that helping children find quiet in the madness of modern life (Mudge, 2018) or an ability to resist capitalist consumerism (Eaude, 2019) are also critical aspects of enhancing children's well-being through spiritual practices. It seems apparent that children's openness to guidance by adults paired with openness to ideas about the supernatural makes children 5 to 11 ripe for being socialized into religious and other spiritual traditions that will frame their experiences of loss.

SPECIAL CONSIDERATIONS IN RISK AND RESILIENCE

The increasing number of children born to mothers who used opioids during pregnancy is of great concern. The 2017 National Survey on Drug Use and Health (Substance Abuse and Mental Health Services Administration [SAMHSA], 2018) revealed that about 8.5% of pregnant women used an illicit drug within the 30 days prior to the survey. Neonatal abstinence syndrome (NAS) following withdrawal of the newborn from opioids has increased between 3 and 10 fold (varying by state) from the early 2000s to 2019 (Brennan et al., 2019). Although there is no clear evidence that these children have specific ongoing medical problems, research to date indicates that children born with NAS have significantly higher medical services usage in each of the first eight years of life (Liu et al., 2019), indicating that they do experience some health impairments. Poorer parenting practices and likelihood of children's removal from parents are associated with parents' opioid use (Winstanley & Stover, 2019) and these factors may also influence medical services use.

ACEs of all sorts, by definition, happen during childhood and generally entail some trauma. Research suggests that not all ACEs have the same long-term health effects. Dose–response influences (intensity of the ACE or frequency) may function differently. For instance, the more categories of ACEs a child experiences (particularly household dysfunction with emotional and physical abuse), the more likely increased negative health effects are found in adulthood. Additionally, the potency of ACEs such as child sexual abuse may create higher risks for negative health effects in adulthood (Crouch et al., 2018). The dose–response finding indicates the importance of providing remediation of ACEs in childhood and preventing future ACEs (Boullier & Blair, 2018). Figure 4.1 illustrates the significant negative impact of trauma on children, emphasizing how imperative it is to prevent ACEs and ameliorate their impact when they do occur. Figure 4.2 lists public policy strategies developed by the Centers for Disease Control and Prevention (CDC, 2019a) that aim to prevent ACEs by strengthening economic supports for families and ensuring positive childcare experiences through home visits after birth and accessible quality preschool and after-school programing connected to primary education.

The CDC recommendations rely heavily on educational resources to prevent and ameliorate the negative effects of ACEs. Primary education provides a site where children can have access to adults who can help to ensure their safety and offer support and guidance. Yet inequitable funding of schools means that this potential is often least available for the children who need it most (Baker et al., 2018). When children move frequently, the possibility of developing caring relationships with adults at school is diminished. Research demonstrates that not only do academic markers deteriorate with moving but the mediating role of cognitive dysregulation likely affects many other aspects of the child's functioning (Friedman-Krauss & Raver, 2015). Good schools with before- and after-school care not only help working parents but allow a haven where children can develop a sense of self-efficacy and meet adults who might identify and/or buffer ACEs. Yet caring, supportive, nondiscriminatory schools can exist only when supported by public policies and funds, a current challenge in the United States.

⬡⬡⬡ Preventing ACEs	
Strategy	**Approach**
Strengthen economic supports to families	• Strengthening household financial security • Family-friendly work policies
Promote social norms that protect against violence and adversity	• Public education campaigns • Legislative approaches to reduce corporal punishment • Bystander approaches • Men and boys as allies in prevention
Ensure a strong start for children	• Early childhood home visitation • High-quality child-care • Preschool enrichment with family engagement
Teach skills	• Social–emotional learning • Safe dating and healthy relationship skill programs • Parenting skills and family relationship approaches
Connect youth to caring adults and activities	• Mentoring programs • After-school programs
Intervene to lessen immediate and long-term harms	• Enhanced primary care • Victim-centered services • Treatment to lessen the harms of ACEs • Treatment to prevent problem behavior and future involvement in violence • Family-centered treatment for substance use disorders

FIGURE 4.2 Strategies for Preventing ACEs. This list developed by the Centers for Disease Prevention and Control identifies strategies for preventing ACEs among children along with approaches to assist families in raising healthy children.
ACEs, adverse childhood experiences.
Source: Centers for Disease Control and Prevention. (2019a). *Preventing adverse childhood experiences: Leveraging the best available evidence.* National Center for Injury Prevention and Control, Centers for Disease Control and Prevention. https://www.cdc.gov/violenceprevention/pdf/preventingACES.pdf

Harvard University's Center on the Developing Child (2019) synthesizes extensive research into three principles designed to reduce risks to children and enhance their resilience and well-being over a lifetime: First, support responsive relationships between children and adults; second, strengthen core life skills (including self-regulation and executive functioning); and third, reduce sources of stress for children and their families.

LOSS EXPERIENCED BY ELEMENTARY SCHOOL-AGE CHILDREN

Impacts and Perceptions of Loss for Elementary School-Age Children

The developmental processes described earlier have great bearing on how children understand loss and their coping tools. Whereas younger children have few tools for processing a loss and benefit most from the security of a steady and nurturing caregiver, school-age children have a variety of newly developed skills and resources for gaining support and processing the loss. Developmental age and skills define a child's experience of loss, and as children continue to develop, they must rework prior losses using their new, more mature understanding. Children who lose a sibling or parent in toddlerhood will need to rework this loss during later maturational stages over their lifespan. As children in later elementary school begin to imagine their futures, they are likely to reexperience their previous losses, realizing that graduations, learning to drive, and so forth, will all happen without the deceased loved one(s). As these secondary losses are recognized, children need acknowledgment and support for renewed mourning from the perspective of the later developmental level, which brings new skills in language, abstraction, and symbolic thought.

Nguyen and Scott (2013) found that bereaved children with higher physical self-concepts (defined as approving of one's appearance) experienced lower levels of depression after a loss. Unexpectedly, they also found that children with a higher math self-concept had increased levels of depression. They speculated that children with high math self-concept may have higher expectations for achievement and that falling achievement in the aftermath of a family death can lead to depression.

Children from ages 6 through 11 tend to express sadness and grief in intense yet rapidly alternating spurts. They may cry one moment and be running around playing the next. Dual process (Stroebe & Schut, 1999) works somewhat differently in childhood. School-age children seem to modulate their emotions by moving into distraction mode more readily than older people. Although often unnerving to adults, children's oscillation from asking serious and detailed questions about the death to giddy play is a healthy and normal response.

Children in the 6- to 8-year-old group tend to remember appearance-related characteristics and enjoy talking about pleasant memories of the deceased (Christ, 2000; Christ & Christ, 2006). They benefit from having concrete mementoes of the deceased. They often speak about wanting to die in order to be with a deceased loved one. This is a form of wishful thinking; it is not suicidal ideation (Christ, 2000).

Children in the 9 to 11 age range seem to have a stronger need for factual information and tend to avoid direct expression of emotions, preferring to compartmentalize emotion or experience it very briefly or in private (Christ, 2000). Occasionally, this may lead to aggression or withdrawal. On the whole, children in this age group seem to benefit from interventions that help them remember happier times, obtain a transitional object associated with the deceased, and affirm their tendency to move in and out of emotion about the loss (Christ, 2000). Because memory acquisition and recall are better developed by ages 9 to 11, these children remember abstract qualities (e.g., kindness) of the deceased.

Death Losses

Death of a Parent

The death of a parent, of course, is perhaps the most life-changing loss an elementary school-age child can experience. In Sweden, where national registries allow life course analyses of an entire age cohort, Berg et al. (2014) found that parental death had a fairly immediate and significant negative impact on school performance and grades. They theorized that school performance mediates (directly influences outcomes) and moderates (modifies the intensity of outcomes) adult outcomes for educational attainment, substance use, and other mental health disorders known to be associated with parental death in childhood. Later, Berg et al. (2016) found that bereaved children experience somewhat higher rates of hospitalization for depression as they move into young adulthood, with higher risk among those who were bereaved at the youngest ages and those whose parents died suddenly. They suggest that long-term negative impacts of parental death may be ameliorated by attention to children's school performance and enhancement of support for ongoing academic achievement, especially in the first two years after the death.

A study of parentally bereaved children from Denmark, Finland, and Sweden found higher rates of early mortality for the children as they aged, with greater risk when the parent died of "unnatural" causes such as suicide or homicide (Li et al., 2014). Li et al. observed that increased risk can come from genetic heritable sources, epigenetic effects of stress during childhood leading to metabolic syndrome or immune system suppression, or social and economic disadvantages after a parent's death. Similarly, Pham et al. (2018) followed bereaved children for seven years in the United States and also found that younger children who lost a parent to suicide, homicide, or other unanticipated death were at higher risk of negative outcomes in adulthood. They noted that depressive symptoms in the first two years after the parental death were common and that a Family Bereavement Program (Sandler et al., 2013) could ameliorate stressors by helping the surviving caregiver provide consistent parenting and support.

Some research indicates that children can experience posttraumatic growth after a parental death (Brewer & Sparkes, 2011). One person who was 9 when both parents died stated that, at her current age of 19, those losses would "destroy" her; she believed that her younger age at their deaths allowed her to "bounce back" (Brewer & Sparkes, 2011, p. 211). Brewer and Sparkes (2011) observed that in the United Kingdom, where the study took place, bereavement is spoken of as a journey, in contrast to the United States, where bereavement discourse often emphasizes return to a pre-bereavement state. Children in the United Kingdom may feel free to follow different pathways for coping rather than feeling obliged to "return to normal." In the United States, therapeutic advice for parents raising a child after parental death also asserts that children can thrive after loss if given the chance to honestly talk about their responses in a context of stable support and routines as well as assurance that the surviving caregiver is coping well enough to provide the consistent care the child needs (Borrenson, 2019).

Children envision deceased parents in ways that continue the parent's presence in their lives (Silverman & Nickman, 1996). Typically, they maintain their connections (continuing bonds) in one of five ways: (a) locating the deceased (in heaven, for example); (b) experiencing the deceased (e.g., believing the deceased parent is watching them); (c) reaching out to the deceased to initiate a connection (e.g., praying to the deceased); (d) remembering (actively); and (e) keeping a belonging of the deceased. Silverman and Nickman see these strategies as critical to the child's coping trajectory. Children who could not "locate" the parent or felt a lack of ongoing connection seemed to have greater difficulty coping over time. They proposed a trajectory of the way children perceived the connection to the deceased parent that moves from (a) seeing the parent as a visiting ghost to (b) holding onto memories of the past, to (c) maintaining an interactive relationship, and finally (d) becoming a living legacy (making them proud, doing well; Normand et al., 1996). Karydi (2018) notes that the surviving parent is most frequently the person who helps children maintain continuing bonds with the deceased parent over a lifetime, and she finds that some adults experience activated grieving for the deceased parent. It seems those children who have help maintaining the continuing bond with the deceased parent find this beneficial in early adulthood, but Karydi suggests that for some, this may also correspond with troubling prolonged grief.

Death of a Sibling

With the death of a sibling, children not only lose a playmate, confidante, and colluder against parents but also likely lose attention due to their parents' grief. Siblings often believe they must stifle their grief to avoid adding to their parents' sadness or irritability. In a study of adults bereaved in childhood by the death of a sibling, Rostila et al. (2017) found a higher hazard ratio of death in young adulthood for the bereaved, though this was partially explained by the same cause of natural death, especially after removing the half of siblings who died under the age of 1. They speculate that similar genetic or other pathological processes may affect each sibling and also note that the higher hazard rate of mortality for children bereaved at elementary school age is rather small. Also using a sample from Sweden, Kennedy et al. (2018) measured stress resilience during mandatory military examinations and found that recruits who had a first-degree relative die during their childhood (7–12) had lower stress resilience scores. The scores were worse for those whose relative died during the recruits' adolescence. In short, children's futures seem to be negatively affected by a sibling's death during childhood, yet it is hard to tease out how much of this is because of similar susceptibility to illness, changes in the protectiveness of families after bereavement, or lack of supportive intervention after loss.

In examining children's reactions to sibling deaths, Packman et al. observed that schoolchildren generally feel "I hurt inside," "I don't understand," "I don't belong," and "I'm not enough" (2006, p. 830). Feeling that they do not belong or are not enough has to do with changes in the parents as they grieve and transformation of the family structure into something unrecognizable. They feel inadequate to meet their parents' needs and expectations. Packman et al. (2006) suggest that promoting continuing bonds can be fruitful for siblings, although they note the exception of siblings who have had contentious, competitive relationships. They employ the language of Devita-Raeburn (2004), who describes "carrying" the deceased sibling along in life. "Carrying" is a way of keeping the memory and relationship with the dead sibling alive over time.

Death of a Pet

Commonly, children in this age range lose a pet, often a beloved one that has been confided in and viewed as a family member. This is often the first death a child experiences and may set a template for how the child processes grief in the future. When this loss is disenfranchised through nonrecognition or demeaning or trivializing the feelings of grief, children are given the message that mourning is not acceptable. A similar message is communicated if a beloved pet merely disappears and is never spoken of again. This may detrimentally affect the child's ability to process grief in the future. Pets provide a unique connection and source of comfort (Sable, 2013). When the loss of a beloved pet is acknowledged, children learn that loss can be observed, discussed, and mourned.

Living Losses: Atypical, Typical, and Maturational Losses

Losses of a Parent(s) Due to Abuse

In the United States, one in seven children experience physical, sexual, or emotional abuse or neglect each year (CDC, 2019b). Additionally, every 9 minutes, child protective services (CPS) substantiates a claim of sexual abuse (RAINNE, 2019). Children who experience abuse endure the loss of the prior trusting, caring relationship with the abuser and often have difficulty trusting relationships or being vulnerable within them in the future. Experiencing abuse in childhood is associated with intimate partner violence (IPV) in adulthood in complex ways. Physical abuse in childhood is associated with both IPV victimization and perpetration in adulthood. Combined with emotional abuse in childhood, it may be even more strongly associated with IPV victimization in adulthood, though gender of the child and types of abuse affect these associations (Richards et al., 2017).

In adulthood, children who experienced sexual abuse have higher levels of depression, dissociative identity disorder, borderline personality disorder, criminal convictions, substance use disorders, and eating disorders (Friedman et al., 2011), and these outcomes seem to be intensified if the individual is also of sexual minority group status (LGBTQ). Yet we should not forget that many sexually abused children thrive nonetheless (Zafar & Ross, 2013).

In one of the few studies to examine the narratives of sexually abused children related while they were still children (derived from trauma-focused cognitive behavioral therapy [TF-CBT] interventions), the primary theme to emerge was their fear of the abuser and of experiencing abuse in the future. These fears for safety were written in each of the 21 narratives examined (Foster & Hagedorn, 2014). Even though most children fear their abuser, they may also continue attempts to gain that person's praise and deny the negative impact on themselves.

Children may lose their parents as a result of CPS removing them from their homes due to substantiated abuse. Christopher Church asserts:

The research on the harm inflicted by separating children from their parents is so unambiguous that Harvard Professor of Pediatrics, Dr. Charles Nelson, told the Washington Post, "If people paid attention at all to the science, they would never do this." But we do this as a matter of routine in the name of child protection—more than 250,000 times per year. (2019, e1)

Our supplementary materials include a reading from the first edition of this book, in which Tara Sinclair traced the long-term consequences for Nina after her removal from her parents, consequences that included Nina's ongoing attachment problems and difficulty trusting others.

Survivors of childhood maltreatment may deny the effects of the abuse in much the same way that people deny the affective impact of a loss. Just as children bereaved in more traditional ways must rework their losses as they mature, children who experience abuse must rework their understandings to recognize, validate, and grieve the losses involved in the betrayal of the parental (or abuser) relationship or the loss of those relationships altogether if they are removed from parental care. If they deny the negative impacts of the loss, they may be unable to continue to rework their understanding of the experience as they mature. Part of healing and being resilient after losses due to abuse involves acknowledging the experience, considering the losses involved in the parental and caregiver relationships, and attending to self-care and healing over a lifetime. In short, mourning the loss of a trusted caregiver's nurture can be as painful as a death.

Loss Due to Parental Divorce

Parental divorce is common when children are in elementary school and places children in some untenable positions. Children often engage in omnipotent and magical thinking and therefore believe they somehow caused the problems between their parents and the dissolution of their marriage. Further, they may be used as pawns between parents fighting over property, financial support, and their children's loyalty. Despite the consistent and loud expert advice to help children through their parents' divorce (Hecker & Sori, 2003), children remain forgotten mourners. The child experiences loss (of the parent who leaves the home and of the former family constellation) but may not quite understand what divorce means. The divorce-related losses of family structure and routine, financial well-being, and assumptive world are powerful. Studies suggest that children whose parents divorce are at somewhat higher risk for relationship instability during their early adulthood, but once changes in economic well-being and parenting problems are controlled for, children whose parents divorce during their elementary school years show few long-term relationship impacts (Fergusson et al., 2014).

Recognizing children's needs for security and stability are keys to intervention. There are few evidenced-based approaches to care for children after divorce, but some note that programs focused on protective factors should be more widely implemented (Pedro-Carroll, 2005). Pedro-Carroll (2005) suggests that support groups allow children to name their own losses and recognize loss and misunderstandings in other children in a supportive environment. Additionally, activities that help children consolidate knowledge about divorce and engage their peers help them normalize the experience. This allows them to get support in validating their losses and promotes resilient adaptation. Sidorsky's reading at the end of this chapter illustrates the deep pain and isolation children could experience in earlier eras when divorce was severely stigmatized.

Loss of Being a Child

Children can be deprived of their childhood by abuse (of every kind), deaths, the impairment of their caregiver, relocation, poverty, life-threatening illness, or differences like atypical sexual or gender development. Although childhood is idealized and children have more worries, responsibilities, and needs than typically portrayed, many in the aforementioned circumstances become parentified: They feel the need to take on the responsibilities, concerns, and burdens of adulthood before their time (Jurkovic, 1997). Although some research finds that parentification can enhance abilities and develop strengths, the general practice wisdom is that families should ensure that children are not burdened with adult roles and responsibilities and that they have room in their lives for play, friendship, and imagination (Chee et al., 2014). Schier et al. (2015) note that emotional parentification can be just as harmful as instrumental parentification (fulfilling adult activities of care) and that depressive symptoms in adulthood are associated with parentification. The losses of parentified childhood are often unrecognized, and losses unrecognized can produce submerged resentment leading to grief later in life (see Sidorsky's observations in both this and Chapter 9 (retirement). Helping families to acknowledge losses and attempt to ameliorate and/or mourn them to some degree may help minimize the internalized rage parentified children may carry into adulthood.

Loss Due to Illness or Injury

Typically, children are fairly healthy, yet in elementary school, they start to venture from their homes into neighborhoods, schools, and other spaces that are not always as safe as one would wish. Due to playground injuries, especially falls, children between 5 and 9 visit EDs more frequently than people in any other age group (CDC, 2012). As a result of inadequate maintenance, the likelihood of injury is greatest in poorer neighborhoods (CDC, 2012). As the reading by McCarthy illustrates, childhood injuries can have long-lasting physical consequences and hidden psychological and emotional ramifications when children feel different or ostracized because of medical treatments. These are losses of competence, mastery, and the acceptance of peers, in addition to the loss of bodily integrity.

Children sometimes have conditions such as cystic fibrosis and sickle cell anemia that affect them from birth, as well as cancers that develop during childhood. Research and professional opinion coincide in recommending honest, developmentally appropriate communication with children, even those who may still be coming to understand the nature of death. In an extensive review of available guidance in caring for children with life-threatening illness, Bates and Kearney (2015) report that many children are not included in discussions about their health because parents resist hearing physicians' explanations of poor prognoses. They observe that this cuts children off from the opportunity to say good bye, to have adults role-model coping responses, or to have their questions answered and fears addressed. Bates and Kearney report that children in elementary school often fear being alone while ill and worry that they will miss their belongings when they die. They suggest that clinicians help parents understand that their wish to protect their child is understandable but that open, honest, developmentally informed communication will best allow children to receive the support, answers, and reassurance they need to maintain trust in the adults around them.

REACTIONS OF OTHERS TO THE LOSS OF AN ELEMENTARY SCHOOL–AGE CHILD

Parents' Loss of a Child

Parents are responsible for the well-being of their children and therefore often have extreme levels of guilt about the death of a child. Rando (1993) asserts that loss of a child consistently correlates with complicated parental grief. The assumptive world is violated when a child dies before a parent, and this leads to a heightened sense of vulnerability.

For parents living through the process of their child's death, the tension between holding on to their child and wanting the child relieved of suffering becomes unbearable at times. Parents cope by focusing on action. These have been categorized as piloting, providing, protecting, and preserving (Price et al., 2011). Piloting involves directing the child's care and treatment decisions, while providing involves actual parental care of the child. Protecting the child from knowledge of the illness, caregivers they perceived as less competent, and other real or perceived threats was problematic: Efforts to "protect" in these ways led to communication failures and anxiety. Preserving the family, both during the child's illness and after the child's death, includes preserving the child's place within the family (Price et al., 2011). This implies that helping parents take constructive action can assist them to cope during a child's course of dying. Bereaved parents report that they listen closely to communications from the healthcare team, appreciate guidance about anticipatory mourning and decisions that must be made during the dying process, welcome bereavement support, wish for ongoing contact with their children's care team after the death, and value opportunities to remember their child (Snaman et al., 2016).

In a developed world, children's deaths are viewed as utterly preventable, through either the miracles of modern medicine or vigilance about preventing risks and avoiding accidents. That children will outlive parents is part of the expected order of life. Yet children will always be vulnerable, and a child's death turns the assumptive world upside down. Often, these deaths are totally unexpected and due to tragic accidents. Other times, the deaths are not only unexpected but unexplained, leading to police and CPS investigations that add trauma to the distress of bereaved parents. These bereaved parents have people judge their culpability and assume how they should grieve and cope, which impairs parents' ability to protect their living children from exposures to the details of the sibling's death (Turner, 2017).

Recent technologies such as Facebook, virtual memorials through funeral homes, and other online spaces appeal to some parents, yet they may also work against the North American norm of "moving on" after a death (Mitchell et al., 2012). Despite taboos about discussion of child death, these virtual memorials proliferate. Mitchell et al. (2012) analyze how commercial websites furnish parents with templates to memorialize a deceased child and in doing so both memorialize and reconstitute the child. In maintaining the websites, parents' and others' postings "[transform] the lived experience of their child's death into forms of sociality which include that absent child's presence" (Mitchell et al., 2012, p. 419). The memorial sites seldom include discussion of the child's death and, unlike memorials for stillborn and neonatal deaths, do not include postmortem pictures. Maintaining a sense of the child in the present is a critical feature of the sites. Others' (even strangers') ability to visit the website and virtually "light candles and leave teddy bears," usually at a small cost, eerily reconstitutes the child as a commodity. The interactional nature of these sites whereby parents wish the (dead) child good night, apologize for not writing more frequently, start charities in children's honor, and "share" their child with others creates a public space very different from typical rituals of death. Mitchell et al.'s (2012) analysis of "online afterlife" (p. 429) suggests that these sites fundamentally change notions of grief and bereavement to be congruent with continuing bonds (Klass et al., 1996) but also move beyond that with expectations of ongoing interactions.

In addition to continuing the bond with a deceased child, finding some meaning in the death is hypothesized to be a critical feature of parents' grief process and eventual healing. Lichtenthal et al. (2013) explored how meaning-making, benefit-finding, and cause of death interact in parents' grief. Not surprisingly, parents whose children died due to violence had a much more difficult time making meaning or finding a reason for the loss, and fewer than half were able to do so; a small fraction (22.9%) identified a benefit after the death ("a silver lining" such as growth in empathy or not taking life for granted; Lichtenthal et al., 2013, p. 320). It is important to note that meaning-making may involve consideration of why the death happened, a type of causal attribution, but not always. Sometimes, the meaning may be related to the benefit that came afterward or to a focus on fate. Of parents whose children died of natural causes, 61% were able to do some meaning-making (an attribution of "God's will," an assertion the child is in a safer place, or an explanation of medical reasons), and benefit-finding was exhibited in more than three quarters of their sample. Symptoms of complicated grief were found in both sets of parents but were more pronounced among those whose child died violently.

A particularly challenging form of parental grief comes after a child dies from complications related to a developmental disability. All parents cope with the loss of the idealized child when a baby is born; parents whose child is ill or has a diagnosed disability feel this loss acutely and chronically (Boss et al., 2011). Although prior theories asserted that parents of children with disabilities had "chronic sorrow" (Olshansky, 1962), others contest that (Green, 2007; Morse et al., 2000). Green (2007) argued that the lack of formal and informal support is what aggrieves parents of children with special needs. In a study of mothers whose children with disabilities died, women often felt that their love for their child and their loss were not validated (Milo, 2005). The study found that members of the parents' social network said things like "Don't you think it was for the best?"—a painful dismissal of their child's value. The bereaved mothers in Milo's study had to navigate a reworking of "Who am I now?" once their role of intensive caregiving was lost. Having wished for relief from the burdens of care, but also loving their child and the gifts the child brought, women struggled to make meaning from the conflicted experience. Milo asserted that mothers coped better if they originally were given an accurate portrayal of the child's prognosis and were encouraged to take control where it was possible. Support groups were once again identified as the intervention of choice. Boss et al. (2011) also suggested that parents coped best by identifying the paradox of loving one's child while also feeling burdened, a hallmark of ambiguous loss and chronic sorrow when parenting children with disabilities.

Parental responsibility is unique to the parent–child bond. Couples often are stressed when each parent grieves differently, both due to gender differences and individual coping abilities. These stresses may threaten the relationship if the mutual support between partners is lost at a difficult time when each hopes to be comforted by the other. Instead, guilt may be displaced into blame, leading to further stress in the relationship. Especially when there are questions about the death, parents' tendency to look for blame and occasionally find it in the other may also take a toll on relationships (Turner, 2017). Even so, and despite the commonly held belief to the contrary, divorce is not more common after a child's death (Schwab, 1998).

Parents also encounter an economic toll after a child's death. Research indicates that the costs associated with funerals and time off from jobs for bereavement leave actually pale in comparison to economic costs associated with "presenteeism"—being present at one's work site but not fulfilling duties or being able to work at typical levels of efficacy and efficiency due to bereavement (Fox et al., 2014). Fox et al. (2014) observe that others have found that overall lifetime earnings of bereaved parents are lower than those not bereaved, but it is unclear whether this is due to ramifications of lowered productivity while on the job ("presenteeism") or the result of changes in bereaved parents' work priorities or capabilities that find them assuming less demanding, but lower-paying, employment.

Forgotten Mourners—The Grandparents

With lifespans extending into the 80s and 90s, many grandparents experience the death of a grandchild. Like parents, grandparents inhabit an assumptive world in which grandchildren outlive both themselves and the grandchild's parents. When grandchildren die, grandparents are believed to experience a double loss in that they mourn the grandchild with whom they often had a special relationship and their child who is bereaved and whom they cannot comfort. Research identifies grandparents as experiencing five aspects of pain: pain from previous bereavements; pain from the loss of the grandchild; the pain of witnessing the son or daughter's grief; the pain of witnessing subsequent negative changes in the son or daughter; and pain that is common to all grief (Gilrane-McGarry & O'Grady, 2011). Providing support for adult children while mourning a grandchild is clearly stressful. New loss triggers old losses, and grandparents are particularly vulnerable to cumulative grief as they likely have accumulated more losses. It is important to remember grandparents when developing bereavement resources following the death of an elementary school–age child.

Losses (Nondeath) Related to Child Protective Services

Sometimes, parents and grandparents lose custody and care of their children due to their removal from the home by CPS. Nixon et al. (2013) empirically confirmed what has long been assumed: Mothers experience deep pain and grief when CPS removes their children. They explored the particularly fraught situation where children are removed from their mother when there is IPV. Mothers' ambiguous grief over not knowing where their child is or whether the child is being well cared for, and their loss of role and identity as a mother, are so destabilizing that one of the mothers actually returned to her abuser looking for comfort (Nixon et al., 2013). They observe that women's parenting has often been controlled within the IPV-plagued relationship and the removal of children is one more experience of subjugation. Sympathy for mothers who have substance use problems or other behaviors that put children at risk is often lacking; thus, these ambiguous losses are disenfranchised and made more painful. The women need support and validation to process their grief.

Whether from death or removal by CPS, the loss of a child of elementary school age violates parental notions that they should have responsibility for care of their child. Grieving these losses requires revision of the assumptive world wherein the child outlives the parent or will always be with the parent. Further, a parent's responsibility to provide care for bereaved siblings adds additional challenge to that parent's coping. Finding ways of continuing the (revised) bond with the child is critical to moving through such loss.

INTERVENTION ISSUES WITH CHILDREN IN ELEMENTARY SCHOOL

Children in elementary school are developmentally primed to engage with peers. It is therefore not surprising that many authors describe interventions with children based on group work. Groups allow children to feel the support of others who mourn similar losses. This validates the loss and allows children to hear from others at their developmental level about strategies for coping with their loss. Most important, group participation shows them that they are not alone and that others have gone through very similar losses and circumstances.

As we observed earlier, children grieve differently, taking dual process (Stroebe & Schut, 1999, 2005) to its extremes; they cry 1 minute and play happily the next, particularly at younger ages. Unfortunately, this makes it seem that they are either grieving "incorrectly" or not grieving at all (Crenshaw, 2002). Children blunt their grief expression in order to protect the surviving parent or siblings from painful reminders and also occasionally due to fears of shaming themselves by showing intense emotions. Clinicians working with grieving children must show themselves as trustworthy, truly hearing and validating the grief, while not pushing or otherwise indicating to children that their emotions should be anything but what they are (Crenshaw, 2002).

Parents generally get bereavement leave (albeit brief), but children are often returned to school fairly soon after a death. It is important to allow space for their dual process to function. For example, assuring that they can leave the classroom to go to a safe space to talk with a trusted adult can help. Linda Goldman, renowned for her work with bereaved children, came to bereavement work from teaching children who had to repeat the first grade. She discovered they often had experienced multiple losses. She used class time to process many of those losses and the children thrived and learned (Goldman, 2015). She advises that bereaved children in elementary school need to tell their story "over and over again" (2017, p. 161); use drawing, storytelling, and acting out the story to project it out of themselves (externalize the problem); have a safe space in the school where they can retreat when overwhelmed; be allowed to get "reality checks" in the face of fears about whether surviving family members are safe; and be given the chance to do memory work and create legacy projects. "What we can mention, we can manage" (2017, p. 171), Goldman asserts, creating the expectation that schools provide the environment where children can speak of their losses, document them, and gain support as well as distraction while they build resilience. Clearly, for children in elementary school, help with processing losses must be available in school, and schools need to support learning while children are grieving.

In the case of a parent's extended, terminal illness, decisions must be made about how to prepare for the impending death. Clinicians have moved toward facilitating attachments prior to a death while also acknowledging the coming loss and using time for anticipatory grieving. Saldinger et al. (2004) question the value of romanticizing an anticipated "good death" (2004, p. 916) and also recognize that facilitating intimacy and optimizing remaining time with the family member may be more important than minimizing the strains of trying to both attach and detach at the same time. They studied the effect of this challenging position on children and found that they did make efforts to stay connected to dying parents, even when the parent was nonresponsive due to illness or acted in a "mean" manner (pp. 926–927). They also found that the surviving parent usually bore responsibility for mediating the relationship between the dying parent and the child to some degree, including participating in legacy projects to maintain memories and connections after the other parent's death. Saldinger et al. (2004) found that the unpredictability of death creates problems when families believe they can orchestrate a positive farewell ritual, particularly for young children who may be frightened by the physical sounds and actions of individuals as they die. They conclude that a formulaic approach to fostering attachment is not useful, but fostering attachment is valued when all parties pursue it flexibly and with sensitivity to the child's needs and developmental capacities. Similarly, in pursuing legacy projects, adults should let children adjust their level of interest at any point in time. School-age children seem to avoid attending to letters and other communications from the deceased parent, preferring to look at gifts from that parent or other mementoes. In time, they become mature enough to handle the direct communications.

Intervention strategies to support children with dying relatives tend to be organized to allow professionals to intervene. A professional who is not part of the family system can interact, sometimes in displaced and symbolic ways, to convey information appropriate to the child's developmental stage, correct misconceptions due to magical thinking, validate the child's feelings and responses, and provide support. The clinician can also help interpret some of the child's behaviors to family members to reduce reactivity and correct misunderstandings. Saldinger et al. (2004) recommended that children and families with a dying parent need provision of information, communication of feelings, promotion of awareness and responsiveness, maintenance of a stable environment, assuring additional support for the child, exposure to the dying parent, encouragement to participate in funeral arrangements, relationship facilitation, and meaning-making. Clinicians in palliative care and hospice have long known that accurate communication with children is critical to their resilience. Even so, a review of extant articles about professionals delivering such care shows that while they aspire to deliver family-focused care, they often shy away from explicit communication with children (Franklin et al., 2019). They often felt unprepared to seek out the children, to understand their developmental needs, to manage their own empathetic and emotional responses to the entire family, and to manage the stresses within the family and the healthcare team as the parent was dying. Franklin et al. observed that these professionals understand the importance of providing such care and supporting the bonds between children and their parents. They recommend that employers and agencies assure appropriate support for the workers themselves so that they can adequately provide support (Franklin et al., 2019).

Play therapy (Boyd Webb et al., 2011) and mindfulness techniques (Burke, 2010) are also commonly used with bereaved children. Play therapy allows children to play out the story of the loss or to engage in the reworking of it as they express the anger, replay differing outcomes, or use the play to ask questions and get correct information from the counselor. Mindfulness-based stress reduction and other mindfulness approaches involve training the child to adopt relaxation practices (visualization and progressive muscle relaxation) that help create an attitude of non-judgmental, patient awareness, sustained and directed attention, and intentional use of the awareness and attention in directed practice (Burke, 2010). In a systematic review, Burke (2010) found that most studies of mindfulness with children in elementary school have focused on feasibility and acceptance of the method rather than its efficacy. Goldman observes, "Today's children face a kaleidoscope of grief and loss issues ranging from school shootings, terrorism, and hurricanes to a parent's deportation, homelessness, or imprisonment. . . . Educators can provide grief vocabulary, resources, crisis and educational interventions, preventions, and 'postventions' in order to create an oasis of safety for bereaved children within the school system" (2017, p. 171). She is right, and children in every school everywhere deserve prepared counselors at school where the children spend the vast majority of their time.

READINGS

Good Boys of Divorced Parents—Part I: Childhood Differences
STEPHEN SIDORSKY

Stephen Sidorsky, MSW, LCSW, has retired as director of mental health services in community mental health. He is currently a part-time lecturer at Rutgers University School of Social Work and teaches in the Continuing Education Program in Social Work.

PART I of II

There is, somewhere, an "iconic" photo of a young boy, maybe 6 or 8 years old. His parents are divorced (have been for most of his life), and the young boy lives with his mother. In the photo, he is neatly dressed in a short-sleeved shirt, hair combed, sitting by the window waiting for his father who is coming for a visit. He waits a long time, perhaps for an hour beyond when his father was to arrive to take him out to lunch, perhaps to a movie or even better, to play catch in the nearby park. His father never arrives, and the young boy steps away from the window, walks over to his bed, and sits down to read a book. There is no talking about this with his mother, except to say, "He must have had to work. Maybe he will come another time."

This story is not so much about a particular phase of life and how a loss was experienced, processed, and resolved or integrated. Rather, it is about a particular kind of loss, how it was regarded (or not), and how it infused itself into my life and colored it for many, many years.

In an odd way, my parents were always "separated." They married in the early 1940s, my father was in the service during the war, and I was born soon after his return. From what I understand, trouble started at that time and only got worse. While I never remember them being together, their actual divorce happened when I was about 6. My mother and I moved into my grandmother's apartment, which was in the same building as ours was, in Brooklyn. The important piece to all this is that no one ever said anything about the separation, the divorce, or our move to the new apartment. Nothing was acknowledged, declared, or explained. There would be no "before" and "after," no recognition that something had happened. Simply, father visited less and less frequently, until it got down to maybe three or four times a year, and eventually fewer than that.

I have since learned that this experience illustrates two types of loss and grief: ambiguous loss and disenfranchised grief. The ambiguity comes from (for a young boy) a disorienting and worrying sense of not knowing what was happening. In the context of ambiguous loss, the person—my father—was physically absent but remained psychologically present. As his absence was never spoken about, was never acknowledged—there was never an instance of "Let's all sit down—we have something to talk to you about"—I was living in a kind of twilight zone—something profound was happening, but since we never spoke about it, we continued to live as if nothing had happened. On one hand, my father seemed to simply fade away and slowly disappear from our lives. At the same time, in his absence, his presence became greater than when he actually came by and spent time with me. My experience—my sense of loss and uncertainty—was very much disenfranchised, in two ways. For one thing, it was ignored and disregarded, as if nothing was happening. Second, there was the feeling that something was wrong with me because my parents were separated—it was as if I was disenfranchising my own sadness and sense of loss, as no one else really acknowledged what was happening.

Strangely (though not so much in the context of ambiguous loss), I felt his presence was greater when he wasn't there, than when he was. I had no siblings, so the family was myself and my mother. My uncle (her brother) lived nearby with his family, and while there was a closeness between us, I maintained a certain distance—a lifelong avoidance of attachment, fearful of another unspeakable loss.

I think this "loss," occurring when it did and during the time when it did (the 1950s), was particularly difficult for several reasons. Coming from a so-called "broken home," as it was referred to in that era, was an embarrassing, almost shameful thing. It set one apart from the other families in this lower middle-class, Jewish community and set me apart from most everyone else. Divorce was not as acceptable as it is today. While there were probably others like me, I knew of only one other person—another boy—whose parents were divorced. Not that he and I commiserated or shared stories. We couldn't as I did everything I could to keep this shameful thing a secret.

Another aspect was my age when this was happening. That 6- to 9- or 10-year-old period is one when you begin to step away from the security and familiarity of family and move into a world of peers, school, playgrounds, and, in my neighborhood, hanging around the candy store. It became difficult for me, given this secret I was carrying around, but also because a part of me felt I needed to stay at home, lest it fall apart even more than it already had.

This loss—or rather, my efforts to maintain this secret—was the central feature, the absolute organizing principle in my young life. From it came my shame, my guilt, the lens through which I viewed the world, understood families, relationships, one's place in the world—whether you "had it" or didn't have it. You were either a "normal person" or you were damaged. Once branded, labeled, classified, and cataloged, that is who you were; you could never really shake it off, or even if you were to, it followed you like a shadow always there, regardless of what you said, how you looked, or what you did, not unlike Hester Prynne's Scarlet Letter. Yet, if she chose to, she could have torn it off, moved away, and started over. Mine was more like the mark of Cain, except that nobody could see it. While I realize now that it was my choice to wear this invisible tattoo, there was no one to talk to about this and no one to show me how to let it go. It was not a question of making a choice—it simply was.

The experience of such a loss (or better, destabilization or disorientation) at such a time in my life—when I was beginning to make attempts to "separate" and develop connections with others outside of my small family—deeply affected how I related to others and structured my relationships and my activities. As my parents were always at odds (regardless of whether my father was "present" or not), I was always "in the middle" or at least felt that I was. Like many children in this situation, I frequently felt a sense of guilt and responsibility for how our life had turned out. Children often believe that somehow it is their fault that their parents are not able to live together or even to get along.

"If only I could be more like this, less like that, my parents would come back together, and we would be a normal family."

While I do not mean to pile on more and more of what led to my experience, I should mention that it was not only in my home that things were ignored. For whatever the reasons were—perhaps I feared being told that I just was not wanted—I never asked my father why he left, if he was ever coming back and, later, why was he visiting less and less, until he just disappeared (when I was about 13 years old). Though I was not aware of this at the time, the impact of no one acknowledging the situation made it more and more difficult and painful to go about the day-to-day business of growing up.

I was not really aware that I felt responsible for this situation. But in the end, I guess I did, since, after all, I did feel that something was wrong with me. Otherwise, why did I carry with me the feeling and belief that no one really wanted to be my friend and that if someone chose me for something, they were doing it so as not to hurt my feelings. This was a feeling I carried for many years, even though I knew it was a distorted, untrue picture of things.

In many ways, I was not really aware of my experience as "a loss." Perhaps if I could have understood it in such a way, even by naming it as a loss, I would have been able to understand it as something that had happened in my life, rather than as the core of my being and who I was. I carried the sense of simply not being "good enough" throughout most of my young adult and adult life. For example, I was very aware of my wish to have a mentor, a guide, a kind of father figure who would help me along. Even so, when I had the opportunity—in summer camp with my counselors, some teachers in high school and college, supervisors, trainers, and directors, who were older than I, at jobs, even therapists that I saw—I both hungered for them, but at the same time eluded their attempts to be helpful. The vulnerability, the fear of being disappointed or abandoned, and, perhaps more than anything, the belief that they were only being "good to me" out of some kind of sympathy always stood in the way.

My growing awareness of this dynamic enabled me to benefit from these mentoring relationships. I made a conscious effort not to dismiss them, but rather to engage and to try hard to be open to what they offered me. In some cases, it worked, in others, not so well, but over time, things became better for me. The core belief remained, however, and was probably strongest when my wife and I considered having children. I truly wondered if this was something I could manage. The good news is that I did manage, and I continue to do so.

So, an important note in thinking about separation and divorce and children: Remember the importance of being open and honest (to the degree that one can) with a child or adolescent, even if it might seem that what you are discussing is awful, heart breaking, or impossible to live with. This does not mean spilling an unfiltered story all over the place, but rather, that talking about things is better than leaving them shrouded in mystery.

Fun and Fall Affect the Future: Childhood Injury's Unseen Losses
CAITLIN McCARTHY

Caitlin McCarthy, PharmD, is a clinical assistant professor in the Department of Pharmacy Practice and Administration at the Ernest Mario School of Pharmacy, Rutgers, the State University of New Jersey. She maintains a clinical practice site in ambulatory care at Henry J. Austin Health Center, a Federally Qualified Health Center in Trenton, New Jersey, where she also serves as the director of pharmacy services.

I lost 2.5 vertebrae—part of thoracic vertebra 2 and all of 3 and 4—when I was 11 years old. Though this loss was only a few millimeters in length, it turned out to be one of the most impactful losses of my life.

One day after school in late spring, I, being the silly and adventurous child I was at the time, thought it might be fun to climb the tree in my front yard. This was at the start of a thunderstorm. While my younger brother rode his bike back and forth in the street, I attempted to pelt him with berries that grew from the tree branches. This soon turned into a full-on berry war. Looking back, imaging the scenario, I still think it would have been a lot of fun had it not been interrupted. However, in an unfortunate turn of events, I took one wrong step, slipped on a particularly slimy bit of sap, and fell down from the tree, landing directly on my back on a piece of root that stuck out from the ground.

The wind knocked out of me; it took a moment to collect myself. I looked up from the flat of my back to see my brother standing over me, staring down with an uncharacteristically shocked look. I had never seen him look that concerned. In a moment of panic, thinking something dreadful must have happened, I stood up and ran into the house to inspect myself. I played quite a few contact sports during my childhood, so I was no stranger to injury. After a quick once over, I deemed the situation to be minor and decided this was not something worth telling my parents. However, a day or so later, I did notice that my back seemed to hurt more than I had originally perceived. It was painful, yes, but it still seemed manageable. It took about a week for me to realize that this was a far more serious injury than I had originally assessed. I vividly remember being in my kitchen, looking up at my mom, and telling her that I thought something was wrong.

The next week, I saw my pediatrician, and three more weeks elapsed before I saw an orthopedist. One MRI later, I was referred to an orthopedic surgeon who happened to be the same doctor who performed surgery on my brother 1 year prior. From the MRI, it was clear that part of my spine had collapsed on itself, but it was not just due to the fall. After two more imaging studies, I finally had my diagnosis. I was told I had an eosinophilic granuloma. I sat next to my mom as the doctor described my disorder. I remember trying to memorize the name, sounding it out phonetically over and over again, E-OH-SIN-OH-FILL-ICK-GRAN-YOU-LOW-MA, while trying to keep up with what my doctor was saying. He said I needed surgery. He said that my tumor was in a difficult location. He said that some aspects of the surgery were experimental. He said they would need to collapse one of my lungs to do the surgery. He said there was a low chance of complication. He also said that I could die. He said that my vertebrae might grow back. He said that I could hope for my vertebrae to grow back by fifty percent. He said there was nothing we could do about the vertebrae themselves except to hope for recovery. It felt a bit surreal when the doctor faced me to ask what I thought. I recall thinking it strange for him to ask a child for permission to perform such a procedure. While I understand now that my parents also had to provide consent, it was both intimidating and empowering to be asked, and I agreed to the surgery.

An eosinophilic granuloma is a benign, solitary tumor of bone. It strikes me as a bit odd to call what I had benign. From a medical perspective, of course, it makes perfect sense. My tumor was not malignant; therefore, it was benign. However, it did not follow the standard definition. My illness was not kind, nor was it friendly. It certainly was not benign.

The summer during which most of the diagnostics occurred were something of a blur. Most of it was spent in doctors' offices, completing tests, and preparing for surgery. While this took away from my usual summer entertainment, I was so focused on finding out what was wrong that it did not bother me much. However, the events of that summer changed me. Prior to breaking my back, I was considered by most of my family and friends to be something of a wild child. I was filled with energy and constantly on the move. The pain I experienced and the thought of surgery tempered my disposition. I became more serious and more withdrawn. However, the most striking changes came after my surgery.

My surgery was performed about 1 week prior to the start of sixth grade. For months after, I felt delicate, a feeling with which I was not very comfortable. It was frustrating. I was no longer an invincible child. Recovery was a struggle. Collapsing my lung for the surgery took a toll. I spent each day exercising my lungs with an incentive spirometer, but it was nearly a year before I felt like my stamina returned. Worse than that was the pain. Going into the surgery, I had an expectation that my pain was primarily due to the tumor, and after its removal, I would feel better. Instead, my pain became excruciating. For the first few weeks, I could not sleep in my own bed. Instead, I would attempt to sleep upright in the reclining chair in my father's work room. The pain kept me awake. I would spend hours willing myself to sleep. Nighttime crying episodes became habitual. They would begin a few hours after my three siblings and parents had gone to bed. The first few nights, I cried uncontrollably, and each night, my mother came downstairs to comfort me until I was too tired to keep my eyes open. Later, I had more control, and I would wait as long as possible until I felt like I was starting to feel insane from the pain and exhaustion. In retrospect, I now know that part of the reason I was crying was due to loneliness. I did not want to have to suffer alone, and I craved the feelings of security that my mother offered. However, one night when I cried, she did not come. The next night, I moved myself back to my bedroom.

I shared a room with my sister and tried to stay quiet out of respect for her. I remember many sleepless nights lying in bed, turning to my side, staring at my wall and wondering "Why? Why did this happen to me? Why does it hurt so much? Why can't I get better? Why am I so sad? Why am I so angry? Why does no one seem to notice? Why can't I just die?" Years later, my sister explained to me that it was in that time that she first noticed my depression.

Going to school soon after my surgery also proved to be a challenge. To help ensure as much growth as possible, I needed to wear a back brace. While I waited for my permanent brace to be constructed, I had a temporary brace that was more like a corset and fit discretely under my shirt. I do not think many of my peers noticed. That changed when my teacher started roll call. When she came to my name, she asked me to confirm that I was the girl with the medical condition who needed the special desk. As someone trying to draw as little attention to myself as possible, the feeling of all eyes on me left me literally speechless. I started to shake my head back and forth. She pressed on, pointing to the large drafting desk that had been set alongside the wall, wedged between two bookcases, and looking away from my classmates. For fear of being ostracized, I lied and told my teacher that she was mistaken. When I did receive my permanent back brace, I realized why the drafting desk would be needed. The sheer size precluded me from using a traditional school desk. It was also clear to me that if I wore my back brace, there would be no way to hide it, and my teacher would realize I had lied. So, instead, I chose not to wear it to school. Somehow this never became much of an issue, something I still wonder about today.

I tried to wear my brace as much as possible when I was at home, though it was very painful and limiting. One weekend, I went to a close friend's house for a sleepover and brought it with me. After hours of being mocked mercilessly and trying to laugh off the insults, my friend fell asleep while I silently cried next to her. I became much more guarded in our friendship after that night. I realized that, for better or worse, she put a large emphasis on appearance. Having very little interest in appearance myself, and certainly no interest in using appearance as a tool to insult others, a wedge was placed between us. While we have grown somewhat distant over the years, we are still friends to this day, so much so that we were in each other's bridal parities. However, that night allowed me to see that though I did not care about my physical appearance, I was very much concerned about how others viewed me in general. I decided to never again wear my brace in front of nonfamily members.

One of my greatest embarrassments was the toll my injury took on my performance as an athlete. Though I played many sports as a child, one of my favorite activities was to play soccer. I started playing when I was 5, and as far back as I remember, I played year-round. My parents and I put a lot of effort into the game, with weekday practices, weekend games and tournaments, off-season private training sessions, and soccer camps.

The year prior to my accident, I tried out for and made a traveling soccer team. Though I loved the game, I never thought of myself as a particularly gifted player and making the team seemed to validate all of our efforts and filled me with immense pride. My injury served to be a huge setback to any progress I had made in that first year.

I attended every practice and put more effort into my training than I had ever before, but no amount of effort seemed to overcome the effect my injury had on my performance. As I recovered, I spent most of my first season back on the sidelines and offering support to my teammates.

My coach gave me the opportunity to play for about 5 to 10 minutes each game, but due to the competitiveness of the league, and my underwhelming performance, I never played in both halves. While unsatisfying, I was relatively at peace with this. I understood that I was having a negative effect on my team's overall performance, and typically, 5 minutes of running up and down the field was all that my back could handle. However, my father did not seem to share my sentiments. One game during half time, my father had an unpleasant conversation with my coach about how little I was playing. I had already played about 10 minutes during the first half, but my father said we would leave if I was not allowed to play in the second. My coach listened to my father and had me start the second half. Five minutes in, I was in excruciating pain, came to the sidelines, and asked the coach to substitute me out. At that moment, my father came to our side of the field and started screaming at the coach for taking me out of the game, not knowing that it was at my request. The coach attempted to defend himself, and when my father learned that I took myself out, he became furious with me, yelling at me in front of my team, the opposing team, and the spectators. To be in that incredible amount of pain, to want nothing else but to be able to perform as my former self, and then to have someone I trusted to support me unconditionally seem to have absolutely no regard for my well-being and humiliate me—it was heartbreaking. I knew my dad had a powerful competitive streak that showed itself that day, and I knew he was trying to advocate for me, but he added literal insult to injury, and although I knew he loved me, I felt devastated.

One thing that makes me grateful for this experience is how it nurtured my passion for music. I never received any formal counseling. Instead, music was my therapy. Breaking my back may have had a significant negative impact on my athleticism, but through that loss I was able to find something else that filled me with a sense of accomplishment. In a time when I felt delicate and helpless, there was still something I could control. I would lose myself for hours playing piano after school and on the weekends. One of my favorite days was when my grandparents took me to pick out a piano of my own, the same piano that sits in my living room today. It has been nearly two decades since my fall, and playing the piano continues to bring me a unique sense of joy and peace.

My back is still broken. Soon after graduating from college, I had a follow-up MRI when my pain was flaring. The good and bad news was there were no changes. My spine did not get any worse, but it also did not grow back the 50% that I had anticipated. I experience daily pain— unremittingly. As to be expected, it waxes and wanes with some weeks harder than others. I often wonder what it would be like to have just one day when I did not experience pain. I think about what I might be able to do if I did not have to live with chronic pain. More than anything, I think about how a life without pain might affect my mood, my energy. Would I feel more confident and have more patience? Or is being shy, insecure, and irritable innate to my personality? Would I feel less sorry for myself? Would I feel as depressed or anxious? I have many unanswered questions, the most lingering of which is why do I feel so ashamed to expose my vulnerabilities? People who know me do not think of me as shy, insecure, or depressed as I work each day to project the persona I want to be. I like to think of myself as being strong. "Tough as nails" is how my high school cross-country coach described me once after hearing about my condition, and I like to think I live up to that description.

Matty's Death and Emmy's Life With Li-Fraumeni Syndrome
ALLISON WERNER-LIN AND CATHERINE WILSNACK

Allison Werner-Lin, PhD, LCSW, is associate professor in the School of Social Policy and Practice at the University of Pennsylvania and a licensed clinical social worker in private practice specializing in bereavement and oncology. She serves as senior adviser to the Clinical Genetics Branch of the

National Cancer Institute, where she oversees psychosocial research on hereditary cancer predisposition syndromes.

Catherine Wilsnack, MSW, LMSW, is a recent graduate of The School of Social Policy and Practice at the University of Pennsylvania and a licensed social worker with specializations in aging and research. She is a predoctoral fellow at the Clinical Genetics Branch of the National Cancer Institute working families affected by Li-Fraumeni syndrome (LFS) and inherited bone marrow failure syndromes.

Li-Fraumeni syndrome (LFS) is a rare cancer predisposition disorder caused by mutations in the *TP53* gene. The mutation is inherited in an autosomal dominant fashion, meaning each child of a carrier parent has a 50% chance of inheriting the variant. LFS is characterized by nearly 100% lifetime penetrance, with syndrome-related cancers occurring from childhood through older adulthood. Multiple, independent, primary malignant tumors often occur in the same individual, with the highest risks for soft-tissue, bone, breast, brain, and adrenal cancers, as well as acute leukemia (https://rarediseases.info.nih.gov/diseases/6902/li-fraumeni-syndrome). Recommendations for *early detection* for all genders are rigorous: frequent regular physical examinations, whole-body and brain MRI, abdominal and pelvic ultrasound, and breast cancer screening starting approximately age 20. Comprehensive screening protocols do result in earlier diagnosis, but the impact of regular screening on survival has not been quantified. Recommendations for *prevention* include bilateral risk-reducing mastectomy for women. Families often experience multiple concurrent diagnoses, both within and across generations, leading to high cancer burden and substantial physical and emotional distress among family members (lfsassociation.org).

The Case of Emmy

Emmy is a bright, curious, 8-year-old with LFS. When she was a toddler, her older brother, Matty, experienced severe and debilitating headaches, blurry vision, and disruption to his balance. Rebecca, their mother, "had that parental instinct that something was wrong." A visit to the pediatrician escalated rapidly to consultation with the ED, discovery of a brain mass, and surgery to excise a medulloblastoma on his brain stem. The nearest comprehensive cancer center equipped for surgical and chemotherapeutic treatment was a 4-hour drive from their home. For the following 6 months, Emmy lived primarily with her father, Fred, at the family's home, while Matty and Rebecca stayed near the hospital to enable his care. Rebecca described "going into Emmy withdrawal," so Rebecca and Fred would swap parenting roles 1 week per month. Rebecca was "torn, so much. But you get into the mode where you do what you have to do."

After Matty's surgery, Fred contacted a distant cousin to learn more about the family's medical history. This cousin was the sole surviving member of his branch of the family tree; the rest had died of various rare cancers. Fred suspected a genetic component and made an appointment with a genetic counselor at the facility where Matty was receiving treatment. The genetic counselor took a multigenerational family history and suggested genetic testing was indicated, but Fred and Rebecca were too overwhelmed with Matty's treatment to proceed. Instead, they had Matty tested 6 months after he finished treatment and confirmed that Fred and Matty both carried a *TP53* mutation linked to LFS. After consulting with the oncology social worker, Rebecca and Fred "waited to have Emmy tested" because they "honestly just couldn't handle the information."

Matty's paternal grandmother, also *TP53* mutation positive, was diagnosed with cancer just after Matty. This timing impacted how Rebecca and Fred shared Matty's LFS diagnosis with her, "because she felt guilty, and she was starting her treatment, and not in a really good emotional state. So, we waited because you can only take so many blows." Eventually, Matty's optimism inspired his grandmother to find a purpose in her own struggle. She would say, "If my grandson can go through chemo and radiation, then I can, too." Their concurrent treatments, however, left Fred emotionally and physically exhausted. With his mother and son in simultaneous cancer treatment for cancers related to a syndrome with which he was also diagnosed, Fred experienced "every little ache and pain, first thing that goes across my mind, 'Could this be my first [cancer]?'"

Over the next 14 months, Matty's doctors identified and excised two tumors during regular follow-up surveillance. To maintain as normal a life as possible for Emmy during this time, Rebecca and Fred "isolated her from some of the worst. She didn't have to see all of the treatments that he had." While their parents were at the hospital for Matty's surgeries, Emmy often stayed with an older neighbor who gave her vague information about what was happening with Matty's care or when her family might return. This left Emmy confused about what was happening to Matty. She missed playing and laughing with her big brother.

End of Life

At a regular surveillance visit, which the family entered "expecting it to be another regular 3-month checkup," physicians discovered Matty had a glioblastoma that was ultimately terminal. Rebecca and Fred were not "ready to just give up" and enlisted Matty in a clinical trial on the east coast that gained him "8 months of quality . . . ; [he] was walking again, back to school full time, getting straight A's, the tumor was shrinking." However, once the tumor grew into his brain stem, "he lost his vision, his hearing, he couldn't swallow anymore, and then he was done."

Matty entered hospice. The hospice social worker, Annie, discussed Matty's end-of-life care decisions with Rebecca and Fred. They struggled to share Matty's terminal prognosis with him and with Emmy because they "didn't want him to lose hope." Using a psychoeducational approach, Annie provided a safe holding environment for Rebecca and Fred to anticipate Matty's death, for Fred to consider his guilt, and to invite discussion with Matty about his wishes. They also needed to discuss the present and future needs of the family's hidden patient, Emmy. Matty died at the age of 13, when Emmy was 10. At the time, Emmy did not understand how Matty could "give up" on what the family referred to as the "cancer fight," and leave her. Through art and play-based therapy, Emmy asked questions about Matty's death and learned more about his end-of-life experience.

Testing Emmy

A year later, Rebecca and Fred decided to pursue *TP53* testing for Emmy and were devastated to learn she carried the same mutation. Rebecca referred to Emmy's diagnosis as belonging to "part of the mutant branch" of the family. "Having to tell Emmy was pretty tough." Emmy started to ask more questions about Matty's death when she began regular screening at age 11, "So that was very real to her when she realized she had to start that process."

Emmy's LFS diagnosis complicated her grief over Matty's death. She had trouble adjusting to her new role as an only child. The family felt no reprieve from the grief associated with Matty's initial cancer diagnosis, remission, or death; "knowing that it [cancer] could happen to Emmy at any time, weighed us down." Rebecca sought counseling for Emmy and for herself, "the only nonmutant in the family." Fred and Rebecca considered every change in Emmy as a signal of cancer. "She had a bout of high fever last year, and we had to have her blood checked every day for five cause her white cells were crazy. All I could think about was leukemia."

Rebecca also took comfort in phenotypic similarities between Fred and Emmy, saying Fred has "a really strong immune system. He's never sick. And Emmy's the same way, which gives me hope that she'll be where he is today, with no cancer at 49."

Though Emmy initially did not want to talk in a group setting, Rebecca persisted in seeking out resources to support Emmy, because "whenever we would start talking about Matty, she would leave the room." Rebecca found a social worker, and the family started to see her regularly in various configurations to grieve Matty's death, learn to live with Fred and Emmy's risk, address

Rebecca's fear of burying them all, and give the family language to talk about their history. After several months, Emmy is cancer free and reconnecting with her memories of Matty. Rebecca reported to the social worker, "Now she talks about him, she's got pictures of the two of them up in her bedroom, and I think she's handling it really well."

Case Analysis

Working with families impacted by inherited cancer predisposition syndromes requires mental health professionals to attend to multiple forms of grief and uncertainty. The combination of profound grief regarding Matty's death and cancer risk for Emmy and Fred is tied together. Families live in a persistent state of loss and change when living with an inherited cancer predisposition syndrome, which requires ongoing, multimodal, and multidisciplinary approaches to bereavement.

Present Losses

Emmy and her parents faced multiple losses before, during, and after Matty's death with limited respite. Initially, Emmy lost her brother and mother for the 6 months of Matty's treatment. This loss remained ambiguous (Boss, 2006), as Matty and Rebecca continued to play a significant role in shaping family life yet were often absent from the home for prolonged periods of treatment and surveillance. The diagnosis of Fred's mother further destabilized the family. Others were bodily losses, such as when Matty regained, relished, and then lost physical function in the months leading up to his death. Fred began to experience his body differently after genetic testing as cancer worry grew. Emmy also lost control over her body as she submitted to regular screening protocols that increased family anxiety and triggered memories of Matty's struggle.

Practice Recommendation

This family would benefit from ongoing medical family therapy (McDaniel et al., 2014) due to the chronic and ambiguous nature of Emmy and Fred's disease risk, the demands of early detection protocols, and the need to balance resources between LFS and activities of daily life. Meaning-making and memory work will help the family adjust to their new configuration, including Emmy's new role as an only child, while remaining connected to Matty's memory. Such work may be balanced with granting permission to enjoy cancer-free, restorative time together, particularly when it includes opportunities to enjoy, rather than fear, their bodies.

Losses Yet to Come

Much of Rebecca and Fred's distress concerned losses they continued to anticipate. Because inherited cancer risk is unpredictable, families are often biased, affecting their ability to interpret risk information. Emmy may anticipate following the pathway of her deceased brother or her healthy father, both carriers of the familial mutation. Like Rebecca and Fred, parents are often responsible for disclosing and discussing cancer risk with children and setting expectations for how the family will discuss loss, risk, and survivorship. These conversations are often challenging due to feelings of guilt at having "passed on" the mutation, yet prompt disclosure generally strengthens trust and cohesion between parents and children.

General Practice Implications

We recommend that parents structure ongoing conversations tailored to the child's developmental, cognitive, emotional, and behavioral abilities to support comprehension, and urge parents to revisit these conversations as children mature. Best practices show that experienced genetic counselors (www.nsgc.org/findageneticcounselor) and mental health providers can guide parents through these conversations (Werner-Lin et al., 2018).

Supporting Emmy

Emmy sustained different losses than her parents, primarily the loss of an only sibling and the promise of a healthy future. After the death of a sibling, children often fear their own death, experience somatic complaints as bids for attention or as a mechanism to communicate with caregivers, and may lose their sense of security in the world. For Emmy, these feelings are intensified due to her shared LFS diagnosis. Since she is younger than Matty, her grief and cancer worry are likely to intensify as she reaches the age Matty was diagnosed and died. A holistic plan of support for Emmy will entail cognitive behavioral interventions to balance magical thinking with survivor guilt. Psychoeducational interventions may help Fred and Rebecca recognize the idiosyncratic ways children like Emmy grieve so they can interpret and respond to her needs. Integrating Rebecca and Fred, who are also grieving, into Emmy's treatment can facilitate open communication about feelings, information, and support needs. Providers must learn about the family's presenting syndrome and associated psychosocial issues, including prevention, treatment, testing, and reproductive options, to help guide their care and to facilitate informed decision-making.

SUMMARY

Children in elementary school change rapidly. Much of their psychosocial growth relates to moving from the family environment to the bigger world as they enter school. Normal maturational (and developmental) losses occur as a result of being judged by teachers and peers instead of being unconditionally loved (ideally) in one's home. This means that children experience gains as they navigate these challenges and develop a sense of self-efficacy or may experience a sense of failure if they are unable to negotiate them. These judgments by teachers and peers can be very challenging when a child has a disability or other difference that creates a separation from the peer group. Even young children who move often leave much behind, and for international immigrants, these losses are intensified as they encounter different norms and language. Often they are leaned on by parents instead of the other way around. Schools need to have social workers, school nurses, and trained teachers to give children the support they need.

When children in this age group lose a parent, sibling, pet, or other significant relationship, they have varied abilities to cope. During kindergarten and first grade, they may not have enough verbal facility to process feelings of loss and may withdraw or become hostile or aggressive if the loss is more than they can process. As they grow, they may be less willing to overtly express emotion but have more ability to verbally process the loss and cope by holding on to important memories and linking objects.

Support groups seem particularly helpful for school-aged children. Although these children increase their social connections, they seldom have networks that include others who have experienced the same loss they have unless they are welcomed into such a group. The opportunity to share experiences helps children feel less isolated and ostracized. Support groups also provide an opportunity for validation and shared problem-solving with peers and offer professional support to help clarify misconceptions and draw out supportive opportunities. Likewise, bereaved parents find the support of other bereaved parents critical to coping.

DISCUSSION QUESTIONS

1. If you were working in an elementary school like Sandy Hook, where a shooter came into the school and killed several students as well as himself, how would you guide the school to handle the first 24 to 48 hours? What guidance would you have for the aftermath once students begin to return to the school?
2. How might you work with children who have recently moved to your school who come from non–English-speaking countries and translate for their parents at school meetings?
3. How could you explain to a school administrator why you believe some students' loss and trauma histories impair their academic work?

KEY REFERENCES

Only key references appear in the print edition. The full reference list appears in the digital product found on http://connect.springerpub.com/content/book/978-0-8261-4964-0/chapter/ch04

Berg, L., Rostila, M., & Hjern, A. (2016). Parental death during childhood and depression in young adults: A national cohort study. *Journal of Child Psychology and Psychiatry, 57*, 1092–1098. https://doi .org/10.1111/jcpp.12560

Boullier, M., & Blair, M. (2018). Adverse childhood experiences. *Paediatrics and Child Health, 28*(3), 132–137. https://doi.org/10.1016/j.paed.2017.12.008

Boyd Webb, N., Heath, M., & Hudnall, G. (2011). Play therapy for bereaved children: Adapting strategies to community, school, and home settings. *School Psychology International, 32*(2), 132–143. https:// doi.org/10.1177/0143034311400832

Christ, G. H., & Christ, A. E. (2006). Current approaches to helping children cope with a parent's terminal illness. *CA: A Cancer Journal for Clinicians, 56*(4), 197–212. https://doi.org/10.3322/canjclin.56.4.197

Goldman, L. (2017). Helping bereaved children in the schools. In R. G. Stevenson & G. R. Cox (Eds.), *Children, adolescents and death: Questions and answers* (pp. 153–186). Routledge.

Harvard University Center on the Developing Child. (2019). *Three principles to improve outcomes for children and families.* https://developingchild.harvard.edu/resources/three-early-childhood-develop ment-principles-improve-child-family-outcomes/

Lichtenthal, W. G., Neimeyer, R. A., Currier, J. M., Roberts, K., & Jordan, N. (2013). Cause of death and the quest for meaning after the loss of a child. *Death Studies, 37*(4), 311–342. https://doi.org/10.1080/ 07481187.2012.673533

Pham, S., Porta, G., Biemesser, C., Walker Payne, M., Iyengar, S., Melhem, N., & Brent, D. A. (2018). The burden of bereavement: Early-onset depression and impairment in youths bereaved by sudden parental death in a 7-year prospective study. *American Journal of Psychiatry, 175*(9), 887–896. https:// ajp.psychiatryonline.org/doi/pdf/10.1176/appi.ajp.2018.17070792

Rostila, M., Berg, L., Saarela, J., Kawachi, I., & Hjern, A. (2017). Experience of sibling death in childhood and risk of death in adulthood: A national cohort study from Sweden. *American Journal of Epidemiology, 185*(12), 1247–1254. https://doi.org/10.1093/aje/kww126

Sheftall, A. H., Asti, L., Horowitz, L. M., Felts, A., Fontanella, C. A., Campo, J., & Bridge, J. A. (2016). Suicide in elementary school-aged children and early adolescents. *Pediatrics, 138*(4), e20160436. https://doi. org/10.1542/peds.2016-0436

5

Grief and Loss in Tweens and Teens

INTRODUCTION

Tweens and teens are neither overgrown children nor immature adults: Their brains are distinctly different from both, making them more sensitive to emotional and social factors. This chapter synthesizes information about how these neurobiological changes affect adolescents' experiences of loss. Adolescence creates the potential for double jeopardy—being both more vulnerable and less willing to indicate a need for help—when faced with grief and loss. This loss can be from a death, a changed relationship, or an experience of social marginalization. The critical task of identity development begins, and romantic and other social relationships with peers become the focus. Gender and sexuality orientations become clearer and may lead to marginalization. Adverse childhood experiences (ACEs), socioeconomic influences, schooling, and anxiety all affect teens' ability to cope with losses. Interventions including Learn to BREATHE and Grief-Help are described as helpful for adolescent grief as they incorporate peers and creative outlets.

OBJECTIVES

After studying this chapter, the reader will be able to:
- Describe the psychosocial, neurobiological, and spiritual development of tweens and teens, particularly the way teens tend to be impulsive, creative, polarizing, and social.
- Describe the facets of risk and resilience that affect tweens and teens.
- Identify why tweens and teens are at "double jeopardy" in their grief.
- Discuss the pros and cons of why group support for bereaved tweens and teens is most effective yet also challenging.

VIGNETTE

Andrea was not sure where to turn for help. She knew people thought of her as "so together," but she felt her life was falling apart. She was focused on her schoolwork, aiming to earn a scholarship to go to a good university, where she could pursue her dream of becoming a physician. She was involved in extracurricular activities and church activities, she volunteered, she babysat, and she had a large group of friends. People did not approve of her boyfriend, however. Greg had recently dropped out of high school to work on cars. Despite that, she knew she loved him, and she was sure they would marry someday. Based on that commitment, Andrea agreed to make love even though she was sure it was not a good idea. Now, she had just learned she was pregnant, and at 15, with two more years of high school to go, this did not fit with her plans at all. Greg was delighted and thought they should have the baby and get married as soon as they were old enough. Andrea had already gone to planned parenthood (PP) and heard her many options for adoption, having the baby, or ending the pregnancy. She was truly torn but hesitant about telling her parents or friends because she did not want them to be disapproving of her for the pregnancy or for her choice, whatever it might be. She trusted her Advanced Placement English teacher and disclosed everything to her, along with the options the PP counselor provided. She loved babies and hoped to have at least two children in her future. Her teacher let her talk about all the pros and cons of each option, just as she had done at PP. The more she talked, the more she realized she could not imagine relinquishing a baby for adoption, nor could she see how to go to college and medical school with a baby in tow. Although heartbroken, she ended the pregnancy early, needing only some pills. It seemed so odd to her that just taking some pills could leave her so sad. Although she felt so alone, she would not take the risk that others would learn what she had done and think less of her. She told Greg she miscarried and kept her secret well past her graduation from high school.

DEVELOPMENTAL TASKS: IDENTITY DEVELOPMENT VERSUS IDENTITY DIFFUSION

Like many life phases, the age range of adolescence is variably defined. Some now consider adolescence to start around age 10 and linger until 25 (Ledford, 2018). Generally, ages 10 to 13 are called the "tween" years or early adolescence. They comprise the years between the concrete operations, cognitive style, and straightforward relationships of childhood and the abstract thinking, idealism, and judgments of a true teen between ages 14 and 18. In this chapter, we use these age distinctions between tweens and teens, employing youth or adolescent to refer to both age groups together. Adolescence is a time of brain changes and consequent changes in hypothetical reasoning and abstraction abilities, growing skills for impulse control (though still not totally developed for most), and a clearer sense of self. By the latter part of the teen years, individuals begin to consolidate their identity and often start to build intense relationships with romantic partners, as well as with close friends. Adolescents take on more adult responsibilities as they complete schoolwork with little parental assistance, take jobs, learn to drive, and even begin to vote. This adolescent period develops into what is called "emerging adulthood," now defined as ages 18 to 25 or 30 (Arnett & Mitra, 2018).

Biological Development

Adolescent brains differ from those of children and adults, and these differences make them more sensitive to rewards and to social interactions while also priming them to take risks and explore new environments (National Academies of Sciences, Engineering, and Medicine [NASEM], 2019). The heightened neuroplasticity of the adolescent brain allows for innovation and creativity unachievable before or after this life phase, as cognitive capacity diminishes as brains are pruned starting in late adolescence and continuing into adulthood (Dougherty & Clarke, 2018). Kleibeuker et al. (2016) trace adolescent creativity and innovation to changes in teen brains that promote divergent and insightful thinking, while still imbued with the multiple neuronal connections of childhood. Neuroscientists report that the adolescent brain becomes more efficient and focused as the proliferation of gray matter in the brain formed during childhood begins to be pruned (thinning of extra neurons; Johnson & Stevens, 2018).

Jokes about "crazy" teenagers are long standing, but newer neurobiological understandings are changing the way we view this life stage. Dobbs (2011) writes, "Troublesome traits like idiocy and haste don't really characterize adolescence. They're just what we notice most because they annoy us or put our children in danger" (p. 48). He ties adolescent risk-taking to the evolutionary need to search for new opportunities and to be open to taking risks to grow. Similarly, Siegel (2013) also views adolescence as an important life stage that promotes creativity, growth, and innovation. He coins the acronym of "Adult-ESSENCE" or "Adol-ESSENCE" to stand for Emotional Spark, Social Engagement, Novelty, and Creative Explorations (p. 12) to describe adolescent core issues. In *Brainstorm* (Siegel, 2013), changing brain structures (particularly, the development and integration of the prefrontal cortex) are tied to the human needs for adventure and connection. Siegel views adolescence as a time when the rigid adherence to rules and safety alternates with impulsivity and risk-taking.

Siegel suggests that adolescence is when the brain integrates. Left and right hemispheres of the brain communicate better, and the cortex develops more neuronal connections with middle structures (corpus callosum, amygdala) of the brain. Integration yields more accurate judgments and allows adolescent and adult thinkers to develop a more socially competent brain with more capacity for balanced judgment (Siegel, 2013). Risk-taking in adolescence contributes to higher rates of accidental death but is also associated with prosocial behavior because teens avoid social risks that alienate them from their peer group (Smith, 2018). Teens begin to weigh their risks more realistically as the brain pruning continues.

Changes in the adolescent brain seem to set the stage for "hardwiring" brain pathways. Neuroscience demonstrates that engagement in learning a language or even a video game lays down neuronal "traces" that enable skills. The "use it or lose it" aphorism is apt as frequently used skills and thinking patterns become "hardwired" (neuronal connections are developed) while unused skills and thinking patterns are lost. This raises concerns about substance use during adolescence as substances such as alcohol, nicotine, and cannabis seem able to change neural structures, including the adolescent's most recently developed frontal lobe, which is responsible for executive functions (Silveri et al., 2016). Although many teens experiment with substance use and physical risks, a common part of the risk-taking associated with adolescence, most do not take life-threatening risks (Smith, 2018). The importance of sleep is also becoming clearer as poor sleep is associated with higher risk-taking behavior in adolescence (Johnson & Stevens, 2018). The combination of poor sleep and substance use in adolescence is associated with a higher risk of developing schizophrenia, particularly when brain pruning differs from the norm (either too fast or too slow; Johnson & Stevens, 2018).

The most obvious biological changes of adolescence have to do with puberty and its accompanying body changes, usually leading to the secondary sex characteristic development that leaves boys looking like men and girls looking like women. Sexual and reproductive functions, such as nocturnal emissions (male) and menses (female), develop even if cultural experience has provided little preparation for full adulthood and reproductive function. Many teens both impatiently wait for and later are embarrassed by these dramatic bodily changes. There is growing evidence that the age of physical maturation is dropping in Westernized countries (Ledford, 2018). Lower levels of exercise and activity, higher body mass index, and obesity have all been implicated in lowering the age of puberty and of menarche (first menses or period) (Ledford, 2018). For gender-nonconforming youth, these changes can be traumatic, bringing them to confront how their gender identity differs from the bodily development taking place (Healy, 2016). These adolescents require special support as they may turn to food restriction to stop unwanted menses or to weight gain to hide bodily changes; they may use hormones such as testosterone or estrogen, either of which can be harmful when not prescribed appropriately and monitored.

The many dramatic biological changes of adolescence create maturational losses because change always involves the loss of the past and present for the new future. These changes may inspire a sense of childhood freedoms lost. For those who mature early, the "out-of-sync" sense may also be experienced as a loss of social conformity, albeit possibly compensated for by the cachet of feeling adult. Across the board, losses are intensely experienced because of the highly attuned and sensitized adolescent brain, which amplifies emotion (Siegel, 2013).

Psychosocial Development

Piaget (1954) identified the hallmark of adolescence as the ability to engage in abstract thinking; ideas themselves can be manipulated, and the individual is no longer reliant on seeing, hearing, or touching objects to consider their interrelationships. Erikson (1959/1980) viewed the psychological task of adolescence to be the development of a coherent identity. Along with a growing ability to see oneself through the eyes of others and to consider how and why one adopts or rejects certain social roles, he emphasized the consolidation of ego identity and integration of a sense of sameness, continuity, and congruency within one's self-concept. According to Erikson, many adolescents regard differences as faults. Although they view themselves as unique and want to differentiate themselves from their family of origin, they also want to fit in with their peers. He observed that a critical feature of adolescence is the tendency to view behavior as identity. For instance, instead of saying that one did not get good grades one semester, adolescents tend to invoke character deficits—"I'm a moron"—that they believe fundamentally define them, rather than viewing poor grades as just having a bad semester. Seligman et al. (1995) showed that attribution of situations to permanent, pervasive, and persistent character traits rather than to temporary circumstances tends to foster a pessimistic attributional style that places adolescents at risk for depression and anxiety.

This tendency to attribute behavior to inherent personal traits may be most harmful to teens who engage in risky behavior and may subsequently be labeled with terms, such as *delinquent*, *no-good*, and *loser*. Such labels can become self-fulfilling prophecies. Teens take in the identity message that they are durably "bad." Erikson cautioned: "[I]f diagnosed and treated correctly, seemingly psychotic and criminal incidents do not in adolescence have the same fatal significance which they have at other ages" (1959/1980, p. 97). Thus, great harm likely results from policies that charge lawbreaking teens as adults and process them in the adult justice system.

Identity development and adaptation plays a significant role in processing loss. Sometimes the losses relate directly to identity: For example, a teen who loses a mother may identify herself as a motherless daughter, with the implication that she has no identity other than as someone bereft. Adolescents who experience multiple losses may come to view themselves as "angels of death," as one tween did, not able to view the confluence of loss as outside of his control. Viewing loss as a fundamental core of identity is hazardous to a coherent and healthy identity.

Adolescence is bound up in peer relationships. As tweens become more aware of the world outside their family, peers gain more influence. Trying on new social roles is as natural as the new body individuals develop during this time. The confluence of new body, new roles, and new friends can be confusing to adolescents as they try to adopt more adult behaviors that may invite negative sanctions (particularly in areas of sexuality and substance use). Yet, if they maintain more child-like roles of dependency, they are urged to "grow up already." Among their peers, they can gain support as they navigate these mixed messages and "try on" potential adult identities. Typically, adolescents are understood to have successfully navigated adolescence once they are capable of committing to relationships and occupational goals (and ideally beginning to work in paid employment).

Gender differences become both more defined (overtly expressed in dress and behavior) and more blurred (blending gender roles) as individuals encounter expectations for the culture-consistent socialization of gender. Gender expression is influenced by peer groups who expose adolescents to varied ways of expressing themselves, often in deliberately androgynous ways. As gender fluidity becomes more common across the globe and the adolescent task of identity formation intersects with broader questions of gender identity and the expression of sexuality, there likely will be greater latitude in both gender identity and sexual orientation in the coming years (Fontanella et al., 2014).

Self-acceptance of one's identity may be especially challenging when teens stray from norms and adopt socially devalued roles. The lack of support for teens who are gay, lesbian, bisexual, transgender, queer, asexual, or otherwise gender nonconforming can be distressing and isolating at a time when they need support for identity consolidation (LaSala, 2015). Other losses occur frequently (e.g., loss of a love relationship, death of a pet, loss of an occupational dream, or other goals). Following a death, adolescents have impaired ability to proceed with "normal" development amid the inherent stresses of loss. Additionally, for adolescents who are themselves seriously ill or dying, pursuing the developmental urge toward independence comes at the tremendous price of forgoing support when their coping capacities are severely challenged.

Spiritual Development

Adolescence has long been viewed as a time of enhanced spiritual inquiry (Cobb et al., 2015). Although only recently examined developmentally (Sink & Bultsma, 2014), the adolescent brain development that enables more abstract thinking seems to enable consideration of spiritual and religious questions as well. Adolescents begin to develop their own perspective rather than adopt without question the training of the adults around them. Dimensions most commonly considered as part of spirituality and religious practice are "existential wellbeing, present-centeredness (mindfulness), life purpose and satisfaction, meaning-making, and spiritual connectedness" (Sink & Bultsma, 2014, p. 152). Higher scores on measures of these constructs are associated with less risk-taking and higher reported levels of general well-being. As a result, some theorize that spirituality can be a protective factor in preventing substance use among teens (Kim-Spoon et al., 2014). Debnam et al. (2016) found increased substance use among those with lower reported levels of spiritual beliefs in a parochial school sample, but they did not find evidence that spiritual beliefs moderated stress in a way that reduced substance use when sample members reported stress (and substance use as a result). Kim-Spoon et al. did find that religiosity (connection to specific religious beliefs and practices, not vague spirituality) seemed protective in lowering substance use by teens exposed to harsh parenting: Those with more self-reported religiosity reported substance use less than those reporting lower religiosity (2014). The evidence is mixed about how protective spirituality or religious beliefs are among adolescents who embrace such beliefs.

Despite high levels of change in identity in adolescence generally, Good et al. (2011) found little change in spirituality/religiosity from grade 11 to grade 12 in a Canadian sample of adolescents. (They acknowledge that this may relate to the short time frame of the study.) Specifically, the only statistically significant change concerned teens who changed from being highly institutionally and personally identified with religious practice (17% of their sample in grade 11) to being more personally (and less institutionally) involved by grade 12 (8%). The clusters of disconnected wonderers and aspiritual/areligious teens were the most stable over time. Cabrera and Stevenson (2017) synthesize research and practice wisdom to suggest that spirituality and religion are more important for urban minority youth because they tend to have an external locus of control that leaves them feeling more vulnerable. Thus, they argue that belief in God's control allows teens to feel that "all is well" (p. 205). It must be said that faith communities have been a source of connection and cultural continuity for many immigrant groups and African Americans historically, so this social solidarity may contribute to the sense of well-being as well.

SPECIAL CONSIDERATIONS IN RISK AND RESILIENCE

Adolescence is full of contradictions and strongly felt emotions. The same development that allows adolescents to innovate and think creatively (Dougherty & Clarke, 2018) also leaves them feeling emotions more intensely and longing for adventure (Siegel, 2013). The still-developing prefrontal cortex and executive functioning mean that their judgments about risk are often less attuned to adult-like assessment of risk. Accidental injury is the leading cause of death among 10- to 24-year-olds (Centers for Disease Control and Prevention [CDC], 2017), closely followed by suicide. In addition, over 60% of U.S. youth have experienced at least one adverse childhood event, with over a third experiencing physical assault (most often at the hands of a sibling) and over 14% of girls (ages 14–17) having experienced a sexual assault during their lifetime (Finkelhor et al., 2015). These levels of risk are not distributed equally; communities of color and those living in poverty have higher risks of ACEs (Bruner, 2017).

Adolescents exhibit resilience as well. Notably, education seems to be protective; people who take middle- to higher-level coursework in their sophomore year of high school exhibit better health in mid-adulthood (Carroll et al., 2017), although Brody et al. (2016) suggest this resilience is only "skin deep" (p. e1) as they found that Black youth who were strivers (seeking to achieve academically) in high school achieved more both scholastically and economically but also had a higher likelihood of developing type 2 diabetes in adulthood. Others suggest that resilience can be promoted by helping tweens and teens develop "roots and wings," through development of competence, confidence, connection, character, and contribution to community (Ginsburg et al., 2011). Another promising finding is that although negative self-schemas are more common in early adolescence, positive self-schemas tend to remain stable across adolescence (or at least over the 7-year study period; McArthur et al., 2019), indicating that investment in helping children and tweens develop positive self-concepts will help them through the more tumultuous years to come. See Figure 5.1 for influences on development over the lifespan.

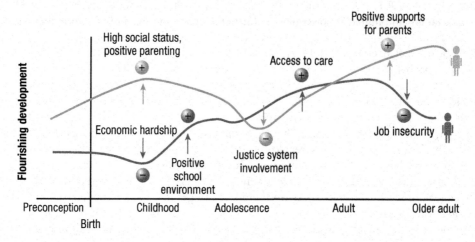

FIGURE 5.1 Societal and Other Forces Affecting Human Development Across the Lifespan. This graph illustrates the forces acting to promote or reduce well-being across the lifespan. We thank the National Academies Press and Halfon et al. (2014) for allowing to use.

Source: Reproduced with permission from Halfon, N., Larson, K., Lu, M., Tullis, E., & Russ, S. (2014). Lifecourse health development: Past, present and future. *Maternal and Child Health Journal, 18,* 344–365. https://doi.org/10.1007/s10995-013-1346-2; National Academies of Sciences, Engineering, and Medicine. (2019). *The promise of adolescence: Realizing opportunity for all youth* (p. 81). The National Academies Press. https://doi.org/10.17226/25388

LOSSES EXPERIENCED BY THE ADOLESCENT

Death Losses

Grace Christ and her colleagues have devoted their careers to exploring the impact of loss on children and adolescents. In a review article, they assert that early adolescents or tweens are "characterized by ambivalent expressions of dependence and independence and sometimes by angry and perplexing expressions of selfish egocentrism" (Christ et al., 2002, p. 1271). By mid-adolescence, which Christ et al. define as 15 to 17 years old, individuals have an ability to assess situational demands more accurately and have developed more empathic abilities. They have greater ability to understand the nature of death, though they tend to maintain earlier developmental characteristics of asynchronous expressions of grief (cycling in and out in a dual process that only gradually becomes more consistent with adult tendencies to maintain longer periods of sadness and anhedonia). Christ (2000) recommends that tweens and teens be told about the nature of a parent's illness even when that disclosure seems to promote anger and withdrawal.

Balk (2011) reviewed reactions to loss in similar age ranges and contends that early adolescents (10–14) tend to be more frightened and overwhelmed by loss, whereas middle adolescents (15–17) tend toward anger and attempt to camouflage their grief. He asserts that older adolescents (18–22) tend to feel either accepted and loved or rejected, with a strong focus on relationships during their mourning. Balk draws on Fleming and Adolph's classic theory (1986) that bereaved adolescents must resolve five core issues: predictability of events, mastery/control, belonging, fairness/social justice, and self-image. In a review of the literature, these and other studies were synthesized, and the conclusion that adolescents are particularly vulnerable grievers was supported. The tendency of youth to withdraw and isolate themselves was tied to

> belief that talking about death is distressing and unacceptable to friends, fear of being considered boring, desire to appear normal, belief in the inability of other people to enter into their feelings because of the exclusivity of their experience, and desire of not being a burden for the surviving parent. Public display of suffering is also perceived as a failure and an inability to maintain their composure. (Punzanio et al., 2014, p. 368)

Adolescents may inhibit their emotional expression because of others' seeming need for support or because they want to present as "adult" (something that they may assume includes little emotional expression). In this sense, teens are said to experience "double jeopardy" (Oltjenbruns, 1996). They often feel compelled to hide their emotional reactions to loss, yet they are deprived of support for processing their loss because they refrain from letting others know about their thoughts and feelings. Lytje (2017) draws upon focus groups with bereaved teens to derive three dynamics: "loss of power over one's own life, feeling different from classmates, and trying to function in school while struck by grief" (p. 292). He suggests a model of loss navigation in adolescence grounded in others' work, integrated with his findings. The model focuses on the adolescent's experiences of dilemmas as they fear being different from their peers, wish to project being in control, and reflect on being in their grief (see Figure 5.2). Lytje views each of these "being" states as a factor that is in tension with the others in such a way that adolescents need to resolve each factor while also experiencing each of the three factors in contradiction or tension with one another. This requires them to temporarily resolve the tension by privileging one "being" factor over another (e.g., electing to be in one's grief even if fearful of feeling different or electing to exert emotional control rather than allowing oneself to be in one's grief). This means adolescents must navigate their internal sense of what feels authentic among the "being" factors while assessing the social world around them to determine how to use their agency to portray the "face" they wish to present. The model integrates well with dual-process oscillation (Stroebe &

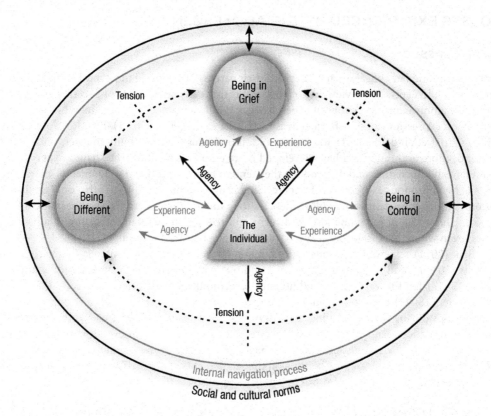

FIGURE 5.2 Model of Loss Navigation in Adolescence by Martin Lytje (2017). This illustrates the tensions between the dimensions of experience the grieving teen must reconcile.
Source: Reproduced with permission from Lytje, M. (2017). Towards a model of loss navigation in adolescence. *Death Studies, 41*(5), 291–302. https://doi.org/10.1080/07481187.2016.1276488

Shut, 2010) while also acknowledging that social aspects of grief mold the experience as surely as psychological and biological influences.

Death of a Parent

The death of a parent not only causes feelings of loss but affects adolescents' family structure, economic security, and life plans (Punzanio et al., 2014). In a small qualitative study of people who were between 16 and 18 when a parent died of terminal illness, Cafferky et al. (2018) found that an initial core experience of these adolescents was the challenge of changing family dynamics including having more responsibility thrust upon them while they were trying to manage painful information about their dying parent. Responses to parents' deaths often entail not only sadness but significant fear/anxiety about how the surviving members of the family will carry on (particularly economically) as well as a heightened sense of vulnerability to other losses. Punzanio et al.'s (2014) review of studies of parentally bereaved adolescents shows that teens' academic performance suffers in the year following the death, and they often have intrusive thoughts about the parent's death. Adolescents seem to need to process both the time immediately preceding the death and the aftermath but differ in their interest in being part of the funeral and other family arrangements after death. Studies suggest that some adolescents elect to distract themselves outside the home, whereas others feel that involvement with the arrangements cements their sense of belonging in the family. Growth and a sense of enhanced maturity also occur among some bereaved adolescents. In short, Punzanio et al.'s review finds that while there are many variations in adolescent responses to parental death, there seems to be a common tendency to avoid overt discussions of the death and its impact with peers/friends, precisely the people of most interest to adolescents. They suggest "the creation of special moments of encounter and dialogue between parents, adolescents, and health professionals: the teenagers can thus take advantage of the opportunity to express their feelings and to revisit certain situations by talking directly with parents and experts" (Punzanio et al., 2014, p. 373). They also note that helping adolescents return to their routines is a key to helping them cope well and that creative memory building is helpful.

Comedian Stephen Colbert's father and brothers died in a plane crash as he was on the cusp of adolescence. He told Anderson Cooper (CNN, 2019) that as one of a large group of siblings, he learned to feel grateful for all that life brings—the good and the bad—that all of it creates the life one lives. He also observed that when his mother died four decades later, he and his siblings felt a revival of the loss of his father and brothers. His experience seems typical in the way he needed to reprocess the varied losses over time, and yet less common was his ability to find meaning and connection in the loss, something he attributes to his family's Roman Catholicism and to his recent adoption of Buddhist traditions of gratitude and mindfulness. Like many, though certainly not all, Colbert's loss led him to consider existential questions (though his extensive reading of Tolkien may have contributed as well). Also, his academic performance lagged as his grief (and Tolkien reading) took precedence after his father's and brothers' deaths. The conversation between Colbert and Cooper is remarkable, and their grief experiences may help youth see that sharing grief helps.

The intensity of adolescence primes such growth. Cait's study of young women who lost a parent during adolescence bears this out. The women she interviewed reflected on religious and spiritual beliefs, with some embracing their faith and others rejecting or revising it (Cait, 2004). Interestingly, nearly all used spiritual beliefs to retain connections to their deceased parent. Many struggled with how to believe in a loving supreme being that allowed the parent to die (Cait, 2004).

When parents have a terminal diagnosis, adolescents are often expected to assist in their care, even as they work to understand the changing family dynamics and medical information (Cafferky et al., 2018). This constitutes an off-time loss, and many felt peers did not understand what they were going through, nor did the youths feel comfortable sharing their (impending) loss as they worried about the stigma of becoming "the one who has the dead parent" (p. 187). Additionally, the youths often felt more vulnerable to illness themselves during their parent's illness and after their death. Mirroring Lytje's model (2017), the adolescents in Cafferky et al.'s study both desired support and pushed it away, trying to carry on with routines in order to feel normal. This strategy, though often employed by teens, leaves their needs unattended when adults assume they are functioning.

Adolescence is a time to figure out who one is and what one believes. Although mourning after the death of a parent, adolescents' reflections on existential questions may allow them to grow and mature (Dehlin & Reg, 2009). Yet they may struggle alone. Linking bereaved youth with one another, supporting faith beliefs where appropriate (Cabrera & Stevenson, 2017), and providing outlets for "normal" youth activities seem critical to helping adolescents cope with parental death.

Death of a Sibling

Sibling bereavement is surprisingly common, affecting nearly 8% of the U.S. population before the age of 25. Yet the consequences of sibling death have not been researched as extensively as parental death or the death of a child (Fletcher et al., 2013). In the sibling relationship, shared family history, similar cohort influences, and tight housing circumstances often lead to close (or at least tightly entwined) connections. Fletcher et al. (2013), examining the "spillover" effects on siblings who experienced the death of a sibling in childhood or adolescence, found that years of schooling are reduced, with subsequent increases in failure to finish high school and reduced earning capacity. These effects were stronger for bereaved sisters than for brothers and included higher likelihood of teen pregnancy. Fletcher et al. postulate three mechanisms for these effects: the siblings' own grief and school impairment, the families' changed structures and ability to support the surviving sibling, and increased existential questioning that may dampen motivation for achievement. In a poignant memoir, Judy Eichinger (2018) recounts her experiences following her sister's death when Judy was a 15-year-old in high school. Although her sister Ruth had been ill for most of her childhood, Ruth's death came as a surprise, and she was excluded from the deathbed due to her parents' wishes to protect her. Yet the family silence over the years combined with adolescent trepidation about disclosure to blind Judy to her own grief until she sought counseling much later following an emotional breakdown. After individual and group counseling and research into sibling grief, she was able to recognize how some parents, like hers, turn toward each other in their grief, essentially leaving the surviving sibling/s to struggle with their emotions alone. When this happens to introverted children (particularly if one becomes the only living child in the family), they may need someone to draw them out of their silence. The combination of double jeopardy (the tendency to silence one's expressions of grief when they most need to be shared) and the lifetime socioeconomic effects noted earlier makes it clear that grief workers must help adolescents process their grief while maintaining their schooling.

Death of a Grandparent

Not infrequently, young children lose a grandparent, but with increasing longevity, this typical first family loss often comes during adolescence. Research in New Zealand (Breheny et al., 2013) traced how grandparents come to "be there" as the grandchildren are born and how this translates into "being there" in ongoing close relationships with the grandchildren as they age. The sampled grandparents avoided "interference" and cultivated enjoyable relationships with their grandchildren, explaining to researchers that they believed all grandparents would enjoy such contact. In the United States, Scherrer (2010) illustrated how grandparents became some of the main supporters of gender-nonconforming youth, showing how intense the attachment between adolescents and their grandparents can be.

Characterized by high levels of support and love and less emphasis on the regulation required of the parental role, these relationships are mourned when grandparents die. In a systematic review of how adolescents grieve after deaths by suicide, Andriessen et al. (2016) found that the closeness of the relationship with the deceased, whether the deceased was a family member (with fears about their own mental health stability if the death was suicidal), and post-loss family stability were factors in the adolescents' grief. They observed that suicide among Western older men is common, raising the likelihood that youth have grandfathers who take their lives by suicide (although their review of the literature found little research on this group). Grief after grandparents' death is often disenfranchised because grandparents' deaths are expected. We believe that adolescents benefit when their grief is validated and they are provided a safe space to remember their grandparent and talk about them. Adolescents may be conscious of their parents' grief and avoid expressing their grief at home. Schools have a special opportunity to provide the place for adolescents to process such grief without fear of making their parents' grief worse.

Death of a Friend

In 2016, almost 14,000 adolescents (ages 10–19) died in the United States, mostly in motor vehicle accidents or due to drug overdose or unintentional injury (Cunningham et al., 2018), with suicide and homicide close behind (CDC, 2017). Each of these deaths leaves parents, siblings, and friends bereft. The death of a friend by homicide is startling, as reflected in Celeste Johnson's reading in our supplementary materials. The sheer surprise and feeling of injustice that come with a friend's sudden death by any means is not only hard for teens to adjust to but often is the first time they experience the death of a peer. It is dramatic and a clear violation of the assumptive world that interrupts intense and intimate friendships that are generally viewed as immortal. Adolescents often have few opportunities to process their grief because of their own reluctance to expose their feelings and thoughts, as they work hard to maintain a facade of normalcy. They tend to use on-line memorial sites to directly address the deceased (communicating as if the deceased receives their messages on those sites; Williams & Merten, 2009). This approach to grief seems to keep some forms of rumination about the deceased ongoing yet also provides a place to process the grief for youth who may avoid face-to-face interactions (Dilmaç, 2018). It is not clear how this movement of private mourning onto internet spaces will affect adolescents over time, but there is some reassurance that adolescents are quite resilient after loss (de Moor et al., 2019) and that grievers benefit from writing their stories (Graybeal et al., 2002). Grief Speaks has developed a resource area for teens who experience the death of a friend (www.griefspeaks.com/id89.html).

Living Losses: Atypical, Typical, and Maturational Losses

Loss of Health

Although it is atypical to be unhealthy during adolescence, teens who are ill struggle with the demands of differentiation and developmental maturation at a time when their health requires them to depend more on adults. Adolescents living with cancer got recognition when the popular movie *A Fault in Our Stars* (2014) showed how teens wish so strongly to be accepted as normal even when dealing with life-threatening illness. In a study of teens who attended a "Tee-napalooza" weekend for teens living with cancer, Stegenga (2014) found that they valued peer support, "hanging out with people who understand" (p. 295), engaging in activities they chose (having autonomy), and seeing people return after treatment (gaining hope). Despite adult fears that teens should not have to talk about their life-threatening illnesses, Lyon et al. (2010) found that teens living with HIV were able to participate in family-centered advanced care (FACE) planning. They had only minor decreases in school performance (in contrast to ill teens who did not get FACE) but were all able and willing to complete an advanced directive (end-of-life planning) and appoint a surrogate decision-maker. Similarly, Zadeh and Wiener (2015) found that Voicing My CHOiCES™ is an end-of-life planning tool useful for teens as well. Together, these studies reinforce the practice wisdom that talking with teens openly about their life-threatening illnesses, treating them as having normal lives beyond their diagnoses, and engaging them in planning their futures are important aspects of their care.

Sometimes, ill health reflects chronic conditions that adolescents must learn to manage as they move from pediatric to adult care providers, a transition that involves taking on more responsibility for their health (Reed-Knight et al., 2014). For social workers helping with this transition, assessing the teen's executive function, self-efficacy, and disease knowledge, and how these interact with social factors such as family conflict and degree of parental monitoring will help identify areas for intervention (Reed-Knight et al., 2014). Also, it is painful for a teen to lose a care provider who was with them throughout childhood. In many cases, these relationships become close, and the person truly kept the teen alive. This loss is often unrecognized and disenfranchised yet may operate to sensitize (or "depress") youth in ways they do not recognize. Ideally, the new providers would welcome the teen into adult care in a way that is not alienating. In a review of transitions from pediatric care to adult care by 18- to 21-year-old youth living with HIV, the authors found that more teens were retained in care when the waiting rooms were youth friendly and when hours allowed for continued schooling (Judd & Davies, 2018).

Loss of Self-Esteem/Identity

Tweens and teens need to build intense and close peer relationships where they feel known and esteemed. It is critical to their identity development that they achieve both a coherent sense of identity and positive assessment by others (NASEM, 2019). Social group identities (racial, ethnic, religious, sexuality, gender, political, ability/skill, etc.) become part of how adolescents typically come to understand their individual identity, with those who feel pride in their identity groups having better outcomes over time (NASEM, 2019). When one's social identity groups or personal characteristics are devalued, youth struggle with identity consolidation and healthy self-esteem, and they may become distraught and impulsive.

Bullying is often an indicator of such devaluation, and adolescents cannot easily or constructively avoid the school environment where it typically occurs. This has had major ramifications for LGBTQ+ teens. Thwarted belonging and perceived burdensomeness, combined with adolescents' neurobiological impulsivity, are theorized to predict raised risk for suicidal ideation and attempts (Stewart et al., 2017). As suicide is a potential outcome of bullying, it must be taken very seriously as a loss of peer acceptance and self-esteem (www.suicide.org/teen-suicide-and-youth-suicide.html). Teens on the whole seem to have a trajectory of suicidal ideation that peaks between ages 14 and 17, and patterns of increasing or decreasing ideation may predict suicide attempts (Rueter et al., 2008). Unexpectedly, males with decreasing ideation are more likely to attempt suicide, while attempts are more likely among females with increasing ideation (at least in Rueter et al.'s Caucasian sample).

Assuring teens that "it gets better" (www.itgetsbetter.org/pages/about-it-gets-better-project) has helped to prevent suicide during the painful years of adolescence when differences seem insurmountable. Although established to help LGBTQ+ youth, the "it gets better" pledge includes a vow to "speak up against hate and intolerance whenever I see it, at school and at work" and to reassure teens in all marginalized groups that it gets better. Adolescents who are out of the ordinary in some way that is important in their environment (bookish in an athletic community; dark skinned in a pale community; from another country) tend to be at risk for feeling a loss of self-esteem. Lowered self-esteem in adolescence is positively associated with depression in adulthood (Steiger et al., 2014), so it behooves us to attend to the marginalization of youth. Adults need to take these losses of peer valuation seriously, help adolescents express their loss, and look for communities of acceptance.

Loss of a Relationship

Establishing close relationships is a critical developmental aspect of adolescence, and romantic relationships are part of this. Yet romantic relationships dissolve so frequently in adolescence that theorists believe that changing romances are part of how adolescents learn to develop, maintain, and dissolve intimate relationships, as well as identify their orientation to gender and sexuality (Collins, 2003). While adolescent romance has often been disenfranchised as "puppy love" (Rowling, 2002), the intensity of grief has negative health effects. In one of the few longitudinal examinations of teens after relationship dissolution, Szwedo et al. (2015) found strong evidence that teens' use of positive coping strategies and perceived friendship competence after a breakup protect teens somewhat from the risk of depressive symptoms over time. That said, consistent with previous research, they found a strong link between romantic relationships in adolescence and depressive symptoms in adulthood. Adolescents need support to mourn not only the relationship but the hopes and dreams they had built while thinking about futures with the partner. These secondary losses must be identified and acknowledged as valid sources of grief. Promoting positive outlooks for the future and supporting other friendships may be of additional efficacy.

Higher Expectations for Responsibility and Independence

Teens experience intensified expectations about academic work and pressure to develop long-term life goals. As children enter middle school and high school, more demands are made upon their time, energy, and ability to conform to educational (as well as familial) imperatives. They are treated by teachers and parents as responsible for their own production of work (or lack thereof) and are expected to be self-directed (NASEM, 2019). Although this is legitimate and helpful to development, the struggle parallels toddler losses: The adolescents embrace their growing independence but may want to avoid the ramifications of being held responsible for their behavior. To no longer be granted fairly unconditional support—financially and emotionally—is a maturational loss, expressed by adolescents in the ambivalence with which they pursue independent/adult roles while wishing for less pressure.

Aspects of Identity Change

Some suggest many adolescents have developed a cynical pragmatism in response to growing pressures to succeed. One example is the phenomenon of "doing school" by working only as necessary to attain achievements and good grades, largely discounting more ideal motivations like self-satisfaction (Pope, 2001). Yet teens also protest gun violence (the Marjorie Stoneman Douglas High School students from Parkland, Florida, March for Our Lives movement is a particularly powerful example; see www.youtube.com/watch?v=sfPrzg_j0WM), advocate action on climatic changes that threaten the world (see Greta Thunberg say "How dare you!" to a UN summit at www.youtube.com/watch?v=TMrtLsQbaok), and fight for educational opportunities for girls in Pakistan and around the world (Malala, nearly assassinated at 15 and Noble Prize winner at 17). These teens exemplify what adolescents can do with the identities they cultivate and the actions they take as a result. In substantial numbers, adolescents bring passionate innovation to bear on a world "Boomers" seem unable to fix. It will be a terrible loss should their passion and idealism wane in the face of adult obstinacy.

Tweens and especially teens must adjust to the maturational losses involved in identity formation. Adolescence is a time of "trying on" different dimensions of identity and then settling into a more consistent identity (NASEM, 2019). Although a positive maturational step, such commitment entails a loss of flexibility. Furthermore, as self-knowledge grows, teens become aware of the discrepancies between the identity they adopt and those that are socially valued. This brings some back into conformance with social norms, as when a teen who experiments with drugs and/or alcohol gets pressure to abstain from teammates in a chosen sport. (These forces for conformity are most efficacious when coming from a valued peer or reference group.) Females may experience a less positive loss due to conformity, often referred to as a loss of voice. The adoption of silence as a safe position from which to avoid conflict (particularly with males) is documented across many cultures (Gilligan, 1982/1993; Iglesias & Courmier, 2002; Jack, 1991). Mixed messages about gender roles are being negotiated at the same time as mixed messages about whether they are maturing too quickly or not quickly enough. Discrepant messages add to the struggles for teens as they work to consolidate identity.

Another major identity issue arises as adolescents mature into serious relationship building. Some discover that their love interests revolve around same sex relationships rather than the more common heterosexual ones. Although a positive development in self-awareness, it can also lead to secrecy and self-silencing (a form of loss) if teens do not believe this identity will be supported and valued by those in their social milieus. Furthermore, even if their social groups are supportive, teens must decide whether to share this aspect of identity since heterosexist culture makes the assumption of heterosexuality until shown otherwise (McGeorge & Carlson, 2011). Under conditions where heterosexist culture includes ostracism of those who love in other ways, teens may hide their authentic loves and become self-destructive as they feel unable to allow themselves to thrive as they are.

LaSala (2015) illustrates how parents can support the recognition of sexuality and protect teens from potential harm. His research suggests that parental knowledge, involvement, and active communication can assist gay teens to adopt safer sex practices. The parental support seems to translate into teens having more self-acceptance and self-care. Unrecognized losses involved in identity formation can add to the possibility of acting impulsively out of a fear of ostracism, yet parental and peer support can be quite protective.

Double jeopardy, the tendency to avoid sharing feelings of loss while being deprived of support since others are not informed (Oltjenbruns, 1996), implies that teens may need support identifying and processing these maturational and other losses. Even when emotional supports are available, teens may not be forthcoming about the ways losses (ended love relationships, abortions, failures in school, etc.) also bring about the end of a fantasy for the future (Rowling, 2002). These disenfranchised losses are unrecognized and occur at a time when adolescents often are assumed ready to handle their emotions on their own. Although all age groups benefit from sharing their emotions with trusted others, tweens and teens may avoid this because they believe these painful thoughts and feelings make them seem less mature. Asking adolescents to talk about their feelings directly is often unsuccessful, yet asking gentle, specific questions (What is it like to be working now? What is the hardest thing to manage now that you graduated? How are you coping with your breakup?) allows tweens and teens to open up enough to begin to reveal and process the painful areas of their lives.

REACTIONS OF OTHERS TO THE DEATH OF AN ADOLESCENT

When adolescents die, it is usually sudden (CDC, 2017). Such losses betray parents' assumptive world and may leave survivors (whether family or friends) with posttraumatic stress disorder (PTSD; Boelen & Spuij, 2013). Following traumatic death, parents must grapple with the unfairness of life and often require a longer-than-usual time to adjust. Adolescent friends or siblings of the deceased, also in a period of rapid development, may still be impulsive and engage in some magical thinking, while also having their grief go unrecognized. The nature of off-time loss—in this case of the promise of adolescence snuffed out just as it starts—causes survivors to grapple with a world where expectations for the future are dashed and grieving is more challenging.

Parents' Loss of a Tween or Teen

Parents are the most common mourners of teens. Traditionally, violent, sudden death, particularly suicide, was believed to raise the risk of complicated grief and PTSD for survivors, especially parents (Rando, 1993). In a study of over a million bereaved parents of an adolescent (ages 16–24 in this study), Wilcox et al. (2015) found that parents whose child died from suicide or accident experienced a tenfold higher risk of absence from work for more than 30 days due to psychiatric illness and a fivefold higher rate for those whose child died of natural causes. Fathers of a child who died by suicide also had increased rates of somatic illness requiring a 30-day absence or more from work. Clearly, parents are strongly affected emotionally and economically by the death of their adolescent children.

Many researchers note parents' relationship tensions when a child dies, spurred by differences in grieving styles, hampered communication, and the fact that both require support at the same time (Rando, 1986, 1993; Schwab, 1998). Yet Klass (1986–1987) suggested a paradoxical effect: Couples experience a profound bond due to the shared loss of a child, yet each is somewhat estranged from the other because each parent had a singular relationship (and subsequent loss) with the deceased child. Grief affects both in ways that it does most mourners, with sadness, anhedonia, lethargy, periodic upsurges of grief, and the need to share stories of the deceased, often in asynchronous ways. Despite consistent findings of lower marital satisfaction after loss, Schwab (1998) reported little evidence to support the widely held view that divorce rates increase for couples whose child dies, a finding consistent with the experience of Compassionate Friends (a support group for bereaved parents, 2020).

As with the death of a younger child, parents' dreams for their adolescent child are part of the loss. Adolescents may be starting to engage with parents in a relationship that is more rewarding than formerly, as the normal rebellions of the tween and early teen years wane. In obituaries, parents commonly observe that a child "was just getting his life together" or "at the beginning of her life" when the teen died. As with making meaning in other losses, parents find hope and solace when they can usefully memorialize a tragedy (Klass, 2005; Klass et al., 1996). The unexpectedness (and avoidability) of most adolescent deaths means that bereaved parents are commonly angry, and we know that anger tends to complicate the grief response and healing (Rando, 1993). Support groups such as Compassionate Friends can provide much-needed continuing support for bereaved parents. Continuity is an important factor as research indicates that many interventions stop long before parents are ready to make effective use of the proffered support (Lindqvist et al., 2008).

Grandparents' Grief After Adolescent's Death

Grandparents may not always be viewed as "legitimate grievers," but they also mourn the deceased teen. In a support group with those whose grandchildren died of cancer (usually an anticipated death), grandparents identified the frustrations of being unable to process their own grief because they were busy supporting the bereaved parents (their children; Nehari et al., 2007). Some grandparents observed that their children pulled away from them to conserve their waning energy as they grieved their child, leaving the grandparents alone in their grief and a bit estranged from their children. Nehari et al. (2007) suggest that support groups for grandparents provide them a place to validate and process their grief. Tatterton (2016) similarly found that grandparents' grief was profoundly influenced by their roles as both beloved grandparent to the deceased child and parent to the bereaved parent, both roles complicated by a poignant sense of helplessness. Tatterton notes that bereavement leave policies seldom extend to grandparents even though they experience a sense of doubled or tripled grief. As with siblings, grandparents' grief is often overlooked as they support the bereaved family, often at the cost of their own ability to mourn.

INTERVENTIONS WITH TWEENS AND TEENS

When it comes to exploring adolescents' experience of loss, research and practice wisdom encourage gentle, specific questions asked by trusted adults. To a vague question about "how things are going," a teen likely will reply that things are "fine." Rowling (2002) suggests the following questions: "How did you react? (Not, What did you feel?) How do you experience your grief? What did the loss mean to you? What strategies do you use to cope that are helpful? What kind of advice is helpful? With whom do you share your loss?" (p. 289). These convey a gentle, implicit demand for an answer while also providing specific guidance about what to talk about, something most teens appreciate.

Although adolescents usually hesitate to share their grief openly, they do seem to benefit from interventions that draw them out with the use of symbolic material such as writing song lyrics or creating artwork (Punzanio et al., 2014). Peer interaction is the most valued activity during adolescence, so interventions aimed at groups of teens seem to meet their developmental needs most fully, even if it is often hard to get them to try a group (Malone, 2012). McFerran et al. (2010) suggest that music provides both a "window" into grief (opening dialogue when sad songs are chosen) and a strategy to consciously use music for mood management. Adolescents can select music that allows them to express their grief or music that distracts or enlivens. Although adolescent groups may seem to avoid overt discussions of grief and loss, using symbolic activities such as lyric writing (McFerran et al., 2010) and focusing on somatic aspects of grief (Malone,

2012) seem more acceptable and effective. Having teens who are later in their bereavement help to facilitate mutual aid groups can be quite effective in allowing recently bereaved teens to feel comfortable. In that scenario, the adult functions to arrange a safe place for the group to gather, to assure confidentiality is understood, and to help student facilitators with planning.

Learn to BREATHE and Grief-Help Programs

Broderick and Frank (2014) suggest that adolescents benefit from learning mindfulness-based techniques to build executive function and manage difficult emotions. A universal approach to teaching the skills of body scan, self-compassion, empowerment, and emotion management (Broderick & Metz, 2009), the Learn to BREATHE program offers skills that may allow bereaved or ill adolescents to cope with the intensity of grief. A more targeted intervention, Grief-Help is a nine-session structured approach using cognitive behavioral interventions that shows promise in treating prolonged grief in older children and adolescents (Spuij et al., 2015). Using exposure and behavioral activation, the intervention challenges avoidance of the discussion of the death and tendencies toward isolation while also providing psychoeducation about grief.

An interesting "intervention" is happening with teens in Israel at the Miriam Rodman School in Kiryat Yam. The teens of the school interview families of young Israeli soldiers who have died and create a life book to give the family. The teens are guided by a faculty mentor in developing these books but are expected to meet with the bereaved family themselves and hear the story of the deceased. The books include pictures, stories, and other mementos of the soldier's life and death. Aside from the powerful and meaningful books created for the family (and for the school's library), the teens also learn to be unafraid of talking with bereaved people and to manage their own emotional responses to both the death and the interview experience. When teens are helped to understand the experience of grief and mourning, they likely move into adulthood more capable of supporting bereaved others and less frightened of managing their own emotions in the face of grief.

READINGS

Losing a Mother: Augusta's Grief
ERICA GOLDBLATT HYATT

Erica Goldblatt Hyatt, MBE, DSW, LCSW, is an assistant professor of teaching and the assistant director of the Doctorate of Social Work at Rutgers, the State University of New Jersey. She is also a clinician in private practice and author of both commercial and peer-reviewed publications.

Loss and Aftermath

Augusta was 15 years old when her mother, Belle, died by suicide. Belle was a deeply loved and highly respected figure in the community where the family lived: As an instructor of physical education at the local high school, Belle integrated both holistic and homeopathic methods of self-care into her instruction. Many of her students were boarders in the high school dormitory, and Belle provided them support as a type of surrogate mother, frequently inviting them for dinner, checking in on them, and welcoming them on long walks along the beautiful nature trail near her home. Though Belle never displayed any prior signs of mental illness, her family had a history of bipolar disorder. As she entered perimenopause, Belle began to display signs of paranoia related to her family's safety, and she told her husband, Mel, that she heard voices telling her what to do (command auditory hallucinations). Mel avoided psychopharmacological intervention, instead consulting a local homeopathic practitioner who prescribed a regimen of acupressure, herbal remedies, and rest. Unfortunately, Belle's symptoms increased in severity, and she ended her life by suicide on New Year's Eve after she was reported missing with one of Mel's firearms. The loss shook the insular community.

Augusta presented to therapy 2 years after her mother's death, at age 17. Her father felt that seeing a therapist was a "last resort." In his overall assessment, Augusta was coping well with the loss. However, Augusta confided to a friend of her mother that she had begun to harm herself and had thoughts of suicide. She was worried that, like her mother, she was going to kill herself. The friend reported this to Mel, who first attempted homeopathy and spiritual counseling. When he noticed superficial wounds on Augusta's arms, he contacted me as a clinical social worker in the community.

In discussing the loss of her mother, Augusta reported that she felt unaffected. Her initial reaction to hearing of her mother's death was of genuine surprise and of her stomach dropping and experiencing a pain in her gut. Augusta recounted that ever since she was a child, she experienced anxiety in the form of stomachaches at nighttime. When she was little, she would awaken Belle and the two would go for calming walks in the predawn hours. In the wake of Belle's death, Augusta experienced these somatic pains again, but she was also in the beginning stages of a new relationship and called her boyfriend to talk her through the discomfort, finding in him an immediate substitute or "security blanket," as she called him. As the relationship evolved, Augusta frequently felt dissatisfied with her boyfriend's lack of physical affection or attention toward her. She frequently felt pressured to become sexually intimate before she felt ready because she was terrified of losing him. Upon reflection, Augusta began to understand that focusing on her boyfriend helped her to maintain a sense of normalcy both in self-appraisal and in the eyes of her peers, whom she felt were critically examining her for signs that the loss had "marked" her in some way. Like many bereaved adolescents I have worked with, Augusta did not want to stand out because of her loss, and because the community was so aware of how her mother had died, she felt especially scrutinized for signs that she was "going crazy too." Typical of many adolescents in Western society (Arnett, 2014), she was existentially preoccupied with *who* she was, and how much of her mother's path would become her own.

As adolescents seek to individuate from their family of origin, it is important for their families to remain consistent with their boundaries and expectations as teens experiment with new relationships, interests, hobbies, and more (Erikson, 1959/1980). Unfortunately, Augusta's father was preoccupied with the death of his wife as well as caring for her younger brother, who displayed more blatant and distressing symptoms following the loss. According to Mel, Augusta was "thriving" following Belle's death, though Augusta reported that she felt very uncomfortable telling her father when she began to experience thoughts of depression and suicide.

Increasingly, Augusta began to avoid her father, also deciding to isolate more from her former group of friends, because she felt they were scrutinizing and judging her. Characteristic of their developmental status, adolescents continuously compare themselves to peers. Even in loss, they may search for cues regarding how to process or behave in the wake of a loss (Balk, 2014). Examining her peers, Augusta believed that her friends were responding to Belle's death with more difficulty than she was. Augusta, on the contrary, felt empty when she thought about Belle and wondered if she was grieving the wrong way. Not wanting to stand out, she continued her relationship with her boyfriend, though she felt deeply unhappy about it.

Intervention

Stabilization, Psychoeducation, and Communication

While self-harm is not uncommon among adolescents (Hawton et al., 2012), it is still necessary to explore whether there is imminent risk of suicidality. When working with families affected by suicide, clinicians should be aware that surviving family members have an increased risk of dying in the same way (National Institute of Mental Health, 2019). In Augusta's case, it was necessary to clarify her risk of suicidality, particularly if she wanted to end her life or whether her intention in harming herself was to "feel something" apart from a lack of emotion, channeling her emotions and psychological responses to her loss into a physical wound. The death of her mother triggered Augusta's questions about death as well as a sense of longing for death to feel *something* and be reunited with her Belle. Initially, Augusta required hospitalization as she reported a loss of control related to her cutting and feeling as though she could not stop herself.

It is essential to discuss the limitations of confidentiality with adolescents, as they may feel especially reticent to involve parents in their treatment. Indeed, this discussion with Augusta resulted in some resistance as she did not want to bother her father. However, as with all adolescents, it was important to model for Augusta that she might not be able to solve problems on her own and should confide in trusting adults who might help her through tough times. Mel was shocked at the severity of his daughter's symptoms but was reluctant to hospitalize her. This was a surprising reaction given his wife's suicide after a lack of psychotherapeutic intervention, but he appeared overwhelmed by assuming the role of mother and father in the aftermath of Belle's death, and Augusta hid her suffering successfully. For some parents of adolescents, as in this case, psychoeducation about adolescent responses to grief is necessary. Mel also required guidance regarding what to expect when taking Augusta for assessment at the local children's hospital, as he feared her being overmedicated. Direct communication with Mel about my concerns for Augusta and clarity about potential implications eased his initial anxiety.

It is useful to work with bereaved teens like Augusta on communicating their feelings to their parents or trusting adults, instead of hiding them. For Augusta, I assigned "homework assignments" of talking with her father to decrease the level of discomfort and embarrassment she associated with telling Mel about her feelings, in an effort to both save face and avoid burdening him. Homework and practice assignments included setting a timer and spending a few extra minutes at the dinner table talking to Mel, taking walks together, creating and practicing a script in therapy that provided wording to ask for help, and finally, role-playing with me and eventually waking her father up in the night when she was experiencing anxiety or thoughts of self-harm. These interventions worked because Mel was able to respond to his daughter's cues and supported her work in therapy. It is important to note that grieving adults respond differently to adolescents depending on individual personalities, relationships with the bereaved, and other psychosocial, environmental, and resource factors. Therefore, it is important to identify healthy adults in a grieving teen's life that can serve as a safe harbor. These may include pastors, guidance counselors, coaches, and others.

Distress Tolerance, Mindfulness, and Coping Cards

To avoid coping by self-harm, substance use, or other risky activities, bereaved adolescents may benefit from psychotherapeutic work exploring how to abide feelings of grief. While taking risks and engaging in experimentation is a hallmark of adolescence, it is important to maintain an awareness of when attempts to individuate are interfering with a teen's burgeoning sense of self. In therapy, it is useful to establish a sense of control and self-efficacy, in addition to managing emotions that can feel overwhelming at times. Much of our therapeutic work centered on Augusta identifying both the similarities and differences between herself and her mother, thus to better appreciate and promote her unique sense of individuality. It was important to confront Augusta's fears of "going crazy like my mom" and to normalize these as understandable anxiety and intrusive thoughts triggered by her mother's death. To expand Augusta's narrative of her mother beyond the unsettling circumstances of Belle's death, I encouraged her to explore moments of comfort and happiness throughout the relationship. Augusta observed Belle's strengths as well as her flaws. She noted that Belle hid her psychosis and paranoia so well from her children that her death was a genuine surprise. While Augusta initially identified this as a strength because she saw it as "the ultimate act of love: shielding her kids from pain," I gently challenged the value of hiding one's struggles and provided a reframe as an example of where Augusta's path was different from her mother, because she was willing to ask for help when she began to harm herself.

Augusta began to explore self-soothing and tolerating urges to self-harm by incorporating exercise, deep breathing, and self-expression through drawing cartoons when she was feeling overwhelmed. Because her mother took her on walks and taught mindfulness in her physical education classes, Augusta felt these would be useful to pursue during episodes where she felt especially empty or sad. I have found that incorporating the "wise mind" perspective from dialectical behavioral therapy (Linehan, 2014) can also be useful with grieving teens, as it helps them to reflect on their experiences without judgment. This was also useful as Augusta worked on observing and describing her grief without judgment, making pros and cons lists of whether to harm herself, and practicing mindfulness on her walks by immersing herself in the peace and quiet of nature.

Coping cards can be useful for teens like Augusta who may feel impulsive and overwhelmed or confused by their emotions in the wake of loss. Because she frequently felt the desire to hurt herself so overwhelming that she cut without the self-awareness to stop, I helped Augusta create her own coping cards. On these cue cards, which she kept in her bedroom and in digital format on her cellphone, Augusta listed triggers for self-harm, including comments by her boyfriend or feeling judged by friends. She then listed several alternatives to cutting herself, including drawing on her arms, immersing her face in ice-cold water, engaging in vigorous exercise, going for a walk, or asking her father for help. Augusta acknowledged feeling resistant to using the coping cards because it felt easier to cut herself, but in time, she began to use them and feel proud of herself when she was able to abstain from cutting for weeks at a time. I have found coping cards to be valuable beyond self-harm episodes for bereaved teens and they can be adapted to the individual. Some clients have included inspirational quotes and song lyrics, names and numbers of immediate supports, positive mantras, and more.

Dual-Process Work: Grief and Restoration

According to Stroebe and Schut (1999), the "work" of grief involves oscillating between experiencing the pain of loss and engaging in restorative practices that help the bereaved adjust to life moving forward. I find that it is truly necessary to adopt a dual-process orientation to facilitate healing for bereaved adolescents. For Augusta to explore the grief of losing her mother, it was necessary to examine how the relationship with her boyfriend served as an unhealthy distraction that impeded experiencing the pain of Belle's death. Augusta acknowledged that by throwing herself into the relationship with her boyfriend, she could avoid thinking too deeply or feeling too much about her mother's death. She was hesitant to end the relationship because she felt that if she did, she would be alone, and without protection from the deeper emotions she was avoiding. Therapy provided a safe, healthy environment where Augusta learned to experience her feelings without becoming overwhelmed, as she worried she would. Adopting a cognitive behavioral perspective helped Augusta identify automatic irrational thoughts such as "I can't handle my sadness" and challenge them with healthier, more nuanced self-talk. Augusta felt safe to discuss the feelings of abandonment connected to her mother's suicide, as well as the coexisting emotions of hurt, confusion, betrayal, but also longing. I find that the cornerstones of my work with all grieving teens are providing nonjudgmental acceptance of the many feelings that accompany loss, encouraging expression, and validating, as well as praising the hard work done to face those feelings.

Similarly, Augusta explored how her mother served as a healthy mentor for students at the high school, and she began to look for other adults she could trust, as well as ways to continue her mother's legacy as a supporter of teens in the community. Augusta learned that two of her peers had also lost their parents in the past 5 years, and they formed friendships based on this shared experience, dubbing their group "The Dead Parents Club." Augusta confided that she felt she could truly be herself with these new friends, and she did not feel judged or scrutinized. Her new friends knew Belle, and they encouraged Augusta to create an outdoor walking club for younger high schoolers in honor of her mother. By doing this, Augusta maintained a bond with her mother by honoring one of her favorite activities. Social ties are extremely important to adolescents as they navigate life post loss, and with the help of her friends, Augusta began to acknowledge a new component of her identity as a bereaved daughter. She was able to feel more comfortable integrating this life-changing event into her self-concept as artist, friend, daughter, and student.

Helping Bridget Feel Safe Again: Surviving Sexual Abuse
ELAINE SHOR

Elaine Shor, MA, ATR-BC, LPC, is a board-certified, registered art therapist and a licensed professional counselor. She has worked in outpatient and inpatient mental health settings. She is presently in private practice, where she specializes in assisting clients in overcoming anxiety, healing from the effects of trauma, and adjusting to life changes due to divorce. Ms. Shor works with children, adolescents, and adults providing services to individuals, families, and groups.

A child entering elementary school is beginning to explore environments beyond her home and people beyond her family. Attending school, visiting homes of friends, and exploring peer relationships are all part of developing a sense of self relative to the world. This is possible when a strong sense of security is provided, allowing the child to venture into a larger world with confidence. However, what happens if some of that safety is taken?

Bridget was 6 years old when she was sexually molested by a close family friend related to her aunt and cousins. She was brought to therapy sessions to help prepare her for a court appearance about her abuse and to assist her in regaining a sense of trust in others and in her environment. Bridget was withdrawn during her first few sessions, appearing younger than her age. She was anxious about appearing in the completely unfamiliar environment of court, feeling especially concerned about seeing her perpetrator and having to be in proximity to him. Bridget felt fearful and helpless. Bridget expressed her fear at each session, and I helped her understand what a courtroom looked like, the people who would be there, and the procedures that would take place. After several sessions reviewing what to expect at court, using diagrams of the room for clarification, Bridget stated she was less anxious about having to appear in court but continued to wish she would not have to do it. Role-playing the court appearance further aided Bridget to feel some control over her environment, something she had lost after the abuse. To reinforce Bridget's feeling of control, I suggested that her mother arrange a visit to the courtroom. The prosecutor arranged it.

The abuse originally took place at Bridget's aunt's home, though the perpetrator did not live there. Bridget was struggling with the fact that her aunt's home was a place that previously provided a nurturing and happy experience for her. As a result of the abuse, Bridget was confused about whom she could trust and was hesitant about entering her aunt's home again. This loss of a sense of safety and concern about feeling protected left Bridget anxious and fearful. However, her parents were loving and supportive, providing Bridget with the needed validation that the abuse was not her fault. This allowed Bridget to gain strength to discuss her abuse with me and to review methods of feeling safe by knowing what to do when someone attempts to touch her inappropriately. Bridget gained an understanding of her lack of blame for her abuse, and she began viewing the court appearance as a way to hold the perpetrator responsible since he was to blame. At this point, the prosecutor informed Bridget's mother that because the perpetrator pleaded guilty, Bridget would not have to appear in court after all. Bridget's parents decided to discontinue therapy sessions at that point. She attended two more sessions; Bridget was relieved about not having to confront her perpetrator and had gained a clearer perspective on her abuse. After 6 months of treatment, Bridget had eliminated for now the feeling of being in danger and felt safe when visiting her aunt and cousins with her parents. I reminded Bridget and her parents that Bridget could return to therapy at any time, if needed.

Effects in Adolescence

Adolescence is a time of separating from parents and venturing out to explore other relationships. This can be difficult for those who have experienced sexual abuse as a young child because early wounds can resurface. Just as losses due to death must be revisited as children mature, it is also important to revisit other losses, such as the loss of safety Bridget experienced. Ten years after her first therapy sessions, Bridget returned to therapy at age 16. She was suffering with anxiety and finding it difficult to attend high school. Bridget felt she could not relate to other students; she felt like an outsider. She found herself having a different value system and a feeling of "differentness" due to her abuse. She often stopped herself from joining friends when invited to activities due to anxious feelings of not being safe. Bridget also stated that she had no interest in dating, fearing her reaction to having a close relationship after her abusive experience. At this stage in her life, where most girls begin transferring their connections from parents to peers, Bridget remained attached to her mother, father, and siblings. She was especially attached to her mother, who was caring and patient with her.

The need to further process the experience of abuse was essential to Bridget's maturation and to enable her to regain her confidence. To do this, Bridget needed to alleviate the strong physical reactions she had when experiencing anxiety. These included nausea, increased heart rate, and headaches. Bridget was taught progressive muscle relaxation and deep breathing exercises to practice daily. She took these exercises seriously and was soon able to confront her anxiety rather than be overwhelmed by it. She learned to step back when anxiety occurred and counteract the messages with statements of reality. This served as a way for Bridget to take back control. At my request, she was able to create a narrative about her abuse, including illustrations. With Bridget's permission, I reviewed the narrative with her mother in preparation for Bridget to share it with her, a trusted witness, at a subsequent session. Bridget was able to read the narrative to her mom, and her mother was able to be supportive. Bridget was regaining a sense of control.

During the next 2 years, Bridget also learned to recognize the abuse as an incident in her life and not something that defined her. Bridget focused on placing this experience in her past so she could develop her identity as a young woman. She began to recognize her feelings of "differentness" as due to the abuse influencing her life, and she was determined to fight against letting the abuse define her. Her sense of safety and control were growing, and Bridget's strength was allowing her to take back her autonomy and reject the anxious feelings. Bridget often revealed her dreams in sessions, some of which suggested some lingering feelings of fault for her abuse and concern about whether she could protect herself now. Art materials were used to explore these feelings, resulting in images of herself as she is now, strong and able to remove herself from any uncomfortable situation. She used her newfound familiarity with a calm center, gained through her practice of progressive muscle relaxation and breathing techniques, to reject her anxiety and remain in the present. The following week, Bridget accepted an invitation to spend the weekend at her aunt and uncle's house, where the abuse took place. She was able to counteract the anxiety she felt by using "reality checks" and talking with her mom. Bridget had a great time during the weekend and was proud she fought against the fear that had previously stopped her from venturing out from the comfort of home.

As therapy progressed, Bridget began to experience intense feelings of anger toward her perpetrator. At one point, she tore up the dress she was wearing when molested and then threw it away. Bridget was getting rid of the remnants of helplessness, identifying with her present self.

She then wrote a letter to her perpetrator, not to be sent, but to further express her anger. During her next session, Bridget created a timeline to represent all the events in her life to concretize the fact that the abuse was only one event. These acts were cathartic and provided a sense of regained autonomy.

Bridget was able to describe her abuse to me during a session, stating that she felt relieved afterward. This further emphasized Bridget's ability to regain her sense of power and not allow the abuse to dictate her feelings or behavior. She was now able to fantasize about being physically intimate with celebrities without anxiety interfering with her fantasy. Bridget felt this demonstrated that she no longer viewed sexuality as bad. About a year later, Bridget began dating a boy she met through friends.

Bridget was very interested in studying acting and stated that she felt at ease during her acting classes when she was able to push past her anxiety. She began to take more risks through her acting. At one point, she was invited by the director of the school to act in a play dealing with sexual abuse. She would not be the main character who is victimized, but she would play a supporting role. Bridget was concerned but excited to be in the production. During a rehearsal, she was overwhelmed with the play's content. She reached out to a teacher who was aware of her history. After speaking with the teacher about her reactions, Bridget decided to take a few days off. She used the time to process her feelings using techniques learned in therapy and returned to rehearsals 2 days later. Bridget then acted in the role without any negative reactions, feeling energized and present.

Conclusion

Bridget was able to use the many resources, internal and external, that were available to assist her in regaining a sense of safety and confidence after experiencing sexual molestation at the age of 6. The loss of trust in others and the loss of confidence in herself were preventing Bridget from fully participating in her life. She lost her confidence and trust at age 6, immediately after the abuse, and again during adolescence. Bridget's perseverance and commitment to treatment moved her forward. The influence of her abuse may appear again in another developmental stage of her life, but Bridget has demonstrated that she is able to take control back and live her life in the present.

SUMMARY

The readings that conclude this chapter bring into sharp relief the developmental aspects of grief and loss in adolescence. Adolescents are poised between the ability of younger children to move rather fluidly in and out of active grieving and the more adult-like experience of long periods of time in the active grieving stages of the dual process, all the while experiencing the heightened sensitivity of the adolescent brain. The tendency toward "double jeopardy," and its paradox of needing more support yet being unwilling to reveal oneself, leaves adolescents particularly vulnerable at a time when depression and impulsiveness may be part of normal development. The unrecognized losses involved in identity formation are also crucial aspects of loss at this age. Whether the struggle is to feel "normal" or to process difference from peers, adolescents are challenged with developing a sense of who they are. Interventions are finely tuned to engage adolescents without having them feel too exposed; they require strict confidentiality, attention to trust building, and encouragement to make use of family, friends, and other support. In short, just as the adolescent is in a liminal position between childhood and adulthood, the practitioner must be poised between the nurturing and active intervention posture one adopts with children and the more peer-like stance one may take with adults. The intensity and malleability of adolescence make it a fruitful and exciting time to help teens make use of the growth opportunities inherent in losses of all kinds.

DISCUSSION QUESTIONS

1. How has the experience of coming out as LGBTQ+ changed in your geographic or practice area over the past decade? How might that affect identity losses for individuals who identify with one of these categories?
2. What on-campus, non-stigmatizing, supportive services might high schools develop for teens who have experienced the death of friends?
3. Discuss with a small group the ways you could encourage teens to reveal that a friend/peer may be considering suicide. How might that process work to assure that the at-risk teen gets intervention in a respectful manner and that the revealing teen is not ostracized?

KEY REFERENCES

Only key references appear in the print edition. The full reference list appears in the digital product found on http://connect.springerpub.com/content/book/978-0-8261-4964-0/chapter/ch05

Bruner, C. (2017). ACE, place, race, and poverty: Building hope for children. *Academic Pediatrics, 17*(7), S123–S129. https://doi.org/10.1016/j.acap.2017.05.009

Christ, G. H., Siegel, K., & Christ, A. E. (2002). Adolescent grief: "It never really hit me…until it actually happened." *Journal of the American Medical Association, 288*, 1269–1279. https://doi.org/10.1001/jama.288.10.1269

Dilmaç, J. A. (2018). The new forms of mourning: Loss and exhibition of the death on the internet. *Omega: Journal of Death and Dying, 77*(3), 280–295. https://doi.org/10.1177/0030222816633240

Dougherty, I., & Clarke, A. (2018). Wired for innovation: Valuing the unique innovation abilities of emerging adults. *Emerging Adulthood, 6*(5), 358–365. https://doi.org/10.1177/2167696817739393

Ledford, H. (2018). The shifting boundaries of adolescence. *Nature, 554*, 429–431.

Lytje, M. (2017). Towards a model of loss navigation in adolescence. *Death Studies, 41*(5), 291–302. https://doi.org/10.1080/07481187.2016.1276488

National Academies of Sciences, Engineering, and Medicine. (2019). *The promise of adolescence: Realizing opportunity for all youth.* The National Academies Press. https://doi.org/10.17226/25388

Punzanio, A. C., Montagna, L., Mastroianni, C., Giuseppe, C., Piredda, M., & de Marinis, M. G. (2014). Losing a parent: Analysis of the literature on the experiences and needs of adolescents dealing with grief. *Journal of Hospice and Palliative Nursing, 16*(6), 362–373. https://doi.org/10.1097/NJH.0000000000000079

Siegel, D. J. (2013). *Brainstorm: The power and purpose of the teenage brain.* Jeremy P. Tarcher/Penguin.

Szwedo, D. E., Chango, J. M., & Allen, J. P. (2015). Adolescent romance and depressive symptoms: The moderating effects of positive coping and perceived friendship competence. *Journal of Clinical Child and Adolescent Psychology, 44*(4), 538–550. https://doi.org/10.1080/15374416.2014.881290

6

Grief and Loss in Emerging Adults

INTRODUCTION

Emerging adulthood, a recently defined life phase, evolved from the coalescence of social changes including lengthening formal education, changes in sexual norms, and most critically, economic changes that made job opportunities more elusive for young adults from 18 to 30. In this chapter, we outline the developmental challenges embedded in emerging adulthood, which is characterized by continued dependence on parents and ends with self-sufficiency. Death losses abound as peers' deaths due to suicide, homicide, motor vehicle accident (MVA), and drug overdose are not uncommon, and parents are more likely to die. Living losses are also extensive, related to economic security, changing identity, and multiple relationships. Social media has changed the way many—but particularly emerging adults—interact, and it provides a platform to validate emerging adults' grief. Emerging adults benefit from grief interventions that leverage their social natures but without requiring that they participate in routinized ways.

OBJECTIVES

After studying this chapter, the reader will be able to:
- Describe the changing societal circumstances that led to the creation of "emerging adulthood" as a distinct developmental life phase and identify its main task.
- Identify how emerging adults are affected differently by losses than younger and older people.
- Discuss how technology generally and social media more specifically are involved with loss among emerging adults.
- Identify the many losses inherent in the instability of emerging adulthood in current worldwide conditions.

VIGNETTE

Latoya was more than annoyed. She had worked her tail off to arrive in college but now felt like the success she expected had turned out to be a joke. She sat in a psychology class hearing about emerging adulthood and wanted to laugh. Maybe White rich kids got to "try out multiple identities, relationships, and jobs" during their college years, but that was surely not her experience. She had worked two to three jobs since she was 16 years old, and now she scrambled each day to put together the money to get through the next week and the time to study. Trying out multiple identities? She wished! Even so, she felt lucky compared with many of her childhood friends, some of whom were in jail; others were tied down with kids, and some others were so busy working to keep up that college was not on their radar. She knew she was "lucky" but that did not mean she had the luxury of the freedoms this phase of life supposedly offered.

Latoya felt economically squeezed and trapped. She guessed many others of her age felt similarly. Maybe after getting her degree, there would be a job with benefits, a decent salary, and a chance to make the world better. She hoped to be a social worker and help kids in neighborhoods like the one where she grew up. Maybe the supposedly improved economy would give her a shot at a good job. But maybe the color of her skin would change those chances too. Her typical optimism was dwindling.

DEVELOPMENTAL TASKS: ADULT SUFFICIENCY OR INSUFFICIENCY

Developmental psychologist Arnett (2000) coined the term *emerging adulthood* to better define the ambiguous period between adolescence and adulthood, then viewed as 18 to 25, now considered to be 18 to 29 (Society for the Study of Emerging Adulthood [SSEA], 2019). Arnett justified this reconceptualization of development by noting how marriage, childbearing, and career formation were coming later in Western, industrialized nations as education and adolescent dependency were prolonged. He predicted that this life phase might extend into the late 20s under conditions of persistent economic weakness, hypothesizing that developmental stages are tied to the economy (Arnett, 2004). By December 2007, when the United States descended into the Great Recession, his term became widely accepted, and in the course of the recession and its lingering aftermath, his prediction was borne out.

During and after the Great Recession, unemployment was very high among those under 30, not returning to prerecession levels until 2017, after the Obama stimulus took effect (Statistica, 2020b). Even in 2020, relatively few emerging adults can find secure full-time employment with benefits and a living wage. Many entered the gig economy or withdrew from the labor force, burnishing work credentials in school if they could. The economic situation has shaped a generation much like how the Great Depression and World War II affected prior generations, and similarly, the damage is not undone easily.

Arnett's (2004) conceptualization included five features that provided a rationale for why emerging adulthood is a separate life phase, not merely a transition: identity explorations (continued and broadened from adolescence), instability (multiple moves/jobs), self-focus, feeling in-between, and anticipating many possibilities. Although these are features of adolescence and can be found in adulthood, they are most frequent and intense among those between 18 and mid-to-late 20s.

In more recent descriptions of emerging adulthood, Arnett and Mitre found that other adult age groups may also endorse emerging adult assertions such as "This is a time of my life for finding out who I am" (2018, p. 6). They maintain the 18-to-25 range although the SSEA has adopted the longer range. We use the broader range, recognizing that many life phases are changeable, and as the economic context changes, we may go back to the shorter range as more are able to gain a true economic foothold. At this point, we see that some people commit to careers, relationships, and stability by 25, but many others still struggle to find self-sufficiency well into their 30s. Despite much individual variation, we focus on the developmental aspects of the life phase in order to frame how those aspects relate to loss and grief.

Biological Development

Neurobiologists assert that brain maturation is not complete until the prefrontal cortex is fully integrated and executive functions are well established—a task most believe to occur by 25. The brain goes through tremendous change from adolescence into the 20s: The hypothalamic–pituitary–adrenal axis evolves, the dopamine system is sculpted, and pruning and integration of the prefrontal cortex is completed (Dougherty & Clarke, 2018; Johnson & Stevens, 2018). This coincides with emerging adulthood as most people complete these processes between 18 and 25. Functionally, the brain becomes integrated to be flexible, adaptive, coherent, energized, and stable by the time these changes are completed (Siegel, 1999/2012). White and gray matter changes in the brain correspond with early emerging adults' search for novelty and intensity until the development of a calmer, focused brain is completed (Dougherty & Clarke, 2018; Weiland et al., 2014).

Psychological Development

Development in emerging adulthood blends the tasks of adolescence and young adulthood and represents a discrete phase of life with the primary task of movement toward self-sufficiency (Arnett, 2004, 2007). Instead of being a time for "settling down," it is viewed as a time of relationship exploration, exploration of gender and attraction identities, and a time of hiatus where those who marry are out of the norm. Expectations of lucrative employment and an independent household were declining due to the prolonged nature of adolescence (Arnett, 2007), but the Great Recession meant emerging adults moved back home after college in the largest numbers ever (Choi et al., 2019). Many of the expectations of adolescent development are now pushed off until age 25 or later. Arnett (2007) classifies the subtasks of emerging adulthood as (a) accepting responsibility for oneself, (b) making independent decisions, and (c) becoming financially independent and notes that this is a time of great instability and explorations of love, work, and worldviews. Additionally, emerging adults tend to be low in "other focus" (taking others' opinions, needs, or concerns into account), and they tend to feel less vulnerable and to take more chances, increasing their vulnerability to substance misuse (Sussman & Arnett, 2014).

Marcia's (1966) classic terms of identity development remain relevant when describing emerging adulthood. It is often a time of moratorium (a time of exploring identities, yet not committing to one). As Marcia observes, it can also be a time when other identity processes occur: foreclosure (commitment to an identity without much exploration), identity diffusion (characterized by avoiding exploration and commitments related to identity), or achieving identity (following exploration, commitment to a stable identity). Emerging adulthood includes many possibilities for experiments in identity and involvement with the social groups that support them.

Aside from identity development and movement toward self-sufficiency, emerging adults typically grapple with beliefs about how the world works—their assumptive world. Lerner (1980) defined belief in a just world (BJW) as "a theory of justice that has as its basic premise the notion that people get what they deserve and deserve what they get" (p. 512). BJW promotes a sense of safety in childhood and young adolescence and evolves idiosyncratically, declining through exposure to life events (Dalbert & Sallay, 2004). Taken to an extreme, BJW has been associated with stigmatization, vengefulness, and judgmental attitudes, but in moderation, BJW is associated with a greater sense of well-being, more effective coping, and less intense negative emotion (Lench & Chang, 2007).

Yet the experience of emerging adulthood itself calls BJW into question. Dalbert and Donat (2015) suggest that when an injustice occurs (such as when working hard in school and life does not yield a good job or adult stability), people with a strong BJW often assimilate that experience to make it congruent with BJW (asserting the injustice was self-inflicted, is not that bad, or is the victim's fault). Quite likely, many emerging adults believe that they are at fault for their lack of achievement, rather than questioning their BJW and recognizing that the world is often unjust and that honest effort may yield little. Dalbert and Donat describe the protective qualities BJW can have for optimism, achievement, and adaptation. After all, the lesson of self-blame is to try harder.

Still, with emerging adults hard up against obvious structural injustices that bar economic success, it may be that BJW is a casualty of their experience. They discover that the world is not fair.

Social Development

Sociologists also recognized early in the 2000s that adulthood required an "ever-lengthening transition" (Furstenberg et al., 2004, p. 34). This transition became emerging adulthood, with 25 taken as the normal age of economic self-sufficiency. Global popular culture has taken up the notion of "quarter-life crisis" to mirror "midlife crisis," and in this realm, 25 is understood as an age of anxiety, depression, and pessimism about success. Buzzfeed has a tongue-in-cheek quiz about quarter life and its discontents in the United States (Misener, 2013), and the United Kingdom's typically proper news invokes the F-word when discussing the quarter-life crisis (Piskorz, 2018). Although crisis is posited to start at 30 for people in China (Keyao, 2016), the similar features of feeling like losers and incapable of achieving adult goals show how broadly the notion has spread. This speaks to the maturational losses emerging adults feel as they lose the socially sanctioned dependence of adolescence without feeling fully adult (Arnett, 2000). *The Huffington Post* reports Quarter Life Crisis stories about the challenges, *ennui*, and frustrations of life at 25. Beaton (2017) writes there about a widespread sense of inadequacy, in-betweenness, and loss in comparison with previous generations and argues that the quarter-life crisis results from not having realistic goals rather than failing to accomplish them. She asserts that her peers wonder "is this it?" and worry that they will have regrets or miss out on the better options in life by "settling" for a good job or other adequate-but-not-ideal outcomes. Although previous generations might disagree about the unique status of emerging adults related to inadequacy, loss, and worries about selling out, emerging adults' explorations of love, work, goals, and worldview do lead to losses inherent in instability and insecurity.

Spiritual Development

Few studies attempt to separate religiosity and spirituality because the constructs have overlapping concepts that make distinctions difficult. Nadal et al. (2018) distinguished religiosity (formal dogmas and practices) and spirituality (idiosyncratic connections to universals) and then measured those constructs in a large emerging adult sample of U.S. college students that was racially diverse and spread across the country. The largest groups were comprised of students identified as religious and spiritual (RAS 37%) or not religious and not spiritual (NRNS 33%). Those who were identified as spiritual but not religious (SBNR 9%) or religious but not spiritual (RBNS 8%) constituted smaller groups. They then mapped how these identities were correlated with positive (e.g., psychological well-being, maturity, prosocial behavior) and maladaptive (e.g., hazardous alcohol use, depression, antisocial behavior) qualities and found that RAS people were higher on positive and lower on maladaptive characteristics, and RBNS were highest on depression. The NRNS group was more moderate with the second highest correlations with positive characteristic variables and the second lowest for most variables indicating maladaptation. NRNS group members also had more risky sexual behavior and alcohol use. The authors were surprised that the RBNS group had the lowest positive variable associations and relatively high maladaptation correlations. After latent class analysis that identified low, moderate, and high R/S groupings (the mixed groups dropped out of the classes), the high R/S group continued to show high associations with the positive variables and low ones with the maladaptation variables. Yet the moderate R/S group had worse outcomes than the low R/S group, possibly indicating more struggles with the inconsistency between their actions and their idealized self (Nadal et al., 2018). Thus, emerging adults exhibit a wide range of RAS identities, and they influence psychological and behavioral outcomes, though not in any simple straightforward manner.

The evocative title "From 'worm food' to 'infinite bliss': Emerging adults' views of life after death" (Arnett, 2008) indicates a similarly broad range of views about religious or spiritual understandings of death. In answer to the question "what happens after death?" 25% of the emerging adults professed belief in heaven and hell, and only this group's members were strongly affiliated with a specific religion (Christian); 15% believed in heaven only and another 15% believed there was some indescribable existence after death. Some said they had no idea what happened after death (21%), 11% believed in no afterlife ("worm food"), and 13% believed in reincarnation or that the deceased returned to a cosmic energy source. Emerging adults comprise a diverse group when it comes to religious or spiritual identities.

Arnett (2000) argued that emerging adulthood is a time when spiritual and religious identifications are solidified. Others argue that religious affiliations are protective (Nadal et al., 2018), but fewer emerging adults are embracing formal religious identifications and practices (Chan et al., 2015). People who identify as gender and sexual minority (GSM) may endure negative judgments from heteronormative and cisnormative voices in society generally but from religious communities particularly. Scroggs et al. considered how emerging adults who participate in GSM group activity and religious group activity experience protective (or not) influences in the context of GSM identity visibility, salience, and integration. Against their hypothesis, people who were more active in GSM groups did not have higher well-being scores, but those active in religious groups did report higher well-being. Those with higher GSM identity integration also had higher well-being. The authors observed that more religious communities welcome LGBTQ+ people now and they suggested that people who identify as GSM and integrate that part of their identity with their religious affiliation may be in communities that affirm them, enhancing well-being (Scroggs et al., 2018).

SPECIAL CONSIDERATIONS IN RISK AND RESILIENCE

As noted, RAS affiliations and beliefs seem to have protective qualities for some emerging adults. Yet risk and resilience factors have many sources. As mentioned throughout this text, adverse childhood experiences (ACEs) are known to be associated with poor health and other outcomes over the life span (Felitti et al., 1998), and emerging adulthood seems to be the point at which these events of childhood begin to have an impact on both risk and resilience. Arnett (2016) observed that people who have ACEs may need to take on more responsibilities and may not have the luxury of identity explorations and postponing adult job responsibilities. In short, they skip many qualities of emerging adulthood because they take on marriage, jobs, children, and other adult responsibilities. Davis et al. (2018) set out to examine how ACEs interact with the characteristics of emerging adulthood. In their sample of mostly White emerging adults recruited on Amazon mTurk, they found only partial support for the hypotheses that higher ACE scores would be associated with lower experimentation/possibilities, self-focus, and educational attainment. They did not find support for the hypothesis that education would mediate ACE exposure and endorsement of the qualities of emerging adulthood (explorations, possibilities, instability, self-focus, and in-betweenness). They found that perceived stress mediated the relationship between ACEs and emerging adult qualities such that more ACEs were associated with increased perceived stress and, in turn, increased stress was associated with lower levels of exploration/possibilities and self-focus. They suggest that people who have higher ACE scores may also have adapted successfully to challenging circumstances, making them look less like typical emerging adults because they exhibited maturity and displayed adult behavior already (Davis et al., 2018).

As in prior life phases, race and ethnicity influence risk and resilience. Particularly striking is the way premature death affects Blacks in every age group, from infant mortality through childhood and adolescence and into emerging adulthood (and beyond). This means that Black community members are more likely to experience multiple deaths of significant others, increasing levels of stress, weathering (high allostatic load leading to "wear and tear" on health), and poor outcomes (Umberson, 2017). Individual statistics about high Black infant (and maternal) mortality are widely known, and we know that Black children have higher rates of asthma and other life-threatening illness and that homicide is the number one killer of young Black men. Yet the implications are bigger than even the horrific statistics. Umberson uses a life course perspective to

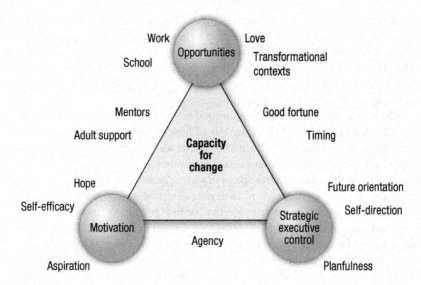

FIGURE 6.1 Factors Contributing to Resilience in Emerging Adulthood. This image (Wood et al., 2018) illustrates the resources that support emerging adults' resilience.
Source: Reproduced with permission from Wood, D., Crapnell, T., Lau, L., Bennett, A., Lotstein, D., Ferris, M., & Kuo, A. (2018). Emerging Adulthood as a critical stage in the life course. In N. Halfon, C. Forrest, R. Lerner, & E. Faustman (Eds.), *Handbook of life course health development* (pp. 123–143). Springer Publishing Company. https://link.springer .com/chapter/10.1007/978-3-319-47143-3_7

argue convincingly that "racial disparities in exposure to the deaths of friends and loved ones is a unique type of stress for black Americans that not only obliterates important social connections, but also launches a cascade of psychological, social, behavioral, and biological consequences that undermine relationships, as well as health, over the life course" (2017, p. 3). These accumulating life course effects mean that people enter emerging adulthood not only buffeted by the losses but without some of the friends and family members who help people navigate emerging adulthood. These racial risks and losses seem to fall most heavily on Black and Native Americans, whereas White, Asian, and Hispanic Americans have fewer losses per life phase and seemingly stronger ongoing social support networks (Umberson, 2017).

Just as some exposure to limited ACEs may add some degree of resilience through learning to cope, other aspects of development may also enhance resiliency. Given emerging adults' tendency to rely on parental support, it is interesting that emerging adults who experience an adverse event and then process it with their parent(s) seem to have a better chance of experiencing posttraumatic growth as a result. There are obviously topics emerging adults are less likely to discuss with their parents (romantic relationships and academic failures), but when they feel comfortable communicating with a parent and believe the parent has trustworthy information or opinions to provide, they seem more resilient (Tian et al., 2016). Their own qualities also enhance resilience. Wood et al. (2018) suggest that motivation, opportunities, and developed executive control combine with hope and self-efficacy (among other qualities) to enhance resiliency and capacity for change. Possessing occupational aspirations and developing relationships with adults and mentors are also protective factors. See Figure 6.1 for a visual depiction of factors promoting resilience.

LOSSES EXPERIENCED BY EMERGING ADULTS

Death Losses

Just as tweens and teens have a somewhat sentimentalized view of death, some assert that emerging adults often have a romanticized view of death that is mingled with changing spiritual and religious views and tends toward rumination (Power & McKinney, 2013). Counter to that view, others find that emerging adults experience fewer grief symptoms than older or younger people and exhibit more posttraumatic growth (Patrick & Henrie, 2016). Not surprisingly, the research literature is mixed, probably because emerging adulthood covers a large range of development, and the characteristic instability of emerging adulthood likely contributes to significant differences within each individual as well as across the broad range of emerging adults. Some may ruminate more like teens, while others may have so many distractions in life that they find little time to exhibit grief.

When coping with the death of a loved one, many emerging adults feel that their BJW has been violated. Surely the death of a close loved one, especially unexpectedly, would cause a reworking of a belief that the world is just and bad things only happen to bad people. Indeed, emerging adulthood itself may challenge one's belief that the world rewards the good and punishes the bad, but the death of a loved one at this time may even more fully confront them with the fact that the world is not always—or even usually—just. They may even come to expect bad things to happen to good people, themselves included, with a subsequent rise in a sense of vulnerability. Such individuals may be at higher risk for longer-term maladaptive coping after trauma and loss (Lench & Chang, 2007). Especially on their first encounter with death, confronted with the injustice of the world (and the secondary loss of security that entails), emerging adults may struggle not only with the grief of the death but with the revision of their assumptive world as BJW is violated.

Despite the challenges of revising BJW, most research finds remarkable resilience on the part of emerging adults (Patrick & Henrie, 2016; Porter & Claridge, 2019; Schwartz et al., 2018). Emerging adults also seem to have a distinctive experience of cumulative grief. Schwartz et al. (2018) assessed maladaptive grief symptoms, resilience, and depression symptoms in a diverse sample of well over 500 emerging adults enrolled in college who had at least one loved one die in their past. They wondered if an earlier loss might promote the development of coping or if a previous loss would decrease resilience after future losses. Their most surprising finding was that resilience did not differ among those who had a past loss, those who had a more recent loss, and those who had both, nor did the presence of depression symptoms. Although there were more maladaptive grief symptoms in the group with both types of losses (past and recent), that differed significantly only from the past loss group, while both losses and recent loss groups were more similar. They interpreted these findings to indicate that even when cumulative loss led to more maladaptive grief symptoms, the high level of resilience in emerging adults was protective (Schwartz et al., 2018).

Death of a Parent

An emerging adult's sense of injustice may be particularly heightened by the off-time loss of a parent. As noted in Chapter 1, off-time losses are challenging because few peers must cope with similar losses. This leaves grievers without company in their grief and without models for how to grieve such a loss.

Before the death, parents and emerging adults may have given mixed signals about the degree of adult responsibility and readiness for independence the emerging adult has achieved. A parental death before these issues are clarified can leave emerging adult children uncertain as to their status as fully functioning adults. Because many emerging adults remain dependent both emotionally and financially on parents, the loss of a parent may also remove critical support. Research indicates that while parents hold emerging adults responsible for finances, requiring that they pay cell phone and credit card bills (Jablonski & Martino, 2013) as well as help the family (driving siblings, etc.), most do not expect full-fledged self-sufficiency. Thus, the death of a parent is not only an emotional loss but an untimely threat to material security.

Newton (2012) explored the coping and support needs of emerging adults after the death of a parent, noting that most still relied heavily on their parents for financial, instrumental (concrete help with chores/needs), and emotional supports. Most reported coping with parental loss by throwing themselves back into school or work quickly, yet "old coping mechanisms were not quite enough" (p. 48). Her respondents reported coping through exercise, strengthened religious affiliations, yoga, and talking with others. Respondents whose parent had died more than 5 years previously were considerably further through their grief than those who had experienced the death more recently. Many of the latter group felt that the loss profoundly shaped daily life. Despite that, none of the 10 participants relied heavily on the surviving parent or family of origin as their primary support, which as Newton observes, fits with the developmental need to become more independent.

Emerging adults processing the death of their parents do so during a very busy phase of life. In interviews with emerging adults whose parent had died during these years, most commented on the difficulty of managing the funeral or estate arrangements while trying to maintain class work (if in college) or multiple job responsibilities (Porter & Claridge, 2019). They observed that others' perceptions of their identity had changed. One participant commented that she was no longer viewed as the tall basketball player but as the girl whose dad died (p. 6). Most indicated a high degree of resiliency and, in contrast to Newton's finding, they reported that their primary supporter was the surviving parent. Porter and Claridge's respondents did not indicate strong interest in using therapeutic resources, but they recommended that support groups designed for emerging adults should target their age group alone and include fun activities to allow some reprieve from focusing solely on grief. They cautioned that such a group should allow attendees to listen to other participants rather than feel forced to share their own stories (Porter & Claridge, 2019).

Carlos (2014) suggests that therapists working with emerging adults who are parentally bereaved may find *Worden's Four Tasks of Mourning* a useful guide for intervention. She advises close attention to issues of termination and helping emerging adults recognize the ongoing nature of grief (to "avoid the illusion of an end to grief") and the tendency toward sudden upsurges of grief, seemingly her version of Rando's (1993) subsequent temporary upsurges of grief reactions (pp. 64–77).

Since Edelman's (1994) book *Motherless Daughters*, people have become sensitized to how powerful that particular loss can be. For emerging adults working on identity processes, it seems all the more powerful. Schultz (2007) interviewed six women 18 to 25 and found that half of them had considered suicide and all of them identified significant ways their sense of identity had changed as a result of their mother's death. Most cultivated relationships with older women who could function as maternal figures and also worked to identify their mother's qualities that they could see in themselves. Pearce (2011) also found that women felt their worlds and senses-of-self interrupted by the death of their mother. Susan (a respondent in the research) reported some ambivalence after her mother's death: She enjoyed the freedom that came with not being monitored and told what to do but was discomforted by the fact that she could not go to university because "suddenly you're on your own that's it, you've gotta work, you've gotta earn, you've gotta support yourself. And there are no other options" (Pearce, 2011, p. 41). Given that emerging adults live on the frustrating verge of a fragile independence, such ambivalence may be more prevalent than commonly reported.

We must never overlook the influence of culture on the experience of parental death. In an autophotographical study, bereaved Korean emerging adults reported more anger at their deceased parent, and more need to protect the surviving parent from burden, than did bereaved emerging adults in Western nations. The respondents who were bereaved in childhood reported a high degree of embarrassment and shame related to the Korean stigmatization of single parent families that extends even to the survivors of a parent's death (Yang, 2012). Additionally, Korean children, especially adult children, are expected to witness their parent's last breath; for those who were unable to do so, extreme regret is part of the culture of mourning (Yang, 2012). Competent support of grievers requires exploration of the cultural norms in which the parental relationship is embedded, including duties to parents in death, dying, and mourning rituals.

Many emerging adults are in college; calls to provide support for bereaved college students were sounded in the mid-1980s (Zinner, 1985) and consistently in the intervening years (Fajgenbaum et al., 2012; Liew & Servaty-Seib, 2018). Although this is often couched within the need for such services when a campus is affected by mass murder or suicide, colleges and universities should ensure the availability of grief counselors to provide support, education, and counseling for all bereaved students in many circumstances, including after the death of a parent. The link between college students' bereavement and their ability to maintain academic and social achievement in college (and their felt attachment to the college/university itself) is affected by the support they receive from their family and the type of coping they do (Cousins et al., 2017). College and university communities need to implement bereavement policies and on-campus support (Servaty-Seib & Liew, 2019). These should be culturally sensitive so as to allow family support in ways not common in that community. For instance, a parentally bereaved Papua New Guinea emerging adult is expected to return home for a month to 100 days of memorial services. University communities must find ways to be more supportive and flexible with such students.

Death of Friends/Lovers

Friends, peers, and intimate partners take on more emotional salience during adolescence, and Arnett (2007) confirms that these attachments remain highly influential during emerging adulthood. Many emerging adults feel their grief to be disenfranchised after such a person dies. Family members and siblings are viewed as the truly legitimate grievers, whereas grieving friends are often relegated to a second-class status.

Because MVAs, suicide, and homicide deaths are the primary cause of death in this age group (Centers for Disease Control and Prevention [CDC], 2017), this makes unexpected and violent deaths common in emerging adult peer groups. Opioid overdose deaths have added significantly to this. Among 15- to 34-year-old African Americans, homicide is the leading cause of death (Dicker, 2016), and the two age categories with the highest murder victim rates in the United States in 2018 were the 20- to 24- and 25- to 29-year-old groups (Statistica, 2020a). This means that emerging adults, particularly in communities of color, are experiencing an extraordinary number of deaths in their social circle. Recognizing the high rate of violent death among young people, medical systems have started culturally sensitive programs that view violent injury and overdose as teachable moments and intervene, often with peer counselors, to connect ED patients to treatment resources and peer support (Dicker, 2016; Mercy & Vivolo-Kantor, 2016). Loss of friends through sudden and often violent deaths leaves emerging adults struggling to make meaning of the loss and possibly at risk for believing revenge will create justice. Regardless of the way a friend dies, emerging adults need support in processing these losses.

In a study of 25 Canadian men of diverse backgrounds who were 19 to 25 years old and who had experienced the sudden death of a male friend, Creighton et al. (2013) found that the majority "man[ed] up" to avoid overt emotional expressions, save anger. Even so, as part of the photo elicitation research, the bereaved men displayed deep emotional responses to their friends' deaths while sharing the photos. Many asserted that men's stoicism is "inbuilt" (p. 38) and they attributed this not only to social norms "taught from an early age—don't cry, it's not your job" (p. 38)—but also to biology—"It just won't connect with tear glands and I think that's just how guys are" (p. 38). As the authors note, this has implications for intervention. Taking photographs for the research inspired the bereaved men to deep expression, suggesting that clinicians and supporters need to recognize that bereaved, emerging adult males may seem stoic but experience life-changing thoughts and feelings that resist verbal expression. Creighton's team (2013) found that most of their respondents integrated the friend's death into their identity by becoming more adventurous (embracing life) or more fatherly (being more protective and responsible) or experiencing a type of rebirth the authors describe as the Lamplighter identity as they now "saw the light" (p. 41) and worked toward finding the good in themselves and others.

Technology and social media have changed the way emerging adults mourn their friends. McBride had the tragic experience of losing both her husband and emerging adult daughter to death in a short time, leaving herself and her surviving daughter to cope with their changed world. Part of that changed world became the focus of her dissertation as she encountered emerging adults' use of social media sites as memorials and community mourning tools. She learned that emerging adults posted for five purposes: (a) for "alternate places and spaces" (p. ii) to grieve and mourn; (b) to allow for ongoing attachment to the deceased; (c) to promote coping and integration of the loss; (d) to foster continuing bonds; and (e) to inhabit a space initially created by the deceased where a virtual community continues to remember the deceased (2019). She observes that families provided space for mourning in the past, and friends' grief was often disenfranchised, yet now, social media creates a space where friends' grief and mourning are expected and honored in ways that seem particularly validating.

Suicide Deaths

Suicide is the second most common cause of death among people ages 15 to 34 (National Institute of Mental Health [NIMH], 2019). Miron et al. (2019) report that in 2017, people ages 20 to 24 had a suicide rate of 17 per 100,000, up from 12.5 in 2000, likely due to opioid deaths classified as suicide. Although both genders had rising rates of suicide from 2000 to 2017, the men's (20–24) suicide rate in 2017 was 27.1/100,000 and the women's (20–24) was 6.2/100,000 (Miron et al., 2019). In the same time period, reported opioid deaths per 100,000 (all ages) went from 2.20 in 2000 to 13.21 in 2017, of which approximately 90% were deemed unintentional, 4% were deemed to be suicides, and slightly over 5% were of undetermined intent (Olfson et al., 2019). Olfson et al. observe that the dramatic rise in opioid deaths likely masks suicides and that people who have nonfatal opioid overdose are at higher risk for suicide in the future. There is some indication that this trend in opioid deaths has begun to level off as life expectancy, which had dipped due to opioid deaths in 2015 to 2017, began to rise incrementally in 2018 (Tavernise & Goodnough, 2020).

Suicide deaths among emerging adults seem to follow one of three trajectories from adolescence through emerging adulthood. Although theoretically there could be four trajectories (stable high rates, stable low rates, rising rates, and declining rates), data from four waves of the Adolescent Longitudinal Health (Add Health) study showed only three trajectories. Following a sample of over 9,000 youth from ages 12 to 18 through 29, Thompson and Swartout (2018) found that the vast majority (almost 94%) followed a stable low likelihood of suicide ideation or attempt trajectory, whereas 5.1% declined with a high likelihood of suicide attempt that abruptly dropped as they approached 22, a pattern they called adolescent limited. A third trajectory, with 1.3% of the sample, followed a persistently higher trajectory (though with a mild decline to age 29), indicating that these youth who struggled with suicidal ideation and attempts in adolescence continued to struggle in emerging adulthood. Suicide attempts were associated with alcohol use, impulsivity, depression, delinquency, and exposure to partner abuse. For the adolescent-limited group, these associations all dropped off as the adolescent moved into emerging adulthood, except for depression and exposure to partner abuse. When these behaviors continue into emerging adulthood, they may indicate higher likelihood of suicide attempts, especially in combination with exposure to friends and family who have taken their lives. The hope is that knowing these associations will allow targeted intervention to reduce the behaviors and hopefully the suicide attempts (Thompson & Swartout, 2018).

Support groups are often suggested for support of survivors of suicide (friends and family). In considering her experience facilitating support groups for emerging adults bereaved by suicide (family members or similarly aged friends), Mead (2020) theorized that emerging adults' developmental needs to move toward adult development are in tension with bereaved people's needs to reflect backward on the lost relationship. She observes that emerging adults must manage work, school, other relationships, and other activities, and this seemingly forces them to process their grief more quickly. She also suggests that emerging adults give voice to their anger and guilt in ways that may interfere with processing grief. She reports that many in her support groups felt the group to be the only place they felt safe to discuss their loss because other friends of their age were not trusted to understand how suicide deaths differed from death due to other causes. She strongly suggests that support groups with individual counseling be available for emerging adults bereaved by suicide. Similarly, their strong developmental preference for autonomy is an impediment to getting emerging adults to make use of therapeutic help when bereaved by suicide or if considering suicide (Wilson et al., 2011). Wilson et al. suggest educating peers to provide informal assistance and monitoring, while also urging use of formal help resources.

Living Losses: Atypical, Typical, and Maturational Losses

Emerging adults experience many living (nondeath) losses, most related to the instability of their life phase. Here, the atypical loss of chronic and life-threatening illness is addressed first due to its significant challenges.

Chronic and Life-Threatening Illness

Chronic conditions such an autism spectrum disorder (ASD) affect many with particularly challenging effects as people reach emerging adulthood. A key task of emerging adulthood is to become self-sufficient, but the majority of young adults with ASD are not able to hold jobs or move away from caregiving parents, grandparents, or others, making this a challenging time for families (Wood et al., 2018). Although ASD encompasses a broad range of presentations, work to foster self-determination and work skills can be an important part of working with families to promote positive outcomes for individuals living with ASD. The emerging adult who struggles with ASD may very much desire independent living and the accoutrements of adulthood while not being able to independently maintain those responsibilities. Helping them to recognize their sense of loss at not being able to achieve those adult-independence milestones is part of the work with these individuals and their families. When independent living is an option, helping families navigate how to "check in" in ways that are acceptable to both parties may also be necessary.

Other emerging adults may have developmental disabilities that affect them both cognitively and physically. Wilkenfeld's reading at the end of this chapter is illustrative of how frustrating these types of conditions can be for the individuals who have them and their family members. Again, emerging adulthood is the point at which hopes for movement into an independent adulthood are often dashed, leaving loss in their wake.

Emerging adults with chronic illnesses from diabetes mellitus to cancer to chronic kidney disease need to receive care (often from parents) at the very point in their development where they wish to assert their independence. This is challenging to them and to their caretakers. Emerging adults coping with life-threatening illness approach death and adulthood at the same time, and their challenges are much different from those of older adults facing imminent death. They need to find ways of living their current lives with peers whose focus is toward the future, while they gingerly hold hopeful expectations of a long life during which they would accomplish adult goals.

When emerging adults are critically ill or dying, their medical and physical care needs usually take precedence over developmental needs. Hospitals may put them on wards with children or much older adults, with whom they have little in common. Although most emerging adults remain connected to their family of origin's home, providers must pay special attention to assessing the type of physical care provider and place where a final illness plays out so that the emerging adult has some sense of control in the home care, palliative care, or hospice planning. In interviews with emerging adults with advanced cancers, Knox et al. (2017) found a pervasive sense of developmental arrest (being stuck) with a strong sense of isolation and emotional distance from others. Respondents described attempts to maintain a sense of normalcy, and many felt an ongoing sense of disbelief that they had life-threatening cancers. They not only struggled with having to rely on parents but also seemed resigned to doing so. They worried about whether time spent working or in school had been "wasted" (p. 404). Although asked about whether they desired support groups, most rejected the idea, assuming that similar to their medical care, they might be put together either with people not in their age group or with similarly aged cancer patients who were more likely to be cured. Many commented that answering the interview's specific questions helped them to process their experience. Kenten et al. (2019), whose study included families, similarly found that young adults worked almost desperately to maintain a sense of normalcy even in the face of significant symptoms and illness. They struggled with having to return to parents for care, and the families struggled with the young adult's return home. Families often lacked the skills needed to provide emotional and instrumental care, and the authors observed that, under the circumstances, the families often could not be "skilled up" in time to be helpful (p. 11). In short, the emerging adults' developmental needs should play a role in determining how care is provided.

Climate Grief

Although not solely the worry of emerging adults, grief about the state of the earth's climate and health has been strongly affecting them. Awareness of global warming, drought, fires, and extreme weather events has been a growing public concern since the 1960s, but scientific consensus has become clear over the past decade about the perilous nature of climate change (United Nations, 2019). In Utah, two emerging adults responded to climate grief by developing a 10-step "Good Grief" support program for those experiencing anxiety and grief about the state of the planet. This was in conjunction with a program called Uplift Climate, which aimed to support those under 30 years who were grieving for the state of the planet (Scher, 2018). Many who attended Uplift Climate meetings express reluctance to have children because of the dire predictions of rising global devastation in the next 30 to 50 years, a concern echoed by other emerging adults (Tomaine, 2020). This type of living loss is not just about the environment and climate but reflects a more general loss of hope as well.

Loss of Self-Esteem

Emerging adults may battle a loss of self-esteem on multiple fronts, some of which are discussed in the following under a loss of economic self-sufficiency. Chung et al. (2014) found predictable drops in self-esteem as emerging adults started college along with predictable rises in self-esteem over the course of college, except for about 12% of their respondents. Self-esteem is also associated with depressive symptoms. A study of depression and self-esteem after relationship breakups returned surprising results: Emerging adults with low self-esteem typically had depressive symptoms regardless of relationship status, but those who had high self-esteem experienced more depressive symptoms and negative ruminations when a romantic relationship ended than those who had lower self-esteem (O'Sullivan et al., 2019). Self-esteem may therefore have both situational and developmental aspects. It may also be associated with the level of parental involvement in an emerging adult's life such that those with "helicopter parents" may not learn their own competencies or develop the ability to cope with adversity (see Dumont's reading at the end of this chapter). They may fail to develop self-esteem, which is commonly based on an earned sense of mastery and self-efficacy. This life phase is ripe for multiple challenges to developing and maintaining self-esteem over time.

Loss of Economic Viability

Before the Great Recession, emerging adults were likely to move into economic self-sufficiency between 18 and 23 years of age, depending on class origin and university attendance, and the maturational losses involved in giving up dependency on parents for economic survival were often experienced as a loss. Such loss still occurs, but today's cohort of emerging adults usually faces it later, because the transition has become far more difficult. According to Urban Institute data, 12% of 25- to 34-year-olds lived with their parents in 2000 and that rose to 22%, by 2017, while the same age group's home ownership rate went from 45.8% in 2000 to 38.4% in 2017 (Choi et al., 2019). The chance to achieve the markers of adulthood—one's own living space, economic viability, privacy—is forfeited when one must remain living with parent/s. Carrying high student debt and low credit scores into young adulthood means fewer opportunities to improve one's economic circumstances. Lost here is an imagined and even expected future of success and security.

Emerging adults and their parents are aware of this, if only intuitively. They report a sense of economic pressure that leads to pessimism about the economy as well as anxiety and depressive symptoms for both groups (Stein et al., 2011). The parents tend to have anxiety and depression related to concerns about their children's career possibilities and potential for sacrificing to assist parents, whereas emerging adults tend to have more anxiety and depression about personal economic pressures (though they were not unaware of the possibility that they may need to sacrifice for parental well-being in the future; Stein et al., 2011).

Although there is growing awareness of the economic structures that work against emerging adults, particularly those without advanced education, this loss nevertheless remains largely disenfranchised by the widely accepted American "just world" myth of bountiful opportunity. As with many disenfranchised losses, the silent self-blame that accompanies it must be exposed to allow emerging adults to mourn their lost expectations, gain strength from one another, and avoid blaming themselves for circumstances beyond their control. They must also be helped to achieve productive work lives that enable a sense of purpose and satisfying independence.

Loss of a Romantic Relationship

The emerging adult, like the adolescent, is involved in exploring intimate relationships. Erikson (1959/1980) defined the crisis of intimacy versus isolation as the major thrust of young adult development and asserted that those who resolve this crisis in favor of intimacy are able to experience love. More than one-third of all types of partnerships (gay, lesbian, and heterosexual) dissolve within 2 years (Neimeyer, 1998). For some young people, the dissolution of a relationship contributes to growth, but for many others "the years of dating represent a seemingly endless series of exhilarating romantic connections, broken by disappointment and occasionally devastating disconnections" (Neimeyer, 1998, p. 23).

Some of the secondary losses from breakups are subtle, such as loss of the self-definition provided by being in a couple. The dissolution of a relationship shifts the view of self, in part because of how others react to the change. Particularly in a world where emerging adults are viewed as having transient dalliances and "hookups" rather than relationships (Katz & Schneider, 2013), relationship loss is often trivialized by family and friends with comments like "you are young and will find someone else." While probably true and well intended, this is not a constructive observation. Even so, emerging adults also seem to grow and reassess themselves by virtue of living through several romantic relationships that end. They develop abilities to self-regulate, assess their needs within relationships, mobilize support when hurting, and cope with stress in ways that enhance their developmental maturity (Norona et al., 2017). Romantic entanglements in adolescence seem to set the stage for emerging adulthood in that those who struggled with depressive symptoms in adolescence exhibit more distress during romantic relationship dissolution in emerging adulthood. Furthermore, women with high degrees of distress after breakups during emerging adulthood tended to have more difficulty in subsequent relationships (relationships that were "current" during the study; Shulman et al., 2017). Like most losses, leaving a relationship is painful and entails adjustments in identity, yet it also brings maturational gains as people learn more about their strengths and weaknesses within relationships and how to adapt in healthier ways.

Social media can make breakups painfully public and even shocking when people learn they are no longer part of a couple when the Facebook relationship status is unilaterally changed or when other relationships are exposed on Snapchat or Instagram. At times, social media provokes the breakup (Clayton et al., 2013). Although current emerging adults still engage in person (Rappleyea et al., 2014), most view social media as a place for all their activities including information about their relationships and the ongoing or discontinued nature of them.

Relationship qualities are affected by the identity issues discussed earlier involving moratorium or achieved identities in emerging adulthood (as well as diffuse or foreclosed identities as per Marcia, 1966). Women in any of the identity categories other than moratorium reported higher relationship intimacy, as did male emerging adults with foreclosed or achieved identity. This implies that women still exploring identity were less likely to engage in high intimacy relationships while men who had committed to identity earlier were more likely to be competently intimate. For those who have established identity (via achievement or foreclosure), romantic partnerships seem to be easier and to create a greater sense of well-being (Johnson et al., 2012).

Losses Related to Substance Use Disorders

Emerging adults are engaging in illicit substance use at ever-greater rates, with marijuana use driving the pace, followed closely by prescription pain reliever misuse (Substance Abuse and Mental Health Services Administration, 2019). Neurobiology seems to make emerging adults more vulnerable to substance use disorders (SUDs; Weiland et al., 2014) due to their attraction to consciousness-altering substances and the potential of substances to damage the developing brain. Stressful life events like the death of a parent or the end of a romantic relationship have been found to increase the likelihood of SUDs (Stone et al., 2012). Social context is associated with SUDs in complex ways. Substance use and abuse tend to develop or intensify during emerging adulthood, which is characterized by new freedoms often unrestrained by the commitments and routines of spouse, parent, and worker roles or held back by older bodies more likely to provide early signals of serious substance-related distress (Waldorf et al., 1992). Many African American emerging adults, particularly males, become subject to regular encounters with racial discrimination, and their substance use rises in response to this stress (Lee et al., 2018). The trajectory of substance use by emerging adults in other marginalized populations may look similar, but that is a question for future research.

When emerging adults develop SUDs, they often lose any self-sufficiency they have achieved. Additionally, they are typically exposed to a high degree of social stigma that disqualifies them from societally valued positions and may actually reinforce their problem (Room, 2005). Depending on the level of use, they may also impair their health and accrue delays in developmental tasks with lifelong ill effects. As recovery is a long process usually marked by relapse, even individuals who stop using may find it very difficult to reclaim the energy and flexibility of emerging adulthood and be unable to gain a foothold in conventional adult society.

In recovery, people with SUDs give up the substance use that mitigated their stress and often organized their social world. Many recognize the losses inherent in having an SUD, but recovery involves many losses too, often disenfranchised. Inherent in recovery are the loss of the friends one hung out with; the rituals of use and the pleasure and stress relief provided by the substances; and the opportunity to blame failures on the SUD rather than oneself. An African saying holds that when someone is asked to give up something valuable, something of value must be returned. This exchange is at the heart of recovery as the losses inherent in stopping substance use are (hopefully) validated by a supportive recovery community and compensated by new opportunity to enter adulthood. Creating such opportunities is outside the scope of typical recovery programs, but there is a long history of attempts to link recovery fellowship and professional treatment with job training and development (Baumohl et al., 2003).

The 12-step recovery fellowships strongly encourage members to change the "people, places, and things" associated with substance use. Mutual help organizations (MHOs) such as Alcoholics Anonymous (AA) and Narcotics Anonymous (NA) are considered successful (even if more by anecdote than systematic research), yet only 10% to 20% of AA and NA members are under age 30, raising questions about their value for emerging adults. A study of the impact of a residential treatment program designed to serve emerging adults found that focusing on decreasing high-risk friendships (substance using friends) and encouraging 12-step involvement helped emerging adults persist in recovery post discharge (Kelly et al., 2014). Even so, while participation in 12-step MHOs seemed to support recovery, it did not directly facilitate new low-risk social network affiliations, probably because few age peers were at the meetings (Kelly et al., 2014). It seems helping emerging adults develop low-risk friendships will need to rely on other means.

Davis et al. (2017) compared treatment groups for emerging adults and found that those in the motivation enhancement therapy and the cognitive behavioral therapy groups did better during treatment than those in the 12-step group treatment, although these differences disappeared at the 1-year follow-up. They speculate that individualized active treatment participation most benefits emerging adults whose peers tend to pull them back into use and who are less drawn to the milieu and routines of 12-step groups.

REACTIONS OF OTHERS TO THE DEATH OF AN EMERGING ADULT

While emerging adults sometimes die of diseases such as cancer (5% of all deaths of those between 15 and 24) or heart disease (3%), the leading cause of death for age groups 15 to 24 and 25 to 34 is unintentional injury, incorporating car accidents, falls/injuries during sports, fires, drowning, and other fatal accidents (CDC, 2017), though overdose deaths are frequent too. As indicated earlier, suicide and homicide are common, and friends are usually from the same age range and often experience not only grief but life-changing reassessments of identity as a result. For survivors, a critical aspect of the death of an emerging adult is the sense that the person was just starting to live an adult life—coming into their own. This loss of potential almost realized permeates the death of many, if not most, emerging adults.

Parents' and Others' Responses to an Emerging Adult's Death

Rando (1993) made a persuasive case that those bereaved suddenly are at higher risk for complicated grief, grief in which the bereaved yearns for the deceased and has trouble moving back into life. In contrast, Jordan and McIntosh (2011) argue that suicide survivors (family and friends of the decedent) who learn to "dose" themselves can better manage their grief by distracting themselves and using delineated time (dose) to focus on their grief. They argue suicide survivors must consciously move toward and away from grief to avoid perseverating on the death narrative and that this will protect against complicated grief. Yet research comparing natural death loss to sudden, unnatural deaths continues to show that those suddenly bereaved are at higher risk for complications of their grief process (Shear, 2015). Shear (2015) observes that some people remain immobilized by their grief, continuing to yearn for their deceased loved one and even having flashbacks. Her model of therapeutic focus on exposure therapy, guided reflection, and goal setting has shown great efficacy with complicated grief.

A common observation after the death of an emerging adult is that the person's "life was just beginning." In obituaries, one is struck by the way this theme jumps out whenever the decedent is an emerging adult. This is not surprising: The developmental stage is one where life truly is beginning to take on the shape of adulthood with forays into work, love, and other life roles. When emerging adults die, parents and other loved ones are often left to grieve not only the person but the potential adult life, the contours of which had just started to emerge.

INTERVENTIONS

As in all grief, to support emerging adult grievers requires the ability to form a supportive, authentic helping relationship to provide psychosocial education about grief and a venue where grievers may tell their stories. Adults are more able to engage in typical talk therapy, but emerging adults can still benefit from activities that assist them to articulate their grief. As Creighton et al. (2013) indicated, using pictures, songs, and other mementoes can allow grievers to speak in ways they might otherwise avoid. Developed for college students, KORU mindfulness training may be particularly useful in assisting bereaved emerging adults (friends and siblings; Rogers, 2013). After finding that attrition was high for many formats of mindfulness training with college students, Rogers and her coleader found that a four-session training and experiential class paired with a commitment from the student for 10 minutes of daily meditative practice appealed to them. Mindfulness skills seem to assist people to avoid rumination and perseveration that interfere with processing grief. It is likely that any intervention aimed at emerging adults' grief needs to be time limited and clear in its goals and activities.

Williams et al. (2018) developed an intervention model based on identifying the common components of evidence-based treatment practices for prolonged grief disorder, posttraumatic stress disorder, and depression. They then did focus groups with survivors of sudden deaths including MVA, homicide, and suicide to examine how the survivors would feel about intervention that used the common components in a modular manner (tailored use of the components pertinent to each griever). Williams et al. identify the common features of the three modalities (see Figure 6.2). They found that those bereaved by MVA were particularly likely to struggle with fears related to traveling by car for a period of time after the death, whereas those whose loved one died by homicide found their grief interrupted and challenged by aspects of the legal case. Yet, despite these differences, most focus group members strongly endorsed an individualized approach that would allow suddenly bereaved people to collaboratively consider the various practice elements and incorporate those "modules" in their treatment. All seemed to support the benefit of psychoeducation about grief, trauma, anniversary reactions, enlisting support from friends, and the distinctive effects of sudden traumatic death. Some were less supportive about exposure aspects of treatment (retelling the story), though others acknowledged that such interventions had assisted them in moving forward in their grief. In short, there was strong support for an approach that allowed traumatically bereaved people to view the practice elements of the three approaches (shown in Figure 6.2) and then to use combinations of those aspects of treatment in tailored ways. This approach seems likely to appeal to emerging adults who may need more individualized approaches as they are also managing unique identity, development, and economic issues in addition to their grief. Such an approach would allow psychoeducation about individuals' particular sets of circumstances in ways that might appeal to emerging adults.

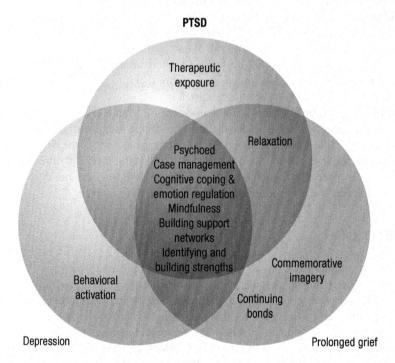

FIGURE 6.2 Common Features of Varied Treatment Models. . This images shows the common features of varied treatment models for grief for use with emerging adults. Williams et al. (2018) developed this figure to help identify which aspects of evidence-based treatments coalesce and could be used for a "modular" approach to treatment.

Source: Reproduced with permission from Williams, J. L., Rheingold, A. A., McNallan, L. J., & Knowlton, A. W. (2018). Survivors' perspectives on a modular approach to traumatic grief treatment. *Death Studies, 42*(3), 155–163. https://doi.org/10.1080/07481187.2017.1370796

There's No One to Call
ELIZABETH WOLF

Elizabeth Wolf is a graduate of the Rutgers School of Social Work where she was named a 2019-2020 Fellow in Aging. Elizabeth's sense of identity is grounded in her role as a family caregiver wherein she has spent the past decade of her life providing care to both her parents who were simultaneously diagnosed with Alzheimer's disease. Elizabeth is passionately invested in the affirmation of personhood in people with advanced dementia. She serves as a volunteer advocate for the Alzheimer's Association and the ambassador to her district congressperson. Elizabeth occasionally publishes about her personal journey at upsidedowndaughter.com.

Jessie and I met through an online photojournalism community comprised of adult children grappling with ongoing losses related to a parent's (or multiple parents') dementia. Our shared circumstance and our geographic proximity magnetized us to each other. Both our mothers had been diagnosed with a type of dementia known as younger-onset Alzheimer's disease when they were in their fifties. She and I met for brunch one morning and tucked ourselves into a booth in the back corner of a neighborhood diner with the promise of bottomless coffee. Both of us knew, though we never acknowledged it aloud, that we would be there for many hours. Jessie and I took turns questioning and bearing witness to the other – each of us frantically searching our memory banks trying to recover bits and pieces. Each of us attempting to construct a path back to a time when we were emerging, and our mothers were just starting to recede.

Tell me everything. I want to know everything about how it happened to you.

Jessie (pseudonym) is a 35-year-old, cisgender, able-bodied woman. She is proud of her patrilineal Italian heritage - her "Dago family" she calls them, laughingly - noting how close-knit they are. As she was growing up, she was surrounded by and constantly engaged with this side of her family, which she shares was "a blessing and a curse." Jessie was a 21-year-old college student in her Junior year of school when her 54-year-old mother was diagnosed with younger-onset Alzheimer's disease, a type of dementia characterized by progressive decline across every imaginable cognitive, emotional, and physical domain. Such a diagnosis is frequently referred to as a "death sentence" within the Alzheimer's community as there is presently no cure for the disease. Once a person receives this sentence, they are lost long before they are gone.

It is profoundly difficult to describe this loss which is indefinable by time or place. It is a loss that lengthens and compounds. A loss that gets lost in itself because it endures for so long "you forget what it was that you even lost to begin with." For Jessie, it is as if pieces of her mother have been slipping away, like grains of sand through an hourglass. When someone that we love and care for is physically present in their body – we can see them and hear them and rest our own bodies against theirs – yet psychologically, chronologically, and emotionally absent as in the case of dementia – we are said to experience ambiguous loss (Boss, 1999). Jessie grappled for words to describe the fourteen and counting years of painstakingly gradual loss - her tear-stained narrative, a smeared "series of losses" – trying to remember: "When did this actually start happening?"

On a journey to find that starting place, Jessie reflected on the unsettling sequence of events that led to her mother's diagnosis and the sense of ambiguity defining that time period. "There'd be times where she'd be really emotional on the phone saying she just wanted to get out…and she started to really withdraw from family events." Jessie worried about her mother, and she wondered if her mother might be depressed or experiencing hormonal fluctuations related to menopause. Jessie desperately tried to pinpoint the exact moment in time when the disease took hold of her mother. She remembered hearing the paranoia in her mother's voice during their phone conversations and recalled her father confiding in her about her mother's increasing frustration with him for unfounded reasons. Jessie's face paled when she recalled the time her mother got lost while driving the short distance home from work.

It was all confounding. At 54 years of age, none of her mother's physicians immediately suspected Alzheimer's disease so it took months and months before they arrived at an accurate diagnosis. Jessie had a gut feeling and described a conversation she had with a friend whose mother was in the advanced stages of younger-onset Alzheimer's disease. That conversation was harshly illuminating for Jessie as she recognized the many parallels to her own experience – paranoia, social withdrawal, forgetting. "I just remember when she started talking about the things that were happening, I was like 'Oh shit'…. And I knew then." Jessie finally had a name for what was happening to her mother.

From the moment of her mother's diagnosis with younger-onset Alzheimer's disease, Jessie felt like they had about a year together before the loss snowballed to the point that it swallowed up most recognizable traces of her mother. She was heartbroken trying to piece together the details of that period, "Umm… there was about a year of her being sick before I would say we lost her… Because it really didn't take long." Jessie clings to the memory of the last conversation they ever had—a simple, everyday conversation where her mother was "most present as herself for the last time." They used to spend hours on the phone chatting about anything and everything. The predictability of being able to reach her mother at any hour of the day in a matter of seconds had long been a source of comfort and support for Jessie. She aches to hear her mother's voice on the other end of the line soothing and reassuring her, but now "there's no one to call anymore."

Jessie was in the heart of emerging adulthood when her mother was ambiguously lost to younger-onset Alzheimer's disease. That is, her body was present, but her previous mothering self was not there. Pauline Boss (1999) calls this ambiguous loss. "Emerging adulthood" defines the developmental period between the ages of 18 and 25, a time of identity exploration and instability according to Jeffrey James Arnett. Jessie notes that she "wore the wound" that the ambiguous loss of her mother scarred her with. How do you grieve for someone who is both there and not there? For Jessie, so many aspects of the woman her mother was had been eradicated by the Alzheimer's disease. Yet, here was the living, breathing body of the woman Jessie was born from.

The confusion regarding how to process this ongoing, accumulating, "absent-present" loss was excruciating for Jessie. She felt like her mother was trapped in a purgatory between life and death, and she herself was helpless to do anything about it. Her mother was the very person she would call on during times of deep distress, so she felt orphaned by what was happening. She was in her early twenties and struggling to develop her own identity while silently suffering the progressive loss of her mother. Yet, she could not even name this as a loss to her friends! The legitimacy of her heartache was frozen by her own uncertainty as to whether anyone would permit her to grieve. How can a society that has not normalized or even recognized the chronic losses associated with Alzheimer's disease bear witness to the grief experienced by loved ones?

The concept "anticipatory grief" is often used to describe the heartache Alzheimer's caregivers face as they bear witness to the painstaking deterioration of their loved one declining gradually toward bodily death. In essence, caregivers grieve for what they know is to come, and they anticipate a resolution to their ambiguity through death loss. Feeling the pull to both embrace the care of their parent while reconciling the differentiation-from-parent—which emerging adulthood requires—convolutes the sense of loss emerging adult caregivers face when a parent is living with dementia. The pain gets tangled into their identity.

Yet, there are ways to repurpose that pain; which Jessie has been doing through her writing. This process has happened in the context of her coming of age as a woman, shifting from a "wounded child" identity into that of a meaning maker. Through various social media outlets, she has created a safe space for processing the many ambiguities of being an emerging adult caring for a parent with dementia. An ongoing embrace of technology and an encouragement toward the online spaces where the dementia grief process is being normalized is critical for Jessie's continued well-being, especially as she continues to navigate the ambiguity of her mother's condition.

Emerging adults who are caregivers are forced to exchange caregiving roles with their parent/s before the typical time. They mourn their chance to rely on the parent for ongoing care while having to provide the care to their parent instead. They are often halted in their journey toward independence because they are needed in their homes of origin. Yet, the irony is that when "there is no one to call anymore," they are thrust into the very self-sustenance that defines emerging adulthood.

Helicopter Parenting During Emerging Adulthood and the Loss of Grit
DEBORAH DUMONT

Deborah Dumont, MSS, DSW, LCSW, has been in practice for over 20 years focusing most of her work on young adulthood. After receiving her MSS from Bryn Mawr College Graduate School of Social Work and Social Research in 1997, she participated in a year-long postgraduate study of Bowen Family Systems Theory at the Princeton Family Center for Education. Ms. Dumont has substantial experience working with trauma, self-injurious behaviors, mood disorders, eating disorders, and other food and body issues. In her work as a doctorate of social work student at Rutgers University, she studied hyperattentive parenting and its impact on young adults and family systems.

Hyperattentive parenting, originally coined helicopter parenting in 1990 by Foster Cline and Charles Fay, describes a distinct style of overinvolved and developmentally inappropriate parenting of young adults (Schiffron et al., 2014). This kind of overinvolved parenting may be, in part, an anxious response to cultural, societal, and technological changes that have impacted the ways parents and their children think about success, the world, and how they communicate with each other (Dumont, 2019). For example, social constructs such as marriage and parenthood are no longer clear initial markers of adulthood in the way they were 50 years ago (Arnett et al., 2014). Without these societal markers, young people have more flexibility to define themselves as adults in a variety of ways, and they may look to parents to help navigate the transition to adulthood (Arnett et al., 2014).

Another reason the term *helicopter parenting* is now well known is that the very people who were parented in an oversolicitous way, born between 1982 and 1995, have now approached or passed through what Jeffrey Arnett calls emerging adulthood (ages 18–25; Arnett et al., 2014). A recent study of colleges and universities in the United States estimated the prevalence of helicopter parenting affecting their students at between 40% and 60% (Somers & Settle, 2010). Parents of millennials are more preoccupied with their children's successes than in previous generations partly because of global changes resulting in a highly competitive economic environment affecting how difficult it is to get into selective colleges and the likelihood of establishing a desired career (LeMoyne & Buchanan, 2011).

In addition to societal shifts and an extremely competitive economy, the advancement of technology has encouraged overinvolved parents to monitor their children around the clock through smartphone apps and trackers, even though according to Western ideals, they should be encouraging autonomy and differentiation. Hyperattentive parenting may be well intentioned for most and may be motivated by efforts to reduce harm and improve chances for success for beloved children, especially in regard to education and future endeavors. Even so, it may, in fact, rob young people of the opportunity to develop in a way that is expected by the adult world. Young adults who struggle to problem-solve, tolerate distress, manage boredom, or accept failure or who lack the grit or resilience to persevere may be suffering from having parents who planned their lives in a way to avoid discomforts and bumps along the way.

There is growing theoretical literature pointing to the ill effects of overinvolved parenting with precollege and college-age youth, yet there is only a small amount of research investigating hyperattentive parenting and its effects (Schiffron et al., 2014). One such (exploratory) study of 317 university students in the southern region of the United States specifically linked overinvolved parenting with mental health issues and found students with helicopter parents were more likely to be medicated for anxiety and/or depression (LeMoyne & Buchanan, 2011). Similarly, Schriffon et al. (2014) surveyed 297 college students in a public liberal arts college in the mid-Atlantic region of the United States and found that helicopter parenting violated a child's three universal psychological needs: autonomy, competence, and relatedness, thus resulting in higher levels of depression. Seemingly, these findings imply a correlation between hyperattentive parents and children's mental health problems. Therefore, it seems important to recognize the loss incurred by young people who were overparented as they attempt to manage adulthood, often without the skills necessary to do so. For some, difficulty negotiating these losses will result in feelings of incompetence and, for others, significant mental health challenges.

Emerging Adulthood

It may be useful to consider what is happening developmentally for young people as they transition to adulthood. Jeffrey Arnett (2014) coined the term "emerging adulthood" to specify an unstable time for some until secure adult attachments (commitment to work and love) are established. Arnett acknowledges the seminal work of Erik Erikson in the 1950s: what Erikson called "prolonged adolescence" has similarities to Arnett's concept of emerging adulthood's lack of adult achievement markers. What were once the primary tasks of adolescence—identity formation and separation from one's parents—appear to occur in contemporary society in late adolescence and early adulthood (Steinberg & Morris, 2001).

In my clinical practice, when I have young people and their parents stuck and frustrated with each other, I have explained adolescent development as similar to toddlerhood. The toddler will veer from the parent, insisting that the parent stay while they move further away often looking back to make sure they are being watched and protected. When they fall, most will size up the parent's reaction to figure out if their attempt to be independent was accepted and whether they are competent enough to handle the fall again. How the parent reacts to the fall may communicate whether the world is a safe place or one to be feared. These normal shifts toward independence are expected in order to develop resilience and a sense of self. Certainly, as young people transition into the college years, they will be expected to manage themselves in a way that is different from what was expected during childhood and adolescence.

The College Years

In my observation, many college students are leaving home for the first time, and although this may be a milestone for some, it can be a developmental crisis for others. Joanne Medalie (1981) presented an analysis of the college years using Erikson's psychosocial tasks and saw the central developmental tasks during college to be divestment (of childhood ties) and investment (in college life), consolidation (of the separation task), choice (of interest and goals), mastery of and commitment to work, and finally anticipation of the future. She saw maladaptive behaviors in college students as they struggled to resolve psychosocial challenges. It may be that in some cases a hyperattentive style of parenting may interfere with the resolution of psychosocial tasks needed for a successful college experience as well as a sense of competence for the future. In fact, college may be the first opportunity emerging adults have to practice life skills, competency, and autonomy as they navigate adult responsibilities and expectations, and how this experience is internalized may impact their readiness to take on adulthood.

Case Illustration

Jennifer is a 19-year-old upper-middle-class, well-groomed, Caucasian female who presented for treatment while on a leave from college. She reported difficulty sleeping, excessive worry about academic performance, concern about how she is perceived by others, and a general fear about "making it" in life. Her boyfriend recently ended their 2-year relationship, which Jennifer considered her first and only significant romantic connection. She also changed her major after finding that despite having been a straight-A student in high school, she did not perform as well academically in college. In addition, she reported ongoing conflict with her college roommate.

Jennifer was the youngest of three siblings. She described her parents' marriage as "okay" but not necessarily the kind of marriage she would want. She explained that her father worked excessively and her mother focused on raising her three daughters and maintaining the home. Jennifer admitted that even as a college student, she relied on her mother to make doctors' appointments, pick out her clothing for significant events, and help her pick academic courses. As a freshman, Jennifer felt a sense of obligation to text her mother about almost everything she was experiencing at college—sometimes texting up to ten times a day. In response, Jennifer's mother honored all of her requests and even offered to call Jennifer each morning to make sure she was awake. Jennifer's mother even contacted the housing department to see what would be involved in changing roommates since Jennifer was unhappy with her current arrangement. Jennifer felt overwhelmed and anxious at college. In essence, Jennifer did not feel competent to manage what she was expected to do as a college student and eventually she took a medical leave after her mother insisted that she come home.

Jennifer admitted that she felt lost when her mother was not involved, but she was anxious and angry when she perceived her as too directive or controlling. Her emotional states often fluctuated with her mother's mood, demonstrating a lack of differentiation. She said most of their arguments had to do with Jennifer's inability to function in the way her mother expected. Jennifer's mother reacted anxiously to Jennifer's difficulties and was fearful she would not succeed without her involvement. Her mother worried about Jennifer's grades, her safety, whether she would secure a summer internship, and ultimately her happiness. Jennifer's mother could no longer tolerate her own anxiety about Jennifer's unhappiness. With family therapy, Jennifer and her parents began to see how Jennifer's neediness was in part an attempt to take care of her mother who felt lonely in her marriage and possibly as a result overinvested emotionally in Jennifer. This may have inadvertently communicated to Jennifer that she needed to be taken care of and was not competent enough to manage the adult responsibilities that go with being a college student. In essence, this robbed Jennifer of the opportunity to experiment and take risks that would have resulted in both successes and failures, thus interfering with her developing grit and seeing her accomplishments as her own.

An important goal in treatment was to help Jennifer's parents see their role in supporting Jennifer to become a young adult with the skills necessary to launch into adulthood. The willingness of Jennifer's parents to consider how the marital tension pushed her father's focus away from the family unit while increasing her mother's focus on Jennifer was important in diminishing the parental involvement. In essence, understanding the role of the family's relationship to Jennifer's functioning was relevant instead of assuming her struggles were the result of individual failures. Her parents eventually saw that their overinvestment in Jennifer's happiness and academic and career success were not as important as her well-being, especially her ability to manage herself as an adult.

Clinical Implications

Understanding the negative impacts of helicopter parenting while also exploring the motivations behind the behavior may benefit programming efforts with young people and their families from elementary school through college. Clinicians can play an important role in assisting parents of children to consider parenting in a way that allows for listening instead of fixing, allowing for boredom and failure, and valuing well-being over happiness and success so that children may evolve into young adults who can problem-solve, tolerate distress, and make decisions—all of which are necessary for adulthood.

Transitions to Adulthood for Individuals With Developmental Disabilities
BONNIE FADER WILKENFELD

Bonnie Fader Wilkenfeld, PhD, MSW, LCSW, is a licensed clinical social worker. She received her PhD from Rutgers University School of Social Work. Dr. Wilkenfeld has extensive experience working in a variety of medical and educational settings, most recently as a social work clinician in a school, hospital, and residential facility for children and adults with multiple, complex physical, and developmental disabilities. Her scholarly interests include impact of the arts on the sense of well-being in individuals with developmental disabilities (IWDDs).

Background

Cerebral palsy (CP) is a chronic condition comprised of a constellation of disorders impacting movement, tone, and posture. This condition occurs in the developing fetal or infant brain and causes functional activity limitations (WHO, 2011). CP manifests in varied ways, and the impact on functioning for affected persons can differ greatly. The motor (movement) disorders of CP are often accompanied by an array of comorbid conditions including sensory, cognitive, and language delays, seizures, feeding problems, and behavioral issues.

The advent of early intervention programs vastly improved the functional abilities of children born with developmental disabilities. Special education for children in the state of New Jersey is legislated through the Individuals with Disabilities Educational Act (IDEA). The IDEA mandates the provision of comprehensive educational programming with instruction in all academic areas for students with disabilities ages 3 to 21 (grades preschool to 12+++). Students receive related services comprised of occupational therapy, physical therapy, and speech/language therapy in addition to social work, because these services are required by the provisions of the IDEA policy. Teachers are fully certified in special education and highly qualified to teach the core curriculum content areas. Students' needs are met through truly individualized educational plans (IEPs), which focus on strengths and developing skills through best practices.

Comprehensive educational programs are regulated through the State Department of Education and accredited by the Middle States Association of Colleges and Schools. All children (through age 21) who reside in New Jersey and meet the criteria for developmental disabilities are eligible for comprehensive services through the Children's System of Care, Department of Children and Families. While the goal is to maximize the child's potential by providing the full range of services, the fact remains that at 21, the emerging adult will age out of the educational program and transition into adult programming. Families then need to apply for services through the Division of Developmental Disabilities (DDD), a state-funded organization for individuals with developmental disabilities (IWDDs) aged 21 and older.

Once identified as an "adult," the focus changes from progress to rehabilitation. Participants in adult programs seek to maintain the function they had achieved at graduation from Children's Services rather than achieve new goals. This reading will focus on a particularly vivid depiction of loss and the ensuing grief reaction that occurs at graduation. Graduation from high school is a very significant life span transition, when typically developing emerging adults individuate and separate from families of origin, becoming independent and self-sufficient. For IWDDs, the transition from Childhood Services into Adult Programming, with its many fewer supports, is quite challenging. Here, I will discuss biopsychosocial considerations along with recommendations for social work intervention.

Marisol's Story

Marisol is a 21-year-old young woman with a dazzling smile and thick dark curly hair. She also has severe CP, impacting all spheres of function including severe cognitive delays. She is in a manual wheelchair that she cannot propel herself; she is nonverbal and incontinent. She requires assistance with all aspects of daily living. Her condition is chronic and cannot be eradicated by any amount of therapeutic or rehabilitative intervention.

The educational program in which Marisol is enrolled implements a Person-Centered Approaches to Schools and Transitions (PCAST) framework. The PCAST program begins at 19, 2 years prior to graduation. At that time, all involved services (e.g., physical therapy, occupational therapy, speech therapy, and social work) partner with the educational specialists to identify the various meaningful components of each students' life. Every student is treated as a unique individual and, as in Marisol's case, those unable to speak for themselves in a traditional manner are provided with opportunities over the next 2 years to develop a specific person-centered profile of what elements in their life contribute to a sense of well-being and quality of life. Marisol and her PCAST team developed this profile, which delineates what is important to and for her, what makes for a good or bad day, who the important people in her life are, and how she can best communicate her needs, and so forth.

Family Adjustment

The parents and family experience pervasive maturational losses. These begin at initial diagnosis of CP (in this case soon after birth) and are reexperienced with every developmental milestone that typically developing peers and siblings achieve. Because the family is out of synchrony with their peers, this is a disenfranchised loss (Doka, 1989, 2002) with negative implications for support and sympathy from others, compounding the grief reaction. The losses are also nonfinite and ambiguous (Boss, 1999). At each typical milestone event in their children's lives, parents whose child has disability(ies) are reminded of their loss of dreams for the future and the lifelong need to renegotiate plans.

During the final year of PCAST, Marisol, her core therapy team, and her family were invited by her social worker to a luncheon PCAST team meeting where all this information is brought together and discussed in order to make decisions about future adult programming. Both of Marisol's parents were present, along with her speech therapist, personal care assistant, social worker, and school instructor. We discussed the various elements that would be part of her Adult program. We did not anticipate Marisol's father's upset emotional reaction to the team's description of what contributes to Marisol's experience of a good day.

At that juncture, it appeared as if the reality of moving on into adulthood materialized before her father's eyes. This is consistent with other meetings of this nature that I have convened; the father often has a greater emotional reaction than the mother. Perhaps this is due to the more hands-on consistent presence of the mother and her ongoing discussions with the care team. Fathers may have more intermittent interactions and may not have had as many opportunities to adjust to and integrate the knowledge of their children's aging, graduation, and transition into adulthood. Parents tend to infantilize their adult children with developmental disabilities. Many parents are not confronted with the disenfranchised nature of the losses an IWDD experiences until a milestone life stage event such as when siblings or other typically developing peers get a drivers' license or graduate from high school. Nevertheless, the emotions are powerful and mixed—parents are proud of all the progress children make but sad at the loss of expectations and being confronted with the chronicity of their child's condition. This was true of Marisol's father.

Upon graduation into adult services programming, the maturational process of entering adulthood becomes all too real. Accepting that their emerging adult son or daughter has achieved their maximum potential means letting go of previous hopes and dreams. The reality of changing the goal of services from progress to maintenance is difficult to accept, and parents may resist.

Losses From Marisol's Perspective

Marisol exhibited her own grief reaction at this PCAST session. Marisol's reaction may have been attributable to her own feelings of anxiety regarding the transition to adulthood, or she may have reacted to her father's grief response. We do not know why, but we do know Marisol vocalized loudly and appeared upset. She started to cry. All of her team members and her parents surrounded her, enveloping her in a loving, safe environment, acknowledging and validating her reaction.

IWDDs often are not acknowledged by others to understand loss and feel grief (Brickell & Munir, 2008; Sormanti & Ballan, 2011). As a result, they may not have the opportunity to express themselves and subsequently be comforted and validated. In actuality, IWDDs do grieve and express their emotions in a variety of ways (Brickell & Munir, 2008) and should be assisted to express their grief (Dodd, Dowling, & Hollins, 2005). Their social workers should become familiar with the way that particular individual expresses grief.

IWDDs benefit from having familiar people around them, helping to maintain consistency and routine as much as possible. However, the transition to adult services creates some very dramatic changes in their routines. They must navigate new spaces and interact with new educators, therapists, and peers. Lunch may be given at a different time, food may be prepared differently, and procedures will differ.

These multiple changes are felt as losses, and they affect IWDDs' social, emotional, and physical functioning. For a smooth transition to occur, these changes should happen gradually, and caregivers must be cognizant that individuals who cannot express their feelings conventionally will do so in other ways.

Interventions

Social workers assisting emerging adults with developmental disabilities and their families should keep in mind that graduation into the world of adult services is always a shock and a traumatic event. No manner of preparation can completely prevent the emotional responses of graduating students and their families. Practitioners should be comfortable providing support and validation to IWDDs and their family's feelings, allowing them free expression in a nonjudgmental environment. Some recommendations to help the transition to adulthood process include the following:

1. Develop a transition team timeline starting at age 14. At 14 (in the state of New Jersey), special education programs are responsible for developing a treatment team summary of transitional considerations for the high school years ahead. The summary presents timelines for parents to consider in regard to obtaining guardianship and for special events such as prom and graduation.
2. Meet with the family periodically to encourage their input in planning and decision-making. This typically occurs at the annual IEP meeting, but ongoing contact with families is recommended throughout the year to strengthen rapport and trust.
3. Encourage the family to seek guardianship starting at age 18. This crucial task is often put on the back burner, but if no next of kin obtains guardianship for a person with cognitive disabilities, then the state considers that individual to be "void of guardian" and in certain circumstances would need to assign one. Families should also consider financial planning and developing a special needs trust for their child with developmental disabilities. This can go a long way toward providing peace of mind that their child will be financially secure should something happen to the parents.
4. Assist the family to identify community supports and help them get their child registered for adult services programs. Families may need additional support and expertise to navigate the various day program options available in their community. Therapists can partner with social workers to help parents evaluate which programs may be a good fit for their graduating child, assessing how their personal needs regarding overall environment, schedule, distance, and program options match what is available.

5. Understand the various grief reactions and provide empathy and support. Listen, identify the issues, and validate the losses. Understand that for those IWDDs with communication impairment, emotions of depression and anxiety may be expressed behaviorally or physically (e.g., sleep disturbances, dietary issues, increase in seizure activity).

6. Implement a person-centered model for 2 years prior to graduation to assist the transitioning student to identify their key team players and develop a portfolio of the varied activities, routines, and features that give quality to IWDDs' lives from their point of view.

7. Address the transitioning student's grief reaction—recognize it in any way it may be manifested—and utilize person-centered approaches.

8. Work with the team, family, and transitioning/emerging adult to ensure a cohesive plan is developed and everyone's voice is heard.

Conclusion

Powerful markers of maturation such as graduations are characterized by conflicting emotions for all families but particularly for those whose children have chronic, debilitating developmental disabilities. Pride in their child's accomplishments is tempered by acute awareness of others who move on to independence, autonomy, and self-sufficiency. While young adults with debilitating developmental disabilities may never achieve independent functioning, they do achieve a sense of autonomy and have unique preferences for what would contribute to their well-being and overall life quality.

Families and graduating emerging adults experience disenfranchised, ambiguous, and nonfinite losses from their own perspectives. The graduating person with developmental disabilities experiences loss from a biopsychosocial perspective like everyone else. Biological/physiological changes can be associated with changes in dietary regimens, menus, and caregivers; psychologically, IWDDs may experience anxiety, depression, and grief due to social changes in peer groups, staff, and environment. These changes can be challenging for typical people and may overwhelm those with sensory deficits, cognitive processing issues, and communication impairments. It is crucial that social workers recognize all aspects and modes of their clients' grief responses, including how they are expressed by IWDDs. Social workers must address these responses as preemptively as possible, enlisting the support of the treatment care/educational team.

SUMMARY

Economic circumstances have forced many emerging adults to avoid committing to work, family, and other goals during their 20s, as was previously common and customary. Continuing semidependence on family of origin means that maturational losses related to moving into independence are postponed and yet emerging adults have legal and other responsibilities of adulthood. In this betwixt and between life stage, emerging adults may mourn their dependence as well as their independence. Their strong sense of a "just world" or a belief that they can control the events in their life may interfere with processing illness or grief until those illusions have been addressed. Meanwhile, when emerging adults die, the nascent achievements and flourishing hopes and dreams for their adulthood die with them. Work with this age group seems to mirror typical approaches to adults (talk therapy) but is enhanced by adding some of the activities and props (pictures) and fun activities that help with teens and other younger populations.

DISCUSSION QUESTIONS

1. How does the economic environment affect both positively and negatively the life phase of emerging adulthood?
2. Why might emerging adults have greater susceptibility to the problems of cumulative losses?
3. What are the pros and cons of moving through emerging adulthood more rapidly and establishing work, financial independence, an intimate partner relationship, and family before the age of 25?
4. How does "helicopter parenting" or other protective parenting of emerging adults impair their motivation and ability to move toward adult accomplishments?

KEY REFERENCES

Only key references appear in the print edition. The full reference list appears in the digital product found on http://connect.springerpub.com/content/book/978-0-8261-4964-0/chapter/ch06

Arnett, J. J. (2004). *Emerging adulthood: The winding road from the late teens through the twenties.* Oxford University Press.

Arnett, J. J., & Mitra, D. (2018). Are the features of emerging adulthood developmentally distinctive? A comparison of ages 18–60 in the United States. *Emerging Adulthood.* https://doi.org/10.1177/2167696818810073

Choi, J., Zhu, J., & Goodman, L. (2019, January). *Young adults living in parents' basements: Causes and consequences.* Urban Institute. https://www.urban.org/sites/default/files/publication/99707/young_adults_living_in_parents_basements_0.pdf

Chung, J., Robins, R., Trzesniewski, K., Noftle, E., Roberts, B., & Widaman, K. (2014). Continuity and change in self-esteem during emerging adulthood. *Journal of Personality and Social Psychology, 106*(3), 469–483. https://doi.org/10.1037/a0035135

Dodd, P., Dowling, S., & Hollins, S. (2005). A review of the emotional, psychiatric and behavioural responses to bereavement in people with intellectual disabilities. *Journal of Intellectual Disability Research, 49*(7), 537–543. https://doi.org/10.1111/j.1365-2788.2005.00702.x

Marcia, J. E. (1966). Development and validation of ego identity status. *Journal of Personality and Social Psychology, 3,* 551–558. https://doi.org/10.1037/h0023281

Newton, C. S. (2012). *The use of support and coping skills among emerging adults following parental loss* (Master of Social Work Clinical Research Papers No. 67). http://sophia.stkate.edu/cgi/viewcontent.cgi?article=1067&context=msw_papers

Porter, N., & Claridge, A. M. (2019). Unique grief experiences: The needs of emerging adults facing the death of a parent. *Death Studies.* https://doi.org/10.1080/07481187.2019.1626939

Schwartz, L., Howell, K., & Jamison, L. (2018). Effect of time since loss on grief, resilience, and depression among bereaved emerging adults. *Death Studies, 42*(9), 537–547. https://doi.org/10.1080/07481187.2018.1430082

Shear, M. K. (2015). Complicated grief. *New England Journal of Medicine, 372*(2), 153–160. https://www.nejm.org/doi/full/10.1056/NEJMcp1315618

Siegel, D. J. (2012). *The developing mind: How relationships and the brain interact to shape who we are* (2nd ed.). Guilford Press. (Original work published 1999).

Wilson, C., Rickwood, D., Bushnell, J., Caputi, P., & Thomas, S. (2011). The effects of need for autonomy and preference for seeking help from informal sources on emerging adults' intentions to access mental health services for common mental disorders and suicidal thoughts. *Advances in Mental Health, 10*(1), 29–38. https://doi.org/10.5172/jamh.2011.10.1.29

7

Grief and Loss in Young Adulthood

INTRODUCTION

This chapter examines young adulthood, which we define as ages 30 to 45, and reviews experiences of grief as a result of both death and living losses. We take up developmental themes of young adulthood (achieving intimacy and fulfilling career goals), and we summarize young adults' common biological, psychological, social, and spiritual developmental changes. For some, successful achievement of young adult milestones is interrupted by risk factors including poverty and marginalization. Young adults' deaths are considered an off-time loss, but deaths from suicide and drug overdose have made this experience more common in recent years. Some experience complicated grief (CG) as a result. Common living losses that derive from divorce and infertility also affect young adults. We review the Gottman Method Couples Therapy (GMCT) and Complicated Grief Therapy (CGT), practice methods to help young adults.

OBJECTIVES

After studying this chapter, the reader will understand:
- Different developmental models of early adulthood and the variety of developmental tasks young adults face.
- Typical biological, psychological, social, and spiritual development in young adulthood while being aware of the diversity of life experiences and the fluidity of life stages.
- Young adults' typical responses to loss and their coping styles.
- How theories of loss and grief can influence practice with young adults.
- Current practices for intervention with young adults experiencing loss.

VIGNETTE

Karen was 39 years old and in a warm, stable, supportive relationship with Joe, who was 43 years old. Joe was divorced and had two children of 12 and 10 years old. The children lived with Joe's ex-wife, Sandy, and Joe had the kids for dinner every Wednesday. Twice per month, Joe had his children stay over on Friday and Saturday nights. His relationship with Sandy was strained but civil.

Karen developed a positive relationship with Joe's children. She was very willing to be involved in their care; however, Karen had always wanted to have her own biological children. She was aware that, due to her age, she might struggle to become pregnant. Karen told Joe she wanted to marry and try to become pregnant as soon as possible. Although Joe understood Karen's desire to marry quickly in order to have children together and was excited about marriage, he was not interested in having more children. Joe said he realized that his decision might mean losing her, but he wanted an honest relationship and did not want to deceive her.

Karen sought counseling after this discussion with Joe. She felt that whatever decision she made, she would incur a significant loss—the loss of the "love of (her) life" or the loss of her dream of having children. Although she loved Joe's children, she felt that was not the same experience she desired and dreamed of as a child. She explained that Joe's children "already have a mom and my role is different."

Yet Karen recognized that even if she broke up with Joe and tried to become pregnant via alternative strategies for insemination, she might not have a successful pregnancy. Karen was not interested in adopting a child or being a foster parent; she wanted the experience of pregnancy and childbirth. She was 2 months from her 40th birthday, and her younger sister was already married with a 5-year-old daughter. Her gynecologist advised that if Karen wanted to have a child biologically, she must move forward sooner rather than later. Feeling she was in a no-win situation, Karen was not sure what to do.

Ultimately, Karen decided to marry Joe. She did not want to be a single parent and did not want to lose their "wonderful" relationship. Karen stayed in counseling for a brief time as she adjusted to the loss of not having her own biological children and the life she envisioned for herself as a child.

DEFINING YOUNG ADULTHOOD

Using chronological markers or legal status to locate persons in "young," "middle," or "older" adulthood is limited by demographic, cultural, and educational trends and by the history in which such trends are embedded. A century ago, life expectancy in the United States was 47 years, and by 2016, it was almost 79 (Centers for Disease Control and Prevention, 2018). In addition to living longer, what we accomplish at different times in our lives has changed. In most developed nations, people finish school, enter marriages or long-term partnerships, and have children later in life than ever before. The later completion of life milestones has resulted in new ways of defining and understanding adulthood.

Adult development is now seen as a "series of developmental challenges that one engages with and revisits across the adult lifespan" (Malone et al., 2016, p. 497). This chapter focuses on young adulthood, which we define as the period of life from 30 through 45 years old. Young adulthood often overlaps emerging adulthood and on the oldest end middle adulthood. For example, it is not uncommon for people in their 20s to achieve what others accomplish in their 30s and 40s, and for people in their 30s to accomplish the developmental tasks more usually achieved after 45. Typically, in young adulthood, people "settle down" into career paths and commitments to significant others. They develop their own lives and create their own families, often with children, and their focus shifts from large circles of friends to newly created families.

Various theoretical models attempt to explain the key developmental tasks faced by young adults. Although there are differences among them, there is also a common theme: Young adults' primary tasks focus on achieving intimacy and pursuing major life goals. Erikson (1950) defined young adulthood as the 20s through early 40s and posited that they go through the developmental crisis of "intimacy versus isolation." He regarded successful navigation of this crisis as necessary to achieve a capacity for intimacy and love. Levinson (1986) conceived of the life cycle as a "sequence of eras" and defined the "Era of Early Adulthood" (ages 22–45) as the time of life when people pursue their major goals in career, family, love, and creative endeavors. Finally, Vaillant (2012), building on Erikson's work, focused on developmental tasks rather than crises. He too identified "intimacy" as the developmental task of young adulthood.

DEVELOPMENTAL THEMES OF YOUNG ADULTHOOD

Biological Development

Young adults typically report good health and are generally active and fit. However, biological aging—defined specifically as the gradual decline of our physical systems (organs, tissues, telomere length, etc.)—is a process that begins as early as 30 (Medline Plus, 2019). Certain aspects of health and wellness seem to peak by 30: Muscle strength, for instance, peaks at 25 and bone mass strength and density at 30 (Weller & Gould, 2017). In contrast to the temporally predictable changes of adolescence, the pace of biological aging is idiosyncratic and thus hard to predict (Moffitt et al., 2017). Belsky et al. (2015) examined biological aging in people 26 to 38. They found that before midlife, "individuals who were aging more rapidly were less physically able, showed cognitive decline and brain aging, self-reported worse health, and looked older" (p. E4104).

Typically, young adults develop less acute eyesight, higher blood pressure, and lower fertility. Especially as they near 40, they need to hold a book at arm's length to read it, or must squint to make out words read in low light or written in small font. Vision changes because the lens becomes harder, making it more difficult to focus on items up close. We become far sighted. This condition, presbyopia, occurs slowly, and many notice it only around 40 (Cleveland Clinic, 2019), when the use of reading glasses becomes common.

Blood pressure increases with age, and although the risk of overly high blood pressure begins to climb at 45, it can occur in younger adults (WebMD, 2020). The American Heart Association (2014) reports that between 20 and 34 years, 9.1% of men and 6.7% of women have high blood pressure. This prevalence rises significantly from age 35 to 44, a cohort in which high blood pressure occurs in 24.4% of men and 17.6% of women. African Americans tend to develop high blood pressure earlier than others, and the condition is more likely to be severe (WebMD, 2020).

The proverbial biological clock ticks away as women enter their 30s because their fertility begins to decline. According to The American College of Obstetricians and Gynecologists (ACOG, 2014), it decreases gradually from 32 to 37, declining rapidly after that point. ACOG recommends that practitioners educate their patients about this, especially in light of findings that after 35, there is an increased risk of pregnancy loss (ACOG, 2014).

Men's fertility also declines with age. This is largely due to decreased testosterone levels (typically starting at 40) and semen quality (Harris et al., 2011). Harris et al. (2011) explain that "aging has a significant impact on male sexual function, sperm parameters, and fertility, which all contribute to decreased fecundability, increased time to conception, and increased miscarriage rates" (p. e189).

Psychological Development

According to Cohen (2006), young adulthood involves a search for meaning and purpose. Similarly, Levinson (1986) called it a time to pursue major life goals. We will put it this way: Young adults must tackle self-reflection and find their place in the world as adults.

These tasks are made quite challenging by the social complexity that comes with the relatively loose grip of tradition in the Westernized countries of the 21st century and the impact on work of accelerating technological change that is apparent the world over. In the West, work and domestic responsibilities are no longer strictly gendered, and compared with even a generation ago, there is much greater latitude in domestic arrangements and family styles. But in spite of historically high levels of education, young adults face careers of enormous uncertainty and specific jobs with very little security. In the era of gig work, side hustles, student loan debt, and shocking rents, choice often seems illusory. Real circumstances sow a lot of confusion, anxiety, and indecisiveness.

Indecisiveness may be due in part to how young adults think. Cohen (2004) believed that postformal thinking could be a factor. Thinking postformally is to assess obstacles or problems rationally and emotionally, and this can lead to "competing and, at times, contradictory solutions" (Cohen, 2004, p. 8). Although adolescents have capacity for certain aspects of postformal thought, it is a quality that matures with age and contributes to wisdom. Adult cognition becomes more abstract and relativistic (Scott-Janda & Karakok, 2016). Adults understand that the world cannot be reduced to absolutes, that it is not black or white, good or bad. This change in thinking style can make decision-making more complicated because multiple options are present in an ambiguous world.

Social Development

The nature of social life and the number of social connections that people have typically change in young adulthood. This shift may result from leaving the student role; involvement in long-term intimate relationships; parental responsibilities; or relocation based on employment or family considerations. In young adulthood, the *quality* of social activity becomes more important than the *quantity*. Interestingly, young adults' success at achieving quality social activity predicts midlife psychosocial outcomes (Carmichael et al., 2015).

Parenthood deeply affects earlier friendships. When young adults become parents, their friends often become the parents of their children's friends, people they see on a regular basis in connection with school, extracurricular, and faith-based activities, and with whom they coordinate their children's play dates. These planned children's activities require considerable parental involvement and limit the time available for seeing old friends from youth who are not embedded in the same social world.

Parenthood also affects relationships with family. Young adults may seek emotional and instrumental support from parents and may thus move closer to them. This is more likely if parents are raising children, especially if they are doing so on their own for one reason or another. In an extensive longitudinal study, Bengston et al. (2002) showed that while family structures have been changing over the years (due to divorce and other factors), family members continue to rely on each other for support.

Spiritual Development

James Fowler (1981) and M. Scott Peck (1987) each proposed a model of spiritual development across the life span. Fowler's Model of Faith Development identified six stages of spiritual growth and Peck's model four. Both observed that adults do not necessarily progress through all stages. Although not tied to specific ages, Fowler's Individuative-Reflective stage and Peck's Skeptic-Individual stage may start in young adulthood. These stages are described as a time when people critically examine their beliefs and may become disillusioned.

Surveys examining religiosity in the United States highlight skepticism about religion among young adults. The Pew Research Center (2018) found that younger adults are much less likely to identify with a religion or participate in religious practices when compared with older generations. However, religiosity is not the same thing as spirituality, and most of today's young adults describe themselves as spiritual and participate in spiritual practices (Alper, 2015).

With respect to religious belief and practice, Lee et al. (2018) proposed seven pathways of religiosity among those who transitioned from youth to adulthood. These differed by gender, race, education, and family formation (having children). Their results showed not only the complexity and dynamic nature of religiosity but also that young adults' level of religiosity—worship attendance and private dimensions of religiosity (inner beliefs)—increases when they have children.

SPECIAL CONSIDERATIONS IN RISK AND RESILIENCE

Racial, ethnic, and cultural identities; exposure to adverse childhood experiences (ACEs); access to resources; socioeconomic status; and other individual and environmental factors play fundamental roles in our lives. We are influenced by current factors as well as the cumulative effect of our life experiences. Research confirms the important influence of these early experiences on adulthood (Assari et al., 2017; Herzog & Schmahl, 2018; Wallace et al., 2016). Throughout life, social support is a critical protective factor in coping with adversity.

This section reviews some specific risk and resiliency factors that affect developmental tasks in young adulthood. This brief summary is by no means an exhaustive accounting of special considerations but emphasizes how identities and environments influence well-being in young adulthood.

Adverse Childhood Experiences

There is growing empirical evidence that adults who have ACEs are more likely to struggle with health and mental health issues, substance abuse problems, achieving healthy intimate relationships, finishing school, and maintaining work. In their review of ACE studies, Herzog and Schmahl (2018) concluded that ACEs affect adults across the life span. Thus, young adults who have experienced ACEs may have difficulties in their intimate relationships and in their careers. It should be noted, though, that not all who live through ACEs suffer poor outcomes in adulthood. Some have the psychological and social resources necessary to cope with adversity. Exposure to positive childhood experiences, also known as counter-ACEs, seems to offset the heightened risk (Crandall et al., 2019). Coping with adversity may build strengths and emotional resiliency (Seery et al., 2010, p. 8).

Racial and Ethnic Inequality and Home Ownership

In the United States, racial and ethnic inequality and widespread discrimination negatively affect primarily people of color, contributing to the intergenerational reproduction of educational and health disadvantages. In turn, these impair young adults' ability to be self-sustaining and meet major life goals that in young adulthood may include the goal of home ownership, especially after starting families.

Many factors contribute to a young adult's desire to own a home. Over time, it is usually less costly than renting, it lets people put their personal stamp on their own space, and it allows them to obtain amenities they desire. As they prepare for children, or in anticipation of having children, they may desire larger, more private housing. However, home ownership is not as attainable as it once was and remains more difficult for Blacks, who historically have had significantly lower rates of home ownership than Whites due to discriminatory policies across generations (Cunningham et al., 2017; PBS, 2003).

Whites and Asians have higher home ownership rates across the whole life span compared with Blacks, Hispanics, and new immigrants to the country (Goodman et al., 2015). Home ownership rates have been increasing for Hispanics, who were not as hard hit by the housing bust preceding the Great Recession that destroyed a great deal of African American wealth. The current home ownership gap between Blacks and Hispanics is projected to grow between 2020 and 2030, when projected rates of home ownership for those 35 to 44 are 40% for Blacks, 48% for Hispanics, and 69% for Whites (Goodman et al., 2015).

Educational Level

Young adults with less than a college education have fewer career choices and more difficulty earning a living. The U.S. Bureau of Labor Statistics (BLS) consistently finds that higher education yields higher salaries for most people (Torpey, 2018). According to data from 2017, those with the highest levels of educational attainment (i.e., doctoral or professional degree) had the highest salaries and the lowest risk of unemployment (Torpey, 2018).

On the whole, African Americans enter young adulthood with less education than age mates of other racial and ethnic groups. They have the lowest 6-year completion rate (45.9%) if they started in 4-year colleges and the lowest completion rate (25.8%) if they started in 2-year colleges when compared with Hispanic, White, and Asian students (National Student Clearinghouse Research Center, 2017). This phenomenon is believed to exist because of poorer educational opportunities in childhood for many U.S. Black children and because socialization into study habits and strategies for coping with marginalization may be limited. When colleges and universities have programs for first-generation college attendees, support for these students can make a big difference in enhancing completion rates.

Parenthood has a big impact on educational attainment. Delaying parenthood increases the chance of completing higher levels of education. According to Biu and Miller, female college graduates have children 7 years later than nongraduates "and often use the years in between to finish school and build their careers and incomes" (2018, para. 3). Delaying parenthood has been a trend occurring across all ethnic and racial groups in the United States; the age of first-time mothers varies by region and educational attainment (Biu & Miller, 2018). Thus, women who delay parenthood may be more likely to complete higher levels of education and, in turn, be better positioned to attain higher-paying jobs and secure financial stability.

LOSSES EXPERIENCED BY YOUNG ADULTS

Death Losses

Off-Time Losses and Unexpected Deaths of Loved Ones

Losing a child, a friend, a sibling, or a parent is less likely in young adulthood than in middle or older adulthood. Thus, young adults, especially those in the early 30s, who experience the death of a loved one are experiencing an off-time loss. Off-time losses can be more challenging to cope with than losses that occur at expected times. Unexpected deaths result in increased incidence of major depressive episodes, anxiety, and posttraumatic stress disorder (PTSD) as well as a prolonged or CG response (Keyes et al., 2014). Keyes et al. (2014) found that unexpected death was the most common traumatic experience reported by participants and the most likely to be rated their worst traumatic experience, regardless of others they had endured.

Life experiences and losses vary by racial and ethnic identity. For instance, African American adults are more likely than Whites to experience the death of a parent or sibling through midlife and more likely to experience the death of a child and/or spouse from young adulthood through later life (Umberson et al., 2017). Income-related health disparities between African Americans and Whites have a lot to do with this. The death rate for African Americans between ages 35 and 49 was higher than those for Whites, and in this age range, African Americans died at higher rates than Whites from heart disease; cancer; cerebrovascular disease; diabetes mellitus; homicide; nephritis, nephrotic syndrome, and nephrosis; septicemia; and HIV disease (Cunningham et al., 2017).

Death of a Parent

The parent–child relationship evolves as children transition into adulthood. These changes, for better or worse, are especially pronounced from childhood and adolescence through emerging adulthood. However, these relationships further evolve as young adults' concerns with independence, intimate relationships, and careers become more pronounced. Yet most of the research about experiencing the death of a parent focuses on children or adults who experienced the death of a parent in childhood. Much less attention has been given to experiencing parental loss while in adulthood. Of the studies that focus on experiencing parental death in adulthood, most explore grief responses of emerging adults or middle age adults, with a gap in the literature for young adults ages 30 to 45 whose parents die.

Yet, as people live longer lives than ever before, parental death can be considered an off-time loss for young adults. Nowadays, "children can expect to share five or more decades of lifetime with their parents" (Leopold & Lechner, 2015, p. 748). Young adults will likely have fewer peers going through the same experience and have less peer support after a parent dies. In addition, for many young adults in their 30s, parents still provide important emotional and instrumental help, including child care. Thus, losing a parent at this time of life may feel like the loss of a safety net.

In a large German study of 2,760 adult children (ages 17–70; median age 31) whose parents had died during their adult years, Leopold and Lechner (2015, p. 755) found "the impact of filial bereavement on life satisfaction" was "a highly gendered and age-dependent process." Daughters who lost their mothers and those who experienced the loss in younger adulthood experienced the largest drops in life satisfaction, with younger (age 30 or so) daughters having the steepest decline. Furthermore, life satisfaction remained low 4 to 5 years after their mother's death (p. 757). Men and older adults were not as severely affected.

Death of a Sibling

Losing a sibling during young adulthood is also an off-time loss. Siblings grow up together and share a multitude of experiences, good and bad. They assume a continuing presence in each other's lives as they get older. They expect to share responsibilities for the care of older people in the family, become aunts and uncles, and be involved with each other in family rituals, keeping collective memories and connections to family histories. And they help each other. Marshall (2017) explains that sibling loss in adulthood is particularly difficult because at this age the sibling is likely to be a "key part" of an adult's support network (p. 108). This bereavement can be devastating (Halliwell & Franken, 2016). Some studies find that adults who experience the death of a sibling are more likely to have CG, report higher levels of depression, and suffer adverse health consequences that include increased risk of death (Halliwell & Franken, 2016; Wright, 2016).

The bereavement is particularly distressing if the sibling's death was by suicide. In a small qualitative study, Powell and Matthys (2013) focused on sibling survivors of suicide, also known as the "silent mourners." The participants ranged in age from 20 to 75 with a mean of 31. Their participants felt that society, and their parents more specifically, often overlooked or minimized the sibling survivors' loss, and family dynamics and communication were negatively affected, causing significant distress for the sibling survivors.

Death of a Significant Other (e.g., Spouse, Life Partner)

The impact of the death of a significant other is influenced by many factors and varies across contexts, but spousal loss in young adulthood is highly stressful and off-time. Few peers experience the same loss, although with the internet and online support sites, it is now easier to find others of a similar age in similar circumstances. Bereaved spouses are usually older adults grieving a death that was chronologically typical, and support groups for the widowed usually attract older adults.

Parenthood has the potential to both help and hinder the grief response and recovery period of the young adult bereaved. Studies have shown that parenting after a spouse's death involves a challenging adjustment to single parenthood and being the lone authority. Even so, being child focused provides a sense of purpose and increased busyness that distracts from grief (Chindley et al., 2014; McClatchey, 2017).

Death of a Close Friend

Although the death of a close friend can be particularly painful, the grieving friend does not often receive the support that family mourners receive. An Australian study using a nationally representative sample of households found that bereaved friends are an important cohort and may "require physical and emotional support in the four years following the death" (Liu et al., 2019, p. 8). Furthermore, the investigators identified the death of a close friend as a form of disenfranchised grief because the (friend) griever receives less social support for their grief because the relationship with the deceased is considered "less than" that of grieving family members.

Experiencing the death of a friend may be more common now for young adults due to two alarming trends: the increase in deaths by suicide and from drug overdose. The latter is a concomitant of the opioid crisis in the United States. The Centers for Disease Control and Prevention's provisional report (2019) for December 2017 to December 2018 showed the first drop in overdose deaths in almost 20 years. The rate had increased each year since 1999 and, in 2017, stood at 21.7 per 100,000 people, 3.6 times the rate in 1999. The rate for those 25 to 34 was 38.4/100,000, and it was 39/100,000 for people 35 to 44 (The National Institute on Drug Abuse, 2019).

Young adults also lose friends to suicide. In 2017, suicide was the second leading cause of death for those 25 to 34 and the fourth leading cause of death for those 35 to 44 (National Institute of Mental Health, 2019). Deaths by suicide differ in method, often by age. According to the Suicide Prevention Resource Center (2019), in 2017, young adults 25 to 44 primarily used suffocation as a means (36%) followed by the use of firearms (30%).

Combined, deaths by overdose and deaths by suicide have contributed to the decline in life expectancy in the United States from 2015 to 2017. Death rates for the 25-to-34 age group increased the most, followed by the 35-to-44 age group (Joszt, 2018). These very troubling statistics underscore the importance of suicide prevention efforts and the adequate provision of mental health and substance abuse services.

Living Losses: Atypical, Typical, and Maturational Losses

Loss of the Ability to Pursue the "American Dream"

In December 2007, the United States fell into the Great Recession. This crisis included a sharp decline in stock prices, a major slump in the value of real estate, and a doubling of the official unemployment rate (a significant underestimate of real joblessness) from 5% in December 2007 to a peak of 10% in June 2009 (Cunningham, 2018). It was the worst economic jolt since the Great Depression of 1929 to 1941, and unemployment did not return to its December 2007 level until November 2015 (Cunningham, 2018). The older members of today's young adult population, born between 1974 and 1986, suffered significant economic setbacks that will affect them throughout their lives. Those born in 1983 and earlier were most disadvantaged, especially if they lacked a college degree or did not finish high school (Cunningham, 2018).

The economy has improved, but the benefits of recovery have not been equally distributed. According to the National Institute on Retirement Security, many young adults in the workforce have nothing saved for retirement due to stagnant wages and persisting high unemployment until 2016. In addition to little or no savings or other forms of wealth, many still have student loan debt. Some have loan delinquencies that damage their credit worthiness (Elliott & Reynolds, 2015).

Particularly unsettling, few young adult workers have jobs with a pension or significant employer retirement contributions. Not surprisingly, many of today's young adults are pessimistic about their financial futures (Kurt, 2018), although some have recovered and young adults remain in their prime working years (Fry, 2018).

Loss of Probability of Having Children (Biologically) Due to Delay of Parenthood

Losing the opportunity to have children biologically due to infertility is upsetting and can be considered a maturational loss for those who are involuntarily childless. Infertility can occur at any age, but rates increase after age 30, especially after age 37 (ACOG, 2014). Thus, delaying bio-logical childbearing until the late 30s (or even 40s) decreases the chance of achieving successful pregnancy. The loss of the ability to have a child biologically is accompanied by related losses, many unseen, unacknowledged, and invalidated by others. For the single person or couple, there may be distress related to unsuccessful attempts to get pregnant, loss of pregnancies, relationship stress and pressure, family pressures, scheduled sex lives, insensitivity from friends and family, and perhaps most private, the loss of the dream of parenting biological children.

There are many possible causes of infertility. Although estimates vary, about one-third of cases are caused by male factor–only infertility (problems with the sperm), one-third are caused by female factor–only infertility (problematic ovum production, structural problems such as tube occlusion or hormonal insufficiency), and the remaining third is caused by a combination of factors or is unexplained (Office of Population Affairs, 2019). These infertility issues also pertain to people/couples who lack conventional conception possibilities (e.g., LGBT+, single men or women). Alternative insemination, in vitro fertilization (IVF), use of surrogates, and other as-sisted reproductive technologies may be pursued, yet these may not be affordable and may not be successful.

Regardless of the causes, involuntary childlessness is a form of disenfranchised grief, often resulting in grief that cannot be openly acknowledged, publicly mourned, or socially supported (McBain & Reeves, 2019). Most of the people dealing with involuntary childlessness are adults—solos or couples—who tried to conceive in their 20s without success and those who have delayed parenthood and are trying without success in their 30s or early 40s.

Losses Connected With Becoming Parents

For young adults who do become parents, through any means, the transition to parenthood has an immediate and significant impact on their lives, adding stress but potentially providing protective factors, too. Becoming a parent is a transformative process and includes "shifts in self-concept, social roles, and daily routines" (Saxbe et al., 2018, p. 1190). Having a newborn or young child disrupts sleep and decreases exercise and other physical activity (Saxbe et al., 2018). For couples, relationships can be more stressful and less satisfying. How couples experience this transition var-ies, and research shows that certain subgroups (e.g., fathers with mental health problems during the prenatal period) are more at risk than others for a decline in relationship satisfaction (Don & Mickelson, 2014). The losses that accompany parenthood—including freedom and previously held social roles—are typical maturational losses.

The baby or young child entering a parent's life is completely dependent on the parent's care, 24 hours per day, 365 days per year. This new full-time responsibility changes the adult's daily routine. Gone are the days when the young adult could hop in the car to pick up that ingredient missed on the shopping list. Instead, the parent must either have someone at home to provide child care or pack up the child and any needed accessories, get the child into the child seat (no easy task), bring the child into the store—and hope the child does not start screaming. Two-minute errands become 32-minute errands, adding the black hole of lost time to a new parent's sense of being overwhelmed. Thus, loss of independence comes with parenthood. Everything must now be scheduled around the child.

Parents have losses related to their social relationships, typically experiencing a shrinking social network. Although new parents may have an increasing connection with their parents or other family members, they often have less connection with and support from their friends. Wrzus et al. (2013) found that adults' social networks reach "a plateau in the mid-20s to early 30s" and afterward adults' circle of friends begins to constrict with no changes "in the size of the family network" (p. 61). When focusing specifically on people in transition to parenthood, Wrzus et al. found significant decreases in the size of social networks. The timing of the transition to parenthood contributes to this. In general, the earlier men and women have children, the harder it is for them to maintain their friendships (Rozer et al., 2017). Parents may decline social opportunities due to a lack of child care, and friends may not want a child brought to the social outing. Childless friends may prefer an adult night out rather than a "family friendly" evening.

Another potential loss associated with the transition to parenthood is a couple's declining satisfaction with their relationship. Partners must adapt and adjust individually and as a couple to the new roles, division of household labor, paid work commitments, sleep patterns, leisure options, changes in sexual interest, and so forth. It is a new life, and they must achieve a new balance. If one parent provides significantly more care to the child, the other may feel pushed to the periphery while the parent providing most of the care may feel unsupported. Shapiro et al. (2020) tested the efficacy of a program promoting fathers' involvement with parenting called "Bringing Baby Home." The study involved heterosexual couples, and results showed that increased participation of fathers in parenting tasks resulted in both parents' increased relationship satisfaction.

The transition to parenthood can also precipitate a developmental crisis resulting in the experience of distress, potentially increasing the risk of psychological disorders (Epifanio et al., 2015). In fact, women may experience their first episode of a major depression during the postpartum period, which can affect their emotional and physical health in midlife and beyond (Saxbe et al., 2018). This too is a loss: the loss of emotional health at an important time in adulthood.

In addition to the typical adjustments and losses associated with the transition to parenthood, couples who identify as LGBT+ have unique challenges to face and concurrently are free from traditional notions of gendered roles and the heterosexual sequence of dating, marriage, and parenthood. Like heterosexual couples, LGBT+ couples must make a multitude of decisions about commitment, cohabitation, marriage, and parenthood. However, if the LGBT+ couple agrees to have children together, complex decisions immediately follow: how to become parents (e.g., alternate insemination, IVF, adoption, etc.), who will become pregnant (if it is a two-woman couple), whether to use a known or unknown sperm donor, and whether or not to use a surrogate and then adopt or adopt through an agency. Each decision carries financial, legal, and emotional consequences to consider. Once an LGBT+ identified couple has a child, decisions must be made about roles and responsibilities without gendered expectations. The positive outcome of this fluidity for many LGBT+ parents is increased likelihood of shared parenting and the larger division of labor in the household (Goldberg et al., 2012). Glazer asserts that "parents must be able to tolerate periods of gender fluidity when they are called upon to engage in parenting tasks that are outside their assigned genders. Individuals who are more comfortable experiencing gender outside the binary may be better able to handle these demands than parents who have a more rigid sense of adequate gender representation" (2014, p. 218).

Losses Due to Parental Divorce

The pivotal developmental task of young adulthood—connecting with intimate partners and maintaining intimacy in long-term relationships—is often more difficult for those whose parents divorced. The impact of parental divorce on a young adult is influenced by many factors, including when in the young adult's life the parental divorce took place.

Parental Divorce Experienced in the Young Adult's Childhood
Children's responses to parental divorce are quite variable and affected by many factors, particularly the parents' adjustment to the divorce, their ability to maintain positive coparenting relationships, changes to the household, and changes in the child's standard of living (Amato, 2014). Children sometimes suffer from resulting ill effects well into their adult years (Jackson & Fife, 2018). Negative effects can include impaired psychological well-being, reduced social competence, and lower occupational achievement (Amato, 2014; Jackson & Fife, 2018). Compared with those from intact families, adults whose parents divorced when they were children have poorer interpersonal skills, cohabit sooner and with less likelihood of marriage, and when married have a greater risk of divorce (Harkonen et al., 2017).

Parental Divorce Experienced in Young Adulthood
There is little research to inform us about the impact of parents' late life divorce on adult children. Likely, though, most adult children of divorce must grapple with difficulties brought on by the dissolution of their parents' marriage. Although young adults are usually independent of their parents and in their own long-term relationships, studies that have focused on those whose parents' divorce identify common issues: They are put in the middle by their divorcing parents; generational role reversals sometimes occur; they get less assistance and support from the divorced parents; and family rituals are disrupted, notably changes in holiday celebrations (Greenwood, 2014; Jensen & Bowen, 2015; Sumner, 2013). These changes all represent loss, whether of accustomed role relations, material benefits, or meaningful rituals of connection.

Losses Due to Young Adults' Divorce

Divorce is not uncommon among young adults. The average age for a first-time divorce is 30, and three out of five divorces involve those 25 to 39 (Lake, 2019). In addition to the loss of the relationship, a divorce can also result in a distressing loss of innocence about the permanence of love and commitment. This often is compounded by a significant decline in each person's standard of living, even the loss of their home. While married, couples' networks of family members and friends begin to merge, but when couples separate, these networks and relationships are often rearranged (Greif & Deal, 2012). Thus, in addition to material setbacks, losses can include friends, family members, shared pets, and social rituals.

Losses Due to Military Service, Including Disability and Trauma

Young adult veterans may have served in one or more of the United States' post-9/11 wars and border skirmishes in Iraq and Afghanistan. Many who served in the military in these wars suffered significant impairment and consequent disability, whether from loss of body parts or traumatic brain injury (Crawford, 2018). Many have had to cope with intense emotional reactions after trauma.

Post-9/11 active-duty veterans have significantly higher disability rates (about 41%) compared with veterans of previous generations (about 25%; Sisk, 2019). This is primarily due to faster evacuation of injured soldiers, which results in the survival with injuries that in past wars would have been fatal. It is also due to greater awareness of the aftereffects of traumatic brain injury (Sisk, 2019).

In addition, post-9/11 war veterans sometimes show signs of a chronic multisymptom illness that may be related to toxic exposures (DeBeer & Corcoran, 2018). Their symptoms include fatigue, sleep problems, difficulty concentrating, irritability, anxiety or depression, and musculoskeletal pain (DeBeer & Corcoran, 2018). They deal with the multiple losses of physical and emotional health and related life changes, often unemployment. In 2018, there were 326,000 unemployed veterans, and 54% were 25 to 54. Not surprisingly, those with a disability had higher rates of unemployment than those without (Sisk, 2019).

Post-9/11 war veterans have often experienced traumatic events. Following trauma, some have anxiety and develop acute stress disorder, the symptoms of which sometimes persist and cause considerable distress. PTSD is diagnosed when symptoms last for more than 1 month and include avoidance of reminders of the event, negative changes in thoughts and mood, and changes in arousal (American Psychiatric Association, 2013). According to the U.S. Department of Veterans Affairs (2019), between 11% and 20% of veterans from Operations Iraqi Freedom and Enduring Freedom have PTSD in a given year. When the veteran returns profoundly troubled and seemingly changed by events during deployment, spouses experience the loss of the person they knew, a classic ambiguous loss (Boss, 1999).

Military families must deal with impairment and disability on top of stressors intrinsic to military life: prolonged separations, frequent moves, residence in foreign countries, and competing military and family demands (Clever & Segal, 2013). Some relocations may be exciting and enjoyable, but each means leaving friends, family, the nonmilitary spouse's employment, and even familiar geography and climate. These changes all produce losses of one degree or another.

REACTIONS OF OTHERS TO THE DEATH OF A YOUNG ADULT

A young adult's death is an off-time loss, which makes coping with it more challenging. In addition, young adult deaths are usually unexpected. The five leading causes of death among those 25 to 44 are (a) unintentional injuries (accidents), 33.2%; (b) cancer, 10.9%; (c) suicide, 10.6%; (d) heart disease, 10.3%; and (e) homicide, 6.5% (Heron, 2018). Three of the five top causes of death—accidents, suicide, and homicide—account for just over half of the deaths in this cohort of (roughly speaking) young adults and are both sudden and unexpected. Death from cancer and heart disease may or may not be sudden, but they are unexpected calamities for people under 45. Therefore, friend and family survivors may have more difficulty coping and may be at risk for posttraumatic stress and prolonged grief (Ingles et al., 2016; Shear, 2012).

For parents of young adults who die, the loss can be particularly hard to process. Adult children are not supposed to die before their parents, and parents should not have to bury their children—no matter the children's ages. If the young adult had been experiencing mental health and/or substance abuse issues, parent–child relationships may have been conflicted prior to death. In addition, if the young adult left behind a spouse or children, there are other ramifications. The past 40 years in the United States have seen a steadily rising number of grandparents raising grandchildren (Gaille, 2017). This trend is a result of adult children being unable to provide care to their own children as the result of their maltreatment of the children, mental health and/or substance use challenges, incarceration, or death (Gaille, 2017).

INTERVENTIONS

Gottman Method Couples Therapy

Young adults may seek counseling as they work toward intimacy, have long-term relationships, and separate from their families of origin. If they seek couples counseling, an approach to consider is the GMCT model. Drs. John and Julie Gottman developed this framework based on Dr. John Gottman's almost 40 years of work and research with couples (Gottman & Gottman, 2019a).

The model aims to help couples in three main areas: friendship, conflict management, and the creation of shared meaning. It is designed to help couples from diverse backgrounds and identities. More important, outcome research has shown the model to be effective for heterosexual, gay, and lesbian couples (Gottman & Gottman, 2019a). Studies have found that couples participating in GMCT improve in communication skills, intimacy, and marital adjustment (Davoodvandi et al., 2018; Rajaei et al., 2019).

The approach begins with a thorough assessment. The first interview is with the couple together, and then interviews are conducted with each individual. Based on the assessment, the couple and the counselor determine the frequency, intensity, and duration of the counseling. After these initial meetings, interventions are used to strengthen the couple's friendship with each other, improve conflict management skills, and help them create shared meaning (Gottman & Gottman, 2019a).

Gottman and Silver identified seven specific principles to improve relationships in their 2015 book *The Seven Principles for Making Marriage Work*. These comprise the levels of the Sound Relationship House and are (a) building love maps (knowing one another's world), (b) sharing fondness and admiration; (c) turning toward instead of away from each other, (d) having a positive perspective (positive affect), (e) managing conflict, (f) making life dreams come true, and (g) creating shared meaning. Gottman posits that each level builds on the next. For example, the first three levels—building love maps, sharing fondness and admiration, and turning toward each other—will enable the couple to have a positive perspective (seeing their partner as a friend not

FIGURE 7.1 The Sound Relationship House. This graph illustrates the main tenets of Dr. John and Julie Gottman's The Sound Relationship House Theory. The theory asserts that there are nine components of healthy relationships. Seven components create the levels of the house—build love maps, share fondness and admiration, turn towards instead of away, the positive perspective, manage conflict, make life dreams come true, and create shared meaning. The two remaining components—trust and commitment—create the sides of the house and bear the "weight" of the relationship.
Credit: We thank Drs. John and Julie Gottman and the Gottman Institute for their permission to reprint this figure.
Source: Reproduced with permission from The Gottman Institute. (2020). *The Gottman method.* https://www.gottman.com/about/the-gottman-method/

an adversary). In addition, Gottman identified two pillars essential to all relationships: trust and commitment. These bear the weight of the Sound Relationship House, forming the basis of stability for the relationship. Figure 7.1 illustrates the Sound Relationship House structure, with the two pillars of trust and commitment and the seven principles of improving relationships depicted as levels of the house.

Complicated Grief Therapy

A relatively small number of people have prolonged grief or CG after a loss. However, losses for young adults are frequently sudden and traumatic, increasing the risk of prolonged grief or CG. In addition, deaths in young adulthood are off-time losses, which also increase the risk of CG. Thus, when working with a young adult who experienced loss, assessment for CG must be a priority.

The CGT model is a structured, evidence-based practice found to be effective in addressing barriers keeping clients from moving forward in their lives after their loss (Shear, 2010; Shear et al., 2005). CGT helps people adapt to their loss by identifying the complications and then facilitating the adaptive process (The Center for Complicated Grief, 2019). CGT includes 16 sessions that focus on seven core themes: understanding grief, managing painful emotions, thinking about the future, strengthening relationships, telling the story of the death, learning to live with the reminders, and remembering the person who died (The Center for Complicated Grief, 2019). Dr. Shear, founder and creator of the Center for Complicated Grief and CGT, developed a manual and an assessment instrument package, which is available at their website (https://complicatedgrief .columbia.edu/professionals/manual-tools).

READINGS

Sheila's Loss of Self
ESTHER GANZ

Esther Ganz is a retired New Jersey licensed professional counselor and licensed clinical alcohol and drug counselor. She received a BS in education from Temple University and an MEd in student personnel services and counseling from Trenton State College (presently The College of New Jersey). She taught for 9 years and practiced counseling for 32 years. Mrs. Ganz's career began at a nonprofit community agency, and she later administered a transitional housing program for single mothers and their children. She served on committees for the prevention of substance abuse and coordination of community services. From 2003 until 2005, she was executive director of the same agency. In 2005, she opened a successful private practice and retired in 2017.

Losing one's sense of self is not often recognized as a cause of grief. It is, however, a life situation that can disrupt an individual's well-being on many levels. If one loses their identity and feeling of self-worth, they may have difficulty making decisions as they once did. They may no longer trust their instincts or opinions and think they are not worthy of others' respect or love. They can feel lost, as if merely going through the motions of life.

To find themselves again, they must allow themselves to experience and express their feelings of loss. After acknowledging the loss and moving through it, they can develop and utilize a plan to rebuild, a little at a time, a sense of who they really are and want to be. Then, even if life is different than before the loss, it may be just as full and fulfilling.

The following case is an example of how a traumatic loss can affect an individual in many ways and how that individual can move through a process of regaining a life after loss and grief.

Sheila was a 48-year-old divorced female who had remained friendly with her ex-husband until he passed away in a tragic accident 1 year before she engaged in counseling. Though the loss of her ex was upsetting, she seemed to have dealt with the loss appropriately. She was in what appeared to be a healthy, committed relationship for the past several months with Joe, who was also divorced and had adult children. Sheila described being close to her parents and siblings. She had no children.

Sheila had been seeing a psychiatrist for a few years for anxiety, depression, and insomnia. There was a family history of these conditions. She had experienced ongoing harassment and humiliation by her new superior at her job. After never having had any negative feedback at work, she was placed on terminal administrative leave. She felt she had no choice but to take legal action. She had worked in the same place at the same position for well over 20 years.

As a result of the harassment, Sheila felt humiliated and ashamed, even though she rationally believed she had done nothing wrong. She began suffering flashbacks and panic attacks. She felt multiple losses. Among them was loss of her career. Sheila was so traumatized that she generalized her anxiety about work to most environments. Her confidence and self-worth were diminished. She was separated on a daily basis from her coworkers, some of whom were good friends. Sheila pulled away from them because of her embarrassment and the stigma she felt. They were also reminders of all she had lost.

In counseling, it became clear that Sheila was "stuck" in her grief. She had given up most of her usual activities, was unmotivated, was isolative except for seeing her parents and significant other, and started to neglect her self-care. She had periods of tearfulness and felt helpless and hopeless. She was not suicidal. Sheila worried about her financial stability, not knowing what the outcome of her lawsuit would be. She wanted to feel like her old self, whom she described as bubbly, fun loving, and enjoying social contact.

Sheila's legal issues caused her much anxiety because they meant having to discuss and face the trauma through depositions and discussions of the incidents that brought her to this situation. She was fearful of having to see her past superiors at mediation and settlement conferences. It was no wonder it was so difficult for Sheila to process her grief because the legal situation was so distracting and demanding. She ruminated about all these things that she could not control and that related to her past. She could not see her future because she was only thinking about what had occurred to her, wishing to change a past that could not be changed.

In counseling, Sheila was able to identify part of what she was feeling as grief. She felt the losses but had not identified them as such. As with most people, Sheila thought grief only applied to the death of a loved one. Coming to the understanding that she was grieving made it possible for her to allow herself to feel the way she felt because she knew that grieving takes time. Sheila processed her grief by feeling it, crying, talking about it, and acknowledging her losses.

Next, Sheila had to identify skills she could use to move on, one small step at a time. First, she needed to shift negative thoughts and negative self-talk to realistic messages. For example, Sheila believed she was doing an excellent job at work and felt she was very productive. Then a new superior made her feel otherwise. In reality, there are supervisors who may like your work and some who may lend constructive criticism before having to take some action. However, according to Sheila, there was no constructive criticism or aid given. She was insulted and demeaned privately and publicly. In taking a step back and thinking about the history of her professional performance, she realized she was making the recent negative feedback her new reality, while minimizing and essentially forgetting her past consistently excellent performance evaluations. In other words, her loss of self-worth was based on a short period of time and on one person's opinion.

As Sheila practiced recognizing negative, unrealistic thinking and reconstructing those thoughts, she began taking better care of her appearance again. She admitted feeling better when she forced herself to dress well and put on makeup when going out on errands, to doctors' appointments, counseling, and so forth. On occasion, she communicated and socialized with a couple of her previous coworkers. One had experienced harassment by the same superior and was also no longer working at their previous place of employment. That coworker's support and their sharing of thoughts and feelings about the experience was invaluable to her. Sheila applied for and got a part-time job a few days a week. This gave her some structure, purpose, and extra money and confirmed to her that she had a good work ethic, even though she did not see this as a future career.

Sheila was able to move through and past her grief by changing her thinking and taking little steps to recover her sense of self. She married Joe, thus becoming an active stepmother. Her mother passed away after a short illness a year after her wedding. Soon after that loss, which she handled well, her case was settled. Sheila was very relieved regarding her financial security and future. She finally felt at peace. She and Joe moved out of state after Joe's work transferred him, and she was happy to enjoy an early retirement, meet new people, and engage in new activities. Her identity was now wrapped up in being a wife, daughter, stepmother, and friend. Sheila had learned that counseling was necessary for her and she consulted with a provider in her new area.

Without the work Sheila did to progress in the grieving process and rebuild her life, her trauma would have followed her to her new environment. She appropriately made the changes within herself before relocating. The skills she developed helped her successfully grieve the loss of her mother and will, hopefully, aid in handling future losses. Though Sheila was on medication for many years for depression and anxiety, they alone could not eliminate her symptoms from grief and trauma. Most think of grief as initiated by the death of a loved one. However, Sheila's loss of her job, identity, self-worth, financial stability, feelings of safety and trust, and coworkers (life as she had known it) presented with the same symptoms. As a result, this required her to utilize the same type of process and skills to overcome her grief.

Blaming Oneself for Heartbreak: A Case of Fetal Alcohol Syndrome
JOELLE ZABOTKA

Joelle Zabotka, PhD, LCSW, LCADC, is an assistant professor, School of Social Work, Monmouth University. In addition to her teaching and research, she maintains a small practice focused on children, families, and parenting with special attention to families experiencing the effects of fetal alcohol spectrum disorder.

Christina (a pseudonym) is a 35-year-old mother of two children, Tiffany (age 11) and Erik (7). She and her husband Paul (43) have been together for 12 years and married for 8. Christina had a traumatic childhood and met her father only a few dozen times in her life prior to his death in 2017. Christina was raised by her mother and stepfather, who were heavy drinkers. She recalled that they went on binges when they would drink for several days straight and she would be left to get herself to school, figure out her meals, and take care of the house. In addition, her stepfather was physically violent and emotionally abusive toward her mother. She witnessed a lot, and her childhood was lost as she worked to manage her own needs while worrying about her mother. Her mother was in and out of ED, due to both her husband's violence and her own impulsiveness. Christina had a vivid memory of her mother's fist going through a window and another hospital stay for broken ribs. She also remembered her mother and stepfather had several stays in rehab. She told me, "I got smarter as I got older—I wouldn't try to break up the fights. We had a neighbor and I'd run across the road and hide." Christina had none of the security and support ideally received from parents during childhood.

When Christina was 12, her mother had an especially frightful fight with her husband. Christina ran from the house and stayed with a friend for several weeks. Child Protective Services

(CPS) was contacted, and Christina was placed in foster care with a cousin of her mother's. Her mother tried to comply with the requirements of CPS, including treatment for her addiction, and job counseling. There were some visits that Christina can remember, but within a year, her mother was no longer in touch, and Christina had lost her mother as well as her childhood.

Recognizing her hurt, Christina's caregiver-cousin got her to counseling. Although her cousin was a nurturing and attentive caregiver, Christina spent her high school years sad and angry. She described herself as "lost and abandoned." In counseling, she learned to verbalize the strengths and positives of her environment and family, while also acknowledging her history. Despite counseling and a supportive home, acting out behavior (staying out late, skipping class, arguing with peers and teachers, alcohol use, and experimentation with marijuana and prescription medications) was rampant, driven by her feelings of sadness, loss, and abandonment. Christina managed to graduate from high school and enrolled in two classes in community college at the recommendation of her cousin. She also got a part-time job in a local retail store, where she was a quiet and diligent worker. Although she had some difficulty with arriving to work on time, she never called out and was a responsible employee. She continued to live with her cousin and attended counseling less frequently. She felt like her life was coming together and that because she was in school and working, she was doing well enough.

Later that year, Christina met Paul through a mutual acquaintance. Their relationship grew serious quickly, and Christina felt loved for the first time in her life. By the time Christina learned she was pregnant, she was already in her fifth month of pregnancy. Christina and Paul were initially overwhelmed at the thought of responsibility for the coming baby, yet they also looked forward to the baby's arrival.

Tiffany was small for her age and difficult to sooth as a baby. Her physical, cognitive, social, and emotional developmental milestones were delayed. Christina consulted with several physicians and other practitioners over several years searching for information, a cause, a diagnosis. All of the doctors agreed Tiffany had global developmental delays, and referrals to physical therapy, occupational therapy, speech therapy, and a special preschool program were completed. As Christina watched "morning TV" one weekday, a segment aired with information about fetal alcohol spectrum disorder. Almost immediately, Christina recognized her daughter's symptoms as she watched the television. As she listened, she remembered the drinking she and Paul did before she knew she was pregnant. She was stricken and distraught, but she contacted Tiffany's pediatrician and before long Tiffany was diagnosed with fetal alcohol spectrum disorder.

Fetal alcohol spectrum disorder refers to a group of physical abnormalities (small, wide-set eyes and a smooth ridge between a thin upper lip and nose), growth restriction, (prenatally and postnatally), and problems of behavior and cognition (Astley & Clarren, 2000; Jones et al., 1973). It results from brain damage caused by prenatal exposure to alcohol. While the facial characteristics may dissipate as the individual grows into adulthood, the behavioral and cognitive effects never completely disappear.

Christina and Paul were crushed. Christina withdrew almost immediately—she stayed in bed for several days following the diagnosis. She was angry, sad, and hopeless. She felt helpless in the face of her guilt, which came in the form of dislike, even hatred, toward herself:

I robbed my daughter from getting married, not going to college, not getting the life that I had. I robbed her and I hated myself. I still don't totally love myself.

Christina's loss of her child's hoped-for future, her loss of her sense of herself as a good-enough parent, and her sense that it was all her fault were all exquisitely painful. Paul withdrew too, but from Christina. He threw himself into life with his children. He was angry at Christina even though he knew she was drinking during the pregnancy. For months, they coexisted without connection, and Christina was afraid her marriage and sanity would be next on her list of losses. Yet, they told virtually no one, and the family floundered while their growing set of losses was hidden from the outside world.

The more Christina and Paul learned about fetal alcohol spectrum disorder and the extent to which it affected Tiffany, the more disheartened they became about Tiffany's current challenges and those in the future. They now envisioned a completely different adulthood for their daughter. Christina had always assumed that her children would earn college degrees, have wonderful careers, marry, and have families. Now she wondered who would take care of Tiffany once she and Paul could not. Who would administer her medications, cook her meals, and ensure her shelter? She ruminated: "I'll never see her married," "she won't be able to have children," and "her life is stolen from her." Christina and her family had lost many things, but most of all, she had lost hope. Instead of the ease of young adulthood routines and work toward promising futures, Christine and Paul had daily crises of caregiving and a sense of impending doom.

Christina believes her healing began several years after Tiffany's initial diagnosis. First, she found an online support group made up of mothers of children with fetal alcohol spectrum disorder. She credits this group with giving her hope, helping her to live one day at a time, and above all, offering understanding. It helped to find she was not alone and was not the monster she had come to believe she was. She disclosed:

> Knowing that I have to do this for her and I have to be able to help her deal with this—things that need to be dealt with . . . I did this. I made this choice. I am the one that chose this. I am the one that put my child in the position that she is in. So that means I am the one that has to try and fight it. Give her the tools and the knowledge to be able to survive this life. I can't fix what I did—there's nothing I can do to make it better—but I think I can make it easier.

Most important for Christina (and for Paul), they had a newfound spirituality, providing them with grace and understanding. Christina related:

> And thank God we found our church almost three years ago. We wouldn't have the foundation and the fortification we have now. . . . Oh yes. And they have nothing but good to say. How do you hold something back like that! My pastor is 87 years old. You would want to give this guy a hug even though you've never met this guy. He is so real, so down to earth. He is so realistic.

Christina described being welcomed by her church's congregation. Her family did not feel judged. The church members offered understanding, tolerance, and flexibility and embraced her family. Christina and Paul, along with their children, continue as active members of their church community.

Conclusion

Through newly formed connections with both her mother's mutual aid support group and her pastor, Christina began to recognize the many losses that she endured, beginning in childhood. Progressively losing her mother's attention and ultimately her presence contrasted bitterly with the losses that struck quickly, such as the realization and confirmation of Tiffany's fetal alcohol spectrum disorder diagnosis. Realizing their need for support through counseling and their church family, Christina and Paul continue to work on their relationship. Tiffany requires round-the-clock supervision and care, and most of her direct care is provided by Christina. The complexity of balancing her daily guilt along with her active caregiving role as a mother for a child with special needs is an ongoing challenge. The family copes by taking one day at a time. Although the worries for the future are always there, Christina and Paul try to stay in the present and work to both mourn their losses while also identifying realistic hopes for the future.

SUMMARY

Young adults self-reflect and try to find their place in the world as adults. They seek long-term intimate relationships, separate more from families of origin, and move into chosen careers. Their ability to achieve these tasks varies widely based on individual and environmental factors.

The current U.S. birth cohort of young adults has some shared experiences. Many struggle economically due to the Great Recession of 2008, which occurred when they were first entering the workforce or not yet secure. Young adult veterans from post-9/11 wars face significant emotional and physical challenges. Today's young adults have also been hard hit by death from suicide and drug overdose.

In addition to environmental circumstances specific to this birth cohort, there are a multitude of nondeath maturational losses young adults typically face as they enter into long-term relationships, transition to parenthood, and seek careers. These losses include, but are not limited to, the following:

- New parents dealing with the loss of freedom and loss of friends
- Involuntarily childless adults dealing with the loss of what might have been and loss of their dreams to be parents
- Loss of intimate relationship through death, relationship breakups, and/or divorce
- Loss of opportunities to have the job desired, earn the salary hoped for, and secure homesteads
- Loss of peak levels of health as young adults enter their 30s

DISCUSSION QUESTIONS

1. After experiencing a recent parental divorce, a young adult comes to your office for help. Given the developmental tasks of young adulthood, what challenges might this client face?
2. Parents seek your help after their 35-year-old adult child committed suicide. What are some of the complicating factors that may affect their grief response, and how may this event affect their relationship with each other?
3. Young adults seek to find their place in the world as they become more separate from their families of origin. How do race, ethnicity, and/or other cultural identities impact young adults in their pursuit of this task?

KEY REFERENCES

Only key references appear in the print edition. The full reference list appears in the digital product found on http://connect.springerpub.com/content/book/978-0-8261-4964-0/chapter/ch07

The Center for Complicated Grief. (2019). *Complicated grief treatment.* https://complicatedgrief.columbia.edu/professionals/complicated-grief-professionals/treatment/

Cohen, G. D. (2006). Research on creativity and aging: The positive impact of the arts on health and illness. *Generations, XXX*(1), 7–15. https://www.agingkingcounty.org/wp-content/uploads/sites/185/2016/07/RESEARCH-ON-CREATIVITY-AND-AGING.pdf

The Gottman Institute. (2020). *The Gottman method.* https://www.gottman.com/about/the-gottman-method/

Levinson, D. J. (1986). A conception of adult development. *The American Psychological Association, 41*(1), 3–13. https://pdfs.semanticscholar.org/5e75/2a77fb59cc48e9eea4b1ef4c53056b0f140e.pdf

Shapiro, A. F., Gottman, J. M., & Fink, B. C. (2020). Father's involvement when Bringing Baby Home: Efficacy testing of a couple-focused transition to parenthood intervention for promoting father involvement. *Psychological Reports, 123*(3), 806–824. https://doi.org/10.1177/0033294119829436

Shear, M. K. (2010). Complicated grief treatment: The theory, practice and outcomes. *Bereavement Care, 29*(3), 10–14. https://doi.org/10.1080/02682621.2010.522373

Shear, M. K. (2012). Grief and mourning gone awry: Pathway and course of complicated grief. *Dialogues in Clinical Neuroscience, 14*(2), 119–128. https://www.ncbi.nlm.nih.gov/pmc/articles/PMC3384440/

8

Grief and Loss in Middle Adulthood

INTRODUCTION

This chapter examines middle adulthood, a pivotal time of life encompassing ages 45 to 65. It reviews experiences of grief as a result of both deaths and living losses. Distinctive developmental themes in middle adulthood are caring for others and contributing to society. We summarize common biological, psychological, social, and spiritual developmental changes. For some, midlife demands may be more difficult due to risk factors including lack of social support and low socioeconomic status (SES). Adults in midlife also experience the death of loved ones more frequently than in their younger years. Living losses, which include the onset of chronic health conditions, divorce, and career transitions, become more common in middle adulthood. We review examples of practice interventions to help adults in midlife: mindfulness-based stress response, Mindfulness-Based Cognitive Therapy (MBCT), and Resources for Enhancing Alzheimer's Caregiver Health (REACH) II.

OBJECTIVES

After studying this chapter, the reader will understand:
- Developmental themes and tasks of middle adulthood.
- Typical biological, psychological, social, and spiritual development in middle adulthood as well as the diversity and fluidity of life experiences.
- Developmental influences on how adults in midlife cope with loss.
- How theories of loss and grief influence practice with middle-age adults.
- Current practices useful for work with middle-age adults experiencing loss.

VIGNETTE

Joe (age 59) and Karen (55) were married 16 years before deciding to separate and divorce. They have no children from their marriage, but Joe has two children (28 and 26) from his first marriage. Karen's first marriage was to Joe.

Karen wanted to have children of her own, but Joe did not want more children. Karen had sought counseling to help her decide whether to marry him anyway and later spent time in counseling to process the sacrifice. After her divorce, Karen reached out again for counseling to help her face and adjust to the loss of her marriage and the many related losses, including friendships.

Karen and Joe had many mutual friends, and over the years, Karen had grown very close to Joe's children. Unfortunately, due to the circumstances surrounding the divorce (Joe had an affair) and the animosity between them, Joe's children and many friends felt they could not invite Karen to social events because Joe would be there with his girlfriend. Since the friendships she developed while with Joe were primarily with his friends, she was bereft after the divorce.

Karen was also dealing with health issues. Two years prior to the dissolution of her marriage, Karen was diagnosed with stage 1 breast cancer. Her tumor was small, and the cancer was localized. She had a lumpectomy to remove the tumor, followed by radiation treatment. Although the treatment went well, Karen had a difficult time emotionally, becoming very anxious before each follow-up with the oncologist. Throughout the process, she never felt Joe was there for her. In fact, they both think this health issue compounded their already significant relationship difficulties.

Fortunately, Karen could still rely for support on her sister and a few close friends. As well, she had worked full-time for the same company for 30 years, and during this rough time, Karen's supervisor provided great flexibility with tasks and hours when Karen was having "bad days." Her coworkers also pitched in when she was upset. Although she was dealing with many losses, her strong support system combined with counseling enabled her to cope and move forward with life.

DEFINING MIDDLE ADULTHOOD

Americans live longer than previously, and middle adulthood is now understood to extend from age 45 through 65. By middle adulthood, many have settled into long-term relationships and careers, are productive in the workplace, and contribute to their families and communities. Typically, midlife adults reach peaks in career achievement and earnings that may also come with more work flexibility and other perks. Of course, many are in jobs that permit limited autonomy and control and yield modest financial support for domestic obligations. Although a time of relative stability for most, it is a time of struggle for many.

Regardless of career success and income, middle-age adults may find themselves "stuck" in the "sandwich generation," concurrently caring for older relatives while still supporting their children (and sometimes grandchildren). Middle-age adults are frequently the primary caregivers of both the younger and the older generations. Their roles as caregivers, and the expectations attached to those roles, are influenced by many factors, including their racial, ethnic, gender, and LGBT+ identities.

DEVELOPMENTAL THEMES OF MIDDLE ADULTHOOD

Middle adulthood is the age of caregiving. Theorists describe this period in different ways, but the central themes are caring for others and contributing to society through work and other activities. Concurrently, adults in midlife contend with their own physical decline, and most experience more deaths of loved ones than they had previously. Thus, midlife can be seen as the "crossroads" of both growth and decline (Lachman et al., 2015).

Erikson (1950) thought middle adulthood started in the 40s and ended in the 60s. He identified midlife as the age of "generativity versus stagnation" when adults seek to create, produce, and nurture in order to contribute to future generations. Vaillant (2012) agreed that generativity was a primary task for adults in midlife, but he identified career consolidation as an important precondition to its success. Career consolidation involves finding a career "as valuable as . . . play." It is assessed using four criteria: contentment, compensation (both income and feeling useful), competence, and commitment (Vaillant, 2012, p. 95). Once adults achieve career consolidation, they can successfully master generativity, the capacity "to care for and guide the next generation" (p. 95). Levinson (1986) had similar ideas about what he called "the Era of Middle Adulthood." Adults in midlife are seniors in their worlds, responsible for themselves and others and for the development of the younger generation.

Biological Development

Adults in midlife must adjust to the signs of middle age that become apparent in their health and appearance. These may include menopause, late postmenopausal stages of reproductive aging, the onset of chronic health conditions, heart disease, and stroke. Changes in hair and skin occur.

Menopause is a biological passage that women typically experience in middle adulthood. It is diagnosed when women have been without a menstrual cycle for 1 year. Although women enter menopause at widely varying ages, in the United States the average is 51. It results from the natural decline of reproductive hormones but is also caused by chemotherapy and radiation therapy, hysterectomy, and primary ovarian insufficiency (Mayo Clinic, 2017).

Menopause often has unwanted symptoms (e.g., "hot flashes," weight gain, thinning hair, insomnia) and can also increase risk for various health issues (e.g., urinary incontinence, osteoporosis). Women can address these issues by lifestyle adjustments and hormone replacement therapies. Lifestyle changes could include embracing a healthy diet and starting or maintaining an exercise program to reduce the risk of osteoporosis and weight gain (Mayo Clinic, 2017). Women are vulnerable to other health issues due to ovarian aging. Harlow and Derby (2015) discuss the importance of looking carefully at women's midlife health, particularly the connection between ovarian aging and bone, cardiovascular, cognitive, and musculoskeletal health. They report that independent of ovarian aging, women in midlife are vulnerable to the onset or acceleration of other health problems, including osteoarthritis, sleep disturbance, and diabetes.

Popular media typically portray menopausal women in negative ways, most often as crazed: exhibiting swiftly changing moods and volatile irritability and anger. In reality, women have varied experiences with menopause. Some embrace it, happy to be done with menstruating. Others see it as a sign of advancing age and have a difficult time accepting it. For those experiencing intense and unwanted symptoms, menopause can be quite difficult.

Men are not immune to aspects of aging reproductive systems. As men age, the prostate, a gland under the bladder through which the urethra goes, tends to enlarge, causing problems with urination. By age 60, about a third of men experience moderate to severe benign prostatic hyperplasia or enlarged prostate, leading to difficulties initiating a urine stream, difficulty emptying the bladder, and incontinence (Mayo Clinic, 2019). Problems with getting and maintaining an erection are also common in this age group, contributing to men's sense of loss of virility and occasionally affecting romantic relationships.

Many middle-age adults deal with the onset of chronic health conditions, defined by the Centers for Disease Control and Prevention (CDC, 2019a, 2019b) as those that last at least 1 year, require regular medical attention, and potentially limit activities of daily living. Examples of chronic health conditions are high blood pressure, high cholesterol, osteoarthritis, prostatitis, chronic lung disease, diabetes, heart disease, and cancer. About half of middle-age adults in the United States have multiple chronic conditions (54% of men; 47% of women), resulting in greater health service use and spending and decline in functional status (Buttorff et al., 2017).

Midlife brings increased risk of heart disease and stroke. According to the CDC (2018), heart attacks and strokes are the leading causes of death and disability in the United States, and approximately one-third of all life-changing cardiovascular events occur between the ages of 35 and 64. Over 800,000 midlife adults in the United States experienced such a life-changing event in 2016 (CDC, 2018). Midlife risk is heightened by failing to use aspirin or statins (cholesterol-lowering medicines) when indicated, and only half of midlife adults have their blood pressure under control. Blacks are more likely than Whites to develop high blood pressure at earlier ages and are also less likely to have it under control (CDC, 2018).

Midlife adults notice changes in their skin. These result from physiological changes (intrinsic aging) and exposure to environmental insults (extrinsic aging). Environmental factors related to skin aging include poor diet and exposure to sun, smoking, and air pollution. Extrinsic skin aging results in coarse wrinkles, rough-textured skin, and loss of elasticity while changes from intrinsic aging include skin becoming dry and thin and the appearance of fine wrinkles (Zhang & Duan, 2018).

Hair loss in men and women can increase in midlife. Androgenetic alopecia is the most common cause of hair loss, but the pattern differs by sex, which affects hair loss and the probability of becoming bald. Specifically, men typically start to lose hair above their temples, develop a receding hairline, experience thinning of hair at the crown, and gradually progress to being partially or fully bald. Women usually do not develop a receding hairline; their hair becomes thinner all over (not just at the crown); and they typically do not become bald. More than 50% of men over 50 have some amount of hair loss (National Institutes of Health, 2019).

Going gray also occurs frequently in midlife. Generally, as people age, their hair follicles progressively produce less color, and after age 35, the hair is more likely to grow in gray (Shmerling, 2019). There was a well-known "50-50-50 rule of thumb" regarding the prevalence of gray hair: 50% of people over 50 have at least 50% gray hair. However, this folk rule has been debunked by studies showing wide variations based on ethnicity and geography (Panhard et al., 2012).

Psychological Development

In spite of the Western cultural stereotype about midlife, it is unclear whether middle-age adults typically experience midlife crisis. Research finds that most in middle adulthood are not in crisis but busy balancing multiple responsibilities at home and work (Dolberg & Ayalon, 2017). Findings from the Midlife in the United States (MIDUS) longitudinal study paint midlife as a "pivotal" period of "balancing growth and decline," when adults play key roles in the lives of others (Lachman et al., 2015, p. 20). This does not suggest that midlife adults are typically in crisis. Cohen (2006) posits that midlife is less about crisis than quest. He specified Phase I—Midlife Reevaluation (from the late 30s through 60) as a time when adults reflect on their lives and reevaluate priorities. Such reflection often leads to new goals and new meaning. Cohen argued that personal discovery is the typical outcome, not midlife crisis.

Frijters and Beatton (2012) found no decline in adults' level of happiness from the 20s through midlife, finding a "wave-like shape" of happiness across the life span that shows adults experiencing a strong increase in happiness at age 60 followed by a sharp decline in happiness after age 75. This was more or less consistent with Cohen, but in contrast to Blanchflower and Oswald (2004, 2008, 2017), who argued that psychological well-being is temporally U shaped, with the lowest levels of happiness and life satisfaction suffered in middle adulthood (Blanchflower & Oswald, 2004, 2017). Blanchflower and Oswald (2008) extended their research beyond the United States and United Kingdom, examining data from around the globe—and found the same results. Average age of low point of happiness varied by country but was everywhere experienced in midlife. After controlling for confounders, they reported that satisfaction is on average lowest at age 49.5. Both with controls and without controls, life satisfaction at different ages in the United States

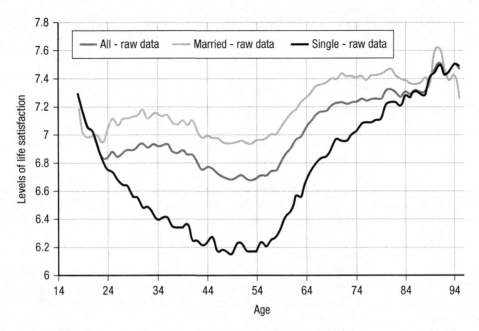

FIGURE 8.1 The U Curve of Life Satisfaction in the United States Based on Age and Relationship Status. This chart illustrates the U curve of life satisfaction for adults based on age and relationship status in the United States. The center line (dark gray) is based on data from all adults regardless of relationship status. The top line (light gray) shows the levels of life satisfaction for married adults. The bottom line (black) shows the levels of life satisfactions for unmarried adults. The vertical axis numbers represent levels of life satisfaction, and the horizontal axis numbers represent age.

Source: Reproduced, with permission, from Graham, C., & Pozuelo, J. R. (2017). Happiness, stress, and age: How the U curve varies across people and places. *Journal of Population Economics, Springer; European Society for Population Economics, 30*(1), 225–264. https://doi.org/10.1007/s00148-016-0611-2

resembles a "U shape" for happiness and a tendency for a midlife low (Blanchflower & Oswald, 2017). Although the MIDUS data did not portray midlife as a period of crisis, it did provide support for the U-shape trend in happiness over the life span (Lachman et al., 2015), and the idea of a slump during a portion of midlife was further supported by Rauch (2018). Graham and Pozuelo (2017) also examined the U-shape trend and looked at how the U curve varies across people and places, recognizing that context matters. As an example, Figure 8.1 illustrates the U shape of life satisfaction in the United States based on age and relationship status (Graham & Pozuelo, 2017). Although married and unmarried adults' level of satisfaction creates a U shape based on age, married adults have higher levels of life satisfaction during midlife compared with unmarried adults.

The authors of the MIDUS study emphasized that midlife should be understood as a mixture of gains and losses in many domains of life (Lachman et al., 2015) and that protective resources that promote resilience affect someone's level of happiness (Lachman et al., 2015). Individual gains and losses are highly variable. Cognitive abilities in midlife vary considerably. Hartshorne and Germine (2015), studying the occurrence of cognitive peaks across the life span, found significant temporal heterogeneity. Some adults peak in high school, others in young adulthood, and still others not until their 40s or beyond. They observed that "there may not be an age at which humans perform at peak on most cognitive tasks" (p. 440). They also explained that cognitive ability is complex, including differing types of knowledge that may be enhanced or diminished in midlife. Crystallized knowledge, which involves the accumulation of knowledge and experience (e.g., vocabulary), generally improves in midlife, whereas acquisition of new knowledge with speed and short-term memory (i.e., fluid knowledge) tends to decrease (Hartshorne & Germine, 2015; Lachman, 2015).

Social Development

Midlife adults frequently have multiple caregiving roles and thus may deal with a heavy load of responsibilities and concerns. Significant shifts in their relationships with children, partners, spouses, siblings, parents, and others may occur as a result of their caregiving roles. Of course, in addition to caregiving, middle-age adults usually have jobs to manage.

As people live longer, an increasing number of middle-age adults care for aging parents and other relatives or friends, the demands depending on the physical and cognitive health of these loved ones. In addition to whatever physical effort is required, caregivers may need to discuss, plan, negotiate, and navigate caregiving responsibilities with those who receive care and those affected by the arrangements. Caregiving is hard and time consuming.

How individuals perceive and cope with the caregiving role and familial expectations of filial responsibilities vary based on culture. In general, people from collectivist cultures, including collectivist traditions within noncollectivist societies, are more likely to emphasize filial responsibility and expect adult children to care for their parents. People from individualistic cultures may feel less responsible for their parents' care.

Using data from the 2015 National Study of Caregiving sample of over 2,000 caregivers 18 and older, Pristavec (2019) explored the burdens and benefits of caregiving. In this sample, caregiver and care receiver had varied familial and nonfamilial relationships with each other. The most common was adult children providing care to their parents (46% of the sample). The largest age cohort of caregivers consisted of those between 40 and 60 (41%). Overall, Blacks were more likely than Whites to have positive and beneficial caregiving experiences. This is similar to findings from previous studies that found that caregivers belonging to minority subgroups, including Black caregivers, experience more benefits from caregiving than Whites. Pristavec observed that "familialism may encourage minority caregivers to accept the role voluntarily, making caregiving less stressful" (p. 1088). Familialism is a collectivist value common throughout the world, though more strongly held in some cultures than in others. Lorene Carey's memoir *Ladysitting* (2019) provides a more complex explication of the caregiving role from the point of view of a working, married, African American mother caring for her grandmother at the end of the grandmother's life. While consistent with familialism, it is laced with ambivalence.

Regardless of the level of care provided to their parents, many midlife adults still have obligations to their children of whatever age. Many have adult children living with them. In 2016, according to the U.S. Census Bureau, 23% of adults 18 to 34 lived with their parents (Vespa, 2017). AARP (2020) conducted a survey of 1,508 middle-age adults (ages 40–64) regarding financial support provided to adult children and to parents. The study found that 32% of adults with living parents provided money to them within the past 12 months and 51% of adults provided money to their adult children aged 25 and older. In addition, AARP found that the money provided by adults to parents or adult children was usually given on a regular basis and involved substantial amounts of money. Of course, middle-aged parents are involved with their children's lives in many different ways, both social and financial, but the important point here is that they often have very full lives that are greatly stressed by their responsibilities to others, and there is loss associated with these responsibilities, as Carey's (2019) memoir makes clear.

Midlife often involves increased responsibilities at work. Having accumulated years on the job, they are the senior employees in their group, or even in their organization (Levinson, 1986). Having ascended to management roles, they are responsible for training and leading others. The workplace or career demands of midlife are often considerable and closely linked to saving for retirement.

In midlife, people seek to balance competing obligations to work, family, and community. Women, in particular, commonly attempt to handle "multiple co-occurring stressors while coping with losses and transitions" (Thomas et al., 2018, p. 1). In addition to the concurrency of stressors, Thomas et al. (2018) identified four common sources of midlife stress for the women in their study: changing family relationships, rebalancing work and personal life, rediscovering self, and securing enough resources.

Spiritual Development

People in midlife are sharply aware of the aging process, and many reflect seriously on the meaning of their lives. Religious traditions provide understandings that guide such meaning-making. In a study of resilience in midlife, McGinnis (2018) found "religious and/or spiritual strategies to be an important component of managing challenges" (p. 216). But they are not panaceas. As Barbara Bradley Hagerty observed, even "people of faith go through the same kind of U curve, the same ennui that you experience psychologically . . . this malaise, this sense that you're praying and no one's listening, that the honeymoon is over" (Woodiwiss, 2016, p. e1).

Today, fewer people in the United States identify with or practice a specific religion. Although still a minority, their numbers have grown rapidly in recent years and more Americans now enter midlife with no religious identification, or consider themselves secular humanists, agnostics, or atheists (Bengtson et al., 2018). This does not mean that they have no spiritual concerns. Fowler (1981) and Peck (1987) each identified stages of spiritual growth that do not presuppose a deity. Although not correlated with specific ages or developmental periods, Fowler's stage of "Conjunctive Faith" and Peck's "Mystical-Communal" stage may best capture the experiences of reflective, spiritually inquiring adults in midlife. Conjunctive Faith means that people recognize that there are paradoxes in life that illustrate the limits of logic. Similarly, Mystical-Communal refers to the recognition of paradoxes and an emphasis on community rather than individual concerns. Although the language is different, the substance here is not far from Cohen's (2006) phase of Midlife Reevaluation.

SPECIAL CONSIDERATIONS IN RISK AND RESILIENCE

Negative life experiences can occur at any age, but adults in midlife typically experience more than when younger. How well midlife adults cope with sometimes serious setbacks depends on various factors that affect resiliency. SES and social support are particularly important.

SES is usually measured by an individual's earnings, accumulated assets, educational attainment, occupation, access to resources, and social status. Higher SES in midlife is associated with higher degrees of well-being (mental health, physical health, cognitive ability, functional and structural brain aging) compared with those with lower SES (Chan et al., 2018). Although money does not buy happiness, it certainly buys protection against many of the consequences of unemployment, divorce, major illness, and other disastrous events that can derail a middle-age life in societies where people must indemnify themselves against hardship. Money brings considerable equanimity to the harried and beleaguered.

Social connections and the social support that flows from them improve the ability to cope with adverse events. In a large study focused on resiliency in midlife, the majority of the most resilient adults reached out to friends and family as a way to cope, either by talking with them or by joining them in social activities (The Hartford, 2019). Those without such relationships usually are less resilient and thus find midlife experiences more challenging.

Personal history also shapes the experience of midlife. As the original adverse childhood experiences (ACEs) study showed, those who experienced multiple ACEs had poorer health and higher risk of harmful behavior such as heavy substance use in midlife (Felitti et al., 1998). It is important to assess such exposure.

LOSSES EXPERIENCED BY MIDLIFE ADULTS

Death Losses

Death of a Parent

Middle-age adults experience more death among loved ones than in earlier years. They usually suffer the death of their father before that of their mother due to gendered differences in life expectancy. Approximately 45% of adults 45 to 49 have lost their father, whereas 26% have lost their mother. The majority of those in later midlife (55–64) have lost at least one parent (Scherer, 2019). Blacks are at a greater risk compared with other groups of losing a mother or father early in life, and this greater risk persists until their mid-50s (Umberson et al., 2017).

The death of a parent at any age is an extremely difficult experience, even when expected. By midlife, however, surviving children are likely the main source of comfort and support for each other and a surviving parent. Especially when there is no surviving parent, they may be expected to take charge of or assist with putting belongings in order and handling the estate. These responsibilities are particularly heavy when there is only one child to bear them.

Although limited, research on parental bereavement during midlife finds negative psychological and physical effects. Marks et al. (2007) found that bereaved adult children tend to mourn the same-sex parent more, with men having more physical symptoms than women. The bereaved, middle-age adult also faces losses collateral to a parent's death. Certain family rituals are no longer possible or are not the same. The surviving midlife children will inevitably be reminded of their own mortality and current signs of aging and lost youth. They will be aware that they are the next in line. If both parents are dead, even middle-age children often feel orphaned and may not welcome the new role of family elder.

Midlife sibling relationships usually change after the loss of one or both parents. Sibling contact tends to intensify, especially after the first parental death, both to share grief and support and to cooperate in aid of the surviving parent (Kalmijn & Leopald, 2018). Kalmijn and Leopald (2018) found that after the second parental death, increased contact was shorter lived than after the first death. In time, sibling relations tended to return to their usual state before the loss.

Death of a Child

The loss of a child is devastating at any age. When a middle-age parent's child dies, it is an off-time death; the child likely had a sudden traumatic death or succumbed to a terminal illness. In recent years, more adult children of midlife adults remain dependent on them financially and/or emotionally, meaning the parent was still in the role of caregiver. These circumstances may affect the grief responses of middle-age parents, and complicated grief (CG) may be more likely. Research suggests that CG is more prevalent among suicide-bereaved families (Tal et al., 2017) and among survivors of other sudden traumatic deaths compared with bereavement after death from a prolonged illness (Boelen et al., 2015).

Death of a Sibling

The death of a sibling may or may not be an off-time loss depending on the sibling's age. Most people in the United States live well into their 70s, so decedents in their 40s or 50s have passed prematurely. A death substantially out of birth order is also likely to be regarded as off-time.

The death of a sibling can be a "disenfranchised" loss (Doka, 2002) if the sibling had a part-ner or children or if parents are still alive. The bereaved spouse, children, and parents are usually taken to be the primary grievers, and most support is provided to them. Surviving siblings, in contrast, are expected to help their surviving parents, nieces/nephews, and the sibling's spouse to handle their loss. They are by custom invisible grievers who must rally themselves to the tasks at hand. This is especially challenging when the lost sibling was a valued confidante and friend or especially important to family caregiving and peacemaking. As Greif and Woolley observe (2015), sibling relationships are nearly always the longest that people sustain, and although they may become closer or more distant after parents' deaths, these relationships may be fraught with ambivalence and long-standing conflicts.

Living Losses: Atypical, Typical, and Maturational Losses

Parental Decline in Physical and/or Cognitive Health

Adults in their 50s usually have parents in their 70s and 80s experiencing physical and/or cogni-tive decline. Families, especially adult children, typically provide most of their care. In addition, adults in midlife may still be caring for children or for ill spouses. The Pew Research Center analysis of Bureau of Labor Statistics data (Livingston, 2018) reports that about 12% of people in the United States are caring for both children and aging parents, most caregivers are in the midlife group.

Caregiving requires considerable time and is a chronic stressor. Any time off is under pres-sure to help the parent in some way, if only to visit. At home, it complicates the management of daily household demands that may include caring for children or grandchildren. When middle-age adults work outside the home, it is difficult to take adequate time off work to provide care. Although the Family and Medical Leave Act provides for job-protected time off for caregiving, unlike the laws of many Western countries, it does not require a paid benefit. Given this burden, it is common that caregivers develop emotional and physical problems (Connors et al., 2019).

Caregivers of parents cope with a variety of notable losses. Obligation entails a loss of free-dom. Time lost to caregiving is time that might have gone to their own interests or relaxation. They also suffer the loss of the parent they knew. They witness the decline up close; sometimes the parent can no longer recognize them or remember their lives together. They lose the child's role, becoming more parental of necessity. And very often, they lose the family home when parents move because adequate care is not possible there.

Care of a Child With Challenges

Instead of seeing their children flourish and become independent, some midlife parents con-tinue caregiving responsibilities due to a child's struggles with health, substance abuse, mental health, and/or developmental disabilities. The multiple losses connected with this situation hit at different times. Parents of children with serious, lifelong impairments of early onset have lost their dreams for the child's life long before midlife and have long known that the obligations of caregiving would extend over a significant period and that the child would never be a caregiver to them. Other parents will encounter these losses only as they consider the consequences of their own aging, and they must plan for their child's welfare while they plan their transition into older adulthood. Some of these parents are simultaneously caring for their own parents.

Midlife adults' coping responses are strongly influenced by their health and available support. Marsack and Hopp (2019) explored the impact of caregiving on 50- or more-year-old parental caregivers of children with autism spectrum disorder. Unsurprisingly, those with health chal-lenges struggled more and had less support and higher levels of caregiver burden.

Divorce (Or the Breakup of Relationships Comparable With Marriage)

The overall rate of divorce in the United States has declined in recent years, yet has increased among those 50 and older (Brown & Lin, 2012; Brown & Wright, 2017). Known as "gray divorce," this trend is associated with the aging of baby boomers (born 1946 and 1964), experiences of divorce earlier in life, and being married for less than 20 years (Stepler, 2017). However, even those married for more than 20 years are divorcing: About one-third of those who divorced after age 50 had been married for 30 years or longer (Stepler, 2017). Numerous losses attend divorce: the family home, economic stability, friendship and in-law relationships, and of particular importance to those in midlife, the security of aging in a predictable relationship.

Along with rising rates of divorce in midlife have come rates of remarriage, which have risen since 1960. According to Livingston (2014) heterosexual adults in midlife (ages 55-64) have the highest rate of remarriage (67%) in contrast to other age groups of heterosexuals. Livingston explains that this may be high due to longer life spans: With many more years to live, people may marry to fulfill ongoing desires for love and companionship.

There are differences in remarriage rates based on gender, however, and heterosexual men's rates of remarriage begin to outpace women's rates of remarriage after they are about 40. For those 55 to 64, 71% of men remarried compared with 63% of women (Livingston, 2014). According to Livingston (2014), only 15% of previously married women wanted to remarry, compared with 29% of previously married men (Livingston, 2014). Recent research affirms these findings. In a study of remarriage after divorce, Crowley (2019) found significant differences between heterosexual men and women over 50 regarding their receptivity to remarriage after divorce. Crowley found that women commonly rejected the idea of remarriage, whereas the men typically wished to remarry. The women wanted to avoid emotional pain and maintain their independence. They wanted a partner with specific desirable characteristics. Men approached remarriage differently: They had unconditional pro-remarriage views (Crowley, 2019).

Loss of Work and/or Career Transitions

Although many midlife adults are experienced employees earning peak salaries and enjoying the perks of seniority, some lose their jobs through layoffs and unwanted early retirement. Job loss in midlife can be particularly challenging, both financially and emotionally. Given that many middle-age adults are also caregivers with added dependents, dealing with a dramatic change in income due to unemployment or underemployment is anxiety provoking and stressful. As well, the blow to self-esteem is considerable, especially when no comparable employment can be secured (Newman, 1999).

Findings from the Health and Retirement Study show that employer-driven separations after employees turned 50 years reached 30%, and as employees enter their 50s, 32% are in short-term, full-time jobs, or part-time positions (Gosselin, 2018). Middle-age adults often have limited employment prospects, especially for positions offering the compensation they need. They are often overqualified or too expensive for available jobs. The longer they remain unemployed in their profession or field, the more difficult it is to get hired. As a result, some take or develop nontraditional or "gig economy" jobs from which income is low or unpredictable and which offer no health, vacation, or retirement benefits. Over time, large problems may loom, as only high-deductible health insurance is affordable, retirement savings are depleted or borrowed against, and mortgage payments get in arrears. This is how many imagined futures are lost.

Loss of Health Onset or Increase of Chronic Health Conditions

As noted earlier, in midlife, people often experience declines in health, and some develop chronic conditions. The readings at the end of the chapter reflect this. In addition to fretting about actual changes in their health, middle-age adults may worry about future decline and think more about their mortality. This is not unfounded concern. The public health service in the United Kingdom warned that four out of five midlife adults (40–60) put themselves at higher risk of illness due to obesity, sedentary jobs, and too much alcohol consumption, all leading to diabetes and other chronic and even fatal illnesses (Pickover, 2016). This is likely true among midlife adult citizens of many developed countries, where access to plentiful food and alcohol, sedentary work and leisure, and lack of regular exercise combine to create significant long-term health risks.

Losses Related to an Adult Child's Life Trajectory

In the United States, the launch or failure to launch of adult children generates typical losses for parents in midlife. When an adult child leaves home to pursue schooling and a career path and family, parents must handle this "empty nest." Conversely, if an adult child does not leave home and is not doing well with school, career, or relationships, parents must handle the loss of the dream they had for their child's life and may have to prolong their roles as caregivers. This potentially results in the loss of freedom to rediscover a life separate from their children, a silver lining in the empty nest. If the adult child struggles with serious mental or physical impairment, the situation is more complex and raises additional concerns.

Losses may also be related to changes in family structure (e.g., blended families, adult children's new families), ages of children (teens, emerging adults, etc.), adult children having their own children, and geographic proximity of adult children. New roles and rituals result in the loss of old roles and rituals. For example, if Labor Day was typically celebrated with a family barbeque at the house but now the two adult children live at a distance, Labor Day will likely no longer be celebrated as it had been in the past. Family rituals change, and the changes can both reflect and promote some degree of family fragmentation.

Loss of the Family Home—"Downsizing"

According to the Joint Center for Housing Studies of Harvard University (2019), people are more likely to relocate in midlife than later on in life. Some middle-age adults decide to pare down their possessions and the space they need because home costs have become a strain, a family-size house and yard are a nuisance to manage, or they have other uses for the money tied up in their home. If children are no longer attending school, staying in a particular town for the good school district may no longer be necessary or beneficial. Midlife adults have numerous housing options, especially if they have adequate financial resources. These include moving into an age-restricted development (e.g., 55+ active adult community, senior housing apartments, a continuing care community), seeking a home in a cohousing development, choosing a smaller residence, or deciding to "age in place."

Moves typically involve losses and can be challenging even if the change is embraced. There are the losses of neighborhood surroundings: neighbor relationships; the house itself (with memories attached) and furnishings and memorabilia that do not fit the new space; favorite local spots; and if the move is of some distance, the loss of local friends. Certainly, the security of local knowledge—from resources to shortcuts—and fixed routines performed without thinking are lost until recreated elsewhere. Changes leave traces of loss, even if only fond memories.

Loss of One's Dreams

Midlife is a time of reflection and reappraisal of goals and achievements. For some, the reality of jobs and relationships does not live up to what they had dreamed. For others, careers may have been successful by most measures yet transcendent goals were unachieved. (In the supplemental material, from our first edition, see Shdaimah's discussion of "cause lawyers," who win many important battles but in midlife understand that they will not see the revolution they hoped to inspire.) Consideration of what family, career, and life goals can still be realized in one's lifetime inevitably involves loss of faith in unlimited potential.

REACTIONS OF OTHERS TO THE DEATH OF AN ADULT IN MIDLIFE

Death of a Significant Other

Widowhood in one's 40s or 50s is an off-time loss that results in serious changes and losses. Because midlife involves caring for others, and its material stability is commonly built on two incomes, losing a partner profoundly affects the imagined and sometimes carefully planned life trajectory. The bereaved must cope with the loss and envision a different future. Lichtenberg (2016) had the bad luck to be widowed twice, first at 25 and then 30 years later. He observed that in midlife, he was much more able to actively participate in his grief, to ask for and mobilize support from others, and to recognize his needs. As a young widower, he experienced guilt and self-blame and had a difficult time mobilizing support. Midlife maturation and greater wisdom permits better knowledge of oneself and one's needs. But regardless of the differences in coping, the later loss required that he envision retirement without his beloved wife, yet another difficult adjustment.

In addition to attending their emotional response to a profound and unexpected death loss, surviving spouses must deal with a multitude of related losses that burden adjustment: a drop in household income, change in handling household tasks, relocation, change from being part of a couple to engaging friends and others as a single person. Parenting and elder care now land squarely on the shoulders of the bereaved spouse. Even if the deceased played only a small role in these responsibilities, likely there were times when they helped or provided some beneficial support that is now lost.

Death of a Close Friend

Losing a close friend of similar age in midlife is also a challenging off-time loss. It entails loss of emotional support from a confidante, even loss of a shared history, especially significant personal experiences that are part of anyone's narrative of life. It may result in the loss of second-order relationships that depend on the lost intermediary link but are nonetheless important. The death of any friend and contemporary, even acquaintances for that matter, can incite worry about well-being and mortality. Miller (2016) writes movingly about the close friends she developed in her feminist circles who died as they aged into midlife. She observes that while we anticipate the deaths of our parents, we assume friendships go on forever, and we are shocked when our intimate contemporaries prove mortal.

Death of the Middle-Age Adult Due to Suicide

Suicide is a problem across all but the earliest phases of the life span. Rates for death by suicide have been increasing since 1975, and in 2015, suicide was the fifth leading cause of death for those 45 to 54 and the eighth leading cause for those 55 to 64 (CDC, 2017). Recent deaths by suicide of famous people—designer Kate Spade, 2018 (age 55); chef Anthony Bourdain, 2018 (61); singer Chris Cornell, 2017 (52); film producer Jill Messick, 2018 (50); and composer Johann Johannsson, 2018 (48)—highlight that suicide can be an issue of concern in midlife, even for highly successful people.

Men in midlife die by suicide more often than women, and their rate of suicide has increased by 30% over the past 25 years; but the increase among women over 50 is even larger (45%; Weller, 2018). A corollary to increasing rates of suicide is that relatives and friends are more likely to experience the death of a middle-age adult by suicide. Grief responses after death by suicide can be complicated and prolonged, and survivors are themselves at somewhat higher risk of suicide. Resources such as the U.S. National Hotline to prevent suicide (1-800-273-8255) and Survivors of Suicide support groups (through the American Foundation for Suicide Prevention) are resources available in the United States to help.

INTERVENTIONS

Mindfulness-Based Cognitive Therapy and Mindfulness-Based Stress Reduction Programs

Most midlife adults experience some decline in health, and many develop chronic health conditions. In addition to changes in health, some middle-age adults experience more losses than earlier in life and have many responsibilities to juggle. The pressure and stress may create or fuel depression. MBCT and Mindfulness-Based Stress Reduction (MBSR) are two promising interventions for these problems.

Initially formulated by Dr. Jon Kabat-Zinn at the University of Massachusetts Medical School in 1979, MBSR was developed to help people with health issues and, more specifically, to relieve pain (UMass Medical School, n.d.). The MBSR program is a group intervention that meets for 8 weeks and involves intensive training in mindfulness meditation with the goal of integrating it into clients' everyday lives. Over the years, research has demonstrated that MBSR effectively mitigates stress, pain, symptoms of illness, and anxiety (UMass Medical School, n.d.).

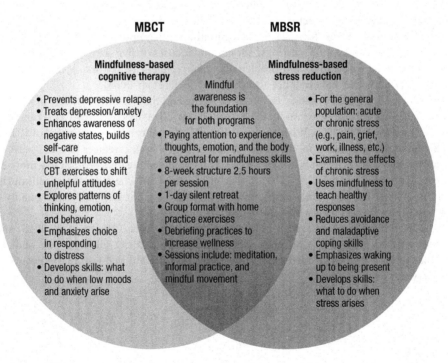

FIGURE 8.2 Understanding Mindfulness-Based Programs. This image illustrates the intersections of two mindfulness-based programs: MBCT and MBSR. The image also illustrates what makes MBCT and MBSR different from each other. CBT, cognitive behavioral therapy; MBCT, mindfulness-based cognitive therapy; MBSR, mindfulness-based stress reduction. We thank the Centre for Mindfulness Studies for their permission to reprint this figure.

Source: Reproduced with permission from Centre for Mindfulness Studies. (n.d.). *Understanding mindfulness-based programs.* https://www.mindfulnessstudies.com/understanding-mbps/

MBCT integrates MBSR with cognitive behavioral therapy (CBT). It was initially developed for treatment of those with recurring episodes of depression and combines meditative practices with cognitive therapy principles (MBCT.com, n.d.). This therapy is one of the "third-wave behavior therapies" and has empirical support for its claim to reduce the risk of depressive relapse (MacKenzie & Kocovski, 2016, p. 126). Recent explorations assessing MBCT's mechanisms of change have yielded disparate findings, even though the efficacy is supported (Alsubaie et al., 2017; MacKenzie & Kocovski, 2016).

MBCT is also an 8-week group intervention. It aims to increase clients' awareness of their patterns of thinking and moods and how these trigger relapses of depression. Mindfulness, used to help clients "disengage" from negative thoughts and depressed moods, is incorporated in the training. Kor et al. (2019) used a modified MBCT approach with family caregivers of people with dementia and found positive and promising results, including stress reduction. These interventions may be useful more generally for people in midlife. As shown in Figure 8.2, MBCT and MBSR are distinct yet share common core concepts and also share similar structure and format (Centre for Mindfulness Studies, n.d.).

Resources for Enhancing Alzheimer's Caregiver Health II

Worldwide, 50 million people live with dementia, a number projected to reach 82 million in 2030, with 5% to 8% of most countries' populations afflicted (World Health Organization, 2019). The burden of caring for loved ones with Alzheimer's falls mostly on midlife adults. In addition to the recent application of MBCT for caregivers of people with dementia, an intervention called REACH II has been found effective in reducing caregiver depression and improving their quality of life (Belle et al., 2006). REACH II is a 6-month, multicomponent, skill-based intervention involving in-person and phone meetings. The content focuses on five areas: safety, self-care, social support, emotional well-being, and problematic care recipient behaviors. A caregiver resource book and access to other materials are also provided (Belle et al., 2006).

Initially funded by the National Institute on Aging and the National Institute of Nursing Research, the REACH project was conducted in two phases (REACH I and REACH II) and tested in six U.S. cities (Belle et al., 2006; Wisniewski et al., 2003). The intervention consisted of 12 in-home and telephone sessions over 6 months that addressed depression, caregiver burden, self-care, social support, and care recipient behaviors. REACH II expanded the intervention to a more diverse group of caregivers. Caregivers in the control group received two check-in phone calls during the 6 months. All participants receiving the intervention had significantly improved quality of life and less depression compared with control group members.

REACH II has been found effective in international contexts (Cheung et al., 2015) and U.S. community-based programs (Cho et al., 2019; Lykens et al., 2014). Of note, Cho et al. (2019) found that some caregivers needed support beyond 6 months and that multiple exposures to the program were beneficial.

READINGS

Becoming a Survivor
DELICATE FLOWER

Delicate Flower is using this pseudonym to protect the privacy she greatly treasures while also sharing her story so others can learn.

I was having a typical, busy September—with a teen starting high school, a small tech business with many clients, and a partner with work travel obligations every other week—and also a persistent worry that I tried not to name or even think about. Several months earlier at my annual gynecological checkup, my doctor had said that the changes in my left breast were nothing to worry about, typical of perimenopause, and my mammogram was clear. I was 56, in good health, and already dealing with occasional hot flashes due to perimenopause. I still was worried, though, and poked the breast in the shower, reassuring myself that it was not a lump. At the urging of my partner, I finally called the doctor's office and spoke with the nurse, who asked me to make an appointment soon. When I saw a different gynecologist in the practice, she, too, did not think it was concerning but sent me for an ultrasound the next week. The radiologist could not "see" anything but could feel what I was talking about. They then connected me with a nurse navigator down the hall, who could make an appointment with a breast specialist. One week later, I met the breast surgeon, and everything changed.

The breast surgeon did a manual exam and a fine needle aspiration, and I read the certainty on her face before she told me that she was sending me for an MRI. Her staff got me an MRI appointment for 6 the next morning. I understood the implications of that urgency and was devastated. I called my partner and went home and cried. How could this be happening to me when I had been so careful about my health, having lost both my parents to cancer in their 60s? The cat lay down in my lap and purred, and I cried until I felt emptied out.

The next 8 days were a blur of imaging tests at different hospitals and unfamiliar medical facilities. I felt numb and like I was living in a nightmare. Small kindnesses from medical people and support staff helped; even a simple offer to sit and wait with me made all the difference. Everything was frightening, especially waiting for the tests to determine where the cancer had spread. It was a tremendous relief when the surgeon called on a Friday night "so we wouldn't worry all weekend" to tell us that there were no distant metastases.

My partner and I went to the appointment with the surgeon together to discuss plans for treatment. We were full of anxiety, and also packing the healthcare power of attorney I had had drawn up before giving birth more than a decade before. We were not sure how we would be treated as an LGBT family by the medical team. We hadn't gotten married and we wondered— would they treat us as life partners who shared decision-making, health insurance, parenting, and all of life's up and downs? Our fears were quickly put to rest, as every member of the surgeon's staff and the surgeon herself gave us hugs (after first asking). When seating us in her office, the surgeon gave my partner the doctor's chair behind the desk and seated herself next to me.

The treatment plan was laid out—chemotherapy, surgery, and radiation over most of the next year. The next hurdle was to communicate what was happening—to our teenage daughter, to her school and advisor, to the wider circle of our friends, and to my business clients. Without a doubt, the hardest conversation was with our daughter. My partner took the lead and thus the emotional burden of telling her, and we all cried together and then distracted ourselves with Harry Potter. What helped the most was that an administrator at our daughter's school had been very public with her own breast cancer diagnosis and treatment, so our daughter had some familiarity with breast cancer and a positive expectation that she could hold onto.

My partner also took the initiative of starting a Caring Bridge site (caringbridge.org), so we could share the story and medical updates with our friends. I learned quickly that repeating the details over and over on a daily basis was exhausting! Although I am an introvert and it is difficult for me to share that much of myself publicly, it was a relief to give out the Caring Bridge URL and to have a flood of love and support from so many people. I learned about others' struggles through Caring Bridge and became closer to people with whom I had had only a business relationship previously. Even people I had known a long time turned out to offer different sorts of support and stories than I expected.

The first part of treatment involved outpatient surgery to have a chemotherapy port inserted. Having only had previous surgery for pregnancy and childbirth, I was very apprehensive.

Ironically, this minor surgery helped calm my fears about the major surgery I would face. The first morning of chemotherapy mere days later brought its own set of fears because I did not know what to expect during the treatment or the side effects to come. I imagined all sorts of scenarios from dying in my sleep to endless throwing up, and yet with all of these potential futures, I did not imagine what actually happened.

My partner and I were in the "chemo suite," where a nurse was attending to me and preparing the many different IV parts of the process (all new to me—saline, antinausea, Benadryl, steroids, and so on prior to the actual chemo drug). It helped that she talked about everything that was happening so I knew what to expect amidst complete uncertainty, and she hooked up an antinausea drug to help prevent side effects from the chemo drug. Suddenly, I couldn't breathe. Instantaneously, I was surrounded by a half dozen people working on me, and amazingly the nurse kept talking to me, giving me details about what she was doing that would help. As my vitals returned to normal, we made jokes about my being a "delicate flower," which helped break the tension, and I learned to trust my medical team.

I had eight rounds of chemo, once every 2 weeks, and it physically got harder as it progressed. It helped to have some emotional support every day: phone calls with friends, cards, chocolate, flowers, books, lists of uplifting or funny movies, dinners, fruit, and errands. All were helpful and helped me get through a very tough (both physically and emotionally) time. It helped that my partner was able to work from home many days and was able to cancel all business travel during my course of treatment. It helped that she took over school transportation and that we walked every day. It helped to remind myself that chemo was ¼ over, ½ over, ¾ over. When I started to lose my hair, it helped that my friend at the hair salon scheduled my appointment after hours so she could shave my head in private. It helped that my knitting friends made hats and my nonknitting friends purchased hats. Feeling like people were thinking about me was the most supportive thing of all, and I felt grateful.

While in chemotherapy, I had looked forward to feeling carefree during the several months in between chemo and surgery. Instead, I mostly worried and worked on getting stronger. I spent spring break with my family in my hometown, enjoying the company of old friends and eating good food. I was still thinking about my cancer all of the time, though, and had started the antiestrogen drug that I would take for years—both a comfort that I would have this protective drug and also a terrifying reminder that the cancer could come back at any time. My presurgery to-do list included updating my financial documents and finding a therapist, yet both of these tasks felt like difficult hurdles to face.

As I prepared financial documents, I once again was reminded that our family is fortunate to have good health insurance. I knew the chemotherapy part of the treatment could easily have been financially catastrophic for most families. I was lucky that my inability to work much during treatment would not financially devastate us. Updating my will was hard too, because it required me to face my fear of dying on the operating table or sometime thereafter from the cancer.

I also knew that I needed a therapist for the long haul to help me handle all of these fears and to help me learn how to live my life after this cancer diagnosis. How does one find a therapist who is a good fit in the midst of all this trauma? I was fortunate to find my therapist by social networking and serendipity—a friend of a friend whose therapist recommended mine. Although this process would not necessarily be accessible to all others (or even result in finding a therapist with experience working with cancer survivors or who is a good fit), checking with friends about therapists they like is always a good first step to locating a good therapist.

I had decided not to have surgical breast reconstruction primarily because of the risk of medical complications. Even so, I had some doubts about this decision prior to surgery. Would I feel differently in my identity as a woman after mastectomy? Talking with my partner about these fears helped. It also helped to review the extensive information about reconstruction provided by the breast center at my hospital. The morning of surgery arrived, and I was afraid of the surgery but confident about my decision. I recovered well, and I was able to go home the next day. In cancer's rollercoaster ride of emotions, I went from cheerful hope immediately after the surgery to feeling crushed days later to learn from pathology lab results that I would need a second surgery that same week to remove more lymph nodes. Talking about it with my partner, my therapist, and old friends helped, followed by distracting light entertainment and then employing some humor with the story (the "2 for 1 surgery special").

Although I had been told that I would experience arm pain, numbness, and range of motion issues, I felt helpless and unprepared for the reality of it. In hindsight, I wish I had had physical therapy scheduled in advance of the surgery so I would have known more concretely what I would be facing. Ultimately, I needed months of physical therapy overlapping with the start of radiation. There has been this constant disquieting overlap: It felt like I was always moving on with the next step of treatment before I had fully processed and dealt with the previous difficult step.

After chemo and surgery (ies!), the next hurdle was daily radiation for 6 weeks while still trying to heal from surgery and to rehab my arm so I could hold the position on the radiation table. I drove myself to these daily appointments and felt empowered that I was able to take care of myself. At first, I was apprehensive about learning "the breath hold" and I worried about the effects of the radiation on my body. By the beginning of the second week, however, I actually began to look forward to seeing the radiation therapists, feeling their kindness, and enjoying our joking around. We even discussed music selections. When I "graduated" and rang their bell, I was actually sad to leave their care and the emotional security of actively having my cancer treated with such a warm and caring group of people.

Now, a year after my diagnosis, I have had a clean MRI, and friends are celebrating the news. I just feel relieved. Many people who gave me so much support during chemotherapy are now not in touch as much, thinking that my difficult treatments are behind me. The reality is that I am struggling to live a "normal" life while still grappling with side effects from the treatments like neuropathy and what it means to live as a cancer survivor. I joined a 5K training group specifically for breast cancer survivors. Talking with these women who really understand, from their own personal experience, has helped me enormously. Complementary therapies—yoga, acupuncture, oncology massage—have also helped me transition from the daily medical appointments to taking care of myself for the long term. With the help of therapy, I am identifying the people and activities that give me strength and purpose.

With this cancer diagnosis, everything in my life has changed—health, irrevocable changes to my body, work life, finances, friendships, family relationships, food and nutrition needs, exercise, and my priorities in determining what is important and what is not. I experience these changes in tangible ways and face the fear of recurrence daily and will live with this uncertainty for the rest of my life. At my 6-month checkup, my breast surgeon encouraged me to reduce chronic stress, increase exercise, and go live my life. My focus now is on nurturing important relationships and making daily choices that bring me small joys, gratitude, and good emotional and physical health.

Losing Health While Staying Engaged
ANONYMOUS

This author chose to remain anonymous, recognizing that her story overlapped with so many other stories—of employers, relatives, and friends—it would be unfair to include them in a story with traceable roots.

I was in my late 40s and had just months ago left my partner of over 20 years. Our parting was not bitter, nor was it consensual. He wanted to continue with couples counseling, and I was done. We had ultimately wanted different things from life. I rented a funky three-story Victorian house, was working on my dissertation, was building a growing consulting practice, and was being considered for the job of a lifetime. I envisioned hiking, backpacking, and cooking, activities I lost track of while living in the battlefield that had once been home. Anything seemed possible.

Then, while on a business trip, I woke up in severe pain, unable to get out of bed. My self-diagnosis of rheumatoid arthritis (RA) was quickly confirmed. A beloved graduate school mentor had RA, and I had seen its quick devastation. I immediately started seeing a rheumatologist and an acupuncturist, eschewing some of the standard medications offered by the rheumatologist. My rheumatologist assured me he would figure out a manageable pain-control regime, although it could take a while to see what worked. He was true to his promise, while in the meantime I learned to breathe through the pain and be patient.

During this time, the ground shifted, nothing was familiar. My closest friend of almost 10 years announced that our friendship had become burdensome, and she terminated all contact. She had had her own struggles with her health and I suspect—but do not know—that my diagnosis heightened her own sense of vulnerability. Over the many years of our friendship, we were each other's "first call" in a crisis. Her dismissal was stunning, and I felt profoundly abandoned and unmoored.

Oddly, the RA diagnosis spurred many changes in my social network. Distant friends were suddenly available, offering a sympathetic ear, problem-solving, and checking in. My mother was unexpectedly devastated at the news, and I quipped to a friend that my mother was acting as if this were a brief, but terminal diagnosis. The intensity of her grief was unsettling, and I kept my distance so I could stay calm.

My soon-to-be-ex-husband was helpful, running errands to the pharmacy, and helping to reduce fall hazards in my new home. He left the door open to taking care of me if I would just move back to the house we had shared. Friends and family encouraged me to go back, at least until the initial health crisis was past.

Although I did not want to go back, it was tough to live alone. I had multiple falls and could be stranded on the third floor of my new house waiting for my joints to calm down enough to safely navigate the stairs. For meals, I often ate whatever I could open, and many things were simply too hard to prepare. I felt like a bear—determined to get to the food but clumsy and leaving carnage in my wake. Alas, ice cream lids turned out to be particularly impossible to remove.

While my emotional independence was at its height—having successfully gotten myself out of my marriage—my physical and financial independence were shaky at best. My standard shift car was difficult to drive—both shifting and braking were hard on my joints. My consulting work was all hourly, and I had days and even weeks when I could not work. I had no savings or income sources that would cover my lack of billable hours, and I worried about money constantly.

Well-meaning mentors cautioned me about letting clients know about the RA, predicting a collapse of my business if people thought I might become unreliable. I had always worked remotely, rarely seeing clients, so they knew nothing about the RA. But the stoic, silent shtick was not working, and I felt dishonest. I made an appointment with a major client to tell her I had RA and also to let her know that I was behind on some important deadlines. I practiced my confession to ensure it was honest but hopeful. She listened carefully, assured me everything would be just fine, and then reached over and gave my very swollen wrists a big reassuring squeeze. I nearly fainted from the pain, but also had to laugh. It was clear she had no idea what I was trying to tell her.

When the pain let up so I could function at the keyboard, I would feverishly work to get on top of past and future deadlines. As part of controlling the pain, my doctor started prescribing oral steroids, which not only brought the inflammation down but also gave me incredible energy. Unfortunately, the energy was neither reliable nor productive, as I could type out pages of nonsense, be impressed by my brilliance, and submit the nonsense to clients. I was losing my ability to judge the quality of my work. Was I also losing my competency?

After the first few months, friends started fading away. The chronic aspect of this was challenging. Lots of people were great in a crisis but unwilling or unable to stay engaged for the long haul. Although friends had offered to help me with typing, I was awkward dictating memos, and very few came back and offered to help a second time.

Although I briefly considered applying for Social Security Disability Insurance, I wanted to work. I contacted the Office of Vocational Rehabilitation (OVR), and they fast-tracked me through their admissions process. I was enthusiastic about my work and a good candidate for their services. They surveyed my office and spent hours sitting silently watching me work, noting situations that were challenging. They ordered specialized equipment and monitored my progress. Their mantra of "key stroke reduction" was transformative. It would be impossible for me to stop using the computer completely, but I could reduce the stress on my joints by typing less.

Soon I was seriously considering taking the strong biologic injectable medication my rheumatologist was recommending. The acupuncturist considered such medicine the antithesis of promoting health, but I was desperate for relief. At $5,000 a shot (which, miraculously, my soon-to-be-ex-husband's insurance paid), it was a momentous decision. I questioned my right to have such a huge financial footprint. I questioned if such therapy could be sustained. I literally had nightmares about giving myself an injection. And I started taking the drugs. Although the medicine made a huge difference in keeping down inflammation, I had already sustained significant, irreversible bone loss. Chronic pain and limited use of my dominant left hand were the result.

The therapist I had seen throughout my separation from my husband proved not to be as helpful as I navigated RA. She became directive and condescending, and I terminated therapy and focused on my meditation practice, guided imagery, and if I could write, journaling. Exercise was tough, and I longed for my pre-RA days of a 4-mile walk before breakfast. Life felt uncertain and unpredictable, but I was moving forward, and I was working. But my ability to work would be tested again.

Fifteen years later life had changed a good deal. I was 60 and had bought a cozy cottage, where I had my office; my consulting practice was thriving; I had a PhD and I was happily remarried. My arthritis was well under control, but I suspected new RA complications. I was seriously fatigued; I was stumbling and had some falls. When full-body tremors started, and I fell three times in short succession, my husband took me to the ED. The diagnosis: Parkinson's disease (PD).

My father died from complications of Parkinson's.

My husband's father died from complications of Parkinson's.

My husband and I thought we knew what we were facing.

We had no idea.

Parkinson's at age 60 is not Parkinson's at age 80.

The first year was an unmitigated nightmare. Told that walking was the key to keeping the PD symptoms at bay, I walked. I also fell. I broke my hand, I chipped my tooth, I imprinted my glasses on my face, and the underside of my chin would never look the same. Nausea from the medication caused daily vomiting and a 25-pound weight loss, despite five different antinausea drugs. And then there were the nightmares. It was unclear if it was the PD or the medications, but I started having terrifying nightmares, screaming while in a dead sleep, hitting and kicking my husband, overturning furniture. I also started sleep walking, waking up confused in different areas of the house.

I was a memorable houseguest.

I knew a good deal about Parkinson's from my father's experience, and Parkinson's dementia was what I feared the most. I decided to face that fear early and arranged for a full neuropsychological evaluation. Confident that I was at the top-of-my-game intellectually, I thought these tests would create a baseline against which to measure cognitive loss in the future. I even looked forward to showing off my mental prowess. But it did not work that way. The tests showed significant loss of cognitive function, especially in my executive functioning areas: planning and sequencing in addition to a significant slowing when processing information. But then the completely unexpected: The tests raised serious concern about my ability to drive. I was distraught. When I sought a different interpretation of the tests from my neurologist, positing that it was too early to me for me to be experiencing such significant executive function challenges, he calmly said "not at all" that almost all of his patients have lost considerable executive function by the first time they see him. Then, with no fanfare, my doctor prescribed medication for the treatment of Alzheimer's. I thought I was literally losing my mind.

So could I work? Would I know if my work was OK? I hated the idea of being the last person to know my work had turned to crap. I still had a very full list of consulting projects on my desk. I resolved part of the dilemma by hiring a small cadre of top-notch colleagues who did similar consulting work and had them "check-my-work" as well as handle some of the more challenging conceptual analysis. They were among the very few who knew the depth of my concern about my capacity to work and were compassionate with me and exacting in their work as ghost editors. We were able to finish all my projects with my dignity intact, but questions about future work loomed.

My relationship with work is complicated: People who have loved me dearly have called me a workaholic. Somewhere in the process of working off a deeply seated inferiority complex, I developed a killer work ethic. I enjoy just about every aspect of work—the sport of it—meeting the impossible deadline, the creative problem-solving, picking the projects and people I wanted to work with, doing work that matters to me and will have long-term impact. My intense focus on work figured prominently in the demise of my first marriage and was well known and accepted—even celebrated—in my second marriage. I planned to work through my 60s, but many of these plans were not going to work if I could not drive. And none of my plans were going to work if I was, indeed, losing my mind.

And then, as if all the worst predictions were being realized, I began being really confused. I had trouble understanding the thread of a conversation or newspaper article. I started mismanaging my finances. I had a few instances where I could not understand what people were saying. When I reported this to my doctor, he suggested that I retire, and with deep grief, I started turning down new work and telling people I was retiring. A few months later, a careful review of my medications indicated that I was taking three different drugs that could each cause memory and confusion problems. As I weaned off the drugs (including the newish drug for Alzheimer's), my mental capacity improved significantly, while faith in my doctor plummeted.

While my mental capacity had dramatically improved with the removal of some of the drugs, the question about my ability to work remained. I could objectively see that short writing tasks that once took a few minutes now took hours. My legendary capacity for focus was impaired, and I frequently lost my train of thought. In addition, my physical capacity to work had diminished. Fatigue remains a serious problem, and two to three naps per day are almost routine.

While friends tried hard to be understanding, the new diagnosis of PD was a real conversation killer. Although most people were supportive and curious about the symptoms, some preferred to keep distance between themselves and any illness. Some brought flowers. Others brought long stories of people they had known who had PD. Good, well-meaning friends ended up saying some very odd things and so I offer this advice to those in similar positions:

- Do not act out a relative/friend's PD tremors—there is no way to do that and be respectful. Believe me, it is not funny—even if I do laugh.
- Do not go into detail about someone's battle with PD, even when you think it will do me good, so I know what is ahead. It won't do me good. It will frighten me, and I will want to avoid you in the future.
- Do not suggest that "this" moment may be the worst that any of it will get. If I don't get any worse than "this" I will become a friggin' medical marvel because everyone loses in the PD game.

- Do not suggest that my medical complexity and prognosis for an early death will at least spare me the worry of saving for retirement.

These terrible attempts at comforting communication were matched only by my poor mother's attempts. She was the daily companion for my father, who died of complications from PD and spent his last 2 years in a nursing home. My mother has repeatedly said that her one comfort is that he died before being completely swallowed by Parkinson's symptoms. She recounts this comfort often, stopping too late to realize that she, too, is wishing me an early death rather than experiencing all that Parkinson's has to offer.

Although I seriously needed counseling, it was remarkably hard to find: Many therapy practices were closed to new clients or did not take my insurance, and I needed someplace close by or accessible on public transportation. The first therapist retired, the second transferred to another office, and the third was a great admirer of my work in the field. After multiple beginnings with a few therapists, I felt like I was running a Parkinson's 101 course. The social worker at the PD clinic was by far the most helpful but was an hour away and had limited availability. Oddly enough, despite the many mental health providers I have seen (who have all taken a thorough history), not one has asked me if I am suicidal.

Luckily, it has been easier to find a community than a therapist. Immediately after my diagnosis, my husband and I quickly joined a large support group that was pivotally helpful and has remained our core of support. We live in an urban area, and there are lots of educational and social events for people with PD and their care partners. These gatherings have been vital to our managing PD in our lives.

So what's ahead for me? Parkinson's is a degenerative disease—which means there will be constant changes in symptoms and constant adjustments to medications. And I will not get better. The focus is to make the changes and the losses a little easier. I take 16 pills a day at 10 different times and 2 inhaled drugs. Each month I take one injection and one infusion. I walk with a cane and also have trouble crossing busy streets on my own because of challenges with depth perception. In the morning, it feels like little cement trucks have filled my shoes to make them just a bit heavier than they were the day before.

It has been 4 years since I was diagnosed and—statistically speaking—in another 4 years, I will need a wheelchair or a walker to get around. My ability to control any of my muscles will continue to deteriorate, making talking and swallowing increasingly difficult and hazardous. My ability to handle stress, already impaired, will lessen as my body makes less and less dopamine, making it difficult to assess danger, or relax after a danger has passed. Although I do not have a tremor (unless it is very early morning and I am late taking my drugs), I do have a spontaneous roll of the hips at odd times that would look much more normal if only I was wearing a hula-hoop!

Not driving has had a big effect on my social life. It is hard to do anything spontaneously, and as friends pick me up and drop me off, I feel like a sullen teenager asking for a ride to the mall. Uber has been great, and my husband and friends very generous in making it easy to ask for rides. Still, this loss puts significant space between me and the world.

The thing that helps at this juncture is taking one day at a time, as trite as that sounds. As a wave of anxiety about the future washes over me, I can screen it quickly to see if it is something I need to pay attention to right now. If not, the thought is dismissed. Having more than 40 years of a meditation practice has helped me hone this, and I am grateful for that training. My bucket list has always been short, so I adjust my desires to my capabilities at any point in time. My hopes of resuming hiking and backpacking are long gone.

I do draw hope from the many new drugs that are coming out to treat Parkinson's. I saw many "miracle drugs" with RA that changed the course of my disease. It could happen again with Parkinson's. I also have slowly embraced the role of talking to people who are newly diagnosed and helping them think through options, formulate questions for the doctors, and advocate for themselves.

My husband has been a great partner through it all—calm, practical, compassionate, and patient. Second marriages are not known to be particularly sturdy when a huge asteroid called "Parkinson's" hits the roof—but he has proved the naysayers wrong. He has joined a men-as-care-partners group and has attended lots of PD social and educational meetings. We are in this together, and that makes all the difference.

John's Story: Healing After Cumulative Losses
SCOTT PONTIER

Scott Pontier, MA, MSW, is a New Jersey–licensed psychotherapist and executive coach in private practice. He has graduate degrees in social work (clinical) and in theology (pastoral counseling). Over the course of his career, he has worked in a myriad of settings, including academia, agencies, corporations, employee assistance programs (EAPs), and a private consulting practice. While his practice is varied, he specializes in working with executives as well as "difficult" couples.

John is a 50-year-old single Caucasian male who lives in New Jersey. He was referred to me approximately 3 years ago by his work-based EAP counselor due to symptoms of grief and depression. John (a pseudonym) has a long history of various losses and the rather quick and unexpected death of his father precipitated his seeing a workplace counselor. John presented with grief and moderate depressive symptoms including difficulty sleeping, poor concentration, procrastination of home and work responsibilities, tearfulness, suppressed appetite, and diminished interest in his hobbies. He is well educated, with both a BS (Dairy Management) and an MBA from an Ivy League institution. He holds a midlevel management position at a large pharmaceutical company. He is verbal and articulate and has a keen mind for remembering dates and details—especially as they relate to his "losses."

John is physically disabled (one of his losses). During adolescence, he experienced the loss of his physical dexterity and balance. He was subsequently diagnosed with spinal muscular atrophy (SMA) type 3 (muscular dystrophy). With the use of a cane, he walks slowly and spastically, unable to navigate most uneven surfaces and stairs. He can drive and lives alone in a single-family home that he owns.

Born into a farming family, John is the older of two sons. His parents were dairy farmers in Pennsylvania until approximately 15 years ago, when they sold the farm and purchased another farm in Missouri (with his youngest brother who went into the farming business). This move constituted another loss for John, as he had grown up in the PA town and it was where his friends and all relatives (including his maternal grandparents) resided. Between mobility impairments and work responsibilities, John was no longer able to see his immediate family regularly after the move.

Over the past 4 years, John has experienced many significant losses in the form of family member deaths. His paternal grandfather died in 2015, his father died in 2016, his dog died in 2016, his mother died in 2017, and his maternal grandmother died in 2018. It was the death of his father and then his dog that led him to seek counseling for his grief/depression.

Influence of Developmental Tasks and Milestones on the Impact of the Loss

John first began experiencing "loss" when he began to fall behind in his coordination and ability to play sports, and his work on the family farm became more challenging. He reports having felt confused, frustrated, and at times experienced shame as his physical abilities began to deteriorate. A brief understanding of his disorder may be helpful.

A primer on SMA:

SMA is a severe inherited disease characterized by the progressive loss of motor neurons, which send signals to control voluntary muscles. As they are lost, the patient's ability to move, swallow, and breathe typically worsens. There are many different types of SMA, based on the gene that is affected. Disease severity and age at onset of symptoms also vary.

SMA type 3 has a later onset and is generally milder than SMA types 0 to 2. It is sometimes referred to as Kugelberg-Welander syndrome. It is inherited in an autosomal recessive manner, which means that an individual must inherit a mutated copy of the survival motor neuron gene 1 (SMN1) gene, critical to the function of nerves that control our muscles, from both their mother and their father to develop the disease.

The symptoms of SMA type 3 usually develop after the child has learned to walk unaided, but they can begin to be evident at 12 months of age. SMA type 3 has two subgroups based on age of onset: SMA type 3a, where symptoms begin before age 3, and SMA type 3b, where symptoms begin after age 3 and usually progress more slowly. Patients with SMA type 3 have muscle wasting, which leads to muscular weakness. As a result, they experience:

- Problems walking unaided, climbing stairs, and running, all of which can worsen with time
- Difficulty standing from a seated or lying position
- Poor balance and an increased risk of falls
- A slight tremor
  (*SMA News Today*, n.d.)

By the time John was in high school, he could no longer compete in organized sports or help with many of the tasks on the farm. He recalls feeling sad as well as frustrated and angry. He made a decision to be as independent as possible for as long as possible. Now, John has been struggling with additional physical loss. He falls with some frequency, and 6 months ago, he broke his shoulder, requiring a hospital stay and a month in a rehabilitation facility until he regained his ability to stand and walk (now with a cane). He understands that with his medical condition, any loss in muscle tone may not be recoverable. This raises the concern of whether it is wise to continue home ownership and live independently. If he does, he will have to sacrifice privacy to engage an aide to help.

Having endured a significant physical disability for several decades—despite his mostly positive attitude—has "set up" John to be more susceptible to loss/grief. Many of the things others take for granted (bounding up stairways, running, getting dressed quickly, taking a long walk, being romantically involved) have not been a part of his life and leave him with a pervasive sense of "losing out" (loss).

Psychological Impact of Loss

John reports functioning quite well and feeling "mostly" happy until several years ago. Soon after his grandfather died, John's father became ill and died rather suddenly. Because John has not been in a long-term romantic relationship and has no children, he remained quite emotionally bonded to his parents, who remained his "family" (unlike couples who view their children as their primary family). This created a deep loss for John, who reports feeling loss of interest, "deep sadness," and the "shrinking of my family."

Soon after John's father died, John's older dog died as well, precipitating John's seeking help. Soon after his father's death, his mother unexpectedly became ill. John made it his mission to find her the best diagnostic services and care—often driving her into New York City. She ended up in a rehabilitation facility near his home, where she remained for several months until she died. His hopes that she would get well again were dashed. She was (as was his father) only in her early 70s.

John reported being "devastated" by his mother's death. They had been particularly close, and he relied on her as his primary confidante and helper. She periodically visited and helped him organize his home and life. After her death, he recounted every event and milestone of her illness and ruminated about what he could have done to keep her alive. He had "bad" dreams in which she asked him to help her. The intrusive and pervasive thoughts caused him to be tearful often and frequently unable to focus at work.

John cycled through the many emotional stages of his grief and found himself angry. He struggled with reconciling "why good people who worked hard ended up dying fairly young and unexpectedly." Sleep was elusive for a few months. Concentration at work diminished, and work felt "unimportant." In our psychotherapy sessions, he would be tearful for most of the time. He expressed a great deal of loneliness: His parents were the people he felt closest to and spoke with most frequently, and now he had no one.

Not long after his mother's death, his maternal grandmother (in PA) died of a heart condition in her early 90s. While John understood better the "timeliness" of her death, it added to the compounding of his grief.

Social Impact of Loss

John's "remaining" family consists of a younger brother (and his wife and children) who reside on and run the family farm in Missouri. While he never felt "close" to them emotionally, the sense of loss is greater now that a void has been created with the death of his parents and grandparents. His sister-in-law is neither friendly nor welcoming. He reports getting along with his brother but states that they don't talk about much other than farming and "my brother is not one to talk much about feelings." He likes his brother's children but senses that the connection is a bit distant and perfunctory. When John visits, he arrives full of expectation but returns sad and disappointed in the "quality" of his time with what remains of his family. They stay engaged with their own lives and livelihood—making little room to include John or make him feel special. John is faced with the "solo" reality of his life on a day-to-day basis.

Friendships are important to John. He maintains connections with college and graduate school friends. His challenge is that all his friends are married with children; they are engaged in their own lives and most do not live near him. The burden falls on him almost exclusively to initiate social engagements (sports events, meeting for a burger, etc.). Although his friends are willing to meet, their own family and life responsibilities mean they rarely reach out to John. While he understands this "intellectually," he still feels sad, lonely, and often isolated. On the positive side, John has been engaged in "adaptive sports" (including biking, skiing, skydiving, boating) and has met others in this forum. Even so, the relationships rarely take on a sense of closeness that extends beyond the events.

Romantic relationships have been elusive. From an early age, John "pictured life with a wife and a few kids" and has a keen sense of disappointment (and loss) that this has not come to be. John has been willing to try online dating and meeting women at work and at business events. While not actually very direct about it, it appears they are not inclined to be with a man with obvious physical limitations. He is an attractive, well-groomed, well-spoken individual; however, his diagnosis and prognosis may be scary, and his awkward mobility may embarrass people around him. We often discuss this loss of love and family in tearful sessions.

John does not profess a faith. He grew up without a faith tradition, though the family loosely considers themselves "Protestant." John does not benefit from a "community of faith" where relationships are often deep and supportive. Many faith communities offer "meals on wheels," support groups, fellowship, and some find belief in a higher power that brings meaning to life (and death), offering a more optimistic outlook.

Interventions

Psychotherapy interventions in this case have been/are drawn from several sources:

- CBT
- Attachment theory
- Psychoeducation

I not only utilize theory and standard therapeutic techniques but also adhere to the school of "one size fits one." I rely on the client/patient to be the guide in what approaches work based on their unique set of circumstances, life context, and personality style.

First and foremost, it has been important to develop a strong, trusting, and caring connection to this individual. The use of open communication, using direct terms (death, dying, dead), summarizing what is being said, and providing space to feel and display his pain have been crucial. At first, John was leery about being specific about what he was experiencing, but now openly discusses and shares his thoughts, feelings, and even haunting images (mother in her bed fading from life). With his disclosures came tears and I gave him permission to grieve and normalized the pain he felt. This was helpful and "freeing."

Primarily a farmer, scientist, and businessman, John wanted a "framework" to understand his emotional struggles. We discussed that there is no predictive path, but we did talk about common responses. Elizabeth Kubler-Ross's framework, which he inquired about, was loosely used with John. I explained that her research was actually focused on one's experience of being terminally ill—which is often extrapolated and generalized by clinicians to encompass individuals experiencing grief as well. John found that normalizing the reactions to grief made his experience more understandable, made him feel "normal," and helped him believe he would move forward from the most challenging times. Even after his parents died, despite logic, he would find himself struggling to accept his parents' deaths. Realizing it was not unexpected—even when not rational—was a comfort to him and assisted him in his grief process.

It was helpful for John to learn to "derail" (a CBT technique) his intrusive and disturbing thoughts and memories at certain times, especially when sleep became elusive, or concentration was challenged when he was "consumed" with painful memories or visual images. He learned to derail by changing what he was doing. (If reading, listen to music instead; if immobile, get up and go to a different room in the house; if driving, play a new station on the radio; etc.)

Learning to journal has been helpful. It provides a mechanism to clarify thoughts and feelings, as well as a method to "get the thoughts out of me and on paper." It also captures a way to chronicle and remember positive life events. The last two seasons, he was able to utilize some of his reflections in a lengthy Christmas newsletter to all his family and friends. He is also in the preliminary process of writing a book about his life—detailing both gains and losses.

Death(s) bring an end to, or change in, rituals and traditions, and this is often emotionally painful. We have focused on maintaining certain traditions (albeit with some changes) and beginning some that are new. Traditions are a form of "emotional glue" that helps hold people together. Reestablishing these have tremendous value. One new tradition that John initiated was flying a nephew out to New Jersey and taking him to several professional sports events for "a guys' weekend."

Finally, as John moves further (in time) from the deaths of his family members, he is motivated to establish new and enhance existing relationships. He has reached out to past acquaintances, taken a few trips to visit old roommates, and traveled to see and visit his brother with more regularity.

Social Supports

While limited, primary social supports have helped John in his ongoing loss experience. His employer provided access to the EAP. The counselor there was sensitive and caring and provided him with support as well as a referral for more psychotherapy. The company has historically been extremely accommodating of his physical disabilities, allowing flexibility to work from home, attend his doctor appointments, and when his parents were ill, take time to be with them as needed. Ongoing therapy has provided John with a consistent and safe source of support. He can openly grieve in session and utilizes the education and tools we discuss. Remaining family and friends provide comfort and help, even if not as actively as he would wish. He continues to cultivate these relationships.

Prognosis

From an early age, the diagnosis of muscular dystrophy challenged John and spurred loss. He experienced losses of mobility, of the family he envisioned, and of his dreams in many areas. In addition, the many family deaths in a short span of time have had a tremendous impact. These factors create a complex grief situation. However, John is by nature an optimistic, can-do person. He steps up to life's challenges (i.e., adaptive sports, graduate degree, travels alone). Life will never be the same, yet John is moving forward. He has demonstrated resiliency during his life, and this will serve him in continuing to process his grief and moving forward productively.

SUMMARY

Adults in midlife are the caregivers in society and are largely focused on others. This can be rewarding and validating yet also demanding. The busyness and responsibilities experienced by middle-age adult caregivers can be overwhelming and may result in low points in happiness and life satisfaction. In many ways, midlife is a tug of war between gains and losses.

Midlife adults may be at the top of their game when it comes to educational attainment, career advancement, and earnings. As the most experienced employees in their companies, they may enjoy the perks and freedoms of seniority yet also may be more at risk to lose their jobs and have greater difficulty finding work. Unemployment and underemployment in midlife—when responsibilities to others are great—can be scary and stressful.

Midlife also ushers in health issues and increasingly the deaths of loved ones. Existential issues—a search for meaning and purpose—may arise as adults in midlife are at a crossroads with these gains and losses, growth and decline, and life and death.

DISCUSSION QUESTIONS

1. After experiencing the death of a sibling, an adult in midlife (age 55) comes to your office for help and a "place to talk." The deceased sibling (52) was married, and his wife and two children are struggling with the sudden and unexpected death of their partner and parent. What may be some issues the client is facing given these circumstances?
2. A middle-age couple, ages 58 and 59, seek counseling services due to concerns about their adult child, 30, who is living at home, is unemployed, did not finish college (after dropping

out freshman year), and has no job skills. The adult child struggles with depression, and the couple worry if they do the "wrong thing" the adult child may take his life by suicide. The couple is unsure what to do, and they cannot agree on next steps. They had planned to move to Florida by age 65 and now wonder if this is ever going to be a possibility. Their life as it is now is not what they thought it would be. What are some of the complicating factors and losses this couple is experiencing?

3. Adults in midlife often provide care to younger and older generations. How do race, ethnicity, and/or other cultural identities impact familial responsibilities and caregiving role?

KEY REFERENCES

Only key references appear in the print edition. The full reference list appears in the digital product found on http://connect.springerpub.com/content/book/978-0-8261-4964-0/chapter/ch08

Cheung, K. S., Lau, B. H., Wong, P. W., Leung, A. Y., Lou, V. W., Chan, G. M., & Schulz, R. (2015). Multicomponent intervention on enhancing dementia caregiver well-being and reducing behavioral problems among Hong Kong Chinese: A translational study based on REACH II. *International Journal of Geriatric Psychiatry, 30*(5), 460–469. https://doi.org/10.1002/gps.4160

Cohen, G. D. (2006). Research on creativity and aging: The positive impact of the arts on health and illness. *Generations, 30*(1), 7–15. https://www.agingkingcounty.org/wp-content/uploads/sites/185/2016/07/RESEARCH-ON-CREATIVITY-AND-AGING.pdf

Lachman, M. E., Teshale, S., & Agrigoroaei, S. (2015). Midlife as a pivotal period in the life course: Balancing growth and decline at the crossroads of youth and old age. *International Journal of Behavioral Development, 39*(1), 20–31. https://doi.org/10.1177/0165025414533223

MBCT.com. (n.d.). *Your guide to mindfulness-based cognitive therapy*. http://www.mbct.com/index.html

UMass Medical School. (n.d.). *History of MBSR*. Center for Mindfulness, Medicine, and Society. https://www.umassmed.edu/cfm/mindfulness-based-programs/mbsr-courses/about-mbsr/history-of-mbsr/

Vaillant, G. E. (2012). Positive mental health: Is there a cross-cultural definition? *World Psychiatry, 11*, 93–99. https://doi.org/10.1016/j.wpsyc.2012.05.006

9

Grief and Loss in Retirement and Reinvention

INTRODUCTION

During working life, people often fantasize about relaxation, adventure, and time to pursue their favorite activities in retirement. In this chapter, we explain how retirement has changed as a result of longer life spans and how intersectional identities and cumulative advantages or disadvantages affect retirement possibilities. We identify protective qualities such as self-efficacy and optimism, as well as problematic aspects of retirement such as declining health or lack of sufficient savings. We examine the living losses of structured time, identity, financial flexibility, work colleague relationships, and spousal relationships. We consider the aspiration to reinvent oneself. This chapter ends with a discussion of interventions currently in use with people as they approach retirement. Three readings about retirement round out the chapter.

OBJECTIVES

After studying this chapter, the reader will be able to:
- Recognize how retirement experiences are sculpted by previous employment, health status, and financial planning.
- Describe how the fantasy of retirement conflicts with the pragmatic aspects of retirement for most people.
- Identify the structural, interpersonal, and self-concept losses that may accompany retirement.
- Analyze the ways reinvention in retirement may apply to people in different socioeconomic and social identity groups.

VIGNETTE

Drew approached retirement as he had approached much of his life: If it was meant to be, it would be, and if not, he would have to figure it out. His father died of cancer when Drew was 17. He decided then that he would make sure he was financially independent, but he was not going to make his life miserable working when he might not live all that long. He was surprised to have survived to his current age of 65 and was stymied by trying to decide whether to retire or wait until 67, when he could get a full retirement benefit. He was still married to Laura, his high school sweetheart, and had worked as a heating and ventilation technician, a low-level banker, a soccer training coach, and a contractor. He never stayed in a job longer than a decade and had nothing to retire on except Social Security benefits. They had two children, both married and on their own. Laura had been home with the children and then worked part-time at a grocery store. She too had no retirement benefits other than Social Security. Drew felt they should be able to kick back and enjoy retirement, but looking at their little bit of projected Social Security income, he was beginning to worry that he and Laura would need to keep part-time employment. He had envisioned traveling and going to every one of his city's professional soccer and football games, but now he worried they would barely be able to meet ordinary living expenses and real-estate taxes. Retirement was not looking at all like he had hoped.

DEVELOPMENTAL ASPECTS OF RETIREMENT: PREPARING

During their working lives, most people imagine retirement as a time to pursue hobbies, travel, renew relationships with friends and family, enjoy grandchildren, linger over meals, and relax without the pressures of work. This is very different than what their forebearers expected. In 1930, prior to the full onslaught of the Great Depression (1929–1941) and before the Social Security Act of 1935, the average life expectancy of men was 58 and of women was 62 (Social Security Administration [SSA], 2020). On the whole, people worked until they died or became disabled. A baby born in 2020 has a life expectancy of 78.93 years, slightly up from 2019 (Macrotrends, 2020), meaning at least another decade of life past a typical retirement age of 65. Approximately 10,000 people turn 65 each day, a number often used inaccurately to imply that 10,000 people retire each day as well (Vandenbroucke, 2019), but many work for years beyond 65. As baby boomers (born 1946–1964) reach 65 in waves, retirements are expected to surge in 2022 to 2024 with a smaller surge in 2028 (Vandenbroucke, 2019). People vary in their retirement ages based on many idiosyncratic factors, yet most approach retirement assuming they will live a long healthy life and have enough money to enjoy it.

The monthly retirement benefit that we call Social Security (SS) started in 1940 when life expectancy was 60 to 65 years and few needed SS for an extended time. The SSA recently observed that people retiring in 2019 were expected to live 15 to 20 years beyond retirement (SSA, 2020). Most people still hope to retire at 65 (though those born after 1960 need to work until 67 to get their full SS benefit). In June 2019, the average monthly SS benefit was $1,470, about 38% of wage replacement value (Center on Budget and Policy Priorities [CBPR], 2019).

Many factors influence the decision to retire or continue paid employment. People may persist in working because they enjoy the work, the friendships associated with it, and both the flexibility and life-structuring properties of the job. Well-educated people with enjoyable careers are especially likely to postpone retirement (Sass, 2016). On the other hand, work requirements of good eyesight and stamina, inflexible work hours, inconvenient hours that limit free time, along with perceived stress, discrimination, or declining health incline people to retire as soon as feasible (Sass, 2016). Retirement planning usually focuses on financial realities, and while this type of planning is necessary, it does not address the qualitative factors noted earlier.

Cultural Aspects of Retirement

Cultural group membership plays a role in retirement. A study by the International Netherlands Group, generally known as ING, reported that although everyone finds planning for retirement daunting, people of color felt less prepared for retirement. In their sample, 54% of Hispanics felt unprepared for retirement (and had an average $54,000 saved, the lowest of the groups), whereas African Americans in their sample had an average of $55,000 saved and 50% felt unprepared to stop working. Asian Americans in their sample had the most savings ($88,000), but 44% still felt unprepared for retirement and 48% of Whites also felt unprepared (SHRM, 2012). This sample came from 2012 and was somewhat anomalous in that it included only U.S. workers with at least $40,000 in assets. Nevertheless, it illustrates that there is substantial variation in the means for retirement across racial and ethnic groups. An insurance company study found differences among cultural groups about when they expect to retire: About 25% of African Americans and Chinese Americans hoped to retire by 60, whereas Korean Americans expected to work well past 70. They also observed that 45% of the group overall hoped to retire before 60, with expectations of decades of life in retirement (Moore, 2019).

Workers' advantages and disadvantages accumulate over the course of their working years, leading to "two worlds of aging" (Crystal, 1982): one group whose members have accumulated advantage and a second group of marginalized people with cumulative disadvantage. Among other liabilities, cumulative disadvantage leads to shorter lifespans (Bosworth et al., 2016).

Cultural group membership clearly influences levels of cumulative advantage or disadvantage. Using data from the Survey of Income and Program Participation (SIPP), Crystal et al. (2017) compared the upper and lower quintiles in retired cohorts from 1983–84 and 2010, determining that the inequality gap widened, concentrating resources in the upper quintile more dramatically in 2010 than in the 1980s. As predicted, people of color, those with lower educational attainment, and single people were concentrated in the lower quintile. This gap between the richest and poorest has major implications for retirement (Crystal et al., 2017).

The situation of Latinx, the largest minority group in the United States, illustrates some of the challenges for members of marginalized groups as they approach retirement. Latinx people have had much lower rates of participation in employer-sponsored retirement plans over the years. Brown and Oakley (2018) find that Latinx workers are somewhat more likely to participate in an employer-sponsored retirement plan than other racial groups when they are offered but they still only have a 31% participation rate (well below Whites' 53%) due to ongoing access and eligibility barriers. Not long ago, Rhee (2013) found that 69% of Latinx people had no savings for retirement (in contrast to 37% of Whites and 75% of African Americans).

Young et al. (2017) observed that the movement away from pension-based retirement and toward self-planning (the need to invest in 401[k] or other retirement saving mechanisms) hurt many people, but particularly African Americans. Using a sample of highly educated African Americans (71% of the sample had bachelor's degrees), they found that financial literacy was fairly low despite high levels of formal education and that those with higher financial literacy were more likely to have begun preparations for retirement. They observed that African Americans typically had few investor role models or sufficient financial understanding to invest independently. Additionally, they found that a household income of $50,000 or more was a threshold predicting that three times more people would prepare for retirement through saving.

Structural and Policy Forces Affecting Retirement Preparation

The policies of governments and employers—the availability and rules of public and private pension plans—affect the way people plan for retirement (Zurlo, 2012). Public plans for the general population are usually straightforward: The age of retirement is deliberately influenced by the size of the benefit at different ages. As in the United States and Canada, the benefit often rises up to a particular age (70 in the United States), with lower benefits available earlier (62 in the United States and 60 in Canada). Thresholds can be manipulated by legislation to adjust for the longevity and age distribution of the population, the cost of benefits, and the need for labor. In many countries, women are permitted benefits at a younger age than men in order to keep men in the labor market, although the trend worldwide is toward gender-neutral retirement ages and higher ages for initial eligibility. In some countries, retirement at a certain age is not just encouraged, but required. For instance, in Israel, people must retire by 67 (it had been 60 for women until 2004), and research indicates that up to a third of Israeli retirees are unhappy about forced retirement (Cohen-Mansfield & Regev, 2018). Finally, some groups of workers negotiate pension rules with their public or private employers. These can be quite complex, sometimes combining age, years of service, and physical impairment to determine eligibility for a benefit that is calculated as a percentage of salary earned at some time in the recent past.

Henkens et al. (2018) raise several as yet unanswered questions (revised here): How do the aspirations for retirement differ from the realities? How will technological advances such as automated financial planning and savings affect retirement practices? How will housing options and decisions influence retirement and vice versa? How can employers maintain productive workers into older ages? How do workers adapt to changes in retirement policies? How does the private pension industry sculpt retirement practices? How does diversity affect retirement sustainability across nations/states? Each of these questions could drive a researcher's life work, yet without answers it is hard to determine beyond gross effects how public and private policies affect retirement decisions and sustainability. For example, although scholars are clear that raising the age for retirement is economically prudent (Munnell et al., 2019), others observe that the vast differences between lower-level earners and upper-level earners make a higher uniform retirement age extremely inequitable and impractical (Brown & Oakley, 2018; Crystal et al., 2017; Johnson, 2018).

SPECIAL CONSIDERATIONS IN RISK AND RESILIENCE

A critical first step of retirement is determining if one can meet responsibilities without ongoing employment income, a situation highly influenced by each person's accumulated advantage or disadvantage. In countries with a strong welfare state, monthly pensions for retirement are comparatively generous, often universal, and healthcare is provided so that people do not fear financial catastrophe triggered by healthcare costs. In the United States, many do not have enough income in early life to save adequately for retirement. In 2019, 25% of U.S. citizens had no retirement savings, and alarmingly, 13% of people over 60 had no savings at all (McCarthy, 2019). Yet, in the United States, financing retirement support falls heavily upon the individual with some help from SS, which was never intended to be a sole source of retirement income. The number of years employed, and particularly the number of years employed by a company that provides a living wage and generous benefits (especially matched retirement savings), define a person's finances in retirement. Employers that offer retirement savings mechanisms provide a strong protective influence in retirement, although defined benefit pensions remain the best predictor of resilience in retirement (Munnell et al., 2019). Ironically, those with substantial retirement savings are the least likely to retire at 65, with many working well past 70 (Sass, 2016). These are well-paid people with jobs they enjoy.

In a 51-country, 10,500+ person study of retirement, Lam et al. (2019) found that the number and variability of social group connections after retirement predicted better quality of life. The larger the number of social groups to which a person belonged, the better their predicted health and well-being in both Western and non-Western countries. Somewhat surprisingly, this effect was stronger in nations with individualistic rather than collectivist traditions. They explained that people in collectivist nations indicated less perceived support from external (nonfamily) social groups because nearly all postretirement support came from family members. In contrast, people from individualistic nations benefited more from access to multiple social groups for support after retirement because they had fewer built-in family supports. For the same reason, they could muster varied forms of help from different people during their transition to retirement, often a time of poorer health and well-being (Lam et al., 2019).

Success in retirement hinges on healthy finances, bodies, relationships, and interests. These protective factors promote resilience in retirement. Good psychosocial functioning at the time of retirement has been associated with multiple healthy aging outcomes (Infurna & Andel, 2018) as well as reduced premature mortality (Wu et al., 2016). Good episodic memory (the ability to remember 3–10 words immediately and after 5 minutes) is also associated with better health outcomes in retirement. Infurna and Andel (2018) demonstrated that cardiovascular disease is highly associated with episodic memory and that those who enter retirement with good episodic memory (especially those who retain it) have a lower incidence of cardiovascular disease, disability, and early mortality. They suggest that good memory contributes to healthy eating, exercise, and appropriate use of needed medications. They cite earlier research indicating that people who maintain complex thinking in their later working years retain cognitive skills more effectively in retirement, thereby promoting physical health.

Poor health is the most challenging problem in retirement. In many societies, and certainly in the United States, medical treatment and supportive care drains limited financial resources. The double whammy of little retirement savings and poor health predicts quick decline. Poor health also limits use of "bridge" employment to shore up finances if necessary.

Bridge employment, first noted in the mid-1980s, refers to work taken on after retirement from full-time employment. For some, it assists in adjusting to full retirement. It can be a new type of job or similar work with reduced hours. As a relatively newly observed phenomenon, research on it is not well developed, and definitional questions have yet to be settled (Bennett et al., 2016). Early estimates claimed that 15% to 50% of retirees in the United States use some form of bridge employment, but Bennett et al. (2016) place that rate closer to 11%.

Distinctions are now made between bridge employment within an existing career and non-career bridge employment. The majority seems to be of the noncareer type as workers gravitate to employment that is more flexible, enjoyable, and less demanding than previous work (Boveda & Metz, 2016). Those who "retire" at earlier ages may move to a new career, called an encore career, and may have the same demands of time and energy that previous work entailed. Using the University of Michigan's Health Retirement Study data, Boveda and Metz traced the retirement trajectories of over 3,700 baby boomers. They found that most continued to work and that, counter to expectations, the financially secure were more likely than others to stay fully employed. The more highly educated also elected to remain employed. As expected, those in poor health were more likely to fully retire. Women were more likely than men to pursue bridge employment, a finding they suggested fit with the demands of women's frequent caregiving and volunteering roles. Another pattern, phased retirement, takes many forms and generally refers to having a planned reduction of hours and duties over time (a year or so). The federal government and some corporations and universities provide these options, but many who wish for phased retirement do not have it available (Kagan, 2019).

Those who have achieved high career status and encounter some pressure to retire seem most likely to use bridge employment, whereas those with higher psychological distress tend to retire fully. Bennett et al. (2016) observed that the predictors for bridge retirement employment were more consistent for people who fully retired than for those who continued employment. A study in the Netherlands found that nonwork characteristics tended to determine who looked for bridge employment but that many who searched for bridge employment were unable to find it (Dingemans et al., 2016). Although phased or bridge employment may seem like a good way to maintain some income and adjust to weaning from work friendships and activities, as indicated in the reading by Walter at the end of this chapter, planned bridge employment and employment-like activities do not always work out.

THEORIES EXPLAINING SUCCESSFUL TRANSITION TO RETIREMENT

Wang and Schultz (2010) examined the literature on retirement prior to 2010 and found that decision-making theories were the foundation for most explanations of postretirement adjustment. Based on the extant empirical literature, they proposed three theoretical models for explaining retirement adjustment. The first draws on life course theory and focuses on interacting factors all working in tandem to affect adjustment to retirement: individual factors (demographics, health, coping abilities, skills), social factors (community norms and expectations), personal history, and work roles. The second, continuity theory, explains that people pursue a sense of continuity and coherence over their lifetimes. People who are able to maintain a sense of continuity in their sense of themselves and their lives will adjust well to retirement. A third theory is based on the adjustment to changing roles during retirement. They find support for each of these theories and suggest that any theory of retirement adjustment must incorporate a person–environment fit assessment as well as a resource perspective, assuming prior resources are carried into retirement. They suggest that decisions about retirement are made with the implicit goals of having adequate resources, continuity of identity, and roles the person finds rewarding. Many have continued to build on their work.

In a systematic review of the international literature, Barbosa, Monteiro, and Murta (2016) identified 26 factors that affect adjustment to retirement, theorizing that these would predict positive retirement adjustment. Factors such as physical health; financial savings; psychological qualities such as self-efficacy, optimism, and extroversion; effective use of leisure time; voluntary retirement; and social integration were positively and strongly associated with a positive adjustment to retirement. Interestingly, factors such as age at retirement, ethnicity, sex, and household composition generally had no strong association or mixed results. It is beyond the scope of this chapter to examine each of the 26 factors Barbosa et al. identified, but they also observed that psychosocial preparation for retirement showed mixed results and did not strongly enhance adjustment to retirement. Research in Israel affirmed this, finding little positive effect for attendees of psychosocial preparation classes and no lasting positive effects after 6 months of retirement (Cohen-Mansfield & Regev, 2018).

Personal characteristics do seem influential. Positing the intuitively sensible notion that resource accumulation predicts adjustment to retirement, Topa and Pra (2018) followed 455 Spanish workers as they approached and attained retirement. Using common standardized measures, they found that people with high degrees of optimism and self-efficacy, particularly a sense that they had control of over retirement decisions, predicted better adjustment to retirement. Financial resources had much more limited influence on retirement adjustment than others typically found, and they assert people's cognitive capacities had no real impact either. A proactive personality seems to assist adjustment to retirement. Maurer and Chapman (2018) characterize proactive people as having qualities of initiation, perseverance, and readiness to grab new opportunities in the face of transition rather than being passive. It is hardly surprising, of course, that those who approach new situations with curiosity and openness manage the uncertainties and change of retirement more easily than those who are frightened and isolated.

Consistent with Lam et al.'s findings (2019), degree of social connectedness is another predictor of good adjustment to retirement. Here, the idea is that multiple connections and activities provide resources to support retirement adjustment. Settels and Schafer (2018) examined how three aspects of social connectedness—broad and varied social network, size of friend network, and social participation—affect retirement, controlling for health, age, education, family composition factors, and gender. They tested whether activity substitution (replacing older working roles with new social and other roles) or complementarity (tendency toward higher or lower social interactions in work and similar patterns after retirement) best explains their findings from data they analyzed from the National Social Life, Health, and Aging Project (NSHAP). They determined

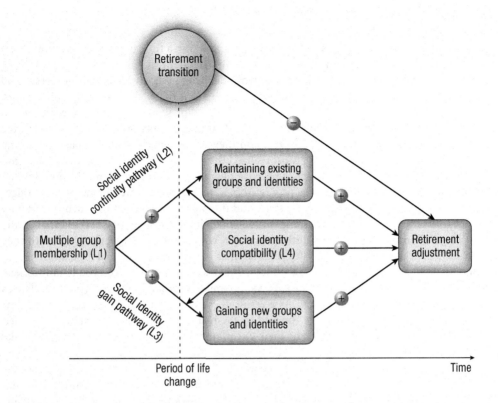

FIGURE 9.1 Forces Affecting Identity and Retirement. The social identity model of identity change (SIMIC) in retirement, developed by Haslam et al. (2019), illustrates how group memberships are protective in retirement.
Source: Reproduced with permission from Haslam, C., Steffens, N. K., Branscombe, N. R., Haslam, S. A., Cruwys, T., Lam, B. C., Pachana, N. A., & Yang, J. (2019). The importance of social groups for retirement adjustment: Evidence, application, and policy implications of the social identity model of identity change. *Social Issues and Policy Review, 13*(1), 93–124. https://doi.org/10.1111/sipr.12049

that activity substitution best fit the data (e.g., those who did best substituted new activities that were similar in intensity and the size of their social network remained about the same). Interestingly, a group of retirees who elected to return to paid work after time out of the workforce showed declines in social connectedness after return to work, but without deleterious effects. It seems likely that return to the often qualitatively intense and deeply embedded relationships of employment may substitute for the quantity of people counted in social networks outside of work.

Haslam et al. (2019) use the social identity model of identity change (SIMIC) in combination with the empirical literature to develop a theory about retirement adjustment (Figure 9.1). Focusing on social groups that create a sense of "us" (family, occupation, sports, leisure, friendship) as resources that define identity and permit its expression, and drawing on SIMIC's assumption that all life transitions require a change in identity, they develop a set of propositions about how the retirement transition affects identity beyond mere role change. The model proposes that multiple group memberships prior to retirement work to buffer adjustment by virtue of their continuity in a retiree's life and because experience with group participation accustoms people to group membership and forming new relationships in different groups. Through (a) maintaining existing group memberships and identities, (b) assuring compatibility (between older and newer group memberships and identities), and (c) assuming new identities and group memberships, the retirement adjustment is predicted to go more smoothly and work out better. Haslam et al. derived a Groups 4 Health intervention, described later in this chapter.

FANTASY VERSUS REALITY

Retirement now tends to be fantasized as a perpetual vacation, a time to fill one's life with leisure activities, or a time to reinvent oneself. This is far from the older retirement expectation of sitting perpetually in a rocking chair, a worn-out survivor of a life of hard work. Yet the new versions of anticipated retirement seem to rest on inaccurate assumptions that yield unrealistic expectations. Goodwin and O'Connor (2014) studied primarily blue-color workers in the United Kingdom during their retirement process. They interviewed their participants originally when they were first entering the workforce in 1960 to 1962, and they reinterviewed those who agreed during their retirement process in the 2010s. Most realized they could not have the perpetual vacation retirement they had hoped for, primarily because financial resources were much more limited than they had anticipated. Many of the new retirees were intensely aware of moving from wage-earning independence to reliance on the state, and this was accompanied by much uncertainty and a degree of fear about their future security. Goodwin and O'Connor observed that in the 1960s, these (then) young men had little interaction with workers and working life until they were socialized into the workforce. Fifty years later, as new retirees, they had little awareness of life in retirement because they knew few retirees. The disconnection between youth and workers and then between workers and retirees kept each population unaware of the typical challenges of the group they were about to enter. As a result, they were unable to prepare adequately for their own futures. Much as they were shocked by the realities of working life when they joined the workforce, they were taken aback by their uncertainty about what retirement might be like (Goodwin & O'Connor, 2014).

Driver (2019) observes that people's fantasies about retirement while still working create anticipatory narratives about retirement. The main retirement narrative in First World countries, she argues, has changed from a story of relaxation after a working life to one of anxiously maintaining productivity and purpose to avoid risking decline and marginalization. Whether through bridge employment, volunteering, or learning new skills, retirees are encouraged to stay active. She believes the change in narratives reflects the neoliberal policy pushes by governments concerned with the cost of cradle-to-grave welfare states if retirement consists of decades devoted to consumption rather than productivity.

Driver (2019) interviewed 49 early career employees in the United States to examine what their narratives revealed about constructed identities and imagined retirements. She found that people use retirement fantasies to construct imaginary selves (i.e., "I am the kind of person who does XYZ and will continue to do so") and to create fixed identities (imaginary, symbolic, and real) that accompany them into retirement. Her analysis of how these narratives reinforce current discourses about productivity and occasionally reflect resistance to master narratives tells us a lot about how fantasies of retirement create the realities that employers or governments wish to promote. Contesting the adoption of producer identities, Driver suggests, can allow more room for Lacan's "project of becoming" (2019, p. 339). Whether the fantasies of a naïve worker yet to encounter the realities of retirement or the indoctrinated worker inculcated with the master discourse of productivity as a vital aspect of retirement, people seem likely to enter retirement with fantasies about how adequate their financial resources are, how much they will be able to continue to earn in bridge employment, how carefree and relaxed they will be, and how healthy they will remain.

In a more recent iteration of the fantasy of retirement, many younger people are exploring the possibility of retiring early. Known as the FIRE movement (financial independence, retire early), the internet is full of young people (30s or so) extolling imminent retirement and financial advisors warning against it (Malito, 2020). Reddit and "Mr. Money Mustache" seem to have sparked the FIRE movement and the belief that it is feasible to save $50 a day to accumulate large sums for investment. Some who aspire to FIRE realize that saving in that way on an ordinary emerging adult's income means that life in their 20s and 30s will likely be meager and unhappy. Furthermore, retirement in one's 40s entails the risk that retirement may be scuttled by the costs of health insurance during the decades leading up to Medicare eligibility. Similarly, long spells of unemployment or other catastrophes can make both savings and early retirement impossible. LaMagna (2019) reported stories of people for whom FIRE failed. Some went from retirement in their 30s and 40s to combining part-time or flexible work to enable some income while not necessarily returning to full-time work. At least one person had returned home to live with parents. For those with the fantasy of early retirement, considerations of the risks and realities are quite important.

LIVING LOSSES LINKED TO RETIREMENT

Retirement is the quintessential maturational loss, and like other maturational losses earlier in the life span, it is often viewed as a positive life event. Yet people go through maturational losses with more ambivalent reactions than they expected to have and often feel unsupported when voicing them. Despite the many fantasies, a reality of full retirement is that there are losses. Some of these (like having to get up and go to work) hardly seem like losses at first but are seen differently with time. Recognizing the losses entailed in retirement permits people to manage them while acknowledging the melancholy, fear, or frustration they may inspire.

Loss of Structured Time

The most obvious change when one retires fully is how time is used. On the first day of retirement, colleagues go to work, but the retiree does not. For many, unscheduled time, the freedom to pursue one's desires, is part of the fantasy of retirement that kept some workers functioning during demanding and stressful periods of work (Heidmarsdottir, 2002). Nevertheless, in some of the earliest writing about retirees, Burgess (1960) commented that these leisure hours become a curse when there is little to fill them with. Many retirees find themselves struggling without the structure of a routine and the resources to make use of their freedom in the fulfilling ways they had imagined, especially when significant others remained in the workforce.

Ekerdt and Koss (2016) found that most retirees identified time sovereignty (the freedom to structure time as desired) as an important feature of retirement. Typically, retirees found ways to structure their time as they adjusted to retirement. Most constructed routines that were more loosely structured, often coordinated carefully with the routines of their spouse/life partner or pet, and encompassing desired activities such as classes or exercise activities. They were quick to create narratives of productivity (and avoidance of "goof-off" days), using routines as a way to "project competence and discipline in meeting the open-endedness of retirement" (Ekerdt & Koss, 2016, p. 1307). Dave Hughes, in his blog about retirement, comments on time in 2 of his 10 truths learned about retirement: He asserts that time management is still needed and that "somedays" need to be "todays" in order to make full use of retirement (Hughes, 2019). In short, the loss of routinized work schedules may be anticipated as an unalloyed positive until there is no routine or structure, at which point it is missed. At this point, most retirees create routines and structures that help them feel integrated into the routines of others in their environments.

Losses Related to Identity

As implied by Driver's (2019) analysis of early career workers' views of retirement, many people are powerfully defined by their occupational identities. For skilled craftsmen, academics, doctors, lawyers, and many others, their occupations are their master identity, and retiring requires a change to being a "former." This threatens identity and constitutes a major loss for many. As earlier editions' retirement readings (and the readings at the end of this chapter) illustrate, grappling with the question of "Who am I now that I'm not ___?" is a central experience of retirement. The master narrative of developing new producer identities consistent with the neoliberalism of our era derives its power from what qualifies as a valued identity.

Preparing for retirement typically involves some planned accumulation of resources. Amabile (2019) suggests four additional tasks: (a) "life restructuring," whereby new routines are established that coordinate with the people with whom one lives; (b) detaching from work and its structures, meaning that one does not keep visiting work virtually or in real life; (c) managing the liminal phase, during which one often carries previous work-related goals into retirement, only to find that one really does not want to expend the energy to accomplish those goals; and (d) consolidating routines and identity for retirement. Amabile asked participants in her study "Would you be more likely to say that your work is what you do or your work is who you are?" and found that for many, the answer is the latter. Those for whom occupation is a master identity benefit from "identity bridging," a process that allows them to maintain some aspect of a work identity from earlier in life. Others may activate a dormant identity, returning to woodworking, sewing, cooking, motorcycle riding, and so forth. Regardless, Amabile asserts that retirees need to find new identities that they value.

Loss of Financial Flexibility

Living on a fixed income when expenses such as healthcare, groceries, gas, taxes, and utilities continue to rise often leaves even well-off retirees feeling apprehensive and frightened. Experts suggest that people should save enough that drawing down 3% to 4% of their savings per year will provide (with SS) 70% of preretirement yearly income (CNNMoney, n.d.). That requires a daunting amount of savings. The going wisdom is that to maintain their standard of living during retirement, retirees should have saved a million dollars (Steverman, 2019).

Yet half of older Americans have not saved anything toward retirement. The Great Recession, reliance on stagnant service-sector wages, student and credit card debt, and the cost of housing, among other factors, have made it very hard to save adequately for retirement (Collinson et al., 2019). Nor is this strictly a U.S. phenomenon: Even in countries with strong retirement pension systems and comprehensive cradle-to-grave healthcare and other provisions, financial fears still affect nearly 20% of retirees (Damman et al., 2019).

The Center for Retirement Research uses a National Retirement Risk Index to monitor the risk of a declining standard of living after retirement. It is currently at 50% (having hit its peak of 53% in 2010), indicating that about half the working families in the United States are at such risk (Munnell et al., 2019). More worrisome, projections show that even if current working people started saving significantly more in 401(k) accounts, this risk would still exist. This is because most households do not have access to employer-sponsored savings plans, which are proven to be the most effective mechanism to help people save. In an era when fixed-benefit pensions have become scarce, built-in savings mechanisms such as employer-facilitated savings and matched contributions help people save for retirement. Munnell et al. (2019) conclude that only by raising the retirement age another 2 years and encouraging significantly more savings will the United States lower the National Retirement Risk Index.

Loss of Work Colleagues

At work, we are usually surrounded by other people. Some are casual acquaintances with whom we interact in passing. People who do similar jobs to our own are usually those with whom we develop often quite close relationships. We share lunches, work discussion, life history, gripe sessions, bathrooms, and office spaces. As Smolowe (2019) puts it, we have situational friendships. Whether by choice or not, these can end abruptly when we retire or wither as our work friends remain working and have little time for us. Acknowledging these social losses and the loss of work identity are aspects of adjusting to retirement (Smolowe, 2019). In her analysis of why seemingly close friends disappear when one leaves a job, Ebonee Thompson (2016) draws on the popular television show *The Office* and her own experiences with being laid off. She observes that although we chat and share intimacies with work friends, these are not the people we would call in a personal crisis. Even so, they are not trivial, and they are lost when we retire. This is a type of ambiguous loss (Boss, 1999) as we know they are still there, yet we no longer have comfortable access to them.

Losses in Cognition

Much current research aims to determine if and why retirement is associated with cognitive decline. The intuitive answer of simple aging has been ruled out. One widely accepted theory derives from the "use it or lose it" theory of neural functioning and maintains that the longer people are retired, the less they use multiple neural pathways. Away from work, the brain's ability to support cognition declines, exhibiting "mental retirement" (Rohwedder & Willis, 2010).

Still, there are different forms of cognition (e.g., memory, executive function, verbal facility), and they may behave differently. Some studies have found that blue-collar workers' cognition seems to improve after retirement and white-collar workers' tends to hold steady (Coe et al., 2012).

The puzzle of cognitive decline after retirement is further complicated by sampling biases. In a sophisticated longitudinal study Clouston and Denier (2017) considered three forms of selection bias that can lead to differing findings about retirement and cognitive abilities. Their findings affirm that retirement is associated with cognitive decline, but that even those who remained employed declined over time. As decline (or maintenance) seemed to follow occupational categories, they suggested that inconsistent research findings result from how different occupational groups were represented in the study samples (Clouston et al., 2017).

Changes in Spousal and Other Significant Relationships

A retiree's spouse or other living partner is intimately affected by the retirement. Retired men are quite well known by their partners to "rattle around the house" rather annoyingly. Grace humorously recalls friends where, after retirement, the husband obsessively alphabetized his wife's spices and walked the stairs multiple times a day (2010, p. 95). These stories are cautionary tales related to couples' retirement planning but like most cautionary tales, there is some degree of reality. Around 2005, when many Japanese men began retiring, a new condition emerged among their wives: Rashes, stomach ulcers, high blood pressure, and depression were soon diagnosed in up to 60% of older Japanese women and given the name retired husband syndrome (the diagnostic phrase *shujin zaitaku sutoresu skokogun* in Japanese literally means "one's husband being at home stress syndrome"; Kincaid, 2015). Largely due to the traditional gender roles in Japan, the return of the husband to the home literally made women ill as husbands treated them as workers and bossily supervised their household work. The cure was deemed to be husbands learning to respect their wives' identity and autonomy and to find other interests (Kincaid, 2015). It is unclear how well that worked.

In light of gender differences in the timing of retirement and concerns about it, the frequent struggles of heterosexual partnerships should not surprise us. Research consistently shows that men tend to focus on retirement as a time of reward and relaxation while women focus on renewing relationships with family and friends and pursuing activities. Furthermore, because career women tend to continue work while career men tend to retire when it is available (Loretto & Vickerstaff, 2015), there are many dimensions of potential conflict.

Damman et al. (2019) explored partners' expectations of retirement, specifically asking about expected financial concerns, relationship problems, or conflict over shared leisure time, both before and after the partner retired (in the Netherlands). Only the financial problems turned out to be worse than expected; the others turned out better than predicted. The research itself might have affected the outcome. In articulating their concern during the first interviews, both partners may have been motivated to work on reducing conflicts as they entered retirement (Damman et al., 2019).

Life partners of all types benefit from a shared and coordinated plan for retirement. Singletary (2018) tells of a woman writing for advice after her husband decided that he would retire after a planned surgery at age 56 with only $30,000 in savings. His 43-year-old wife was distraught that she would need to earn more and support them both. Her plan had been that each of them would work to retirement age, but his health made her plans inconsequential. This is a dramatic example of unchosen circumstances, but if partners differ in how they wish to spend time (e.g., one expects togetherness, the other solitary pursuits), where they live (beach and mountain fantasies are sure to clash), or how they spend money (luxurious travel vs. frugal home activities), there will be problems. Difficult losses may accrue if partners do not discuss expectations of retirement in advance.

Housing Decisions

At least for married, male wage earners, decisions about retirement are often predicated on the value of housing as a sunk cost and potential savings vehicle (Ondrich & Falevich, 2016). Most continue working if their housing does not create wealth; others retire if the housing value and retirement savings together allow them to feel safe doing so. They may return to work if "housing shock" (a drop in value) creates financial vulnerability (Begley & Chan, 2018). Most retirees elect to stay in their current housing for the initial year of retirement as they wait to see how finances settle out. However, joint retirement creates new possibilities for where to live. Retirees may want to move closer to family or seek better weather. They may want to downsize in order to allow more travel and less house care. Financial planners recognize that psychological, practical, and financial factors all play a role in these decisions, and they suggest that couples plan a "housing continuum" that addresses plans to modify the family home to be mobility accessible or to plan to move to a "service-enriched" area (Timmermann, 2014, p. 29) at the point where needed household assistance and health services are likely to increase.

A few healthy, adventurous retirees make major changes in their housing upon retirement. Some take to the road by recreational vehicle or even cruise ship after ridding themselves of (or storing) possessions (DeCarbo, 2018; Greene, 2012; Zane, 2014). Some move into a "small house" (Reiland, 2018) to reduce costs, and others move to other countries. These choices are possible when health, mobility, and interests coincide and family ties do not preclude them. Of course, any of these decisions carry the possibility of loss as connections to neighborhood, home, possessions, and community are disrupted or even severed permanently if a change is not planned to be feasibly reversed.

REINVENTION

When health, finances, and other resources are in good shape, the promise of retirement includes time to pursue hobbies and interests, volunteer, care for family, or in other ways contribute differently to one's community. Zweig (2019) suggests that people consider their identity deeply as they approach retirement. Examining how prior and current work roles define the core of who one is defines the core of the questions Zweig (2019) suggests retirees consider.

This examination helps to frame the activities one plans to pursue in the future as well as to anticipate losses that may accompany retirement. Retirement may be the time when one can regain roles and parts of identity that were sacrificed to work for many years. Perhaps spiritual meditation or brisk walks required more time than one had, or awareness of popular culture or the news required more "bandwidth" than one had, or one's work consumed all the intellectual or physical capacity one had. In retirement, that time and "bandwidth" can be devoted to these activities. These reinventions are also a form of maturational loss (and gain) as one adopts new activities and identities and also loses the prior work identity.

Many books and websites provide coaching for this transition from working life to retirement, nearly all with the implicit or explicit assertion that the best is yet to come. For people whose retirement savings or health do not support travels and adventure, being able to create a bit more flexibility in schedules and give priority to one's interests may be a welcome form of reinvention. Robin Ryan was a career counselor who changed gears to help others reinvent themselves in retirement. After a 2-year fight with breast cancer, she wrote a useful book to help people think about planning for a joyful, fulfilling retirement, often by discovering volunteer and community activities that contribute to the greater good (Ryan, 2018).

INTERVENTIONS

People yearn for retirement and seem to understand the need to plan for it, yet most planning interventions seem minimally effective. In Israel, an intervention to help plan for and then adjust to retirement showed little difference in (and some deterioration in) outcomes of mastery, depression, and positive feelings about retirement (Cohen-Mansfield & Regev, 2018).

Most interventions focused on retirement involve financial planning. Research showed that North Carolinian public employees intended to plan, but those who were "impatient" (taking a hypothetical windfall of $1,000 immediately rather than waiting a year for $1,200) were less likely to plan (even when intending to do so) than patient people, who not only plan but save more as well (Clark et al., 2019). Financial advisors blame lack of financial literacy and the American tendency to overspend and under-save for the poor preparation of so many in the United States. In an intervention with three groups of employees—bankers, manufacturers, and contractors—to prod planning and saving despite these tendencies, Horwitz et al. (2019) aimed to "address the employee's unique money scripts, values, goals, and motivation toward change" (p. 265). They intended to help workers unengaged in retirement planning to be partially or actively engaged. They promoted active savings using cognitive behavioral financial therapy, motivational interviewing, and solution-focused financial therapy, along with encouraging visualization of a desired retirement goal. They successfully got 38% of the unengaged group to begin planning and overall participation rates increased by 39%, so the intervention was deemed successful.

Few interventions have shown strong efficacy at this time, though a planned scoping review of retirement interventions is planned for 2020 (Rodríguez-Monforte et al., 2019). Even so, Haslam et al. (2019) developed an intervention from their SIMIC theory of retirement. Focus on social group membership is primary. The intervention, Groups 4 Health, or G4H, applies the four lessons of the SIMIC retirement theory. The program content starts with Schooling (educating about SIMIC and the importance of social group membership to health) and moves to arenas incorporating the lessons: (a) Scoping—mapping current social group membership and identifying groups that are not compatible with one another (such as groups with differing political agendas) and identifying which help the participant continue to grow; (b) Sourcing—developing skills to maintain and utilize current groups and reconnecting with previously important social groups; (c) Scaffolding—using current group memberships to build new social connections and promote engagement, focusing on groups that are synergistic with one another; and (d) Sustaining—reinforcing the messages of the group a month later as a booster session to troubleshoot and encourage maintenance of skills for social group engagement (Haslam et al., 2019). These groups are being "trialed" and to date have not been rigorously evaluated, but the authors believe they show promise, particularly for retirees who are not socially integrated prior to retirement.

READINGS

Good Boys of Divorced Parents—Part II: Aftereffects
STEPHEN SIDORSKY

Stephen Sidorsky, MSW, LCSW, has retired as director of mental health services in community mental health. He is currently a part-time lecturer at Rutgers University School of Social Work and teaches in the Continuing Education Program in Social Work. Part I was in Chapter 4.

Part II

So, looking back on my early years, these were the cards I was dealt: a lingering fear of abandonment; a feeling of never being "good enough," harboring a shameful secret that I always worried would be exposed; and an ambivalence about relationships, especially when it came to male figures.

Despite all of this (or perhaps because it fostered the wish to do things really, really well), I was quite successful in my field and was always seen in a very positive light. I always moved up, became a manager, supervisor, director, trainer—yet the feeling of inauthenticity was always there . . . that if they truly knew . . . if they found out who I really was . . . if they learned that secret shame.

I am aware of another way that I dealt with this fear (or inability) to allow myself to be really open to others and connected to them. Thinking back, I always had one foot out of the door, something to go to if I felt I needed to disconnect. I had my full-time job, but I also had a second one on the side. If I felt threatened in one, I could flee (in my mind) to the other. I had different groups of friends but was very careful to keep them separate from each other—not that they would tell stories about me, but as my way of keeping a safe distance. It all seemed to be about balancing my world on the thin edge of a razor blade—never to fall off, but never resting too comfortably on that edge, to avoid being hurt.

Over time, the source of the shame dissipated and no longer was an issue. In some settings, it was almost looked upon as if I had some first-hand knowledge about something that people could learn from. Unfortunately—and this is the part that I hope people can learn from—it was not easy to see myself in a different way. That sense of not being "good enough," of something being wrong, remained with me long after my childhood.

Well, it's important that I tell you that things have, in the end, turned out well. I believe that my sensitivity to so many of these dynamics and experiences gave me a deep awareness of others' feelings and experiences and living. This particular kind of understanding helped me not only as a social worker, but as a husband, a parent, and a friend. My marriage has been a strong one, and we have raised two very fine children, one of whom has "given" us four wonderful grandchildren. Time and the inevitable positive reinforcement of good experiences with good people helped me to take more chances and to be the kind of person that I would have liked to have there for me in those days. My own history led me to be very careful (perhaps, sometimes, too careful), in my role as spouse and parent so as not to make the mistakes that I had to grow up with. Also, parenting my children enabled me to "do it right" the second time around, so I remain grateful for having the opportunity for that.

I am currently retired from practice, but teaching in a graduate program in social work, focusing on (what else?) aging and loss. I am able to recognize some important turning points, many of which are reflected in my work life, though they appear in my personal life, as well.

One was my father's death when I was 42 years old. He had remarried and had been living in Florida with his second wife of many years. We had spoken several times a year, and I had visited them a number of times, but as always, I came away feeling somewhat empty and disappointed. I knew about the dynamic of always hoping that "this visit will be different," but it never was. As had been the case throughout my childhood, each visit felt not like a reunion, but rather an awkward meeting with a stranger who, upon reflection, I really wouldn't wish to know and who didn't seem too interested in me. When his wife called me about his death, I did not have much of a reaction (she essentially told me how hard it would be for her without two SS checks). The timing of his death, though, was startling. He died 1 week before I was to begin a new job, which was an exciting and meaningful move for me. Did his death free me to move on toward becoming the person I wished to be or cast a shadow over this significant step that I was taking? Probably both, though how to break it down would require more energy than I wish to spend.

During my career, I was laid off twice—within a period of 3 years. Both instances came out of nowhere and were with organizations in which I had placed a deep trust and where I expected to be treated fairly and honestly. I was disappointed in each of these dimensions. While both instances were due to financial issues within the organizations, these experiences still evoked the sense of abandonment and of not being good enough. While I could have responded as I did when I was younger, I recognized that this was my work life, I had my family to support, I had to put whatever feelings I had aside and move forward, which I did. The several positions I had from that time on required initiative, assertiveness, creativity, and a willingness to take risks. I was able to draw on strengths I did not know I had and welcomed the support of family, friends, and colleagues who were more helpful and encouraging than I could have imagined. It revealed that the "sedimented beliefs" (a term used by Ernesto Spinelli in his *Tales of Unknowing*) about myself that I had grown up with were not as strong as I had believed, and in many cases were simply untrue. This was freeing for me not only in my work, but in my roles as a husband, father, and friend.

My mother's death was also significant for several reasons. On a personal level, it was very liberating as I no longer was the "only child" who had to look after her. While my wife frequently told me how my mother tended to drain me when I visited her or tended to her financial and medical affairs, it wasn't until after her death that I realized how true this was and what a weight was lifted from me. Coincidentally, just as my father had died as I began a new job, so, now, did my mother, 13 years later. I had become a very different person by then, though the irony of this certainly was not lost for me.

Another "sedimented belief" that I had lived with was thankfully shattered during the course of my last position as director of a mental health center outpatient unit, where I managed over 30 employees and close to 2,000 patients at any given time. While I still had doubts about my ability to succeed in this position, I did succeed, and it was where I completed my "agency" career. During that period, I had the opportunity to teach at the Rutgers School of Social Work and realized that this role was my true calling. My attitude could have been "Look how many years you spent on something that was not in tune with who you are!" However, now my view is "How lucky to have found something special that you enjoy and are able to do!"

So, there are several things I have learned from the experience I have been relating. I noted earlier how important it is to tell children what is going on. As difficult as it might seem, one's imagination may only make it worse.

Another lesson is the importance of recognizing that we all react and respond in different ways and at different times to events in our lives. What may seem trivial to you may be an extraordinary experience to someone else. Expand your perspective, ask questions, and listen.

Avoid imposing your meaning or your response on to an event or situation. Perhaps if someone were able to hear and validate my experience, some of the shame, embarrassment, and sense of "differentness" would have been less toxic.

A third lesson is to understand that our experiences can have long-term effects on our lives. The passage of time can be curative, but only to a degree.

I agree with Pauline Boss that ambiguous loss is the most difficult kind. It often is never resolved; there may be no closure and even if there is an ending to the story, the damage has been done, and one may forever be diminished by it. Ambiguous loss can shadow you wherever you go and color so much of your everyday life. It can become an "invisible tattoo"—only seen at certain times or under certain conditions—but inevitable, always there. I do believe that if someone had sat down with me and told me what was going on and what I could anticipate, it would have made a world of difference.

Kenneth Doka's concept of "disenfranchised grief" is crucial to understanding how one may react to loss and destabilization. Perhaps if I had someone to talk with, someone who could clarify and validate my experiences, things might have been easier and less mysterious. Disenfranchised grief really doubles the effect on an individual, whether an adult or a child. If no one is here to support the reality of your experience, you begin to doubt it yourself—in effect, disenfranchising your own grief. It is making the space and the time and the willingness to listen to another's experience that is so important here. In the end, perhaps, this is what Freud really meant by the "talking cure."

Ella's Retirement
ROBIN WILEY

Robin C. Wiley, MSW, DSW, is a licensed clinical social worker with over 24 years of experience serving various populations, including older adults. Much of her work focuses on bringing attention to concerns faced by older adults and informing professionals and family members about how to be supportive. Check out her website theexperienceofaging.com for more information.

At 60 years old, Ella (a composite of similar cases) had worked almost 35 years in the business finance industry. She toyed with the idea of retiring for 5 years. When her company offered a retirement incentive package that Ella felt was worthwhile, she decided to leave the job she had worked at over half her life. She also recognized it was becoming increasingly stressful for her to get to work daily. She experienced some medical ailments that caused her to move a little slower, especially in the morning. Climbing stairs was becoming a dreaded chore at work. In short, Ella felt ready to retire from the physical demands of work, and the retirement incentive package came at just the right point in time—she felt blessed.

Over the years, Ella built significant, meaningful friendships with many of her coworkers. They participated in various community-based activities together several times per month. She also mentored many of the younger employees in her department. She enjoyed witnessing the professional growth of the "up and coming" staff. Ella worked long hours as a salaried employee. She was in a managerial position and relished her assigned duties, always "going the extra mile" to assure quality work. She typically worked 50 to 60 hours per week. This included, at times, going into the office on Saturday. Most weekends, she made plans with her husband or had some coworker-related activity to attend. Being financially stable, she and her husband went out to dinner weekly and attended plays and shows at least twice per month. These activities were in addition to the social activities with her coworkers; her life was full. Ella made a six-figure salary, along with a yearly bonus, so finances were of no concern while she was working.

Ella and her husband have two grown children, both married with small children of their own. They both live in other states but tend to visit during the holidays. Ella and her husband typically take vacation time to visit them each year, and visits to other places of interest were not uncommon.

On Ella's last official day at work, her coworkers honored her with a luncheon, where they presented her with a plaque for her years of dedicated service to the company. Various coworkers recounted their fond memories of working with Ella over the years. Ella went home that evening feeling excited, knowing she did not have to set her alarm clock for the next morning. The weeks that followed her retirement were filled with an occasional errand, or routine doctors' visits. It felt good to not feel rushed all of the time. She and her husband, also retired, spent most of the day watching television in the living room. During a visit to the doctor, Ella was asked how she felt her retirement was going. She disclosed she felt bored and, at times, sad. She reported feeling like she lacked direction and purpose in regard to all her newfound free time.

Retirement is a great milestone to achieve. However, it requires planning. Work encompasses a large amount of our daily and weekly schedule, and our position at work often becomes a large part of our identity. Ella had moved up the ranks into management. She was proud of her strong work ethic and her accomplishments within her company. She had not quite realized how fully intertwined her life was with her coworkers and her work life. She thought she was well prepared for retirement, but it came with various losses and limitations she had not considered.

Ella managed her finances, along with her husband's. Thinking of her own work as supplemental to her husband's and having successfully negotiated the financial changes after his retirement, she thought it would be smooth sailing. However, in retirement, Ella was not really prepared for the mental stress now associated with finances. She and her husband had savings, but she was concerned about being on a fixed income. She worried if their savings would last for their lifetimes. She realized they needed to develop and stick to a budget. How would this impact their ability to maintain the lifestyle they had become accustomed to? Wondering whether they would have enough money in their older age made her wonder if they needed to cut out the extras that made life enjoyable now. This became increasingly worrisome to Ella as the days passed.

Ella was still very astute and more than capable of doing work at the company prior to retirement. Physically she was moving slower and felt more tired at the end of the day, but mentally she could hold her own. In retirement, her brain was not being stimulated, and the idle time in her daily schedule left her restless and searching for something to occupy her time. She stared at her husband, at times, as he sat, contently, watching his favorite television shows. He also gardened and had a weekly card game with his friends. She attempted to join him in certain activities but found them unfulfilling.

What did she like to do? She enjoyed working. Two months into retirement found her having regrets. She had not considered all the time she would have available. Ella felt herself becoming more sullen as day after day she began to stay in bed longer in the mornings. She felt that the longer she stayed in bed, the less time she would have to figure out what to do with her time. She wanted to reach out to coworkers to plan some activities but worried about the costs. Ella missed the daily interaction with coworkers. She wondered how one coworker's relationship had turned out and debated reaching out to another whose parent was ill. Participating effectively in meetings or working hard on a project to meet deadlines were all tasks she had enjoyed. Now there were no coworkers or accolades for work accomplished.

At the suggestion of her doctor, Ella went to see a therapist to discuss her concerns and alleviate some of the emotional symptoms of depression and anxiety. She was having difficulty accepting and adjusting to the new dynamics in her life as a result of retiring. In therapy, Ella processed her feelings about retiring. Her strengths were acknowledged and validated. Ella was outgoing, a natural leader, and she possessed many skills that would benefit her as she aged. Ella and the therapist created a plan with varied options for how Ella could occupy her time in ways that felt meaningful. They considered her daily schedule, how to maintain her social connections, seek activities to continue being active, and strategize to alleviate some of her financial worries.

A year later, Ella and her husband decided to move into a 55 and older community. They decided that downsizing from their larger home would be more cost efficient over the long term. She made friends in the development and now makes it a point to see different friends at least once a week. She decided to work 2 days a week at a small, family-owned business to supplement her income. This not only allowed a bit more flexibility with finances, but also used a nice chunk of time in a way that brought her satisfaction. Ella also became more physically active. She decided to get a dog to encourage herself to walk outside more often. She also enjoyed the responsibility of taking care of a pet. She worked out a budget that allowed her to afford a community outing with friends or her husband once or twice a month. Vacations were not as frequent, but her part-time job allowed for the extra funds for such pleasures. Ella enjoyed researching free community activities to attend, and she liked the kudos she got from her husband and friends as they praised her ability to find fun and free events. Ella still has some downtime that she tries to fill with reading or searching the internet. She acknowledges the adjustment to retirement and aging is ongoing but realizes she has options to increase her ability to cope adequately.

My Retirement/Reinvention Story: How I Tried to Buffer My Losses
CAROLYN AMBLER WALTER

Carolyn Ambler Walter, PhD, LCSW, is a professor emerita at the Center for Social Work Education at Widener University, where she taught MSW and PhD students. Dr. Walter is a coauthor of Grief and Loss Across the Lifespan: A Biopsychosocial Perspective *(2009, 2016) and the author of* The Loss of a Life Partner: Narratives of the Bereaved *(2003). She is coauthor of* Breast Cancer in the Life Course: Women's Experiences *and the author of* The Timing of Motherhood.

During the spring semester of 2009, after 2 years of weighing the pros and cons, I finally announced my retirement plans to the Widener University faculty and administration at the Center for Social Work Education. My colleagues were not surprised as many knew I was approaching the big "65" and that my health insurance would be secured. After serving on the faculty for 26 years, I knew I needed to prepare for this period in my life—fully aware that I had been extremely emotionally and professionally involved in my academic career.

To protect myself from my fear and uncertainty around possible loss of my professional identity, I agreed to stay on for the upcoming fall semester to teach two courses: one was my "baby," Grief and Loss across the Lifespan, and the other was a doctoral seminar on teaching methods and skills. Although the latter course required a new preparation during my first summer of "freedom" from course prep, I was glad to do it—this was a course that I had always wanted to teach. Teaching had been my true passion and was very satisfying to me for more than 30 years. If this course was well received, I assumed that I would have another part-time assignment in which to immerse myself—further buffering my concerns about loss of professional identity. I loved teaching this seminar to seven highly motivated doctoral students who appreciated my Socratic teaching style as well as my use of experiential exercises to enhance student learning. By the end of fall term, I was basking in my glow from such a positive teaching experience. However, when the program director decided to assign my new course, which I had designed, to a junior faculty member, I was angry. Friends and colleagues supported me in believing that I had been "screwed."

This was my first clue that postretirement might be more rocky than I had anticipated. No matter how hard I tried to design teaching experiences that would be satisfying to me, I was left feeling disappointed. During the spring semester of 2010, I began my first experience without classes to teach. I had contracted to teach my beloved grief and loss class during the fall 2009 semester. This enabled my husband and me to escape the cold Philadelphia winter to travel in warmer climates. During the spring semester, I felt quite fulfilled as I enjoyed some of my travel dreams by journeying to Australia and New Zealand. For the first time in my career, I was warm for some of the winter season—my arthritic joints loved the warmth! I also continued with my small private clinical practice—my clients seemed okay about my staying in touch with them as needed.

When the fall semester rolled around, I was happy to teach one course and continued to dabble in nonprofessional pursuits. This included serving on the steering committee for the newly launched Philadelphia chapter of The Transition Network—a national organization designed to help women over 50 cope with various life transitions. This organization has become an integral part of my life since retirement. I also began my involvement in helping to create a Philadelphia chapter of the Life Planning Network, a national organization devoted to helping both men and women design a satisfying life post full-time retirement. I would now have another opportunity to use my skills with grief, loss, and transition issues with the retirement community.

My research on loss and resilience had informed me that maintaining ongoing connections with the teaching profession, as well as assuming leadership positions with new professional groups, would serve me well in coping with my loss of a full-time teaching career and leadership positions on the faculty. Upon reflection, I recognize that my involvement in these new semiprofessional organizations brought me comfort and helped to buffer losses. It is also apparent to me that the rhythm and pace of the academic calendar continues to provide comfort and enjoyment as I create ways to live my life in terms of a fall and spring semester!

By the spring term of 2011, the University of Pennsylvania had invited me to coteach a doctoral student seminar on preparing students for their dissertation work. This sounded promising, but their other offer to teach an alumni course on teaching methods and skills was even more enticing! At last, I would be able to utilize the course preparations from the doctoral course on pedagogy at Widener. Again, I thoroughly enjoyed teaching this seminar, which was very well received by the alumni to whom I had been quite helpful. The course evaluations gave me high marks across the board. However, what I thought would be a "perfect" solution to my retirement/reinvention journey was short lived when funds for these alumni classes "dried up" due to belt tightening at Penn. It was now apparent to me that this reinvention process involved surviving mood swings from that of elation and joy to feelings of disappointment and anger. I recalled that the retirement literature discusses these dramatic swings when you are revising your identity. For several years, I continued to chair a few doctoral dissertation committees, but this did not satisfy my hunger for classroom teaching. Most of this time I had equated classroom teaching and writing books (I had authored and coauthored four by this stage) with making a difference in society.

I think it was about my third year into partial retirement that I realized I could not control this murky phase of my life. Just as the literature on reinvention suggested, this part of the journey tends to move in "fits and starts" (Schlossberg, 2009). Leaving a job or career involves multiple transitions and usually leads to a life qualitatively different from one's working life (Schlossberg, 2009). As discomforting as the fits and starts can be, they are the essence of the "work" one does in creating a new life. However, I still was quite frustrated with trying to balance various parts of my life.

At about this time, Judith McCoyd and I were approached by our publisher to develop a second edition of our text, *Grief and Loss Across the Lifespan*. We were both pleasantly surprised that the text had done so well in the market. We enjoyed creating our first edition but soon realized that producing a second edition may not provide that same type of creative fulfillment. However, we immersed ourselves in redesigning our chapters, based on new research published since the first edition in 2009.

Concurrently, other demands began to pull on my time. My husband was diagnosed with cancer and my granddaughter was born in Philadelphia. Although I had already been a very happy grandma to my Boston boys, the new joys of actually being involved in more weekly care were intoxicating! In addition, we both experienced growing desire for more involvement with our 8 grandchildren scattered along the east coast. To add to the mix, the realities of increased medical issues with aging set in with severe arthritis in most joints. Balancing my life became even more difficult with increased time and energy devoted to doctor appointments as well as necessary wellness tasks of caring for an aging body. My friends and I speak about how this can become a full-time job!

During the final revisions of our second edition of *Grief and Loss Across the Lifespan*, I was barely "holding on." Several months prior to these final revisions, we had decided to give up our suburban life to move into the city to enjoy all of the cultural opportunities that awaited us. This move involved downsizing from a large townhome to a much smaller, city town house with lots of steps! Adjusting to city life took more of a toll than I anticipated. I was very tired, anxious, and depressed, having moved from the Delaware County suburbs where I had lived for 42 years! I had raised my two children there, launched my teaching career at Widener University, where I had helped develop a now thriving MSW program and had buried my first husband at age 48.

My new home office space was more crowded and disorganized, filled with boxes of notes and articles I had collected for our second edition. At this point, writing felt like a burden, without much creativity. As the final deadlines for that second edition approached, my husband and I were scheduled to leave for our now 8-week winter sojourn to warmer climates. I knew I needed more time to make revisions for my chapters, so we asked the publisher for a month-long extension. This allowed me to make the final revisions from our rental apartment in Florida. Prior to this request, I had never asked for an extension during all my years in college and my graduate education; even my doctoral dissertation was completed during the timeline I had set with my chair. I felt extremely frustrated by this decision, but felt I had no choice. Again, I experienced disappointment—this time with myself. Learning to balance all of these parts of my life was becoming more and more complicated.

Experimenting with a new activity or organization (usually in the fall or beginning of spring semester) and hoping that this new endeavor will provide a new direction has become a consistent pattern for me. This is the new rhythm of postretirement. As I write this memoir, I am becoming more content with the uncertainty of this life phase. Plans have to remain flexible. Often, changes beyond our control force us to journey in a new direction. This is actually an apt commentary on my entire life journey and one of the real lessons of my current phase of life!

This summer, I discovered how my immersion in a creative-memoir-writing experience has changed my direction for now. Making a difference to me can mean creating a memoir for my children and grandchildren so they can learn about their father and biological grandfather in more depth. What it means to matter has taken on a different form for me. Helping my 18-year-old grandson with college stressors or helping my granddaughter discuss her worries and fears over ear piercing or medical injections is now every bit as important as the teaching and writing I have done in the past.

In the fall of 2019, I am quite content with not knowing whether teaching gigs will materialize. I am currently preparing to teach one session of a semester-long course our Life Planning Network has created, "Restoring Your Life after a Loss." I believe that other possibilities will emerge! Additionally, I have enrolled in an improv/acting class. I am stretching myself in new ways and it feels good!

References used for this reading:

Schlossberg, N. (2009). *Revitalizing retirement: Reshaping your identity, relationships and purpose.* American Psychological Association.

SUMMARY

With retirement comes the anticipated positive benefit and the below-the-surface losses typical of most maturational losses. Under the best circumstances, it allows those who have marshaled sufficient resources to move into a next chapter of their lives, where they have more autonomy in using their time and resources. Many pursue passions they had little time for in the past, and others get the chance to reinvent themselves for another period of life in which their own interests can take precedence. For those who are marginalized economically or unhealthy, retirement may signify a failure if they are unable to actively pursue adventure, volunteer work, or family involvement. Retirement is a fantasy of working life that comes with sobering realities.

DISCUSSION QUESTIONS

1. A 60-year-old friend works in a tech sector at a high managerial level and has already accumulated 2 million dollars in savings. What advice do you have for her about what she might need to consider if she decides to retire early? How would this advice change if your friend were 40?

2. A new client arrives in your office saying he has been feeling lazy and "somewhat depressed" after recently achieving his life's goal of retiring and buying a yacht. He is financially stable, reports a solid relationship with his husband (both 67 years old), and both are "on the same page" about activities they want to pursue during retirement. What areas do you think you need to assess and what intervention/s do you think will most likely be effective?

3. Think about your own hopes for retirement. At what age do you think you would ideally retire and what do you think you will do with your time?

KEY REFERENCES

Only key references appear in the print edition. The full reference list appears in the digital product found on http://connect.springerpub.com/content/book/978-0-8261-4964-0/chapter/ch09

Barbosa, L. M., Monteiro, B., & Murta, S. G. (2016). Retirement adjustment predictors—A systematic review. *Work, Aging and Retirement, 2*(2), 262–280.

Bennett, M., Beehr, T., & Lepisto, L. (2016). A longitudinal study of work after retirement: Examining predictors of bridge employment, continued career employment, and retirement. *The International Journal of Aging and Human Development, 83*(3), 228–255. https://doi.org/10.1177/0091415016652403

Boveda, I., & Metz, A. J. (2016). Predicting end-of-career transitions for Baby Boomers nearing retirement age. *Career Development Quarterly, 64*(2), 153–168. https://doi.org/10.1002/cdq.12048

Clouston, S. A., & Denier, N. (2017). Mental retirement and health selection: Analyses from the US Health and Retirement Study. *Social Science and Medicine, 178*, 78–86.

Collinson, C., Rowey, P., & Cho, H. (2019, April). *What is "retirement"? Three generations prepare for older age.* TransAmerican Center on Retirement Studies. https://transamericacenter.org/docs/default-source/retirement-survey-of-workers/tcrs2019_sr_what_is_retirement_by_generation.pdf

Ekerdt, D. J., & Koss, C. (2016). The task of time in retirement. *Ageing and Society, 36*(6), 1295–1311.

Haslam, C., Steffens, N. K., Branscombe, N. R., Haslam, S. A., Cruwys, T., Lam, B. C., Pachana, N. A., & Yang, J. (2019). The importance of social groups for retirement adjustment: Evidence, application, and policy implications of the social identity model of identity change. *Social Issues and Policy Review, 13*(1), 93–124. https://doi.org/10.1111/sipr.12049

Infurna, F., & Andel, R. (2018). The impact of changes in episodic memory surrounding retirement on subsequent risk of disability, cardiovascular disease, and mortality. *Work, Aging and Retirement, 4*(1), 10–20. https://doi.org/10.1093/workar/wax020

Kincaid, C. (2015, May 3). *Retired husband syndrome*. Japan Powered. https://www.japanpowered.com/japan-culture/retired-husband-syndrome

Lam, B., Haslam, C., Haslam, S., Steffens, N., Cruwys, T., Jetten, J., & Yang, J. (2018). Multiple social groups support adjustment to retirement across cultures. *Social Science and Medicine, 208*, 200–208. https://doi.org/10.1016/j.socscimed.2018.05.049

Loretto, W., & Vickerstaff, S. (2015). Gender, age and flexible working in later life. *Work, Employment and Society, 29*(2), 233–249. https://doi.org/10.1177/0950017014545267

Ryan, R. (2018). *Retirement reinvention: Make your next act your best act*. Penguin Books.

Sass, S. A. (2016). *How do non-financial factors affect retirement decisions?* Center for Retirement Research. https://crr.bc.edu/wp-content/uploads/2016/02/IB_16-3.pdf

Timmermann, S. (2014). The home and its role in a retirement plan: Making decisions about where to live and how to pay for it. *Journal of Financial Service Professionals, 68*(1), 26–29. http://search.proquest.com/docview/1494128677/

Wu, C., Odden, M. C., Fisher, G. G., & Stawski, R. S. (2016). Association of retirement age with mortality: A population-based longitudinal study among older adults in the USA. *Journal of Epidemiology and Community Health, 70*, 917–923. https://doi.org/10.1136/jech-2015-207097

Zurlo, K. A. (2012). Private pension protections since ERISA: The expanded role of the individual. *Journal of Sociology and Social Welfare, 39*(4), 49–72.

10

Grief and Loss in Young-Old Adulthood: The Third Age

INTRODUCTION

This chapter examines the beginning years of older adulthood, which we define as ages 65 to 84, and reviews experiences of grief and loss during this time of life. Although many older adults experience health-related changes, many remain active, social, and stay in relatively good health. Some may continue to work in paid or volunteer positions. For those content with their lives, these can be the "golden years" of adulthood—after retirement but before disability—that provide a chance to enjoy newfound freedoms. Good adaptability in older adulthood not only depends a lot on health status and social support but also requires an adjustment to aging (AtA) that avoids the internalized ageism that jeopardizes resistance to the depression, loneliness, and existential concerns that often arise as "third agers" accumulate losses. We review practice interventions to help older adults, including the Dual-Process Bereavement Group Intervention (DPBGI) for widowed older adults and the Meaning in Loss Group (MLG).

OBJECTIVES

After studying this chapter, the reader will be able to:
- Describe the difficulties in defining older adulthood.
- Explain biological, psychological, social, and spiritual aspects of older adulthood while remaining aware of the diversity of life experiences, health, and quality of life.
- Depict the impact of ageism on physical and emotional well-being in older adulthood.
- Explain how theories of loss and grief can influence practice with older adults.
- Describe possible interventions useful for work with older adults experiencing loss.

VIGNETTE

Robert (74) and his wife Evelyn (72) have three adult children in their early 50s. They retired about 9 years ago, eventually selling their house in New Jersey and moving to Florida for the lower cost of living and warmer weather. Their children and their families remain in New Jersey so Robert and Evelyn have few in-person visits with them. Instead, they have built a very social "new life" for themselves in their 55+ "active adults" community. Both enjoy sports—Robert plays golf and Evelyn plays tennis—and both enjoy going out with other couples for dinner or other social events.

Robert and Evelyn would like their children to visit more, often reminding them of the beautiful weather and the extra bedrooms they have available for guests. Evelyn worries that they "don't care" because they seldom make the trip. The children get frustrated and remind their parents that they work and have children in school and cannot "zip down" to Florida whenever they choose. The children believe that because Robert and Evelyn chose to move, they will need to come to New Jersey if they want to see family more often.

This "debate" has caused family tensions. Evelyn has mixed feelings about living so far from the family and is looking into communities farther north (e.g., Delaware, North Carolina). Robert disagrees with the idea of moving because they will still be a distance from the kids and will not have year-round good weather for outdoor activities. He believes they need to make decisions based on their own desires, not the children's wishes.

In contrast, Robert and Evelyn's close friends from New Jersey, Eddie (78) and Pam (76), have been struggling with declining health and finances. Eddie retired 13 years ago, and Pam never worked. They have two adult children in New Jersey and decided to stay nearby to be actively involved in their grandchildren's lives. Because they refinanced their house several times, along with high property taxes, they still have mortgage payments, a challenge on their fixed and limited income. In addition, Eddie struggles with hypertension, coronary artery disease, and atrial fibrillation. Pam needs knee replacement surgery. The orthopedic surgeon will start with her right knee within the year and replace the left knee soon after.

Due to these constraints, Eddie and Pam generally stay home except when visiting their children and grandchildren. Eddie wants to sell the house, downsize, and move to a town with lower taxes, possibly joining Robert and Evelyn in Florida. Pam wants to stay in their "family home" close to their children and reminds Eddie that their physicians know them and she does not want to start anew with other providers. Additionally, Pam does not like hot weather, preferring a temperate climate.

Both couples have weathered similar life transitions and gained freedom from work commitments and schedules. Along with more choices, though, came more disagreements between husbands and wives and between each couple and their adult children. Health status, an important factor in adapting to older age, limited some of the choices available for Eddie and Pam but has not yet impacted Robert and Evelyn.

DEFINING OLDER ADULTHOOD

Bernice Neugarten was a pioneer in the study of aging. She introduced the term *young-old* (which she defined as ages 55–75) and *old-old* (75+; Neugarten, 1974). The young-old typically enjoyed good health, were free from work and family responsibilities, and were politically active. Neugarten thought they were potential "agents of social change" (1974, p. 187). In contrast, the old-old often led narrower lives due to declining health and were more likely to depend on others. Neugarten (1974) used age to distinguish the young-old and old-old, acknowledging that although "chronological age is not a satisfactory marker," it was "nevertheless an indispensable one" (p. 191). She explained subsequently that the categories of "young-old and old-old were originally suggested as a gross way of acknowledging some of the enormous diversity among older persons" (Neugarten, 1979, p. 48).

Neugarten's distinction between young-old and old-old was a constructive step toward disaggregating the category of older adulthood, which at that time encompassed everyone 55 and older. It is not unusual now for people to live into their 90s or become centenarians, making a single age category for older adulthood sorely inadequate. Some scholars have thus divided older adulthood into three age categories: the "young-old" (65–74), the "middle-old," (75–84), and the "oldest-old" (85 and older; McInnis-Dittrich, 2014). However, all age categories are imperfect. Aging is highly contextualized, and the diversity of experience and its consequences increase as people get older. How, then, to capture categorically the diversity of older adulthood?

In Peter Laslett's *General Theory of the Third Age* (1987, 1991), older adulthood is comprised of the Third Age and the Fourth Age. These categories are largely consistent with Neugarten's terms. Laslett described the First Age as a time of dependency (childhood) and the Second Age as one of independence and responsibility. He bounded his categories by defining the life context more than specific age groups. Laslett's Third Age is a time for personal fulfillment after retirement, with older adults enjoying good health and remaining independent. In contrast, the Fourth Age marks a time of decline, dependence, and death. In contrast to Neugarten, however, Laslett only identified the age at which an adult entered the Third Age: the year of retirement, which varies by country but is usually around 65. Laslett did not identify an age at which older adults entered the Fourth Age. Rather, he asserted that everyone has an individual aging trajectory based on health and level of function that defines their sudden or gradual entry into the Fourth Age. For some, the Third Age lasts only a few years, while for the most fortunate, it can last decades.

Due to changing demographics and advances in healthcare and longevity, the age ranges attached to the Third Age and Fourth Age are also dynamic. As we move into the 2020s, the Third Age is typically held to span the ages of 65 to 80 or 85, the Fourth thus beginning at 80 or 85, the years when many people decline significantly.

Attempts to categorize older adults by age all share the assumption that they experience at some age a shift in health and quality of life (QoL) that creates a distinct era of life. In this respect, categories imply an underlying stage theory of aging. Stage theories have more metaphorical than empirical value, however, and considering the tremendous diversity of the older adult population, there is still debate about the utility of age-based categories to describe it.

In view of the trend toward later retirement in the United States, a related question concerns the age of entry into older adulthood. The cultural signifiers are quite inconsistent. AARP was formerly called the American Association of Retired Persons, but membership was (and remains) available at 50. Active adult living communities are available to those 55 and older. Social Security retirement benefits become available between 62 and 70 depending on one's year of birth and how large a benefit is desired.

This text uses a modified version of the age-wise subgroups of older adulthood. We devote a chapter to retirement and reinvention that spans a broad age range, overlapping with a chapter on middle adulthood (45–65) and this chapter, which takes up the Third Age (65–84), which we understand as the beginning passage of older adulthood. In the following chapter, we examine grief and loss among those in their Fourth Age, or the "oldest-old" (85+). Still, these categories cannot adequately contain the typical experiences of older adults. Many factors bear on aging singly or in combination at chronological points, which differ considerably among people. Laslett's insistence on individual trajectories of aging seems wise and should be kept in mind.

DEVELOPMENTAL THEMES OF OLDER ADULTHOOD, AGES 65 TO 84

Whatever the diversity among them, older adults find their Third Age to be full of gains and losses. Many have a more positive outlook, improved self-esteem, and emotional stability. Free from work demands, they can pursue personal goals. At the same time, however, they may experience some decline in cognitive functioning, the development of chronic health conditions, and the deaths of loved ones (Barnes, 2011).

Cohen (2006) proposed a series of human "potential" phases emphasizing older adults' ability to be creative, explore new ideas, and make changes. Two phases—"liberation" (mid-50s to mid-70s) and "summing-up" (late 60s into the 80s or beyond)—coincide with the Third Age. During Cohen's phase of liberation, the older adult has "a sense of personal freedom to speak one's mind" and the concurrent freedom from work demands as many enter partial or full retirement (Cohen, 2006, p. 8). During the summing-up phase, "plans and actions are shaped by the desire to find larger meaning in the story of one's life" (Cohen, 2006, p. 9).

Some developmental models assert that older adults' primary task is reflection, as in Cohen's summing-up. Erikson (1950) posited that beginning in their mid-60s, older adults contend with the crisis of "integrity versus despair." This was his eighth and final developmental stage and involved reflection on one's life and dealing with mortality. If one resolved regrets and felt satisfied, Erikson believed that a sense of integrity would be achieved. The alternative was despair. Prior to achieving "integrity," Vaillant (2012) argued that an older adult must complete an additional task: becoming the "keeper of the meaning," which involves passing down traditions to future generations. Promoting wisdom and justice is at the heart of this task.

Biological Development

The Third Age brings physical change. Senses become less sharp, orthopedic changes occur, and chronic health conditions become commonplace. Health status varies widely based on individual factors (e.g., genetics, lifestyle choices) and environmental factors (e.g., access to healthcare services, exposure to pollution).

After 60, various diseases of the eye become more likely and may impair vision: glaucoma, age-related macular degeneration, and cataracts, most notably (American Optometric Association, 2019). Those with other health problems, especially diabetes and hypertension, are at greater risk for these and other eye problems. Hearing loss also becomes more common after 60. Approximately one-third of those 65 to 74 and almost half of those over 75 have difficulty hearing (National Institute on Deafness and Other Communication Disorders, 2018). Most lose their hearing gradually in both ears, a condition known as presbycusis that has many causes but usually results from changes in the inner ear that occur with age (National Institute on Deafness and Other Communication Disorders, 2018).

Other sensory changes likely occur, particularly diminished keenness of smell and taste, usually as a concomitant of age but also due to dental problems and sinus problems. Loss of taste is likely to begin after 60 (Takahashi, 2019), and the sense of smell, which influences taste, begins to diminish after 70 (MedlinePlus, 2019). This can lead to less enjoyment of eating and less interest in food, potentially leading to unwanted weight loss and nutritional deficits.

After 65, many more people develop significant high blood pressure or hypertension, which is directly related to other serious health problems. Hypertension is the leading cause of cardiovascular disease and premature death in the United States (Bundy et al., 2018). For those 65 to 80, high blood pressure and arterial stiffness are usually related and pose major risks for both cardiovascular complications and cognitive decline (Benetos et al., 2019).

Type 2 diabetes (formerly called adult-onset diabetes) also becomes more common with age. Type 2 comprises 90% to 95% of all diabetes cases (Healthline, 2020), and although it can be diagnosed at any age, it is most likely in middle or older adulthood. It can result from numerous interrelated factors that include genetics, race, ethnicity, weight, and an unhealthy lifestyle (e.g., little exercise and poor nutrition). According to the American Diabetes Foundation (2018), approximately 25% of adults over 65—12 million people—have diabetes.

Diseases that cause cognitive decline and dementia also occur more frequently as people grow old. Dementia is not a specific disease, but a cover term for over 100 conditions that cause cognitive challenges, including memory loss (Alzheimer's New Jersey, 2020). Alzheimer's disease (AD) is the most common form of dementia (Alzheimer's New Jersey, 2020). Late-onset AD refers to the condition diagnosed after 65. There are many risk factors for it, but the three most important are age, family history, and carrying the e4 form of the *APOE* gene. Age, however, is the biggest factor: AD affects 3% of people 65 to 74; 17% of those 75 to 84; and 32% of people 85 and older (Alzheimer's Association, 2019).

Dementias like AD create practical and emotional challenges for the affected person and their loved ones and caregivers, who grieve prior to the literal death of the AD sufferer. Indeed, some authors assert that special grief interventions are warranted (Blandin & Pepin, 2017; Silverberg, 2007). Blandin and Pepin explain that predeath grief of dementia caregivers (known also as "dementia grief") is a specific type of anticipatory grief that can entail "specific hindrances" to the natural grief process because the person with dementia experiences "disruptions in communication and impairment in awareness" (p. 3). With other terminal medical conditions, the caregiver usually has an opportunity to resolve conflicts and share feelings with the person who is dying, but this is less feasible with people affected by dementia. Further, dementia grief is characterized by ambiguous loss (Boss, 1999): The person's body is present even if they are not psychologically present.

Due to the specific challenges of dementia grief for caregivers, Blandin and Pepin (2017) developed the Dementia Grief Model, theorizing an iterative grief process. They identified three states within the grief process: separation, liminality (feeling ambiguity), and re-emergence (adaptations to a new reality), hypothesizing that for caregivers of people with dementia, grief cycles through these states in a recursive rather than linear manner (p. 6). Each of these three states has a "dynamic mechanism" that helps move caregivers forward through the grief process. These mechanisms are acknowledging the loss, tolerating difficult feelings, and adapting to the new life circumstance or reality of the loss (p. 6). Therefore, helping caregivers acknowledge losses and express ambiguous and difficult feelings assists them to cope with grief. Using the main tenets of Blandin and Pepin's Dementia Grief Model (2017), McCoyd adapted the graphic to include rings of intervention and risk. See Figure 10.1 for details.

Serious and even life-threatening illnesses, including cancers and Parkinson's disease, become more common as people move through older adulthood. The median age of any cancer diagnosis is 66. For colorectal cancer, it is 68; for lung cancer, 70; and for prostate cancer, 66 (National Cancer Institute, 2015). Further, in 2017, slightly over 57% of all people who died from cancer in the United States were over the age of 70 (Roser & Ritchie, 2020). Age is also the most significant risk factor for Parkinson's disease, a neurodegenerative disease resulting in the progressive loss of muscle control and motor function. The cause is unknown, but most who develop it are 60 or older (Heyn et al., 2019).

Psychological Development

Third-Age adults have the life experience and skills to adapt to life's challenges. According to Carr and Gunderson (2016), the "developmental processes in adulthood shift how" third agers assess their "goals, responsibilities, and values," and they "become better at centering" their lives (p. 84). They understand how to align their lives with their priorities and are willing to do so.

Many third agers enjoy improvement in their emotional well-being. They experience improved self-evaluation, better self-esteem, increased satisfaction with life (subjective well-being), reduction in anger, improved emotional stability, and a beneficial change in the ratio of positive to negative emotions (Barnes, 2011). Emery et al. (2020) assert that older adults' positivity may result from less negative rumination (i.e., dwelling on the meaning of negative moods). They found that adults 60 to 85 had significantly lower negative rumination scores compared with those 19 to 39 but found no difference between the groups on positive rumination (i.e., recurrent thoughts about positive affective states).

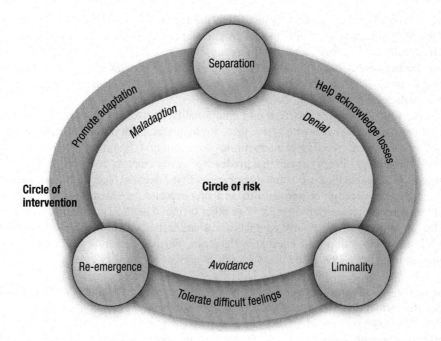

FIGURE 10.1 Adapted Dementia Grief Model. This graphic is an adapted illustration of the Dementia Grief Model. Using the main tenets of the Dementia Grief Model (Blandin & Pepin, 2017), McCoyd created a new graphic that includes rings of intervention and risk.
Source: Adapted from Blandin, K., & Pepin, R. (2017). Dementia grief: A theoretical model of a unique grief experience. *Dementia, 16*(1), 67–78. https://doi.org/10.1177/1471301215581081

Studies of happiness across the life span also support the notion that the Third Age is a time of relative contentment. Some studies found that across the life span, happiness is U shaped, peaking in youth, dipping in middle age, and improving after age 50 to 54 and beyond (Blanchflower & Oswald, 2004, 2008). Other researchers found that life span happiness takes a wave-like shape, increasing at 60 but declining sharply after 75 (Frijters & Beatton, 2012). One might interpret this as a marker for onset of the Fourth Age.

Social Development

Older adults typically maintain active relationships with family and close friends but invest less energy in peripheral relationships (English & Carstensen, 2014; Wrzus et al., 2013). As a result, the number of social partners declines, which could result in less social capital, an important resource for health and well-being (Muckenhuber et al., 2015). Yet focusing more on close relationships and letting go of peripheral ones results in a greater concentration of satisfying relationships (English & Carstensen, 2014). Socioemotional selectivity theory (Carstensen, 2006) posits that this helps older adults regulate their emotions. English and Carstensen found that "older adults described their network members more positively and less negatively than younger adults (i.e., there was an age difference in the emotional tone of social networks)" (2014, p. 8). This is important because "the emotional tone of social networks affects people's daily emotional experiences more than the size of their support system" (English & Carstensen, 2014, p. 9).

Social connectivity is influenced by proximity to family and friends, neighbors, neighborhood services, community events and gatherings, and so forth. Third agers tend to remain where they are. According to the Joint Center for Housing Studies of Harvard University (2019), only 3.6% of all adults 65 to 79 and 3% of those over 80 relocated in 2017 to 2018. Renters moved more frequently: 11% of those 65 to 79 and 8% of those over 80. When family members or friends move, third agers can find themselves separated from important members of their social network. Social media platforms and visual communication technologies can be used to maintain contact, albeit disembodied.

Spiritual Development

Religiosity differs from spirituality. Its concerns are with a person's belief system, values, behavior, and participation in a faith organization. Spirituality is variously defined, but a broad and useful definition holds that it concerns the search for and achievement of meaning in life, a primary task for older adults.

A growing body of research finds that spirituality may benefit older adults, offering a framework to guide daily living and provide support during difficult times (Bailly et al., 2018; Thauvoye et al., 2018). Bailly et al. (2018) interviewed French third agers at three points in time, starting in 2007 when their average age was 76, with follow-ups in 2009 and 2012. They found that participants' measured levels of spirituality were stable over time; that women reported higher levels of spirituality than men; and that older adults who reported high levels of satisfaction with social support and high levels of flexibility (i.e., ability to be adaptive) also reported high levels of spirituality (p. 1745). The causal relationships here are unknown, but the findings are intuitively compatible. Similarly, an exploratory study in Belgium of aspects of spirituality among people over 70 (mean age 76) found that well-being was predicted by connectedness with the transcendent (one of their dimensions of spirituality) and connectedness with others (Thauvoye et al., 2018).

Fowler's six stages of spiritual development are not specifically linked to chronological age, but third agers in the midst of evaluating their lives and searching for purpose seem poised for Fowler's last stage: "universalizing faith." This involves a willingness to "sacrifice the self" for the "sake of a more inclusive justice and the realization of love" (Fowler, 1981, p. 200). As a practical matter, third agers may be well positioned existentially and practically for this stage of spirituality. In the Third Age, adults often evaluate their lives and search for purpose. Concurrently, they have time available to give back to the community in various ways.

SPECIAL CONSIDERATIONS IN RISK AND RESILIENCE

In getting older, we are subject to risk factors that negatively affect cognitive, physical, and/or emotional well-being. Protective factors, on the other hand, offset adversity to some extent and help us adjust to aging. We review some important risk and protective factors here, but this is not a comprehensive consideration.

Despite improvements in healthcare over the years in the United States, disparities in the relative health status of racial and ethnic minorities remain alarming. For example, African Americans have double the likelihood of diabetes as Whites, and the highest incidence among African Americans is among those 65 to 75 (Office of Minority Health, 2019, para. 2). Native American and Alaskan Native people also experience poorer health status and higher prevalence of disease than Whites (Indian Health Service, 2019). These health disparities in turn affect the average age at death and average life expectancy. Figure 10.2 depicts the average age at death by race/ethnicity and gender in the United States in 2017 (Centers for Disease Control and Prevention, 2019). Non-Hispanic Blacks (men and women) die at younger ages than other racial/ethnic groups. Women, however, outlive men within their same racial/ethnic group.

Life expectancy is also different for those belonging to certain racial/ethnic groups. Asian Americans have the highest life expectancy (86.7), followed by Hispanic Americans (82.9) and White Americans (79.1). In contrast, non-Hispanic Blacks' average life expectancy is 75.5, and Native Americans' average life expectancy is 75.1 (Carlson, 2019). Although the Third Age can be

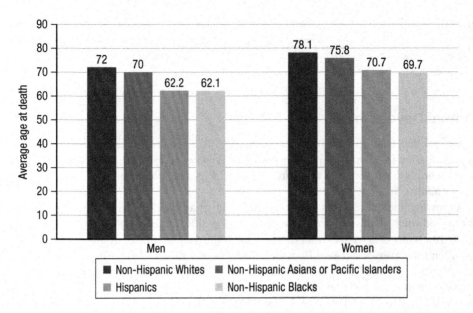

FIGURE 10.2 Average Age at Death by Race/Ethnicity and Gender, United States, 2017. This bar graph illustrates the average age of death based on gender and race/ethnicity in the United States, 2017. The average age of death is the sum of age at death for all deaths from each group divided by the total number of deaths from that group. This graph is adapted from a diagram used in the *Morbidity and Mortality Weekly Report* of the Centers for Disease Control and Prevention (2019).
Source: Centers for Disease Control and Prevention. (2019). QuickStats: Average age at death by race/Hispanic origin and sex- national vital statistics system, United States, 2017. *Morbidity and Mortality Weekly Report.* https://www.cdc.gov/mmwr/volumes/68/wr/mm6831a4.htm

golden for some, others face steep declines into premature death, especially those whose health has been compromised by poverty and exposure to environmental toxins, which make them likely to be in poor health.

LGBT+ older adults experience significant health disparities and are an at-risk group (Fredriksen-Goldsen et al., 2014, 2017). The Caring and Aging with Pride: The National Health, Aging and Sexuality Study collected data from over 2,400 LGBT+ adults (ages 50 to over 100) and found that (a) lesbian, gay, and bisexual people have higher rates of poor mental health and disability than heterosexuals; (b) risks of cardiovascular disease and obesity are higher for bisexual women and lesbians than for heterosexual women; (c) gay and bisexual men are in poorer general health than heterosexual men; and (d) transgender people had higher rates of victimization, disability, stress, and poor health than lesbian, gay, and bisexual people (Fredriksen-Goldsen et al., 2014).

However, many older adults in the LGBT+ community have good health and display resiliency (Fredriksen-Goldsen et al., 2014, 2017). Positive appraisal of one's LGBT+ identity and available social resources contribute to good mental health, which is associated with good physical health, largely due to more health-promoting behaviors (e.g., exercise) and fewer health risk behaviors (e.g., smoking; Fredriksen-Goldsen et al., 2017).

Older adults in prison comprise another group facing distinctive challenges. The inmate population 65 and older grew at a rate 94 times the overall prison population from 2007 to 2010 (National Commission on Correctional Health Care, 2017). Older adult inmates experience "disproportionately high rates of chronic conditions and lower self-rated health and many suffer from mental health conditions" (Flatt et al., 2017, p. 1106). They tend to develop their chronic health conditions earlier, and they tend to be more complex (Canada et al., 2019). The U.S. prison system is ill equipped to handle a burgeoning group of people who, if in the community, would likely need to be in long-term care facilities receiving 24/7 skilled nursing care or living at home with in-home services. In reality, those released from prison have access to few services. Only 9% of social service organizations provide support for older adult inmates or for those being released (National Commission on Correctional Health Care, 2017).

In the United States, as in many developed countries, ageism is commonplace and influences the emotional and physical well-being of older adults. Ageism is the "stereotyping and discrimination against individuals or groups on the basis of their age" (World Health Organization, 2019, para. 1). It takes many forms. Ageism can be directed at young people, but youth is idealized in many important ways, particularly with respect to beauty, sexuality, and health, while older adulthood is devalued. The result can be internalized ageism, which occurs when the messages we give ourselves about aging are consistently and largely negative. Rather than embracing entry into older adulthood, we dread it and deny it. As Bernard Baruch once said, "To me, old age is always fifteen years older than I am" (goodreads, 2020).

The World Health Organization (2019) reports that internalized ageism erodes older adults' emotional and physical well-being. Stereotypes of older adults doing less and being isolated and in decline can become self-fulfilling prophecies. Internalized ageism can also affect physical health. Attitudes about aging are associated with cardiovascular health and life expectancy: Those with negative attitudes about aging had greater cardiovascular responses to stress and worse health behaviors (Levy et al., 2009) and lived 7.5 years fewer than those with positive attitudes (Levy et al., 2002).

The impact of internalized ageism varies among social groups, but the cultural denigration of aging bodies seems particularly injurious to women and gay men. In a small qualitative study of older (age 50+), single, gay men's "body talk," Suen (2016) observed that the participants found it hard to escape negative messages about the aging body. Suen's participants asserted nonetheless that they still look good in contrast to older gay men who do not take care of themselves. This important distinction reinforced "an ageist discourse" (p. 397). Similarly, Wight et al. found that midlife and older gay men often feel devalued in their later years, "denigrated or depreciated because of aging in the context of a gay male identity" (Wight et al., 2015, p. 200).

A growing body of research has found men more likely than women to benefit from positive stereotypes of older adulthood. Women worry about aging more and are perceived as older than men of the same age (Lytle et al., 2018). Lytle et al. found that women reported "greater endorsement of negative stereotypes, less endorsement of positive stereotypes, and [had] significantly more anxiety about aging than men" (2018, p. 5). This self-criticism was associated with lower psychological well-being for both African American and European American women (Sabik, 2015). European American women who reported greater perceptions of age discrimination had worse self-reported health and lower body esteem, but these associations were not significant for African American women. Sabik speculates that African American women, having faced a lifetime of racism and sexism, may have different responses to discrimination.

Conversely, protective factors can inoculate against the worst effects of stress and adversity and help maintain QoL, a multidimensional concept that refers to "the general satisfaction with life or its components" (Eva et al., 2014, p. 218). Eva et al. conducted a study of third agers (mean age 73.8) that explored risk and protective factors for QoL. Self-esteem, perceived social support, and self-efficacy (i.e., agency and control over one's life) were protective factors. Risk factors included depression, anxiety, and loneliness. Valued social connections are consistently associated with better health, QoL, and other positive outcomes.

LOSSES EXPERIENCED BY OLDER ADULTS IN THEIR THIRD AGE

Death Losses

Death of a Spouse/Life Partner

Older adults typically suffer the death of a spouse or life partner. Since death in these years is more likely to result from a protracted illness than a sudden trauma, widowhood is usually a process, not an event (Carr & Jeffreys, 2011). Responses by the widow vary widely but are most influenced by the nature of the relationship, the nature of the death, and the surviving spouse's social supports (Carr & Jeffreys, 2011). In general, social connectedness that survives beyond the spousal relationship promotes well-being and resilience, as we have seen in other contexts (Ermer & Proulx, 2019).

Intrapersonal factors also affect the bereaved person's response. Studying patterns of adaptation to spousal bereavement, Spahni et al. (2015) found that "successful adaptation is primarily associated with high scores in psychological resilience and extraversion, conscientiousness, agreeableness and openness, and low scores in neuroticism" (p. 466). Similar to previous studies, they found that the bereaved fare better as time passes.

Although not discussed often, those widowed in older adulthood contend with the loss of sexual intimacy with their partner. Radosh and Simkin (2016) explored "sexual bereavement," mourning the loss of sexual intimacy when a partner died. They examined whether women anticipated missing sexual relations if they were predeceased by their partners. Of 104 partnered women, mostly heterosexual, all over 55 and over half 66 to 75, they found that 72% anticipated missing sex with their partner, 67% would want to initiate a discussion about this with friends, and the majority would want friends to initiate the discussion.

Death by Suicide

In the United States, suicide rates have been increasing and in 2017 hit a 30-year high (Piscopo, 2017). Young third agers (age 65–74) have lower rates of death by suicide than younger age groups (Heron, 2019), but beyond 74, the rates of suicide increase with age (American Association for Marriage and Family Therapy [AAMFT], 2019). Specifically, there were 15 deaths by suicide per 100,000 individuals for those 65 to 74, in contrast to over 17 deaths by suicide per 100,000 individuals for those 75 to 84, and the number continues to rise for those over 85. These numbers may be underreported because of "silent suicides" (e.g., self-starvation or dehydration; AAMFT, 2019).

To analyze suicide among older Australians, Koo et al. (2017) used the Queensland Suicide Register. They found significant differences in the prevalence of certain risk factors between the young-old (65–74), middle-old (75–84), and oldest-old (85+). They detected gender differences, finding that suicide rates for men climbed as they got older while suicide rates remained low and stable for women. The young-old were more likely to have psychiatric disorders and a higher lifetime prevalence of suicide attempts. Bereavement was the life event most commonly associated with suicide in all three age groups.

In addition to psychiatric disorders and bereavement, other risk factors for suicide among older adults include substance abuse problems, chronic pain, declining function, disability, dementia, cognitive decline, and social isolation (United Health Foundation, 2020). Even long-ago adverse childhood experiences (ACEs; e.g., childhood abuse, parental psychopathology, parental loss) can underlie suicidal behavior in older adulthood (Sachs-Ericsson et al., 2016). Unfortunately, suicide attempts by older adults have higher completion rates than the attempts of younger people. Older adults are more likely to plan ahead and use lethal means; they are not found as quickly, nor do they recover as easily as younger adults or youth (Karlin, 2014).

Death of an Adult Child

As people live longer, parents are more likely than in prior generations to experience the death of an adult child, although it remains an off-time loss. Losing an adult child during one's Third Age can have numerous ramifications beyond dealing with the emotional reactions of immediate family: seeing grandchildren (or great-grandchildren) less frequently; losing connections with surviving in-laws; worry about who will care for the surviving parent(s) when help is needed; or conversely, who will care for the grandchildren if there is no surviving parent.

Death of Contemporaries

Third agers typically experience deaths among their contemporaries, both family members and friends. Gathering together for funerals may become commonplace and catching up with friends may include discussion of who died recently. These losses feel close to home. With each additional death, there is a cumulative emotional effect for grieving third agers and further thinning of the network of relations on which they rely. Research on these matters is quite limited, but Holland and Rozalski (2017) report that psychiatric symptoms are experienced by a sizable minority of surviving older adult siblings, who because of their age may also be in poor physical health.

Living Losses: Atypical, Typical, and Maturational Losses

Social and Physical Changes

As they transition from work to retirement years, third agers typically have related changes in their roles with friends, family members, and former colleagues. For some, these changes and concomitant losses can affect their AtA. AtA is a measure of the psychological adjustments to such changes (von Humboldt & Leal, 2014). In a systematic review of AtA in late adulthood, von Humboldt and Leal (2014) found that self-efficacy, self-acceptance, and mental and emotional engagement were positively associated with AtA. Physical impairment, negative life events, and trouble integrating the past were associated with poor AtA.

Loneliness and Social Isolation

Loneliness is not the same as being alone or socially isolated and is not necessarily improved by company. Loneliness, rather, is the subjective emotional state of feeling alone, whereas social isolation is a lack of social support and lack of access to information and resources (Williams & Braun, 2019). Schutter et al. (2019) found that higher neuroticism and lower extraversion in women, and lower agreeableness in men and women, were associated with loneliness but that a person's social network had little to do with the sense of loneliness.

Coping With Illness and Disability

Third agers are at higher risk for illness and disability than in their younger years. How older adults view their health, cope with health problems, and manage their changing health status varies widely. Tkatch et al. (2017) found that five themes emerged in their study of perceptions of health and keys to aging successfully among people 65 to 85: (a) a lack of congruence between objective (i.e., clinical) and subjective (i.e., self-report) health status; (b) defining health to include psychological well-being; (c) social support; (d) resilience; and (e) maintaining independence. Regarding incongruence between actual and reported health status, the authors hypothesized that "for some participants who had been healthy for most of their lives, it was confusing and frightening to deal with 'newer' concerns and health conditions. Conversely, many of the objectively unhealthy participants had been dealing with multiple health issues for years and had developed strong coping mechanisms" (Tkatch et al., 2017, p. 489).

Losses Related to Life-Threatening Illness

Due to the prevalence of chronic and life-threatening illnesses among them, adults 65 to 84 often receive palliative care and hospice care services, and/or they have loved ones receiving them. Palliative care aims to comfort someone who is ill. Specifically, it is "focused on providing relief from the symptoms and stress of the illness" with the goal of improving "quality of life for both the patient and the family" (Get Palliative Care, 2020). A palliative care team is multidisciplinary, providing medical, social, and emotional help. Recipients of palliative care need not be terminally ill and may be receiving curative treatment at the same time. For example, someone with prostate cancer may receive curative treatment (e.g., radiation therapy) while simultaneously receiving palliative care treatment for bone pain (e.g., through the use of steroids or pain medication) and may also receive emotional and practical help from the palliative care team (e.g., supportive counseling, referrals to services).

Hospice services include palliative care but are provided once a patient is considered terminally ill, defined by a prognosis of 6 or fewer months to live (National Institute on Aging, 2017). Hospice care includes comprehensive comfort care with a multidisciplinary team of providers but is designed for those no longer getting curative treatments. Simply put, all hospice care is palliative care, but not all palliative care is hospice care. A more detailed explanation of hospice care is part of Carol Wallinger's reading at the end of this chapter.

Both palliative care and hospice services can be provided at home or in a facility. Although they greatly help both patients and their loved ones, when a physician recommends hospice the reaction is sometimes "no, not yet!" or simply "no." This may express unreadiness to face death, but studies of the underutilization of these services find misunderstanding of them to be the most significant factor (Davison et al., 2016).

REACTION OF OTHERS TO THE DEATH OF THIRD AGERS

Adult Children

Typically, adult children lose at least one parent when one or more of them are 65 to 84. These adult children may have children grieving the loss of their grandparent(s). This places some burden on the adult child to "be strong" for their children. The bereaved adult children may also have to bear up to caring for a surviving parent who may be grieving and in poor health. This is a particular challenge when the surviving parent relied on the deceased spouse.

In addition to coping with the death of one parent, some adult children must also contend with the repartnering of the surviving parent. It is now common for adults to enter new relationships late in life. Simhi-Meidani and Koren (2018) conducted a small qualitative study in Israel that focused specifically on how adult children 37 to 60 years old dealt with their parents' repartnering after the death of the other parent. They found that the adult children grappled with loyalty conflicts as they both mourned the deceased parent and tried to be supportive of the surviving parent's new life.

INTERVENTIONS

Dual-Process Bereavement Group Intervention for Widowed Older Adults

The dual-process model (DPM) of bereavement has been the foundation for some bereavement support groups for widows. Stroebe and Schut (1999) proposed the DPM, which theorizes two oscillating processes after a loss: loss orientation (i.e., dealing with the loss itself) and restoration orientation (i.e., adapting and adjusting to new roles, life challenges). Those who are able to oscillate flexibly between loss-oriented (LO) and restoration-oriented (RO) tasks will have more favorable bereavement responses. A systematic review of various DPM-based interventions found that they seem more effective than traditional grief therapy (Fiore, 2019).

Chow et al. (2019) sought to evaluate the effectiveness of a bereavement group for widows based on the DPM. They assigned participants in 12 Chinese community centers to a DPBGI or a LO bereavement group intervention. Both involved weekly 2-hour sessions held for 7 weeks and were followed by a 4-hour outing in the 8th week. Of 215 widowed older adults contacted and assessed, only 125 completed interviews pre- and postintervention along with the 16-week follow-up. Although the loss-based group helped reduce grief and depression, the dual-process group reduced grief and depression plus anxiety and loneliness.

Meaning in Loss Group

Neimeyer devised an MLG based on his meaning-making model of bereavement. It shows promise as a group intervention that could benefit third agers. Synthesizing the meaning-making model, previous workshop projects (e.g., The Mustard Seed Project; Neimeyer & Young-Eisendrath, 2015), and narrative procedures (e.g., Directed Journaling), he designed a 12-session weekly group (Neimeyer, 2016).

The sessions promote two processes: each client's telling of the "event story" of the loss and how it affects their life, and accessing and affirming the "back story" of the relationship with the deceased. The process of telling the event story is introduced in the early sessions, and the process of telling the back story is introduced in middle and later sessions. The MLG uses a recurrent structure featuring dyadic interaction of group members, whole group processing and discussion, and homework assignments. Psychoeducation about grief, theories of grief, and sources of meaning are also integrated into the group sessions. An early trial of the MLG in Montreal was successful, and subsequent trials of MLG are under way (Neimeyer, 2016). Interventions allowing bereaved people to process their grief together seem to have both utility and efficacy.

READINGS

Ginny and Karen: Aging Together
CAROLYN A. BRADLEY

Until her retirement in December 2019, Carolyn A. Bradley, PhD, LCSW, LCADC, was an associate professor and the MSW program director in the School of Social Work at Monmouth University, West Long Branch, New Jersey. Her research interests are in aging and how sexual orientation impacts the aging process. Dr. Bradley also maintains a small clinical practice. This case study was developed through a Gero Innovation Grant from the CSWE Gero-Ed Center's Master Advanced Curriculum Project and the John A. Hartford Foundation grant awarded to the School of Social Work at Monmouth University, New Jersey.

Ginny, a 78-year-old White female, and Karen, a 76-year-old White female, have been partners for 48 years. Ginny was a college English professor, and Karen was a nurse and a supervisor in a large metropolitan hospital. They have been retired for about 10 years and live together in a home they jointly own.

Ginny and Karen describe themselves as "complementing each other." Ginny was always more reserved and serious, whereas Karen was outgoing and sociable. Ginny managed the finances. Karen managed their social life. They report that they have had "a wonderful life together," having traveled extensively and enjoyed the varied cultural activities that living in a metropolitan area provides.

Both women were raised in Irish, Catholic families and have fairly large extended families. Ginny enjoys a close, affectionate relationship with her siblings and their families. Karen is cut off from her siblings, who were not able to accept her lesbianism, but Karen remains nominally Catholic. Ginny became an Episcopalian and actively practices her faith.

Both women have enjoyed relatively good health over the years. Ginny has always been less active and slightly heavier than Karen. She has been on medication for high blood pressure for many years. She experiences some problems with ambulation due to being overweight and having knee problems. Karen has not needed medication but reports some problems with arthritis in her back and shoulders that she attributes to her career in nursing.

Recently, Karen reports changes in Ginny's attitude and behavior. Ginny seems more reserved than usual, often appearing confused and unable to perform daily routines. A consult with their family physician revealed that Ginny was experiencing episodes of TIAs (transitory ischemic attacks or "ministrokes"). These episodes have impacted Ginny's ability to manage the couple's finances. Karen, having never shown any interest in this aspect of their life, has very little knowledge or understanding of what assets they have.

Ginny's family wishes to be involved in determining her medical care. Karen has always felt somewhat overwhelmed and at times intimidated by Ginny's family. Ginny is the only female in her family and has three younger brothers. Karen grew up in a family of girls with an alcoholic mother and a father who abandoned the family.

The family physician, who has known the couple for 20 years, recognized how anxious Karen has been at Ginny's medical visits. The physician suggested a mild antianxiety medication for Karen. Karen agreed that some medication to assist her in adjusting to the changes with Ginny might be helpful. The physician never asked about any alcohol use, and despite her own medical background, Karen did not share any information regarding her daily use of alcohol.

Ginny's brothers are now suggesting that the couple sell their home and move into an assisted living facility. The brothers feel that Ginny is no longer able to manage the couple's finances. They report that in the 6 months since Ginny's diagnosis, Karen has become moody, difficult to deal with, and withdrawn.

Discussion

The family presented for counseling to resolve care issues. What became apparent during assessment, and with a few sessions, was the sense of loss experienced by both women. Ginny's diagnosis and subsequent inability to fulfill the many roles in which she overfunctioned created overwhelming anxiety for Karen. The dynamics of the couple's relationship had been upset by the well-intentioned but somewhat intrusive suggestion that Ginny's brothers should now be more actively involved in their sister's care. This suggestion was particularly hurtful to Karen as it negated her professional experience as a nurse.

Growing up in an Irish family as the oldest child and the only female, Ginny had enjoyed a position of power and respect with her siblings. Her brothers would often seek her input prior to making decisions on a variety of matters. Roles within the family were starting to reverse. Ginny, who had always prided herself on her razor-sharp intellect and problem-solving ability, was becoming increasingly aware of her confusion and inability to follow or remember conversations.

Both women had enjoyed successful careers during which they were respected and responsible for decision-making. While Ginny was more understanding of her brothers' desire to become more actively involved with her care, Karen was extremely insulted. Their suggestion exacerbated Karen's long-standing discomfort with Ginny's brothers, whom she described at times as "loud, uncaring, and sarcastic." The difference in interpretation of the brothers' suggestion added to the growing tension between the women.

An immediate area of concern was Karen's combined use of alcohol and antianxiety medications. Although no one in the family had expressed any issue with Karen's substance use, I wondered if it was a contributing factor to what had been described as her moody and withdrawn behavior. I met with Karen alone to assess her individually so as to not create any more issues with

Ginny's siblings. We quickly identified Karen's fear of abandonment and her trepidation as she anticipated multiple losses resulting from Ginny's diminished, and diminishing, capacity.

We also discussed the couple's support from their social network or "family of choice" (that circle of friends who provide much of the support that may have been lost due to cutoffs by one's family of origin). While Ginny had been able to maintain a close, loving relationship with her brothers, Karen had lost all contact with her family. We were able to identify supportive friendships for Karen to cultivate. She had been reluctant to build those relationships because she wanted to protect Ginny from judgment regarding her lessening cognitive abilities.

Interventions

The initial work with this family involved resetting boundaries and establishing the primacy of the couple relationship. The brothers' desire to be of assistance was acknowledged as understandable but perhaps premature at this point in Ginny's condition. The brothers' assistance was "put in reserve," and the couple was acknowledged as capable of making care decisions independently. This action was important as it affirmed the validity of the relationship and dismissed the notion that Ginny and Karen were "a couple of helpless, old ladies," which Karen suggested was how the brothers saw them.

To dispel fears held by both Ginny and Karen about the diagnosis and progression of Ginny's condition, a consult with a neurologist was obtained. This exam ruled out a brain tumor and indicated no signs of dementia. It confirmed that the TIAs at this juncture were manageable with medications. This information reduced anxiety in both women.

Karen, after a few individual sessions, was ready to discuss her substance use with Ginny. Ginny, while understanding, was not enabling and was very insistent about Karen's need to address this issue and reduce or stop her use of alcohol and antianxiety medications. She clarified her need for Karen "more than ever" going forward, and this seemed to lessen Karen's fears about losing her position as the primary person in Ginny's life. Karen accepted a recommendation for individual outpatient treatment for her prescription medication and alcohol abuse.

A major aspect of the work was to expose the family "secret" of Ginny's TIAs to the couple's family of choice. This created a sense of relief and access to much-needed support for Karen. With Ginny's permission to talk about the TIAs with friends, Karen's sense of isolation and fears of abandonment lessened. Family secrets among intimates, whether about illness or substance use, detract from a family's functioning and ability to provide support, and opening the fact of Ginny's illness allowed optimal support from the couple's friends. Opening the secret of Karen's substance use to Ginny allowed her to support Karen's recovery.

When couples retire, there are frequently role losses, yet many find great enjoyment in sharing social activities together. As aging and health conditions bring unavoidable losses to capacities, relationships must change as well. This may entail loss of the partners' ability to fulfill customary roles or loss of some social capacities. Helping couples recognize and mourn those losses while also working to enhance support from families (whether of origin or choice) as they work through a healthy adjustment to new roles is a critical aspect of work with aging couples.

Saying "Yes We Can Do That!" What Is It Like to Be a Hospice Nurse?
CAROL WALLINGER

Carol Wallinger, JD, RN, CHPN, is a clinical professor at both Rutgers Law School and Rutgers School of Nursing Camden and an adjunct professor at Cooper Medical School at Rowan University. Carol teaches professional communication at the law and medical schools and interprofessional ethics at the nursing and medical schools. She also is a board-certified hospice nurse. Carol concentrates her work on teaching professionals and students to translate their work across disciplines via interprofessional education experiences, using interdisciplinary theories of written and oral persuasion and advocacy.

I am often asked about what it is like to be a hospice nurse. Before I can even answer, most people asking that question say, "I'm sure it must be very [sad] [hard] [gut-wrenching]." My initial answer is always the same: You might be surprised how joyful and fulfilling hospice nursing is, for a multitude of reasons. First, most often by the time I meet a patient, the hardest decision has been made; that is, the patient and family have already decided to sign on to use the hospice benefit. Second, because the patient has a limited time to live, as hospice nurses we are able to say "yes" to an almost endless list of requests and wishes. Very often, the hospice social workers are involved in making these wishes come true. This is part of what makes the work joyful. Consider this list of events that have been facilitated, some at the hospice inpatient unit, and others at a patient's home or choice of venue: a patient's wedding; a son or daughter's wedding held on the unit; high school and college graduations; when a young girl wanted one last "camping trip" with her dying dad, the tent was set up in our lobby; many, many birthday and anniversary celebrations in the large communal dining room; visits from all sorts of pets; final conversations with an incarcerated parent or child; and coordinating care with a hospice in another state so a patient with a morphine pump could travel to his favorite beach for a family reunion. Sometimes loved ones have been estranged from each other for many years but, upon learning of the patient's choice to use hospice, want to talk one last time. We will do what it takes to make that possible. It is fulfilling to make these wishes come to fruition. Here, I will answer some of the questions people often have.

Hospice is all about making the end-of-life journey peaceful. My greatest professional satisfaction is attending/facilitating/assisting (it is so hard to define the role!) the deaths of patients to ensure that they were comfortable until the last moment and that all those remaining behind are at peace with how the end-of-life experience went. In other words, I work to assure the journey is as peaceful and comfort filled as possible. Of course, I cannot change the outcome, nor fully assuage the grief of all those who loved and will miss the patient. Some hospice nurses use a "labor and delivery nurse" analogy: In labor and delivery, the baby is coming out one way or another, and the nurse's role is to make the journey as safe and comfortable as possible for the mother and baby. Likewise, in hospice, the patient's death is expected, and our job is to make the journey as safe and comfortable as possible for the patient and the loved ones.

How Do You Know the End Is Coming?

A patient's peaceful death experience can do much to assist the survivors in their grief. Often our job is to explain the dying process to those loved ones. One way to divide the end-of-life timeline is between "approaching death" and "actively dying." Patients who are approaching death, and have 1 to 2 weeks to live, may develop a wide range of symptoms showing that the body is slowly shutting down. These include temperature fluctuations unrelated to infection; a new cough; confused conversation and visions of deceased relatives; agitation and restlessness, often unassociated with pain management; a sudden increase in pain that is out of proportion to any physical changes; intense fatigue; and/or a sudden lack of interest in food or liquids.

We say patients are actively dying when we believe they have days to hours to live. Sometimes, prior symptoms intensify, and sometimes, new symptoms appear. These can be secretions in the back of the patient's throat (rattle); irregular breathing with frequent pauses, some lasting 20 to 30 seconds or more; a moaning sound might develop during the exhalation phase of breathing; a sudden increase in labored breathing; sudden vomiting where there has been none before; hands and feet become cool and sometimes mottled; and most often, the patient generally becomes less responsive. Most patients pass through a period of unconsciousness and irregular breathing before dying, but occasionally an alert and oriented patient will die suddenly, without a loss of consciousness or irregular breathing. Early on, I try to prepare the patient and loved ones for both possibilities because it is impossible for me to know ahead of time which path the patient will take.

During the dying process, many families ask about the next step in the process, and sometimes, they ask how much longer we think the patient will live. While some believe these types of questions signal that the loved ones are "ready for it to be over," I believe these questions mean that those present are actively involved with the patient and paying close attention to how the patient's condition is changing. They are "being present." I have found that answering these questions immediately and with transparency calms patient and family anxiety. By transparency, I mean that I always say that I am happy to give my best estimate of how long the patient might live, as long as the person asking understands that I am wrong about 50% of the time. Most people easily understand this limitation and are grateful for any estimate. Often loved ones ask that same question to multiple nurses on the unit, and often we find out that we gave remarkably similar estimates.

How Does the Hospice Benefit Work?

Hospice is a service that can be a place. The care is provided by an interdisciplinary team that includes chaplains, social workers, nurse practitioners, nurses, certified nursing assistants, physical and musical therapists, volunteers, and doctors. Most patients receive services at home, but temporary placement is available for those with acute severe symptom management issues. Also, a few hospices are residential, and they offer a more home-like level of care, different from acute inpatient hospice. Benefits can also be provided to nursing home residents. The Medicare hospice benefit is designed to support loved ones/family members/nursing home staff because they are always the primary caregivers. The hospice benefit does not provide private duty or one-on-one nursing care.

Two doctors must certify that the patient has a prognosis of less than 6 months to live. Unfortunately, and perhaps because of that requirement, most eligible patients do not consider hospice services until they are 1 to 2 weeks from the end of life. Often patients have heard from others that using the benefit requires them to "give up" and that sounds very final and is disconcerting. While signing onto hospice requires the patient to agree to "forgo curative treatment," the truth is that the decision is easily reversible should the patient have a change of heart. Families, though, often do not understand how the benefit works. Hospice provides a complete menu of services, but most patients never have time to use many of them. Admission nurses work closely with social work staff to get patients admitted and comfortable as soon as possible, but if the patient dies within the first 7 days on hospice, the chaplain, for example, will barely have had time to establish a relationship with the patient and family.

In July 2019, Edo Branch, the president and CEO of the National Hospice and Palliative Care Organization (NHPCO), reported that "a significant concern for us at NHPCO continues to be the number of Medicare beneficiaries (40.5 percent) who received hospice care for 14 days or less, with 27.8 percent accessing this person- and family-centered care for a week or less" (NHPCO, 2019).

Which Families Are Great to Work With, and Which Challenge the Hospice System?

The families easiest to work with are those with everyone "on the same page" or "on board" with the hospice decision once it is made. The care of hospice patients is greatly facilitated when loved ones respect the patient's decision, even though they might not agree. Even when everyone agrees, there will be moments of intense sadness and tears, and we are there as an interdisciplinary team to provide support. The support family members provide for each other while the patient is declining is an invaluable treasure.

In addition, it is easier to work with families that rally around the patient and put aside whatever interpersonal differences they may have had in order to make the patient's last few months, weeks, or days peaceful. In the best-case scenario, those in the room with the patient are present in the moment, even if that means sitting in silence, holding the patient's hand.

Also in this "easier" category are patients and families that have had time to adjust to the news that the patient is nearing the end of life. This benefits both the patient and the loved ones. Loved ones who have had time to ponder the loss of the person (often referred to as anticipatory grief) also have time to share with that person before death. Patients who have some time can get their affairs in order and leave less chaos for those left behind. That can be comforting to both the patient and the loved ones. Our social workers have assisted many patients with end-of-life documents, including wills and powers of attorney.

The saddest cases may involve people who suffer a catastrophic brain injury while their body is strong. Death will take longer in those cases, and the waiting can be hard on everyone, including the nursing staff, even though the family may be accepting of the outcome from the day of the injury.

One very challenging situation occurs when family members are in conflict about the patient entering hospice. This can happen, for example, when an adult child lives far away and has not been involved in the day-to-day management of the patient's diagnosis and treatment/symptoms prior to the election of hospice. The adult child may be confused about why the patient chose to stop curative treatment, and may actively reject the patient's choice of hospice care. They may also decide to weigh in about care options that have already been considered and rejected. This adds to the tension we try to minimize.

Another challenging situation occurs when the family has a dysfunctional communication system as part of their history. The life or death nature of hospice will magnify any communication issues. Some families bond over hospice situations; some fracture from the stress. Sometimes there are unresolved emotional issues between family members that they now seek to "resolve" through the patient's end-of-life situation. I have seen siblings fight physically over what is the best plan of care for a patient or at whose house the patient should spend the last days of life. In those situations, it can seem as if the siblings are trying to prove who loves the patient most. The team, particularly the social workers, are usually called in to ameliorate the conflict, but no one can change long-standing family patterns during a time of crisis.

The most difficult situation for the hospice team occurs when the person holding a valid power of attorney (PoA) acts against the patient's wishes once the patient can no longer speak for himself or herself. PoAs have revoked hospice and taken the patient back to the hospital for active but futile treatment, or called 911 when the patient became unresponsive, rather than calling hospice staff as instructed. Both situations subject patients to painful and invasive treatment they sought to avoid by electing hospice. PoAs may need to be reminded that the legal intent of the PoA is for that person to do what the *patient* would have wanted.

Pain Management Challenges

Controlling a patient's pain at the end of life is a major goal of hospice care. As the patient's body gradually shuts down, the patient's pain experience changes, and the hospice team must make adjustments based on those changes while taking into account many other factors, including fear, depression, and cultural influences. Pain management also can be a source of misunderstanding for both patients and loved ones, and occasionally a source of conflict. While most patients and families readily accept the hospice provider's recommendation for which type and dose of analgesic medication will treat the patient's pain while minimizing side effects, often the recommendations include the use of narcotic medications such as morphine. Some fear the use of narcotics because of concerns about addiction, although most patients are only on the hospice service for weeks to months. Occasionally the use of narcotics will be rejected outright because of belief that the "patient is not that sick yet" or that the use of narcotics means that the patient will die immediately after the first dose. Such fears may lead to families choosing a lesser category of medications, such as Tylenol, that may not be sufficient based on the patient's condition, such as bone cancer, which can be particularly painful. The team approach to hospice care is a crucial tool to address and allay these fears, thereby providing the patient with the best hospice experience.

What Are Counseling Supports for Patients and Families on Hospice Like?

Patients and loved ones need emotional support, and that is provided primarily by the hospice team, which consists of nurses, social workers, chaplains, and hospice volunteers. Hospice has a long tradition of providing volunteer and peer support. I believe that patients and families would be well served if there were more volunteers available to do individual emotional support, both before and after the patient's death. Most hospices use volunteers to visit with patients, but more could be done with peer support of family members as well. Hospice always provides bereavement care after the death in the form of support groups and limited individual meetings with bereavement care staff. Indeed, this is required by the Medicare hospice benefit.

What Is the Best Advice for Taking Care of Yourself as You Do Hospice Work?

Hospice work is very fulfilling professional work, and I feel that for me, at least, it is a true calling. The work can be emotionally draining though, and it is important to watch for signs of moral distress and burnout. I rely on other hospice staff members, especially the chaplains, to be sounding boards when I need to discuss the work. We also hold monthly remembrance meetings where we take turns reading aloud the names of those that died on our service in the last month, and contributing our memories. Especially when there is a difficult family situation with a patient on the service, it is important that those on the team not become isolated. There are weekly team meetings where staff can support one another. Another source of comfort is the hospital ethics committee. An ethics consult can be used to help the staff work through a difficult moral choice, such as the situation discussed earlier where the PoA revokes the hospice benefit and returns the patient for acute care. In short, the team provides support to one another as well as to patients and their families, another reason why hospice work can be joyful.

SUMMARY

This chapter examined the beginning passage of older adulthood, which we define as the Third Age (ages 65–84), recognizing that the Third Age ends when health declines. For those who are healthy, the Third Age of life can be the "golden years" of adulthood, providing an opportunity to enjoy more freedom and preserving control over their lives. Although many third agers do experience some decline in health, many remain active and social and continue to work in paid or volunteer positions.

The most important protective factor for QoL in the Third Age is having a positive support system. Important risk factors include internalized ageism and serious, chronic health problems. Belonging to certain subpopulations increases the risk of chronic health conditions, disability, and a hastened death.

Third agers experience many death losses as well as living losses, yet most are resilient and able to cope and adapt. Intrapersonal strengths (e.g., self-esteem, self-efficacy, and extroversion) and social support help in the bereavement process. Although many have a shrinking social network during this life stage, this is likely a result of investing more time in relationships that are close and most satisfying at the expense of those that are peripheral.

DISCUSSION QUESTIONS

1. After experiencing the death of a spouse, a 75-year-old man comes to your office. The client relied heavily on his spouse for social life and connections to others. Thus, in addition to dealing with the actual death, the client is also struggling with a perceived lack of social support. After asking more, your client acknowledges he has some family and friends who live nearby. In addition, the client is healthy and civic minded and has always wanted to be more involved in the community. What additional understanding of the client would be helpful before exploring with him possible avenues to enhance his social connections?
2. For whom are the Third Age of adulthood not "golden years"? What initiatives on individual, program, and policy levels could be taken to improve the lives of those people?
3. Think about how you anticipate your own older adulthood. Do you have mostly negative, positive, or mixed views of older adulthood? What factors have influenced your view?

KEY REFERENCES

Only key references appear in the print edition. The full reference list appears in the digital product found on http://connect.springerpub.com/content/book/978-0-8261-4964-0/chapter/ch10

Barnes, S. F. (2011). *Third Age—The golden years of adulthood*. San Diego State University Interwork Institute. https://pdfs.semanticscholar.org/edb8/7cdde01d9de4012de68da9c787b053eebb01.pdf

Chow, A. Y. M., Caserta, M., Lund, D., Suen, M. H. P., Xiu, D., Chan, I. K. N., & Chu, K. S. M. (2019). Dual-process bereavement group intervention (DPBGI) for widowed older adults. *The Gerontologist, 59*(5), 983–994. https://doi.org/10.1093/geront/gny095

Cohen, G. D. (2006). Research on creativity and aging: The positive impact of the arts on health and illness. *Generations, 30*(1), 7–15.

Laslett, P. (1987). The emergence of the Third Age. *Ageing and Society, 7*, 133–160. https://doi.org/10.1017/S0144686X00012538

Laslett, P. (1991). *A fresh map of life. The emergence of the Third Age*. George Wiedenfield and Nicholson.

Neimeyer, R. A. (2016). Meaning reconstruction in the wake of loss: Evolution of a research program. *Behaviour Change, 33*(2), 65–79. https://doi.org/10.1017/bec.2016.4

Neugarten, B. L. (1974). Age groups in American society and the rise of the young old. *Annals of the American Academy of Political and Social Science, 415*(1), 187–198. https://doi.org/10.1177%2F000271627441500114

Neugarten, B. L. (1979). Time, age, and the life cycle. *American Journal of Psychiatry, 136*, 887–894. https://psycnet.apa.org/doi/10.1176/ajp.136.7.887

11

Grief and Loss in Older Adulthood: The Fourth Age

INTRODUCTION

This chapter concerns those 85 and beyond who are the "oldest old." Often called the "Fourth Age" of life, a time of decline and disability, this life phase begins whenever health starts to decline dramatically, and for some this is well before 85. With this important exception in mind, we use the terms *oldest old* and *Fourth Age* interchangeably. Acceptance of advancing age and its accompanying decline in health is a central developmental theme of the fourth age. Protective factors include adequate access to services and social support, nutritious food, spiritual beliefs, and regular exercise and activities. Risk factors for poor outcomes derive mainly from failing health. The oldest old are at greater risk for death by suicide than other older adults. Losses of self-efficacy and social connection are correlated with depression. Death losses and the anticipation of one's own death pervade their lives.

OBJECTIVES

After studying this chapter, the reader will understand:
- The fourth age of life.
- The biological, psychological, social, and spiritual aspects of the fourth age.
- The impact of physical and/or cognitive decline on the emotional well-being of the oldest old.
- The theories of loss and grief that can guide practice with the oldest old.
- The possible interventions useful for work with oldest-old adults experiencing loss.

VIGNETTES

Annie

Annie is an 89-year-old widow who has lived alone since her husband's death 20 years ago. She is the youngest of four, and her siblings—Harry, Billy, and Betty—are also deceased. Billy and Harry died about 10 years ago, and Betty died 2 years ago at the age of 90. Annie's circle of friends has dwindled over the years as some died and others experienced worsening illnesses or dementia. Annie has four children, eight grandchildren, and two great-grandchildren. Fortunately, one of Annie's children and two grandchildren live nearby and help her with food shopping, errands, cleaning, and transportation to medical appointments. Annie is financially stable. Her house was paid off many years ago, and although she has a fixed and limited income, she can meet her expenses. Her children outfitted her house with devices to help her remain there (e.g., raised toilet seat, fixed handrail on her tub, shower seat), and her bedroom is on the downstairs level.

Annie has had no cognitive decline but suffered a stroke 2 years ago that left her with some right-side paralysis. After the stroke, she had physical and occupational therapy but walking unaided is a challenge so she relies on a walker for stability. She often feels unsteady and has fallen twice since her stroke. The first resulted in two broken ribs and the second a broken wrist. As a result, she feels less secure and more vulnerable. She is also less able to do certain household tasks (e.g., cleaning the tub) and gave up driving a year ago.

For now, Annie can live in her home, but she worries about what will happen when she needs more help. She cannot afford an assisted living facility (which would triple or quadruple her expenses), and she cannot afford the substantial "buy-in" of a continuing care retirement community. Annie's children do not have room for her to join them but assure her they will provide for her care no matter what she needs.

Peter

Peter, 89, was widowed for the first time 50 years ago when his wife Diane died of ovarian cancer at 45. They had three children together before her death. Although Peter adored Diane and was committed to her and their family, after her death, Peter fell in love with Sam (a man) and "came out" to his adult children. Fortunately, they were accepting and truly liked Sam. Peter and Sam lived happily committed to one another, until Sam died.

Peter and Sam had moved to a rural community in the Midwest to have privacy and enjoy the open spaces. Over the years, Peter's relationships with his children grew more distant. Although he talks with each of them by phone once or twice a month, he seldom sees them. Peter used to visit them but no longer travels well by plane. Their busy lives limit his children's visits. The closest neighbor is 3 miles off, the closest shops (including a pharmacy) is in 15 miles, and the nearest hospital is 22 miles away. His children worry about his distance from others, and they have noticed that he seems sad and lonely when they speak with him. Yet Peter is determined to remain in the home he and Sam shared.

DEFINING OLDER ADULTHOOD: THE FOURTH AGE

Peter Laslett (1987, 1991) described the Fourth Age of life as a time of decline, dependence, and ultimately death. It follows the third age of retirement, activity, and optimally fulfillment. Laslett defines the Fourth Age in terms of functioning. Just as the first age of dependency (childhood) and the second age of responsibility and independence (adulthood) are based on functions rather than age-dependent phases, the third and fourth ages have to do with levels of health that either allow chosen activities (third age) or no longer permit independent action (fourth age).

To define the Fourth Age as a chronological period would ignore the large variation in individual decline, but the oldest-old typically experience significant decline. About 21% of those 85 and older need help with personal care compared with 8% of those from 75 to 84 (Tableau Public,

2018). According to McInnis-Dittrich, the oldest-old are "most likely to have serious health problems and need assistance in more than one personal care area, such as bathing, eating, dressing, toileting, or walking" (2014, p. 2). Almost half of those who live in skilled nursing facilities (SNFs) are over 85 (HealthinAging, 2018). SNFs provide 24-hour skilled nursing services to residents requiring a high level of care.

By definition, then, the Fourth Age denotes a period of decline, differentiating it from "positive" aging and perhaps reinforcing the "othering" of older adults and inadvertently devaluing them. It is important to keep in mind always that the process of aging is quite variable; many factors, including a person's acceptance of aging, affect the last years of life. Yet, with advanced age, the reality of steep decline is profoundly connected with grief and loss.

DEVELOPMENTAL THEMES OF THE OLDEST OLD AGE

Biological Development

Jaul and Barron (2017) examined age-related diseases and public health implications for people 85 and older. Sensory changes are very common: about one half of those over 85 have hearing impairment and severe visual impairment increases from 23% at ages 85 to 89 to 37% at 90 and older. The prevalence of osteoporosis (loss of bone density) and loss of muscle mass and strength increase similarly. Combined with other accumulated chronic conditions, these changes contribute to functional declines with advanced age (Jaul & Barron, 2017). Furthermore, people with these impairments are disabled by their environments when signage or text is small, noise levels obscure conversations, and doorways and stairs limit use of mobility assistance devices.

Chronic health conditions increase in number and severity among the oldest-old: 80% of those over 85 have at least one chronic condition and half have two or more; 59% have at least one activity of daily living (ADL) limitation (e.g., problems with ability to bathe, dress, or eat) in contrast to 35% of people 75 to 84 and 25% of those 65 to 74 (National Prevention, Health Promotion, and Public Health Council, 2016). The prevalence of conditions such as high blood pressure, atrial fibrillation, coronary heart disease, and cardiovascular disease (CVD) increases with age. CVD affects 89% of males and 92% of females over 80 (American Heart Association, 2019).

Due to age-related changes and chronic conditions, the oldest-old are at high risk for mobility disability, slow walking speed, falls, and frailty (Jaul & Barron, 2017). Mobility disability—difficulty walking or climbing stairs—is the most common disability among older adults in the United States (United States Census Bureau, 2014). Mobility is affected by the loss of muscle strength and mass, stiffer joints, and gait changes that typically come with advanced age, and these limitations make falls more common. Falls are the leading cause of both fatal and nonfatal injuries for older adults (National Council on Aging, 2018). In 2016, those 85 and older had the highest annual rate of falls and the highest death rates from falls (Burns & Kakara, 2018). Figure 11.1 shows the overall fall death rates for older adults in the United States, rates that have increased by 30% from 2007 to 2016.

Psychological factors such as balance confidence and "fear of falling (FoF) avoidance behavior" may best predict future falls (Landers et al., 2016). FoF can impair older adults' balance and postural stability. They use "stiffening" strategies that can be beneficial during simple tasks but detrimental in those more complex or demanding. Stiffening strategies actually reduce the range of motion, resulting in shorter strides and reduced gait speeds. FoF can also prompt restricted and reduced activity to avoid falling, thus leading to further loss of muscle mass and strength, and ultimately increasing the risk of falling again (Young & Williams, 2015). With the loss of mobility may come multiple losses: self-sufficiency, self-esteem, and social life, potentially leading to social isolation and loneliness.

Frailty, a significant concern for older adults, gets much attention from numerous health and social care professions. There are multiple screening tools to assess it but no agreement on a

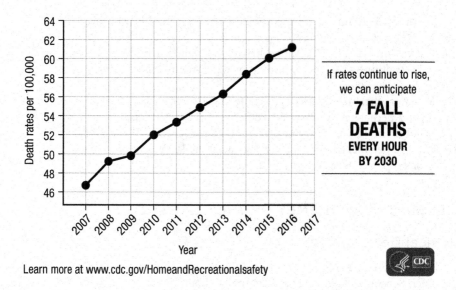

FIGURE 11.1 Fall Death Rates in the United States Increased 30% from 2007 to 2016 for Older Adults. This chart illustrates the rising rates of deaths as a result of falls for older adults from the year 2007 to 2016. *Source:* Centers for Disease Control and Prevention. (2017). *Important facts about falls.* Home and Recreational Safety. https://www.cdc.gov/homeandrecreationalsafety/falls/adultfalls.html

standard instrument (Hoogendijk et al., 2019). Age alone does not create frailty, which is a syndrome of decline (Walston, 2019). However, age is a risk factor. Although 7% to 12% of people over 65 are considered frail, this increases to about 25% among those 84 and older (Johns Hopkins Medicine, 2020). Frail older adults are more vulnerable and less able to adapt to illness or trauma.

With advancing age, cognitive decline and dementias, including Alzheimer's disease (AD), become more prevalent. "Mild short-term memory loss, word-finding difficulty, and slower processing speed are normal parts of aging," but not all cognitive functions decline with age (Jaul & Barron, 2017, p. 335). Of importance, Jaul and Barron observe that wisdom and acquired knowledge do not decline and that normal cognitive aging does not lead to dementia.

Dementia may be caused by certain health conditions, injuries, or infections. Now called major neurocognitive disorder, it is not a specific disease but an umbrella term for a syndrome with symptoms including memory failure, problems with language comprehension or expression, and impaired executive function (Ellison, 2019). In contrast, AD is a specific disease causing progressive cognitive decline and dementia.

AD accounts for 60% to 70% of dementia diagnoses in the United States (American Speech-Language-Hearing Association, 2020). Vascular dementias comprise the next largest category in North America and Europe, representing 15% to 20% of cases. The incidence of vascular dementias increases dramatically with age (Wolters & Ikram, 2019), as they are associated with stroke and atherosclerosis (American Heart Association, 2019). Perhaps due to better control of vascular disease, rates of vascular dementia in North America and Europe have fallen in recent years (Wolters & Ikram, 2019).

The percentage of people with AD also increases with age. The 17% prevalence rate among those 75 to 84 rises to 32% for the oldest old (Alzheimer's Association, 2019). Genetics, environment, and lifestyle are all implicated in AD, but much is unknown about its causes. AD is progressive. Those in the early stage have memory lapses that mimic the typical cognitive declines of aging (e.g., trouble coming up with the right word or name, planning, or organizing; losing or misplacing things). In this stage, the person generally functions well and can live independently. In the often long middle stage, symptoms progress from mild to moderate (e.g., forgetting parts of one's own history, confusion about where one is, not knowing what day it is, wandering away from home), and the person usually needs more care (Alzheimer's Association, 2020). In this stage, the person may become more irritable or angry, perhaps getting frustrated when trying to remember things. The late stage brings severe symptoms that include losing competence in daily living and thus requiring 24-hour care (Alzheimer's Association, 2020).

With the growing population of older adults with AD, memory units or AD special care units are expanding. People diagnosed with AD sometimes move into a care facility with a memory unit available, anticipating a need for daily, round-the-clock care at some point. To anticipate need is also to anticipate loss, in this case the loss of cognitive capability and the resulting loss of self-efficacy, self-esteem, and independence.

Psychological Development

Accepting advancing age and the accompanying decline is a central developmental theme of the Fourth Age. Despite decline, Cohen saw positive potential for those in what he called the "encore" phase of life between the late 70s and death. In these years "plans and actions are shaped by the desire to restate and reaffirm major themes" in their lives and to "explore novel variations on those themes and to further attend to unfinished business or unresolved conflicts" (2006, p. 9). The desire to "live well" can have a positive impact, "influencing decisions to have family reunions and other events" (p. 9). Thus, as the oldest-old face decline, some remain motivated to get as much satisfaction from life as possible. All is not bleak.

Erikson (1980) identified "integrity versus despair" as his eighth and final developmental stage, one he viewed as starting in the mid-60s and lasting until death. He defined the major task of this stage as reviewing and accepting the whole of one's life, both the accomplishments and failures. He believed that this process yielded wisdom. Vaillant (2012) also believed that developing a sense of integrity was the last developmental task of life. He asserted that this involves attaining "some sense of peace and unity with respect to both one's life and the whole world, and the acceptance of one's life cycle as something that had to be" (p. 95). Westerhof, however, countered that "there is only limited evidence that life review is a naturally occurring developmental task that serves to come to terms with life's finitude" (2016, p. 1). In fact, life review as a process of reflection occurs throughout the life span, especially during times of change. Throughout this text, we emphasize that people who take time to reflect on who they are after a loss can achieve new understanding about life generally and their own in particular.

As Erikson declined, he thought even more about aging. After his death at 91, his wife, Joan, synthesized his notes and her own experiences and wrote new chapters for *The Life Cycle Completed*. In the extended version, Joan Erikson, 93 at the time, suggested a ninth stage of life wherein an older adult confronts all eight stages again, acknowledging how they converge. When old, she observed, one must "garner and lean on all previous experience, maintaining awareness and creativity with a new grace" (Erikson & Erikson, 1997, p. 9).

Social Development

The quantity and quality of social connectedness, social support, and social activities vary widely among the oldest old, largely due to their health and the health of their friends and family members, but also as a result of their housing circumstances. About 29% of all community-dwelling older adults live alone; that rises to 50% for those over 85. Women account for about 70% of those living alone, mostly due to different rates of mortality (men tend to die earlier) and remarriage (men are more likely to remarry; Kaplan & Berkman, 2019). Living alone does not mean the person will be lonely, loneliness being an emotional state that can be felt in a crowded home. Nor does living alone always result in social isolation, which is caused by various factors including proximity to others; quality and frequency of social contact; health status; and other factors that can disrupt social relationships.

Even when fourth-age adults are lonely or isolated, they may still want to "age in place" at home. This can contribute to loneliness and isolation, and family members, especially, may insist they would fare better in a long-term care facility, where they can live with others and easily attend social activities. Although this can certainly benefit some experiencing decline, it may not necessarily improve emotional well-being or alleviate loneliness. Residents of long-term care are often lonely, and this is associated with poor self-rated health, dependence on others for help with daily living, mobility impairments, lower cognitive functioning, depression, and poor psychological well-being (Jansson et al., 2017). Furthermore, it is common for residents of long-term care facilities to voice frustration with their lack of influence or control; the paternalistic attitudes and communication styles of staff; loss of privacy and identity; the tenuousness of new relationships; and isolation from family and friends (Theurer et al., 2015).

Spiritual Development

Spirituality and religiosity seem to serve as protective factors for the oldest-old. When dealing with life challenges and losses, some seek new or renewed purpose in life, finding this through religion and spirituality (Browne-Yung et al., 2017). This may improve emotional well-being. Lucchetti et al. (2018) report that involvement in religion/spirituality is "usually associated with lower levels of depression, substance use/abuse, and cognitive decline and better quality of life, well-being, and functional status in older persons" (p. 373).

Similarly, Fortuin et al. (2020), in their qualitative study in the Netherlands with people 79 to 100, found that affirmative religious narratives were positively correlated with positive narratives of aging. They explain that there are three master narratives on aging: one that focuses on active aging (positive image of aging representing independence); a second focused on decline (negative view of aging representing dependence); and a third narrative focused on inner growth that transcends the two conflicting narratives and represents interdependence. A focus on inner growth through religion/spirituality can provide older adults a "way out of the polarity" of seeing aging as all good or bad (Fortuin et al., 2020, p. 19). The narrative of activity, while providing an ideal vision to pursue, does not help adults cope with the decline that accompanies the fourth age. On the flip side, a narrative of decline does not provide solace or support. The narrative of inner growth emphasizes interdependence, accepting things that cannot be changed, and "instead of [focusing either] on activity and generativity or on the loss of abilities, the narrative of inner growth perceives the opportunity of repose that emerges in later life as a possibility for inner growth and reflection" (Fortuin et al., 2020, p. 20).

SPECIAL CONSIDERATIONS IN RISK AND RESILIENCE

AD and other dementias are important risk factors for reduced quality of life and well-being in older adulthood, and more specifically, for being a victim of elder abuse. Approximately 10% of older adults have been mistreated, and it is more common among those with dementia (Mosqueda et al., 2016). As Nerenberg (2019) explains, this is a hidden population because (a) participants in research must give consent, and many of those with dementia would be unable to do so; (b) abuse against those with cognitive impairments was not included in the National Elder Mistreatment Study; and (c) cognitively impaired victims of abuse may not realize their mistreatment or be able to express it.

The cognitively impaired among the oldest-old are some of our most vulnerable citizens, and we must find better ways to intervene on their behalf. Mosqueda et al. (2016) identified three domains in their Abuse Intervention Model that become sites for both assessment and intervention. The first domain is the "vulnerable older adult," who is identified as someone with impaired physical function, impaired cognitive function, and/or emotional distress or mental illness. The second domain is the "trusted other" of the older adult. It is important to assess the person's dependence on the vulnerable older adult, their emotional distress or mental illness, and their impaired physical function. The third domain involves assessment of the "vulnerable adult's context," attending particularly to social isolation, low-quality relationships, and valued cultural norms. By assessing these domains, appropriate interventions can be developed to help prevent abuse. For example, we know that an adult in the early stage of AD (mild dementia symptoms) has a higher risk for financial abuse if they have a loved one who has debt, is financially dependent, or is under emotional duress, especially when there is no oversight of the vulnerable person's finances. In all work with vulnerable older adults, especially those with dementia conditions, the risks of abuse (financial or physical) are high and care providers should attend to each of the domains to assess risk. It is also important to identify assets (strengths and resources) that may help the vulnerable adult.

Although 90% of financial abuse of older adults is perpetrated by family, friends, or caregivers, it is also undertaken by scammers (Khalfani-Cox, 2017). Only about 1 in 44 cases of financial abuse of older adults is reported despite the large amounts of money lost. All states have an agency, easily located through the National Center on Elder Abuse (ncea.aoa.gov), to which one should report concerns about any form of abuse.

Older adults are a heterogeneous group, their differences related in important ways to the social circumstances that have shaped their histories, especially social inequalities. Settersten (2017) observes that individual differences and social inequalities result from a "time-based process," inequalities increasing due to social stratification, accumulation of advantage, accumulation of disadvantage, and the position of the disadvantaged relative to the advantaged (p. 4). The temporal process—the life course—that produces these differences is significantly gendered. Those whose gender identities are "more complex" attach "different social meanings to age and aging" (p. 4). Thus, due to both individual differences and social inequalities, some individuals benefit from protective factors as they enter their fourth age of life, but others' accumulation of disadvantages places them at higher risk for declines in health and well-being.

Being physically active and eating well (mostly fruit, vegetables, and low-fat protein) can strengthen muscles, reduce weakness, and reduce the risk of frailty (Johns Hopkins Medicine, 2020). Thus, fourth agers who exercise and have access to nutritious foods reap health benefits, whereas those who do not have enough food to eat or do not have easily accessible nutritious foods suffer from food insecurity, defined by the U.S. Department of Agriculture (USDA) as having "limited or uncertain access to adequate food" (2019, para. 5).

The USDA measures food security regularly, categorizing households into high food-secure (all household members have access to enough food); marginal food-secure (some members express anxiety about food shortage but no change in food intake); low food-secure (some household members report reduced quality, variety, or desirability of diet but no reduction in food intake); and very low food-secure (one or more household members report disrupted eating patterns and reduced food intake; Gundersen & Ziliak, 2015). Gundersen and Ziliak found that food-insecure older adults were more likely to be in only poor or fair health, have more limitations in ADLs, and more likely to be depressed. In fact, the "effect of being marginally food insecure on having a limitation in an ADL . . . is roughly equivalent to being fourteen years older" (2015, p. 1835).

In addition to exercise and good nutrition, satisfying activities such as creating art protect the well-being. Cohen (2006) examined the impact of creativity on the health of older adults who were 80 on average when the longitudinal Creativity and Aging Study began. All were active in the community, but the intervention group participated in a program run by professional artists. Members of the intervention group showed "powerful positive intervention effects, with the benefits being true gains in health promotion and disease prevention" (2006, p. 13). Subsequent studies found similar benefits. Meeks et al. (2018) found that involvement in performing arts organizations has lifelong benefits. The 65 and over group in their study had higher levels of autonomy, environmental mastery, and self-acceptance compared with the younger group. Kaufmann et al. (2018) found that listening to music also "increased life engagement and [promoted] better health among older Americans" (p. 270).

Cohen (2006) asserted that supporters of people who are aging need to look at the "4 S's" to address health and illness instead of the customary focus on the "2 S's." The 2-S focus in medicine looks only at *signs* and *symptoms*. Cohen advocates two additions: *skills* or strengths and *satisfactions* (interests and activities that bring satisfying feelings). Including these additional factors permits more holistic, strength-based assessments and interventions.

In addition to involvement in the arts and other activities, access to services and resources is important to older adults' health and well-being. Those who live in rural communities may be at a disadvantage when it comes to accessing care. Due to many factors, "rural communities have a higher prevalence of chronic disease, a higher disability rate, a lower prevalence of healthy behaviors, and a widening gap in life expectancy relative to the nation as a whole" (Skoufalos et al., 2017, p. S3). More than 20% of older Americans live in rural areas; Vermont (65.3%) and Maine (62.7%) have the highest percentages of rural older adults (Smith & Trevelyan, 2019).

Poverty is a grave concern for older adults, rural or urban, and for the oldest old especially. Poverty reduces access to food (creating food insecurity), access to healthcare (creating health disparities), and choices available with physical/cognitive decline. The poverty rate increases with age in the United States: 7.9% of those 65 to 69 live in poverty; 8.6% of those 70 to 74; 9.3% of those 75 to 79; and 11.6% of those 80 and older (Congressional Research Service, 2019).

Aging in place requires careful attention to home safety. Some modifications—such as removing throw rugs (a fall hazard)—are simple. Others, though, are more involved and costly. For example, standard doorframes are too narrow for wheelchairs or walkers; bathrooms may not be accessible; uneven outdoor pathways are hazardous. Alterations to address such safety concerns improve living conditions but only for those who can afford them.

Technologies such as smart home devices and communication platforms also help community-dwelling older adults. They mitigate concerns about safety, self-care, and social isolation that accompany efforts to age in place. A life-alert system signals distress to responders via a wearable push button or built-in sensors; smart medication dispensers automatically provide the right pills at the correct time; smart stove shutoff products prevent asphyxiation; social media and visual communication platforms help older adults stay closely in touch with family members and friends. Specially designed computer systems or smart home devices can provide convenience, connection to others, and entertainment for older adults. The use of such technologies depends on finances, condition of the home, and an older adult's openness to new technology and ability to use it. It is common for younger family members to insist on the installation of what their elders regard as undesirable "gadgets," and this raises the issue of self-determination, of course.

Centenarians (those who reach the age of 100) and super-centenarians (110 and older) may be a distinct group of the oldest old who share some protective factors for aging. Those who live this long tend to spend their entire lives in good health. They do not avoid physical decline but seem to be able to "compress morbidity until the very last moments of their lives," experience a slower process of decline, and maintain resiliency longer, perhaps due to specific genetic features (Borras et al., 2020). Researchers exploring the immune systems of super-centenarians have found that they may achieve "exceptional longevity by sustaining immune responses to infections and diseases" (Hashimoto et al., 2019, p. 24242). The causes of extremely long life remain largely unclear, however.

LOSSES EXPERIENCED BY OLDER ADULTS IN THEIR FOURTH AGE

Death Losses

Death of a Spouse/Life Partner

Widowhood becomes commonplace in older adulthood. In the fourth age, as in all phases of life, the death of a life partner is devastating. In a small, qualitative study of the widowhood experience of a group of the oldest old, Isherwood et al. (2015) found widowhood to be associated with "diminished social networks and concurrent challenges related to ageing and health which impacted upon support needs and social participation" (p. 188). Similarly, Brittain et al. (2015), using data from the Newcastle 85+ study, found that the recently widowed were at higher risk for loneliness than those widowed 5 or more years previously.

Death by Suicide

Considering all age groups, those over 85 had the second highest rate of suicide in the United States in 2017 (American Society for Suicide Prevention, 2017). Within this group, White men account for most of the deaths (AgingInPlace, 2020). Furthermore, the number of suicide deaths among the oldest old may be underreported by as much as 40% due to "silent suicides" from self-starvation, self-dehydration, and overdoses.

Decline in physical health and recent bereavement are the two risk factors for suicide in the oldest old. Using data from the Queensland [Australia] Suicide Register, Koo et al. (2017) found that the oldest old had the highest suicide rate compared with the young-old and middle-old groups and were more likely to have impairments in various health domains, reduced independence, and reduced mobility (p. 1301). The authors reported that their findings were similar to previous research showing that the oldest old struggled with health conditions and described their lives as "revolving around burden and loss" (p. 1304). Notably, the suicide attempts of the oldest old are the most likely to be successfully completed (AgingInPlace, 2020).

Living Losses: Atypical, Typical, and Maturational Losses

Loss of Physical and/or Cognitive Health

With the loss of health come many related losses. People lucky enough to have been healthy throughout life feel loss when they require regular medical care and come to be the sort of person "under a doctor's care." Other losses accrue: the loss of mobility, independence and customary housing, social network, and social activity. These losses impair emotional health and undermine self-esteem and sense of value to others. With increasing dependence comes diminished autonomy and, for some, hopelessness and depression.

Loss of Driving

Age alone should not determine when someone should give up driving. In general, adults and their loved ones make this decision based on the functioning and residual skill of the older adult driver. In 19 U.S. states, adults over a certain age must comply with extra license renewal requirements, which usually include testing of eyesight and reflexes. States may require passing an eye exam, a written test, a driving test, and more frequent and in-person renewal. The strictest state, Illinois, requires a road test for renewals at age 75 and subsequently. Some groups (such as the American Automobile Association) advocate policies to improve the safety of all drivers and oppose requirements solely based on age. Some (such as AARP) offer driver refresher courses to help drivers stay safe on the roads (Bergal, 2016).

Most older adults are safe drivers. They drive cautiously, and by multiple measures have good safety records as a group (Bergal, 2016; Tortorello, 2017). Their safety record aside, when older adults are involved in a crash, they are more likely to be injured or killed than those who are younger (Bergal, 2016). The charts in Figure 11.2 illustrate the mileage-based rates of injuries and deaths for the drivers, passengers, and others outside of the vehicle in relation to driver age.

Typically, older adults determine for themselves when to give up their license. Before this extreme, many decide not to drive at night or in bad weather. Multiple losses are incurred if an older

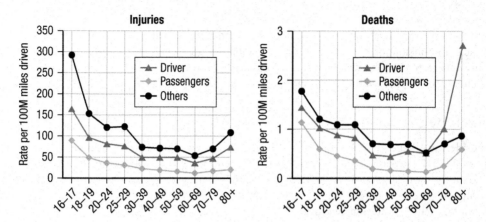

FIGURE 11.2 Mileage-Based Rates of Driver Injury and Deaths, Rates of Injuries, and Deaths of Their Passengers, and Rates of Injuries and Deaths of Other People Outside of the Driver's Vehicle in Relation to Driver Age. These two charts illustrate the number of crashes per 100 million miles driven. Each chart has three lines showing differing rates of injuries and deaths depending on if the person was the driver, was the passenger, or was outside the vehicle. These rates are in relation to the age of the driver.

Source: Reproduced with permission from AAA Foundation. (2017). *Rates of motor vehicle crashes, injuries, and deaths in relation to driver age, United States, 2014-2015.* https://aaafoundation.org/rates-motor-vehicle-crashes-injuries-deaths -relation-driver-age-united-states-2014-2015/

adult decides to give up driving: independence, self-efficacy, the freedom of spontaneous action, mobility, and participation in common activities are some examples. Older adults who give up driving must plan carefully and may become more dependent on friends and family members and come to feel burdensome. There are few transportation options in rural areas, so ceasing to drive effectively isolates people without the resources to use a taxi or ride service. Even then, in rural or urban areas, those with mobility problems will worry that the driver will not be able to assist them properly. Accommodating public transportation services (or transport specifically for older adults) can provide for older adults, but they are unlikely to offer the same flexibility and ease of travel achieved by private automobiles.

Loss of Home/Need to Move/Homelessness

The oldest old typically prefer to stay in their homes. Prior to 85, some may have chosen to move into age-restricted housing (over 55 communities), to a new state or region for lower costs, to a smaller home to downsize, to shared housing, or to a continuing care retirement community (CCRC), but after a time, these places become the home in which they would like to stay. Only 2.9% of those over 80 moved in 2017 to 2018. Although older adult renters move more often than older adult homeowners, only 8% of renters over 80 moved in 2017 to 2018 (Joint Center for Housing Studies of Harvard University [JCHSHU], 2019).

When the oldest-old move, it may not be a desired change. Some moves result from declining physical and/or cognitive health and are likely to be to an assisted living (AL) facility or SNF. Declining older adults already residing in a CCRC may have to move from their independent living (IL) apartment to the AL unit or to an SNF if the CCRC has one. Moves within the CCRC from IL to a higher level of care can be difficult and costly. Residents are sometimes stigmatized by such a move and excluded socially due to individual pejorative attitudes or because of the physical isolation of their new setting and temporal differences in its routines As well, a higher level of care concentrates those with often obvious and sometimes upsetting symptoms of decline.

Potential visitors often find these environments painful, even frightening to behold (Ewen et al., 2017; Zimmerman et al., 2016).

Institutional care is especially difficult for survivors of trauma, who can be triggered by feeling physically vulnerable, rooming with a stranger, being dressed and bathed by staff (sometimes several people each day), and having no privacy. Fortunately, on November 28, 2019, the Centers for Medicare & Medicaid Services entered the final stage of implementing trauma-informed regulations for Medicare- and Medicaid-funded SNFs and other nursing facilities. These promote trauma-informed care by trained and competent staff (Davis, 2019).

Some older adults move because of financial struggles. They may lose their homes, and some may become homeless. In general, homeowners over 80 are much better off financially than those who rent, having far greater wealth even if their incomes are similar. The difference between homeowners' and renters' financial well-being is striking and race related as there is a 27 percentage point home ownership gap between Blacks and Whites (JCHSHU, 2019). People who rent have less by way of savings and no equity to draw on if needed. They may need to incur high-interest credit card debt. Unfortunately, older adults' debt levels, the number of cost-burdened households, and the homeless among them have increased over the years (JCHSHU, 2019). Housing losses can be demoralizing and life threatening, especially when they affect frail people.

REACTION OF OTHERS TO THE DEATH OF AN OLDER ADULT

Worldwide, people are very likely to be disabled in the years before death. In China, disability presages the end of life and impairment in ADLs increases in each of the last three decades of life; prospectively, 28% are predicted to be disabled in the year prior to death in their 80s; 48% in their 90s; and 62% if they live beyond 100 (Liu et al., 2018). In the United States, people also tend to be disabled prior to death, with prevalence rates of ADL disability rising steadily with each decade of age starting in the 50s, but rising sharply in the 80s and 90s. ADL disability shows a sharp rise in the 2 years prior to death (Smith et al., 2013), and a third of older adults will experience disability in their last year of life. Of those who live into their 90s, half will have ADL disabilities that require assistance in the 2 years prior to death and two-thirds will need such assistance in the 6 months prior to death. ADL disability rates are higher among women and people with lower net worth.

That many of the oldest-old experience a significant need for care prior to death affects how others experience that death. When someone has been disabled and isolated due to care needs, others find that death natural and expected. For those who have been providing care within a family setting, feelings of relief may rival those of grief. Ambivalence is common.

In the Fourth Age, attachments often have loosened, and people may no longer interact in the vital and reciprocal ways of earlier in life. Family caregivers may adjust to their loved one's decline by working to stay connected while letting go, which Langer (2017) describes as a "major developmental task" for adult children caring for aging parents.

Ambivalence, looser attachments, and relief from caregiving mean that survivors of a fourth ager's death may not feel the intensity of grief they might have if the death had occurred earlier. Yet, regardless of age and length of illness, losing a parent is hard, and a myriad of contextual factors influence survivors' reactions. For example, Moss and Moss (2018) focused specifically on multiple siblings' experiences (mean age 52) of their parents' deaths (mean age 82). They found that various factors influenced the meaning of the loss and the impact on the siblings' grief responses. These included the quality of the sibling–parent relationship, sibling gender, life-course experiences, and the impact of parental death on personal identity. The siblings described the end of their parents' lives in similar ways but experienced the loss differently.

INTERVENTIONS

Acceptance and Commitment Therapy

Acceptance Commitment Therapy (ACT) (pronounced as the word *act* not the letters of the acronym) is a therapeutic approach developed by Steven C. Hayes that aims to help people discover what they value in life and lead lives that matter. In brief, it is an action-oriented approach comprised of six core therapeutic processes: contacting the present moment (be here now); defusion (watch your thinking); acceptance (open up); self-as context (pure awareness); values (know what matters); and committed action (do what it takes; Harris, 2009, pp. 9–11). Clients are encouraged to accept their inner emotions and unpleasant thoughts or experiences rather than viewing them as problems. Language is an important part of this approach, for how we describe a problem can change our experience of it. Clients then work to make the behavior changes necessary to commit to living life. Harris (2009) explains that an important core message of ACT is to "accept what is out of your personal control and commit to taking action that enriches your life" (p. 2).

ACT shows promise with older adults. For the oldest-old, who struggle with the loss of independence, declining health, and symptoms of depression and anxiety, becoming more "present" and accepting of feelings can help them take value-directed action. Studies specifically focused on using ACT with older adults to combat depression, anxiety, and coping with chronic pain found positive results (Barban, 2016; Roberts & Sedley, 2016). ACT seems effective for residents in long-term care. In a pilot study with 41 residents (average age 85.3) of an SNF, over the course of 12 sessions participants improved in scores on depression and anxiety compared with a wait-list control group (Davison et al., 2017). Each session included a mindfulness segment, work toward clarifying values, learning to watch one's feelings (defusion), accepting one's feelings, and developing an action plan. A few participants did not find the intervention useful as it did not help them change troublesome environmental circumstances (staff interactions and tensions), but most believed the intervention helped them overall.

Life Review Therapy and Reminiscence Therapy

Life review therapy (LRT) was developed by Robert Butler (1963), who asserted that there is a "universal occurrence" whereby older adults review their lives. Life review can contribute to "late-life disorders, particularly depression" but also "participates in the evolution of such characteristics as candor, serenity, and wisdom among certain of the aged" (p. 65). LRT assumes that if older adults look back on their lives, reflecting on both good and bad memories, they can face and resolve unfinished business and achieve peace. Therapists applying LRT use many interventions, and the goals of LRT can vary (e.g., decrease depressive symptoms, decrease anxiety symptoms, foster well-being). Depending on the client and goals, some therapists opt to focus on a certain time of life or a certain theme (e.g., purpose and values).

Despite these variations, LRT is a structured approach guiding individuals through life stages for a specified number of sessions (usually eight). When difficult memories arise, cognitive reframing is used to help the client come to terms with their past (Rubin et al., 2018). Three active principles of Life Review Interventions were identified by Maercker and Bachem (2013): life balance (promoting a balance of positive and negative memories; finding meaning (even with negative experiences including trauma); and elaboration of memory (and in the case of trauma, memories are processed into a narrative). The focus is on integrating life history, and the therapy has been found effective in treating depression (Maercker & Bachem, 2013), fostering the development of personal meaning and ego integrity with terminally ill older adults (Alon, 2018), and improving quality of life for older adults (Sharif et al., 2018).

LRT differs from reminiscence therapy (RT), although some use the terms interchangeably. RT tends to be a less structured and more spontaneous process of recalling positive memories

(Rubin et al., 2018) and focuses on accessing and narrating these positive memories, not on resolving conflicts or reconsidering unfinished business (McInnis-Dittrich, 2014). It intends to improve mood but does not promote insight or conflict resolution. There are different RT approaches. One is to move in the chronological order of a client's life. Each session is devoted to an era of the client's life and the client recalls positive memories from that era. Clients could also be asked to bring in props from that era, such as photos. Another approach is to select a safe topic such as favorite foods and talk about that theme across the life span.

A Matter of Balance: A Falls Prevention Program

While there is no single solution for fall prevention or the FoF, many promising and effective programs have been developed in recent years. One such program—A Matter of Balance (MoB)—was developed to reduce the FoF through standardized education (providing information on risky behaviors and environmental hazards that lead to falls); cognitive components (improving perceived control over falling); and exercise (both balance and strength training (Chen et al., 2015). Chen et al. (2015) found that in contrast to the comparison group, participants in the MoB group were less likely to fall. The benefits of the MoB program have also been found in AL communities (Reynolds et al., 2019).

Animal-Assisted Therapy and Animal-Assisted Activities

Animal-assisted therapy (AAT) and animal-assisted activities (AAAs) are becoming increasingly popular in the United States to improve people's emotional and physical well-being and decrease loneliness. With the increase in use of AAT and AAA, the science of human–animal interaction has also grown. This explores how people's relationships with animals improve health and well-being and promote healthy aging.

AAT and AAA show promising results anecdotally, but research is limited because of methodological challenges such as the lack of standardized measures for pet bonding and outcomes (e.g., loneliness) and difficulty operationalizing the degree of involvement between people and the animals (Gee et al., 2017). Despite the methodological drawbacks, Gee et al. (2017) found that AAAs (including pet ownership) are associated with improved cardiovascular health and reductions in depressive symptoms (including for those residing in AL and SNFs), anxiety, and loneliness.

READINGS

Untouchable Loss: Marion's Story of Her Missing Self-Esteem
LAUREN SNEDEKER

Lauren Snedeker, LMSW, LSW, DSW candidate, is a licensed social worker in New York and New Jersey. Lauren works extensively with older adults and their families by providing case management, counseling, home visits, group therapy, and emergency support both in the community and in facilities. Lauren is passionate about telling the stories of the aging population to debunk myths and help better educate professionals on best practices.

Marion is an 88-year-old woman living in a three-bedroom apartment in a quiet neighborhood in the Bronx, New York. Marion is widowed and has two adult daughters who live out of state.

She has been living alone for almost 20 years. She volunteers several times a week and leads an active life; however, due to recent falls in her home, Marion has home care every day to help with tasks and getting to and from her volunteer job. I visit Marion every 2 weeks for support. Recently, Marion disclosed that she feels "down" about herself. When I asked more, Marion stated that she feels like she has lost her self-esteem. As we age, there are numerous, perhaps expected, losses that occur as a result of biology; however, losing one's self-esteem is not always visible to workers in the gerontology field.

Discussion of the Experience of Loss

I knocked on Marion's door and Layla, Marion's caregiver, answered, smiling, and encouraged me to come in. Layla escorted me to the living room, where I sat and waited for Marion, so we could begin our biweekly visit. Marion had raised her two daughters in this apartment and had experienced the death of two husbands there. The apartment is full of memories and pictures of Marion and her family travelling the world. Her daughters take turns visiting once a month for a week. Marion came into the living room slowly, feeling for the tops of furniture for balance, and sat beside me on the couch. "How ya doin', honey?" Marion asked. I assured her I was doing well and asked her how her week was going. Marion frowned and shared a recent negative experience at the senior center. An incident occurred where she felt unwelcome by several ladies at her usual lunch table because Layla was with her, and there was not enough room for them both to sit down, according to the ladies at the table. Marion described feeling judged because of needing Layla's support in public. She adjusted her blouse then and patted her chest, ensuring the black cord connected to her LifeAlert was hidden. "Getting older is a blessing," Marion stated, "but needing so much help makes you lose your confidence, especially when you have these constant reminders. It makes you feel bad about yourself."

Even though Marion and many others may appreciate a long life, aging is not easy. It is a journey on which you may find yourself needing to learn how to do things differently, over and over again. For example, Marion has had to learn how to use a rolling walker as a result of falling. This was difficult because the walker can be hard to maneuver in doorways, and it symbolizes her decline not only to herself but also to her peers and society in general. Marion has also had to adjust to having Layla do things around the home that she herself did independently up until a few months ago. After living alone for 20 years, Marion initially appreciated the company Layla offered. Nevertheless, coping with having someone in her personal space for such long lengths of time was not easy. Layla's presence began the decline of Marion's self-esteem because she represented to Marion what she could no longer do.

Developmentally, aging represents change, and changes are losses. Many believe the myth that because these changes are expected (e.g., reduced physical ability), they are easier to prepare for and cope with. Such is not the case. Furthermore, loss of self-esteem as a result of these changes is not as readily recognized as a loss. Marion confessed that she felt "less than" around the senior center acquaintances because they do not have the same needs she has. According to Marion, they do not have caregivers like Layla and do not need walkers. Because she can no longer do things independently and benefits from having Layla around, Marion identified feeling less confident when at the center. She feared the judgment of others for needing such support.

I worried how these feelings would further impact Marion. She could start to feel more depressed as a result of having low self-esteem connected to these biological changes. She could lose the fiery motivation that is so ingrained in her personality and decide to lessen her daily activities. Marion might withdraw from socializing as a result of her low self-esteem, causing her to be at risk for isolation and a host of other negative health impacts. Furthermore, this withdrawal could also impact her adult children, who might find her more dependent. Marion's losses could begin to accumulate and cause her to feel hopeless, or as Erikson described, in a state of despair. Marion's cumulative losses include her deceased husbands, physical abilities, health, friends, and now her self-esteem and sense of self. During this visit, I thought it imperative to begin intervention strategies to preserve Marion's self-esteem and enhance her quality of life.

Interventions

First and foremost, with loss, especially a loss such as self-esteem, it is crucial to validate the client's sense of loss. I began validating Marion's disappointment in her peers at the senior center for being so critical of her sitting at their table with her caregiver, Layla. It was important to prevent Marion from feeling disenfranchised about this experience. Society often expects a lot out of seniors, for instance, accepting changes in one's abilities just because it is expected. The truth is that getting older and experiencing loss is never easy.

After validating Marion's feelings of lost self-esteem, I began discussing with Marion what she liked about the senior center and highlighted all the free work she provides to them. I reminded her that she was a crucial member of the center, and how without her, many of the daily tasks might not get done. I tried to show Marion how valuable she was to the center while also hearing from her how important the center was to her. "I like learning, exercising, and talking to people in my age range about different things happening in the world. I can't imagine not having the center and I don't know how I would spend my days without it. I'd probably just watch TV all day, which does not sound fun. I've always enjoyed people and going out," Marion asserted. We talked about how Marion could return to the senior center and perhaps sit at a different table during lunch with Layla. Marion agreed that there were other members with their caregivers there, and she considered how she could start sitting there as opposed to with the rejecting women. We also discussed how Layla could consider taking a walk during lunch time as she did not need to help Marion with her meal. Layla agreed and stated she could eat in the office or another room because she had become friendly with the staff there.

Interventions with individuals experiencing loss must be paced appropriately. I followed Marion's lead in terms of discussing her loss of self-esteem and through conversation, learned that she did not want to lose her connection to the senior center. By validating her role at the senior center, I hoped to boost her self-esteem and sense of self. I then included Layla, Marion's caregiver, in the conversation, which also helped to strengthen their relationship, highlighting how Layla also wanted to support Marion. It is not realistic to think that Marion will always feel her best while she continues to decline physically; however, it helps to provide a space for Marion to discuss these losses, validate that they are real and deserve to be mourned, and gently offer ways to help make Marion (or any client) feel better while living through these changes due to aging. We must anticipate that not every conversation will go well, and some clients may be less interested or receptive to discussions about loss. Some may not identify certain experiences as losses. The most important thing is to recognize your role as the social worker or counselor and the support you can share with your client. It is important to cultivate the strength you have for continuing with this work because our senior clients deserve our care and support.

An Expression of Loss and Coping in the Aged Adult
MARY KAY KROWKOWSKI

Mary Kay Krowkowski is a registered nurse who has worked in geriatrics for more than 40 years. She is a graduate of Boston College in the School of Nursing and has a master's degree in health advocacy from Sarah Lawrence College. She is certified in care management and has been on the Board of the

Aging Life Care Association. She serves on the Board of Directors of the National Academy of Certi-fied Care Managers.

Background

Frances was a woman of 89 years when I first met her, 4 months after her reluctant agreement to move to an IL apartment within a "5 star" CCRC. It was 5 years since her husband's death. Her sister, Agnes, had lived nearby for 40 years, but her memory was declining, and she was moved to a dementia unit near her daughter to provide a safer setting for her care. At 89, Frances spoke frankly of her losses (of friends and family). She rationalized the losses as "expected," but each additional loss took its toll on her emotional strength. Her daughter, Patty, lived 3 hours away and wanted to create a support system for her mother before an emergency health event occurred sud-denly. All of this was very logical and methodically planned; Frances hesitatingly agreed.

Frances had been fortunate financially, socially, educationally, and physically throughout her life. She was well spoken, insightful, reflective, and determined. She drove herself 100 miles to her new IL apartment with her canoe on the roof of her car, expecting to continue her life as she had been—with a little bit of help with organizing and lifting boxes.

The idea to leave her home and move to a "community" was not hers. Eight years earlier, she had done research on CCRCs when her husband's health was waning. She admitted it was easier to consider a move when she could point to her husband as the one who needed the care. But Frank died suddenly, and the move to a CCRC was put aside.

Over the years as a care manager, I have worked with many families who had a loved one with significant dementia, mental health issues, medical instability, or unmanageable housing is-sues that provided a specific reason to make changes quickly. Frances did not fall into any of these categories when I first met her. So, when Frances's lack of ability to cope with her new environs became unmanageable for Patty from afar, she called to ask for guidance.

Care managers are often called upon when family members are unable to convince their par-ent or spouse that a change is needed. We are called out of fear, frustration, and lack of knowledge as to how to intervene in a collapsing elder-care situation. Again, Frances did not fit the "typical" profile. She was angry, resentful, uncooperative, and her energy was focused on being resistant to staff; she disliked the parking rules, the meal options, and the physicians affiliated with the independent level of care. These things were all out of character, according to her daughter. Patty was constantly getting backlash on the phone and hoped that consulting a care manager/care coordinator would help her to get Frances to make friends, settle in, and adjust.

Care managers always begin with a "global assessment." In order to work together, we discuss history, assess strengths and coping skills, and determine personal goals in order to discern a place to gain some "buy-in" by the client. Upon meeting, it was obvious that Frances felt coerced into the move due to the family's concerns that "something was going to happen someday." Patty was trying to recreate a new support system, and recreate stability after Frances's husband's death and Frances's sister's move. Patty assumed that because Frances had done the research and chosen this CCRC, she would be amenable to the move. She failed to realize that Frances did not see a current need and the time frame was not of her choosing. That was a significant piece of the problem.

Social History

Frances had been a librarian and her husband had a career in finance. They had 4 children, 1 of whom lived with multiple sclerosis and lived adjacent to a sibling in a distant state. Patty, the clos-est in proximity, was Frances's Health Care Power of Attorney and lived 3 hours away. Frances always had a fun-filled, active social life and enjoyed camping, canoeing, theater, and classical music. She was quite proud of the fact that, before she met her husband, she had bought and physically built a cabin in rural Pennsylvania. She had recently relinquished that home due to the difficult terrain and its remoteness. She was eminently proud of her independence and self-reliance. Her stories resounded with involvement, humor, accomplishment, and enjoyment. This helped me understand Patty's concern with Frances's change in temperament and difficulties adjusting.

While at her home, Frances had been fully functioning, integrated into daily activities including cooking, reading, shopping, visiting, and calling friends. In her view, she had been aging very successfully, in a way that was consistent with her life history, character, and personality. From her perspective, moving to a CCRC compromised all that.

Psychological adjustments

Frances had the "Welcome Wagon of Greeters" gathering around her at first, but after 3 months, daily calls from Patty and visits from the greeters all started to fade away. Despite the beautiful setting with meals and activities, Frances said she was "keeping a stiff upper lip" and pushing herself to attend evening concerts and lunch dates. She felt that everyone else looked happy and well adjusted to this routinized system, but she did not and could no longer keep up appearances. True to her life story, she resisted the idea of being a "stereotypical" elder living in a facility. She would get into her car and try to challenge herself to leave the facility grounds and incorporate herself into the surrounding community. She got lost on two occasions, and on the second was returned by the police. Patty encouraged her mother to relinquish the car "since she did not need to use it anyway." "Everything was there for her at the CCRC, including transportation." This discussion became an angry exchange between mother and daughter.

Frances was highly alert, attentive, and oriented; had insight; and demonstrated humor, creativity, and abstract thinking. But her short-term memory was sometimes inconsistent, perhaps partially due to her anger, but there seemed to be more that needed on-going observation. I wanted to assess if memory loss was also brewing. Her long-term memory was accurate and detailed. Her frustration and sadness were clear. What began to happen next came to be that "unexpected emergency" Patty had anticipated.

Medical changes

In January, 4 months after the move, Frances attended a theatrical production at a local theater and was getting back on the transportation bus to return to the CCRC for the evening. Frances, whose strength and stamina had always been part of her pride, stepped up on the bus, and missed grabbing the handrail. She fell backwards off the step, slamming to the ground, and required a trip to the ER to ensure that no fractures or injuries had occurred. Because it was January, Frances was in a heavy coat that seemed to help prevent serious injury.

But an 89-year-old does not simply walk away from a traumatic fall, despite negative scans and exams. Patty called me to get an "outsider's perspective" on the changes she sensed were happening to her mother. Frances was staying in her room more, having meals delivered to her room, having memory recall difficulties, neck pain, hip pain, repeated x-rays, but no diagnosable injuries. In our first two meetings after the fall (which I spaced 2 weeks apart), there were subtle but discernible changes: less safety awareness, more irritability, repetition of topics, more isolation, and a decline in her problem-solving abilities. Frances was animated when she spoke, as was her normal. But her hands and wrists, in particular, were in constant motion. In fact, as we continued to talk, Frances adjusted herself every 20 to 30 seconds, as if she was sliding down in her chair. When I brought it to her attention, she said she did not notice and that she had no pain when sitting. She had some neck and lower back soreness, but no real pain. I asked her if she wanted to come across the room to look at some things I had brought as a way to assess her transfer from the chair without making her self-conscious. Her transfer demonstrated less fluidity of movement and less steady balance than before, subtle but notable.

Medical Interventions

Over the next 4 months, Frances's dystonic movements increased and intermittent slurred speech episodes developed, including sudden episodes of hypersalivation and difficulty swallowing that led to frightening choking. There did not appear to be a trigger factor for these episodes, which increased her fear and isolation.

Frances returned to the ER three times and saw a local orthopedist and a local neurologist for more scans. The lack of explanation for her decline led to a consult with a neuromovement specialist at a prestigious medical center in a much larger city. All of this resulted in a "best guess diagnosis" of senile chorea, a rare movement disorder that mimics the rapid onset of Huntington's chorea. According to the movement specialist, the fall from the step off the bus was the sentinel event that was witnessed, but there had likely been other movement and strength changes that had been treated dismissively. Senile chorea has no cure, and symptom management is the only treatment, with muscle relaxants, an antidepressant, and an anticholinergic for the hypersaliva-tion. Frances would not accept any treatment, disbelieving that her physical disabilities were likely permanent and could worsen.

Psychological Analysis

As with any initial "global assessment," the first job is to ask questions without the client feeling interrogated, to listen between-the-lines, to develop rapport and enough trust to open conversations about matters beyond what most family members are comfortable discussing. Frances was well able to state the changes in her life and the feelings of loss with relative ease.

Albert L. Meiburg is a pastor and college professor who has worked extensively with older adults and describes a clinical strategy for dealing with their changes and losses. He utilizes the developmental tasks for older adults constructed by Havighurst and extended by his student, Evelyn M. Duvall (1967):

1. Finding a satisfying home for the later years.
2. Adjusting to retirement income.
3. Establishing comfortable household routines.
4. Nurturing each other as husband and wife.
5. Facing bereavement and widowhood.
6. Maintaining contact with children and grandchildren.
7. Caring for elderly relatives.
8. Keeping an interest in people outside the family.
9. Finding meanings in life.

Meiburg states that the first step in working with this age group is listening, representing re-spect and closeness (Meiburg, 1985, p. 139). This validates their grief and helps those adjusting to change and loss. Meiburg states that in this listening, the clinician needs to look for the "endur-ing meanings" in the older adults' life stories that illuminate their strengths. This helps identify productive coping options and solutions. To illuminate ways to cope with the present, he utilizes Robert Butler's constructive "life review" process to acknowledge the client's previous successful systems (Meiburg, 1985, p. 139).

Erikson calls this developmental task reaching "integrity" or "rightness" about the life one led. Clinicians must help people recognize they have made good choices in the past and can do so again. Respecting their story, not correcting, approving, or disapproving episodes in their life, are the supportive and guiding interventions that are effective. Erikson describes "integrity" as accepting one's life as having been meaningful and appropriate. "Failure to accomplish this task is responsible for the fear of death (despair), the feeling that time has run out, that there is no chance to start life over." "The achievement of integrity produces the 'virtue' of wisdom" (Meiburg, 1985, p. 125).

Even so, health problems can impair dignity through increased dependency, disfigurement due to surgery or use of a walker, and incontinence, with the need for product use that can cause shame (Meiburg, 1985, p. 39). Frances strongly feared these changes. The other loss that Frances faced was the move itself. Downsizing also entails a loss of privacy, ownership, and autonomous space. Her rapid changes in functional abilities and living situation threw Frances into feelings of despair, helplessness, and anger.

Conclusions

I share Frances's case study here because her situation did not appear to require an extreme or dramatic intervention when we first met. She certainly was going through Havighurst's textbook developmental tasks of an older adult: acknowledging and adjusting to decreasing strength and asking for help with lifting and carrying during her move; caring for others and being needed (especially by her surviving sister); adjusting to the loss of her husband; maintaining contact with her children and grandchildren; and finding continued meaning in her life with established hobbies and interests. Two specific things exacerbated her difficulties adjusting. First, her self-identity was insulted by her move to a setting where she viewed those around her as recipients of care rather than as independent, as she viewed herself. Second, her sudden and rapid decline in functional ability made her a recipient of both medical and physical support, something that did not reflect her view of herself and disintegrated her identity further, throwing her into what Erikson would describe as "despair" (1963, p. 269).

Frances's self-respect was grounded in her independence. Yet she also was a good friend and sibling and she had anticipated being able to enjoy her retirement with a strong sense of self-worth. She acknowledged that these productive roles were lost as she was no longer a caregiver but had to be a care-receiver.

Jess Love's developmental tasks for the oldest adults are the need to be heard; express anger; tell their story; be needed; apologize for regrets and ask for forgiveness; and find orderliness to cope with change (Love as cited in Stancil, 2019). Akin to these developmental tasks, Levinson uses the concept of "seasons of adulthood" that also utilize the "life review" to find meaning and value in what has transpired in order to begin to anticipate death. "The seasons theory of human development stipulates that the work of growth in late adulthood is precisely to prepare for death via making peace in the inner being as well as in other relations towards finding conciliatory coherence when looking over one's lived life" (Moon, 2005, p. 18).

Frances needed to cultivate a sense of belonging to this new community and adjust to her new health status in order to reach a level of self-acceptance. Her personhood had always been defined by productivity, not receivership. She was angry, disappointed in herself, and looking for someone to blame. As a care manager, my work with Frances started with listening to her frustrations, her anger, and her resentment, validating her feelings. I listened to the story of her life, her accomplishments, her expectations of herself, her sadness that she could not continue caring for her sister, and her humorous stories about her sisters and husband and empathized with how it felt to be the strongest left standing in her generation of the family. Frances realized over time that she did not have the patience for her sister's dementia symptoms, and she was able to express the sadness she felt that she could not "save" her husband.

Patricia Weenolsen, a "life span developmental psychologist" created the loss/transcendence paradigm, emphasizing that "all the leave-takings of one's life have been prototypes of the final one, and how one has transcended the others may be of help now" (Weenolsen, 1988, p. 304). This framework acknowledges the intensity of the innumerable losses in life. Life review utilizes the opportunity to look at the whole as an integral part of the acceptance of life-ending changes. Erickson et al. evoke a person like Frances: "Those who have been rich in intimacy also have the most to lose" (1986, p. 332). Frances had had a rich life and her anger reflected her resistance to the extensive losses she was facing at 89. "Old age is necessarily a time of relinquishing—of giving up old friends, old roles, earlier work that was once meaningful, and even possessions that belong to a previous stage of life and are now an impediment to the resiliency and freedom that seem to be requisite for adapting to the unknown challenges that determine the final stages of life" (Erickson et al., 1986, p. 332). As Moon states, "the notions of aging, loss, reflection in older adulthood, adaptation, disengagement, renarration, transcendency [sic], and acceptance . . . [are] quite a list of things to accomplish, at any age" (Moon, 2005, p. 27).

The final blow, her loss of mobility, became an opportunity to help Frances learn that her selfhood was in her humor, ability to make friends, and ability to enjoy the concerts and trips. We were able to interview and hand-pick an aide, giving Frances control of who she would agree to allow in her company to assist her physically, including what hours she would schedule. Frances resisted the medications and refused the antidepressant for a long time. Eventually, she acknowledged that the medications did improve her mood and even her mobility.

Working with Frances's daughter was also important. I provided an "outsider" perspective, explaining the source of Frances's anger while supporting the "push" to move her to a safer environment. With the unfortunate health losses rapidly after the move, the mother–daughter relationship improved and gave Frances and Patty time to ask for forgiveness for the contentious words they had exchanged.

Frances continues to live in the IL section of the CCRC. A consistent aide comes to the apartment several days a week to get Frances out for shopping and help her plan and stay on schedule. Frances's memory is not as strong as a year ago, but her humor, personality, staunch independence, and determination remain intact. She takes medications as prescribed, and the chorea symptoms are less problematic.

SUMMARY

Most of the oldest old experience physical and cognitive decline and suffer the loss of independence. Some are frail and at high risk for falls, hospitalization, and poor health outcomes. Depression, loneliness, and social isolation are additional factors that often affect the adjustment and well-being of the oldest old. Those who are able to exercise, eat well, partake in satisfying activities such as creating art, and maintain a close social network may be better positioned to adjust well to aging. Finding meaning and purpose may also help older adults accept the cumulative losses they experience.

DISCUSSION QUESTIONS

1. A 93-year-old client moved into the SNF where you work. She has no cognitive challenges but is frail, has had multiple falls, and has trouble with mobility. She decided reluctantly to move into an SNF because she feels she can no longer live alone and cannot afford full-time live-in care. She needs nursing care, so AL was not an option. After living alone for 30 years

after her spouse died, she is not happy to be sharing a room with a stranger, being awakened to take medication early in the morning, or being forced to eat at certain hours. She feels sad, hopeless, and frustrated. How can you work with this client to help her adjust to her new living environment?

2. An 86-year-old, community-dwelling client is still driving. Her daughter is concerned for her mom's safety and wants her to give up her license. Her mom has not been in any ac-cidents and only drives locally, in daytime hours, and in good weather. The daughter asks you for guidance. She wonders, should not her mom stop driving at this age? What factors besides age are important to consider? What potential losses might the mother experience if she gave up driving?

KEY REFERENCES

Only key references appear in the print edition. The full reference list appears in the digital product found on http://connect.springerpub.com/content/book /978-0-8261-4964-0/chapter/ch11

Cohen, G. D. (2006). Research on creativity and aging: The positive impact of the arts on health and illness. *Generations, 30*(1), 7–15. https://www.ingentaconnect.com/content/asag/gen/2006/00000030/00000001/art00003

Davison, T. E., Eppingstall, B., Runci, S., & O'Connor, D. W. (2017). A pilot trial of acceptance and commitment therapy for symptoms of depression and anxiety in older adults residing in long-term care facilities. *Aging and Mental Health, 21*(7), 766–773. https://doi.org/10.1080/13607863.2016.1156051

Gee, N. R., Mueller, M. K., & Curl, A. L. (2017). Human–animal interaction and older adults: An overview. *Frontiers in Psychology, 8*, 1416. https://doi.org/10.3389/fpsyg.2017.01416

Isherwood, L., King, D., & Luszcz, M. (2017). Widowhood in the fourth age: Support exchange, relationships and social participation. *Ageing and Society, 37*(1), 188–212. https://doi.org/10.1017/S0144686X15001166

Koo, Y. W., Kõlves, K., & De Leo, D. (2017). Suicide in older adults: Differences between the young-old, middle-old, and oldest old. *International Psychogeriatrics, 29*(8), 1297–1306. http://doi.org./10.1017/S1041610217000618

Maercker, A., & Bachem, R. (2013). Life-review interventions as psychotherapeutic techniques in psychotraumatology. *European Journal of Psychotraumatology, 4*(1), 19720. https://doi.org/10.3402/ejpt.v4i0.19720

Mosqueda, L., Burnight, K., Gironda, M. W., Moore, A. A., Robinson, J., & Olsen, B. (2016). The abuse intervention model: A pragmatic approach to intervention for elder mistreatment. *Journal of the American Geriatrics Society, 64*(9), 1879–1883. https://doi.org/10.1111/jgs.14266

Nerenberg, L. (2019). *Elder justice, ageism, and elder abuse.* Springer Publishing Company.

Young, W. R., & Williams, A. M. (2015). How fear of falling can increase fall-risk in older adults: Applying psychological theory to practical observations. *Gait and Posture, 41*, 7–12. http://dx.doi.org/10.1016/j.gaitpost.2014.09.006

12

Conclusions

INTRODUCTION

In this final chapter, we summarize the main themes of the text, focusing on the ways postmodern theories of grief allow us to tailor interventions to meet the needs of individual clients. We review frequently unrecognized maturational losses and propose that they are a form of disenfranchised loss. We review the utility of the dual-process model and reinforce how continuing bonds transformed our understanding of grief processes. We close by reminding clinicians to attend to their own needs and recognize that knowledge of grief and loss does not allow them to bypass the pain and meaning-making work that is entailed in grief. Ultimately, meaning-making is a critical aspect of grieving, regardless of the type of loss.

OBJECTIVES

After studying this chapter, the reader will be able to:
- Synthesize literature about postmodern grief theory.
- Understand how maturational losses fit within the concept of disenfranchised grief.
- Be aware of the intersections of trauma and grief theory.
- Deliberate about changes in the *Diagnostic and Statistical Manual of Mental Disorders,* Fifth Edition (*DSM-5;* American Psychiatric Association, 2013) related to diagnosis and grief.
- Identify forms of self-care that support good practice.

ENDINGS

We began with the premise that the destabilizing force of loss is an inevitable part of human existence and central to life and growth. We also recognized that some grievers mourn for the rest of their lives and do not grow from loss. Still, research and clinical experience reassure us that most individuals cope with the distress of loss and learn lessons of empathy and resilience. They often learn about their ability to survive deep pain and that they are more resilient than they thought. We believe that people can process loss more readily when they talk with someone who is supportive, calm, and nonjudgmental. We know that those supportive others, whether professionals or close friends, will provide better support if they gently ask specific questions of the griever rather than offering a vague invitation to talk.

This text is organized around the further premise that bio–psycho–social–spiritual development and societal contexts have structuring effects on grief and loss. For organizational purposes, the text chapters are defined by age groups, but within each chapter we observe the wide variations that can occur in terms of age and other markers of a particular developmental phase. This is a good reminder to us all that every person's loss experience truly is unique, framed by their developmental stage, the environments that have shaped them, the attachment/s they feel to the lost entity, their coping styles and the type of their loss (e.g., sudden, expected). We provide guidelines for how each of these factors may influence a person's grieving experience, but these guidelines are not prescriptive. Indeed, this text was born of reaction against stage theories and others that ascribed uniform responses to all grievers. We hope that by reflecting on the ideas and information in this text, the reader feels more competent to help grievers in ways suited to their individual circumstances.

ACCOMPANYING THE BEREAVED IN THEIR GRIEF

Many students feel unsure of their ability to work with bereaved people and believe they must remove a client's sadness or in some other way, work magic. In truth, sadness is a normal part of human existence and a customary response to loss. Losses related to attachment, to status and resources, and to meaning or valued goals inspire pain and likely contribute to the high rate of diagnosed depression in the Western world (Horowitz & Wakefield, 2007). Yet these losses and concomitant feelings are common across all cultures and throughout human history. We trust that most bereaved people will be helped by the practitioner, friend, or family member with the courage, curiosity, and compassion to sit with them calmly and truly listen to their stories and feelings. Their curiosity guides them to ask the gentle questions that the grievers need to help them tell their stories. The listener must do so without raising anxiety from the pressure to make magic happen. Such an impossible expectation compromises calm, intent, quiet listening, and gentle probing of the bereaved's thoughts, feelings, and actions.

It is very important that supporters actively help the bereaved tell the stories of their losses and what they mean to them. This is the opposite of saying "I'm here if you want to talk"—an offer grievers seldom pursue. Good support entails asking questions about what led up to the death or loss, what happened during the death or ending (and how that affected the bereaved), how the bereaved was thinking and feeling immediately after the death or loss, how that differs from current feelings, and what fears the person has about moving through life without the loved one or lost entity. Most important, these questions should be posed gently, and one must respond with interest, empathy, and patience. Asking specific questions provides both guidance and permission to begin to talk. There is no magic here, but over time, the bereaved usually are able to make meaning of the loss and create a story with a narrative line that allows them to feel that the experience is understood and contained.

Of course, losses can threaten long-term well-being and may evoke intense sadness. The *DSM-5* is clear that if grieving people begin to have extreme symptoms that meet the criteria for major depressive disorder, they should be referred for psychiatric evaluation. Yet the removal of the "bereavement exclusion" and the decision not to include prolonged or complicated grief as diagnoses in the *DSM-5* have left clinicians with more questions than answers about when loss responses and grief require psychiatric treatment rather than supportive counseling. Wakefield (2013) has neatly explained the history and rationale of *DSM-5*'s removal of the bereavement exclusion and the great difficulty it creates for grievers and their caregivers. Although the bereavement exclusion had long been criticized as too narrow (divorce and job loss can provoke depressive symptoms, too) and also too short (the 2-month bereavement exclusion of *DSM-III* and *DSM-IV* does not recognize that most grievers experience such symptoms for at least 6–12 months), the removal of the exclusion has led to even greater concerns. These can be summed up in Allen Frances's words (Frances is the editor of *DSM-IV TR*): "Many millions of people with *normal grief*, gluttony, distractibility, worries, reactions to stress, the temper tantrums of childhood, the forgetting of old age, and 'behavioral addictions' will soon be mislabeled as psychiatrically sick" (italics added; Frances, 2010). Indeed, Wakefield (2013) expresses similar concerns that we share: Normal grievers may be diagnosed and medicated rather than supported in their grief. We urge readers of this text to approach grief as a painful but normal process and resist the tendency to pathologize it.

The exclusion of complicated grief and prolonged grief in the *DSM-5* also causes consternation for grief therapists. Nearly all clinicians recognize the constellation of symptoms described as prolonged grief (Holland et al., 2009) or those indicating complicated grief (Shear, 2015) and the tendency of these mourners to remain stuck in their grief, often with intrusive thoughts, intense yearning for the deceased, and ongoing avoidance of discussion of the death or the deceased. The *International Classification of Diseases 11 (ICD-11*, 2019) added prolonged grief disorder (PGD) to recognize that mourners benefit from diagnosis and treatment when they experience ongoing debilitating grief. Aside from the greater intensity of sadness and intrusive thoughts, the *ICD-11* describes it as lasting longer than 6 months and exceeding typical cultural norms. The continuing tension between overpathologizing normal grief and facilitating treatment for debilitating grief ensures that these diagnostic issues will remain thorny.

Structured approaches to treating mourners with out-of-the-norm grief reactions—exposure therapies (especially telling the story of the death) and cognitive behavioral methods to reappraise negative cognitions—have been empirically tested and exhibit good efficacy, using many of the interventions discussed previously in this text (Bryant et al., 2014; Shear, 2015). Shear (2015) identified the core components for treating complicated grief as (a) establishing the lay of the land; (b) promoting self-regulation; (c) building connections; (d) setting aspirational goals; (e) revisiting the world; (f) storytelling; and (g) using memory.

The myth that the pain of grief can be avoided is seductive, but grief is painful, messy, and temporarily debilitating. Many of the lessons of grief have to do with what one can bear and survive—lessons only learned when one must do so. We are inclined to help grievers attend to their physical well-being, to allow as much emotional expression as fits the individual within a dual-process model context, and to support grievers in coping with their pain. If a griever is suicidal, still quite debilitated after 4 to 6 months, has strong feelings of worthlessness, or is unable to eat and sleep more normally after several weeks, then a referral for psychiatric evaluation makes sense.

MATURATIONAL LOSSES AS DISENFRANCHISED LOSSES

Children and adults experience various maturational losses, some as a direct result of normal growth and aging and some related indirectly to the maturational stage an individual inhabits. These losses are common in each (loosely defined) age group but often receive little support from others precisely because they are considered normal. These losses and the grief that follows are not validated by societal norms in the ways that allow people to grieve losses deemed legitimate (worthy of sympathy or support). Although not included in Doka's (1989, 2002) five categories of disenfranchised loss, we assert that many maturational losses are indeed disenfranchised. Although we believe that all change involves loss, we do not hold that all maturational losses must be actively mourned. Simply, they deserve recognition as destabilizing and potentially growth-producing events. When people recognize the great or small losses that affect them, they are better able to recognize how irritation, sadness, hypervigilance, or other reactions are related to the loss and may thus cope more effectively.

People can also experience disenfranchised maturational loss when expected developmental achievements are not met. For example, a significant proportion of emerging adults have not been able to establish independent households. We view this delay of developmental achievement as a form of maturational (and disenfranchised) loss. These two categories of maturational loss—loss due to new developmental milestones attained and loss due to nonattainment of expected achievements—both cause a low level of sadness and irritation that can be managed better if recognized as sequelae of a loss. Unfortunately, when unrecognized, these losses can lead to self-blame and a sense of being odd rather than to recognition of the loss, coping with the ambivalent feelings and moving forward.

The first maturational loss is leaving the safe uterine environment from which all humans are thrust without intent or control (addressed in 1929/1999 by Otto Rank in *The Trauma of Birth* and in 1986 by Judith Viorst in *Necessary Losses*). As infants age, they lose the total, unconditional care of their parent(s). Most children then move to school environments, where they are judged, sometimes for the first time in their lives. None of these are viewed as losses requiring support from others, yet they do seem to entail experiences of (unrecognized and disenfranchised) loss as unconditional positive regard is replaced with parental expectations and academic demands for achievement.

Other maturational losses may be recognized but are disenfranchised nonetheless. For example, young adults who transition from depending on their family of origin for support to independent living seldom have support for the losses they experience as they create a new life. In emerging adulthood, the loss of a romantic relationship is often not validated by friends and family, both because it is a normal event of the developmental phase and because the future holds many more opportunities for relationships.

Adults who become parents often do not anticipate the losses their relationship will endure. A new child demands energy and attention the couple once gave each other. The birth of a child is in most cases a happy event and is normatively defined as such. As a result, family, friends, and perhaps the couple themselves are unable to recognize the sadness and grief they may experience as the result of "losing" each other. Alternatively, when a woman suffers a miscarriage, friends and family often say "Don't worry, there probably was something wrong with it" or "You'll have many opportunities to have other children," thereby disenfranchising the loss and indicating that support is unnecessary.

Loss of employment is seldom validated as a loss, yet, as decades of research show, this can be a severe loss, particularly in midlife, when it interferes with the basic developmental task of generativity and is therefore a maturational loss of the second type: nonattainment of an expected developmental achievement. Furthermore, no societal ritual recognizes this loss or provides a socially sanctioned time for grieving and recovery. This is complicated by expectations that unemployed adults be continuously motivated to seek new employment efficiently at a time when they feel a sense of shame and self-doubt. We suggest that these types of cumulative losses may contribute significantly to the U.S. "deaths of despair" epidemic.

At some point, adults typically move from the home they have created. For some, this may be liberating, even joyous because they are moving to a place that permits a more satisfying life. The desirability of the change minimizes accompanying losses and any need to mourn them. But for others, leaving a home is a severe loss that entails reduced access to lifelong friends and abandonment of the familiar environment, which is a powerful symbol of achievement and trigger for important memories. This loss often goes unrecognized unless it results from financial distress or ill health, when it is acknowledged as a secondary loss.

Because they have suffered losses and been resilient, older adults often are understood by themselves and others as able to weather any loss. Individuals may disenfranchise their own grief and have little patience with it. But these cumulative losses, especially if not processed due to self-disenfranchisement, may lead to greater pain. We believe it is important to recognize these hidden and disenfranchised losses as they form an emotional foundation on which further losses pile up, possibly to the person's detriment.

IMPORTANCE OF THE DUAL-PROCESS MODEL OF COPING WITH BEREAVEMENT

We wrote in the Introduction of the importance of understanding the dual-process model of grief (Stroebe & Schut, 1999, 2010), in which the bereaved oscillate between two modes of functioning while adapting to loss. In one, the bereaved yearn and search for the absent person or lost object while focusing on the loss (loss orientation [LO]). In the other, grievers focus on rebuilding their lives by engaging in new relationships, activities, and other distractions that move them away from active grieving and into their futures (restoration orientation [RO]). This cycling allows needed time for both processing the loss and necessary respite. In early chapters, we noted how children utilize dual process, rapidly moving back and forth between LO and RO. Although adults are often uncomfortable with children's responses to death, children model well how to move between the two states without judgment or second-guessing the process that will help them heal.

Adults often have a much more difficult time permitting this movement between active grieving and distraction or looking forward. We believe this to be a place where grief theories (and therapists) have been problematic: As we observe in the first chapter, many believed the "grief hypothesis" and believed that all therapeutic work after bereavement must stay focused on active grief work (focus on LO). We see, however, that clients benefit when the grief counselor is able to model and give permission for tears *and* distractions: to focus on both the grief and the rest of life.

Work with grievers should always include attention to RO in measures that meet the client's needs. A good grief practitioner understands that the movement between active expression of grief and engagement with the other parts of life allows the griever to find new balance. Whatever the loss, grievers need to "re-learn the world" (Attig, 1996, 2015), and this oscillation process seems to enable re-learning and finding a new balance. Using the dual-process model as an intervention strategy, a practitioner might guide active grievers to focus on restoration and to guide those who focus only on the future to consider some of the events, feelings, and thoughts of the period before and during the loss.

IMPORTANCE OF CONTINUING BONDS

Continuing Bonds by Klass et al. (1996) was a landmark contribution to grief theory. They clearly defined that continuing the relationship with the deceased is a principal component of grief work, effectively challenging the idea that disengaging from the lost loved one was the function of grief and mourning. In fact, Klass et al. (1996) view continuing bonds as a resource to enrich functioning in the present and future. Unlike older Freudian conceptualizations of grieving, their understanding posits no zero-sum exchange with regard to the emotional energy available for investment; the bereaved can invest in new relationships while still grieving. Joyful new relationships can coincide with treasured memories of and bonds with the deceased loved one. Derived from this is the helpful idea that the relationship with the deceased changes over time; the deceased may actually be viewed as helping to support the bereaved in building new relationships. This is comforting to many bereaved adults who previously thought they had to "let go" of one relationship prior to forming a new one. As with many other findings, the importance of continuing bonds challenges the necessity of "closure" in the experience of grief.

Unlike death losses, where the continuing bond can be enhanced with linking objects (Volkan, 1985) and other memories, parents who have a perinatal loss are stymied in continuing their relationship with the lost baby. They fear that others will not recognize their loss of one relationship when another (a new pregnancy and healthy baby) comes along. Affirming the ongoing relationship to the baby they dreamed of having (and lost) and differentiating it from a new pregnancy and/or baby enhances work with a bereaved couple by giving the couple leave to fully embrace the new relationship.

The practice of continuing bonds is also challenging in the loss of a relationship. When a love relationship ends, the person experiencing the loss often wishes to maintain the relationship with little change. Part of the work of acknowledging a loss is the transition into a new type of relationship that reflects the changed bond. Thus, the continued bond can consist of memories when no relationship continues, or the bond can be transformed if there is an ongoing relationship with the ex-lover. The changed nature of the bond is the basis for the continuing bond. Foster children struggle somewhat similarly with continuing bonds with birth families and foster families; they must determine what bonds with family of origin can safely be maintained and which must end with a revised bond. In all of these cases, bonds are transformed, but the "lost" entity is not forgotten.

As people reinvent themselves, they may also continue bonds with their former professions, work colleagues, and work sites. Yet the bond must change, and the new relationship with paid work must evolve. Nearly everyone knows someone who stayed active in their work for too long, failing to accept the loss and transform their bonds to work ties in time. The transformation of bonds is a critical aspect of continuing bonds.

MEANING-MAKING AS A PROCESS OF GROWTH

Just as grief and loss are ineffable dimensions of human experience, we inevitably try to make meaning in our lives. Neimeyer (2019) remains an important voice in the work that demonstrates the critical importance of meaning-making in adaptation to grieving and methods for assisting grievers. Whether using the mnemonic shortcut (p. 85) of Bracing (providing support), Pacing (helping modulate and contain grief work), and Facing (being able to confront the story) or providing a full case study, few have demonstrated the power and function of meaning-making through narrative work as well as Neimeyer. He explains that efforts to preserve a coherent self-narrative are disrupted by the loss of significant others upon whom "our life stories depend" (Neimeyer et al., 2002, p. 239). When bereaved individuals create stories where the loss has meaning, they begin to see how to move forward with a revised narrative of how to function without their loved one. Going on being—merely surviving—propels the bereaved to keep putting one foot in front of the other and keep retelling the story until the past is again woven with the future.

Practitioners cannot make meaning for clients. After helping clients tell their stories of bereavement, they may help by asking a deeper set of questions. Questions such as "Where did you find surprise sources of strength?"; "What untapped strengths have you discovered?"; and "How has this loss experience changed your life?" can help clients begin to make meaning from their experiences. Practitioners can help clients who have suffered disenfranchised losses by validating their grief and helping them make meaning of the societal response as well as of the loss itself. Bereaved clients may find that loss is the impetus to reassess their spiritual and/or emotional lives while reevaluating their priorities in a way that makes meaning and leads to a new self-image. Although we would hesitate to ask most grievers if their loss has a silver lining, helping them identify what remains good (or improved) in life is often an important aspect of helping them make meaning.

The struggle to make sense of the loss and the discovery of some "life lesson in the loss" (Neimeyer et al., 2002, p. 240) are among the best predictors of eventual adaptation. Walter's research (2003) with bereaved widows, widowers, and partners found that participants who made meaning from their experiences were able to move forward in their lives. Frustration increases for both individuals and families who are unable to redefine the loss and tend to focus on the "negatives of the situation and wish that things were different than they are" (Neimeyer et al., 2002, p. 248).

TRAUMA AND GRIEF

Trauma from adverse childhood experiences (ACEs), particularly if paired with trauma related to a recent loss, may produce reactions both similar and different from typical grief trajectories. People exposed to trauma, especially in childhood, tend to stifle affect as a result, and may not *seem* to be grieving. We know that the accumulation of ACEs is associated with health and mental health problems as well as substance misuse (Felitti et al., 1998), but it seems as well that some optimal number of ACEs (two to four according to Seery et al., 2010) may promote development of coping capacities. Grief and trauma can contribute to better coping, and both respond well to interventions that use development of a full narrative as a central component of treatment.

Trauma is the result of events that threaten a person's life, health, or well-being, threats certainly felt when people lose a loved one or livelihood. Earlier versions of the *DSM* focused on trauma as the result of life-threatening events that for many provoked symptoms of reexperiencing, avoidance, and hyperarousal in their wake. The *DSM-5* broadens the range of events that provoke trauma (sexual violence has been added) and the criteria now include avoidance, reexperiencing, persistent negative change in mood and cognition, and arousal and reactivity.

Recent research indicates that post-traumatic stress disorder (PTSD) and prolonged grief disorder (PGD) have different symptom profiles that sometimes overlap after renewed exposure to trauma and loss. In research with Mandaean refugees and asylum seekers in Australia, Nickerson et al. (2014) showed that traumatized individuals who had also experienced recent loss had recognizable clusters of symptoms. Their sample included 16% who combined PTSD/PGD symptoms (primarily psychogenic amnesia, restricted affect, and loss of meaning), 25% who exhibited primarily symptoms of PTSD (intrusive memories, avoidance of thoughts/activities, and hyperarousal and less restricted affect), 16% who showed symptoms primarily of PGD (longing and yearning, bitterness, and difficulty accepting the death, with some intrusive memories and other discrete PTSD symptoms), and 43% who were asymptomatic and classified as resilient. These categories and their definitions provide a way to distinguish PGD from PTSD, which is very useful for assuring efficacious treatment.

In another study considering how childhood and adult trauma may interact, Fossion et al. (2013) explored how "Formerly Hidden Children" (FHC) in World War II (WWII) Belgium coped with loss in adulthood. FHC were Jewish children hidden during WWII and living under persistent, life-threatening circumstances. Fossion et al. compared FHC who were currently bereaved adults with bereaved adults who had also lived in Belgium as children during WWII (but not under threat) and found that the FHC group had less resilience than members of the control group. They posit that early trauma makes adults more vulnerable to later life stressors and bereavements. They suggest that reinforcing resilience after each trauma or loss and helping individuals develop a renewed sense of coherence will protect resilience over time.

The typical symptoms of PTSD (dissociative symptoms, numbing, and hypervigilance) may mask typical grief responses, making it difficult to distinguish what treatment is needed for the trauma and what for the grief. Yet a reassuring aspect of this tangle is that both trauma and complex grief share an intervention strategy: Successful treatments for both encourage the individual to tell a repeated and coherent story of the loss and/or trauma (exposure). Combining this with psychoeducation to help adjust expectations about grief and trauma is part of the work as well. Developing the coherent story helps individuals "re-learn the world" (Attig, 2015) and may promote meaning-making that yields a sense that the world is predictable and fairly safe again, a necessity for recovery from trauma in its many forms.

The Winnicottian notion of the safe holding environment is important here. For Winnicott, the holding environment consists of fundamental "caregiving activities and processes that facilitate growth and development" during infancy and which is repeated in therapeutic environments (Winnicott, 1953/1965, p. 33). Therapeutic holding environments may provide the bereaved with the sense of safety necessary to move back and forth between the LO and RO of the dual-process model. When clinicians provide a space of safety and nurture, individuals are better able to process their trauma and grief.

GRIEF COUNSELING EFFICACY

The field of grief counseling is undergoing continuous critical examination. At the 30th Annual Conference of the Association for Death Education and Counseling in April/May of 2008, during the panel presentation "Research That Matters 2008: Does Grief Counseling Work—Yet?," Currier et al. (2007) argued that there is not much evidence that grief counseling makes a difference. However, the lively discussion that ensued made clear that research had failed to consider the client–worker relationship. Because variables of empathy, positive regard, and authenticity have been so critical to understanding positive outcomes in research on other therapeutic methods (Lambert & Barley, 2002), it is logical that research on grief counseling should proceed similarly. Supiano (2019) illustrates how evolving grief theory allows clearer operationalization of concepts and more rigorous research to assess the efficacy of interventions. We suspect that future research will demonstrate the vital importance of the relational aspects of grief counseling, along with tested methods of intervention, and that these will show efficacy as research becomes more refined.

As we imply here, we believe clinicians' relational abilities will be the key to the efficacy of grief therapy. The clinician's ability to bear witness to the bereaved's pain is a critical feature of intervention with individuals coping with loss. Again, this requires that practitioners exude a calm, confident presence, implicitly sharing the hope and expectation that the bereaved will feel better by telling (and retelling) their painful stories of loss and grief. It also comforts and helps when the clinician aids the bereaved to discover ways to continue the relationship with the deceased (or affirm ways already found). Using metaphors of healing (sometimes a wound must be cleaned and made more painful to be able to heal; long journeys to rewarding destinations often have difficult stretches) can also help grievers understand why the grief clinician asks them to revisit painful stories and emotions. Clinicians must never collude in avoiding discussions that will ultimately help the bereaved move forward. Bravely forging a relationship where the bereaved can speak freely and is helped to allow their grief narrative to unfold is key to efficacious grief work.

GRIEF AND THE CLINICIAN: CAUTIONS

You Cannot Bypass Grief

Nothing that readers learn from this text will change the way they experience grief. Many "experts" believe they can use knowledge to bypass painful phenomena as though to be forewarned is to be sufficiently forearmed. Grief does not work that way. Grief takes its time and feels as overwhelming for the expert as it does for anyone else. Just as trauma counselors cannot serve as their own therapists and need to be conscious about being "a healing counselor rather than a wounded healer" (Rudick, 2012), clinicians of all disciplinary backgrounds benefit from support (professional or personal) from someone not affected by the loss and able to intervene as we have described. We coarsen life and demean our attachments whenever we expect grievers (ourselves included) to deny their own mourning.

Take Care of Yourself

We have included information for grievers about the importance of regular exercise, exposure to sunlight, proper nutrition (attending particularly to vitamins B6 and B12 and omega-3 and -6), relaxation and meditative practices, spiritual supports, and close friendships. These elements of self-care are just as important for the caregiver, whether a friend, family member, or clinician (Rudick, 2012; Vachon, 2015). A useful tool available free online, the Professional Quality of Life Scale (ProQol), allows people to assess their levels of compassion satisfaction (the satisfaction derived from caring for others), burnout (feeling hopeless and overwhelmed about work), and secondary traumatic stress (exposures to the stories of others' traumatic events; available at www.proqol.org/ProQol_Test.html). It helps professionals keep tabs on their own levels of each subscale to encourage appropriate self-care and professional consultation. We suggest that professionals in practice self-administer the ProQoL regularly to catch compassion fatigue and burnout before it impairs their ability to provide competent grief counseling.

Vachon (2015) synthesizes years of research about self-care for those providing hospice and palliative care services. She asserts confidently that those who take care of themselves are more able to avoid burnout and compassion fatigue. "Venting" about negative aspects of the job, living stoically with work stress, and/or watching a lot of television or using substances *are not* good forms of self-care. Rather, Vachon encourages particular attention to the pleasure and fulfillment one gets from extending compassion to others ("compassion satisfaction") along with exercise and physical activity, willingness to take time off, meditative and reflective practices, exquisite empathy with good boundaries, and resilience. She suggests spiritual practices as part of a good self-care plan.

When an airplane cabin decompresses, each passenger must secure an oxygen mask. Self-care is the oxygen of grief work. In grief work, as in trauma work, we must help contain our clients' grief and trauma, be fully with them in a calm and confident manner, and be enlivened rather than debilitated by the encounters that constitute this work. We ask you to care well for yourselves so that you can provide important care, treatment, and empathy to the grievers you meet along your way (Professional Quality of Life Measure, 2012).

DISCUSSION QUESTIONS

1. If someone asked you what theories or concepts define the work you do with grievers, what theories would you invoke? Why?
2. How do you typically feel when someone is "leaning" on you for comfort and care?
3. What is an example of compassion satisfaction from your own life?
4. What is your favorite self-care practice?

KEY REFERENCES

Only key references appear in the print edition. The full reference list appears in the digital product found on http://connect.springerpub.com/content/book/978-0-8261-4964-0/chapter/ch12

Attig, T. (2015). Seeking wisdom about mortality, dying and bereavement. In J. M. Stillion & T. Attig (Eds.), *Death, dying, and bereavement: Contemporary perspectives, institutions, and practices* (pp. 1–16). Springer Publishing Company.

Doka, K. J. (Ed.). (2002). *Disenfranchised grief: New directions, challenges and strategies for practice*. Research Press.

Horowitz, A., & Wakefield, J. (2007). *The loss of sadness: How psychiatry transformed normal sorrow into depressive disorder*. Oxford University Press.

International Classification of Diseases 11. (2019). World Health Organization. https://icd.who.int/en

Klass, D., Silverman, P. R., & Nickman, S. L. (Eds.). (1996). *Continuing bonds: New understandings of grief.* Taylor & Francis.

Lambert, M. J., & Barley, D. E. (2002). Research summary on the therapeutic relationship and psychotherapy outcome. In J. C. Norcross (Ed.), *Psychotherapy relationships that work* (pp. 17–32). Oxford University Press.

Neimeyer, R. A., Prigerson, H., & Davies, B. (2002). Mourning and meaning. *American Behavioral Scientist, 46*(2), 235–251. https://doi.org/10.1177/000276402236676

Professional Quality of Life Measure. (2012). *The ProQol measure in English and non-English translations.* https://www.proqol.org/ProQol_Test.html

Seery, M. D., Holman, E. A., & Silver, R. C. (2010). Whatever does not kill us: Cumulative lifetime adversity, vulnerability, and resilience. *Journal of Personality and Social Psychology, 99*(6), 1025. https://doi.org/10.1037/a0021344

Shear, M. K. (2015). Complicated grief. *New England Journal of Medicine, 372*(2), 153–160. https://doi.org/10.1056/NEJMcp1315618

Stroebe, M. S., & Schut, H. (1999). The dual process model of coping with bereavement: Rationale and description. *Death Studies, 23*, 197–224. https://doi.org/10.1080/074811899201046

Stroebe, M. S., & Schut, H. (2010). The dual process model of coping with bereavement: A decade on. *Omega: Journal of Death and Dying, 61*(4), 273–289. https://doi.org/10.2190/OM.61.4.b

Vachon, M. L. S. (2015). Care of the caregiver: Professionals and family members. In J. M. Stillion & T. Attig (Eds.), *Death, dying, and bereavement: Contemporary perspectives, institutions, and practices* (pp. 379–393). Springer Publishing Company.

Index